THE ELOQUENT OBJECT

THE

ELOQUENT OBJECT

THE EVOLUTION OF AMERICAN ART
IN CRAFT MEDIA SINCE 1945

EDITED BY MARCIA MANHART AND TOM MANHART

COORDINATING EDITOR, CAROL HARALSON

THE PHILBROOK MUSEUM OF ART, TULSA

ILLUSTRATIONS OVERLEAF:

Fiesta Basket, ca. 1981, John Garrett
Fabric, vinyl, paint, mixed media, 54 x 36 x 36
Collection of Joe Franko and Maggie Shelton,
Los Angeles, California

Garrett was raised in southern New Mexico in a household where American Indian pottery and basketry were collected. His early experiences are fused with the harsh, high-tech, urban images of his current home, Los Angeles. *Fiesta Basket,* suggesting parties, confetti, brash light and sound, is a container for the spirit of the urban cityscape.

Red Wing, 1984, Ron Nagle
Earthenware, glazed, 3 x 2½ x 11/2
Private collection,
Los Angeles, California

Library of Congress Cataloging-in-Publication Data

The Eloquent Object.

    Includes bibliographies and index.
    1. Decorative arts — United States — History — 20th century. I. Manhart, Marcia, 1943-   . II. Manhart, Tom, 1937-   . III. Philbrook Museum of Art.
NK808.E46   1987   745'.0973   87-50325
ISBN O-86659-006-4

FIRST EDITION

Designer and coordinating editor: Carol Haralson

Production assistant: Carl Brune
Editorial assistant: Rickye Dixon

Printed in Japan by Dai Nippon Printing Company.

Distributed by The University of Washington Press, Seattle, Washington.

MADE POSSIBLE BY A GRANT FROM Mobil.

Also generously supported by the National Endowment for the Humanities, the National Endowment for the Arts and the State Arts Council of Oklahoma.

CONTENTS

PREFACE

The points of view expressed in the pages to follow represent a broad spectrum of attitudes and experiences. Marcia Manhart and Tom Manhart write from the viewpoint of ceramists trained in the studio craft movement whose lives have been indelibly affected by the evolution of American art in craft media. Marcia Manhart, Executive Director of The Philbrook Museum of Art, also speaks as the head of an institution concerned with the preservation and presentation of fine art; Tom Manhart, Associate Professor and Chairman of the Faculty of Art, The University of Tulsa, has taught in a university art department for twenty-six years. From their combined personal history comes an account of the craft movement that provides both an emotional and historical framework for the chapters that follow.

Rose Slivka also writes from direct experience. However, her firsthand observations were made not in the American heartland but in New York City, home of the Abstract Expressionist movement of the 1950s — a movement that, although it began in painting, contributed significantly to the freeing of craft from utilitarian function. Slivka's well-articulated ideas about craft were formed between 1955 and 1979, when she was "on the front line" as editor of *Craft Horizons.* She now edits the quarterly *Craft International.*

Unlike the Manharts and Rose Slivka, Horace Freeland Judson does not come from within the craft movement. He is a historian and critic — chiefly of contemporary science but from time to time of literature and the visual arts. He is the author of *The Eighth Day of Creation,* a history of the principal discoveries of molecular biology, and *The Search for Solutions,* an introduction to the art of scientific discovery, among other books, and is presently Henry R. Luce Professor of Science and Writing at the Johns Hopkins University. In "Breaking the Frames," he draws on his background in science to present some provocative thoughts on the way we react to art objects that are outside our previous experience. Penelope Hunter-Stiebel, a member of the curatorial staff of The Metropolitan Museum of Art for thirteen years and now a principal of the New York art gallery Rosenberg & Stiebel Inc., follows Judson's observations with an overview of attitudes toward craft in Western civilization, as they have been expressed through royal patronage, architecture, the interior decoration of private residences, and other forms of historical evidence. Hunter-Stiebel's essay leaves off where modern museum history begins — an appropriate place for Jonathan L. Fairbanks to embark on a discussion of the role of the museum curator with regard to the collection and presentation of craft art objects. Fairbanks is the Katharine Lane Weems Curator of American Decorative Arts and Sculpture at the Museum of Fine Arts, Boston. Mary Jane Jacob is also a museum professional; she is chief curator at the Museum of Contemporary Art, Los Angeles. However, her thoughts on craft art stem less from her curatorial responsibilities than from personal and enthusiastic observation of recent trends in American art such as the Pattern and Decoration movement of the 1970s. In "The Idea of Crafts in Recent American Art" she presents a fresh view of the playful — and purchasable — new East Village art forms and their relationship to craft. With John Perreault's essay comes a distinct break in voice: Perreault was for seven years senior art critic for the SoHo News, Inc. and has written for *Art News, Art International, Art in America,* and *ArtForum.* He is director and curator of Newhouse Gallery, Snug Harbor Cultural Center in Staten Island, New York. Perreault's notes on art and craft criticism are droll and perhaps surprising.

Lucy R. Lippard, whose essay begins the third section of the book, is author of *Get the Message? A Decade of Art for Social Change,* the recent *Overlay: Contemporary Art and the Art of Prehistory,* and many other books and essays. She is a frequent visiting scholar to numerous universities. Her passionate interest in the vitality of Third World and non-mainstream American art (and the possibilities they represent for better cross-cultural understanding) is apparent. George L. Aguirre also writes about cultural pluralism but he does much more in his refreshing and unusual essay: he illuminates that moment in the creation of art that is both private and universal and exists apart from national affiliation, race, or gender. Aguirre is an artist-photographer currently living in Spain. He has recently exhibited work at El Museo del Barrio, New York; Café Unión, Madrid; and the Ateneo de Guadalajara, Spain; and has been written about in *Popular Photography, Arte Fotográfico, Icónica,* and other journals. Formerly Aguirre was an officer of the Exxon Education Foundation, where his involvement with arts and education was wide and varied.

The pair of essays that conclude *The Eloquent Object* explore a dimension of the subject that is seldom addressed. Ronda Kasl is a young art historian recently graduated from the New York University Institute of Fine Arts and currently working in the painting conservation laboratory of The Metropolitan Museum of Art. In "Artifact and Fiction" she looks at work by artists who are not only making objects but constructing worlds within which those objects function as if they were ritual objects. Edwin L. Wade explores the idea of ritual or sacred function from the viewpoint of an anthropologist. Wade, curator at The Philbrook Museum of Art, was formerly assistant director and collections manager at the Peabody Museum of Archaeology and Ethnology, Harvard University. Drawing on his anthropological background and his extensive study of tribal societies in the American Southwest, he brings an unusual point of view to the analysis of contemporary craft. Wade is the author of *Magic Images: Contemporary Native American Art, As in A Vision: Masterworks of American Indian Art,* and other publications, and is editor of the recent book *The Arts of the North American Indian.*

The variety of voices heard in these eleven essays, the breadth of viewpoint and background, is expressed even in the use of language. You will see the words *craftsman, craftsperson, craftsmaker, craft artist* all used interchangeably, as are *fine art, high art,* and "art in noncraft media." Such variousness signals the fluid and evolving state of current attitudes.

Narrative captions that accompany illustrations of artworks also vary in voice and viewpoint, suggesting the many ways that craft art is perceived by contemporary writers and observers. The majority of these captions are the work of the essayists, with the exception of Horace Freeland Judson and John Perreault. Some captions were also written or researched by Janice Bawden, Dr. Linda C. Hults, Nancy Large, and Jerri Jones. With each illustration is factual information recognizing the work's collection source, dimensions (height preceding width, in inches), date made, and materials — information that, taken cumulatively, comments interestingly on the evolution of the movement. For basic information about the makers of the works represented in the book (and in the exhibition) *The Eloquent Object,* see the artist index, which gives birthdate and place, university degrees and/or other training, and other information for each artist. In this index is recorded the fascinating fabric of interactions — who was mentor to whom — the allegiances and influences and cross-fertilizations that tell an important part of the story of this movement that is only two generations old.

We believe that in variety is strength and that the multi-faceted identity of a movement still in transition is best recorded in a multiplicity of voices. That is what you will hear in the pages to follow. We hope that one or more speaks eloquently to you.

Carol Haralson
Coordinating Editor

ACKNOWLEDGMENTS

T
he idea for *The Eloquent Object* began to take shape in
1980. In some ways the earliest stages of such a project,
when ideas are young, is most delicate. We were very
fortunate in that stage to have the intelligent support of
many friends and colleagues, including Judy Cunningham
Ansteth, Ronda Kasl, Ben G. Henneke, Jr., Susan Petersmeyer
Henneke, Jerri Jones, Myrna Ruffner, the late Janet B. Stratton, and Jesse
G. Wright, Jr., who was then director of The Philbrook Museum. In
thinking back to the beginning, we thank especially Pat and Harley
Manhart, who have always been cornerstones for our visions; our
mothers, Eva Patrick Manhart and Ruth Correll Yockey; and Kent L. Yockey
and Elizabeth Volkman for years of enduring support. Though fully
understanding the extraordinary challenge of the undertaking they
encouraged us to go on, trusting in the power of possibility.

Our next step was to broaden our base, to reach outside our area of
the country, and to present our ideas to key figures in the craft art
movement. We traveled to artists' studios and galleries, talked with private
collectors, museum directors, historians, and critics whose support we felt
was pivotal to our success. We were pleased and grateful to find a
willingness to listen and we welcomed constructive responses from Ellyn
Berk, Alexander Milliken, Lois Moran, Paul J. Smith, and Mildred
Constantine in New York; Helen Williams Drutt in Philadelphia; the late
Rachael Griffin and Kenneth Shores in Portland; Robert Gray in Ashville;
Lynn M. Jorgenson in San Francisco; Lloyd Herman, Michael Monroe and
Eudora Moore in Washington, D.C.; Hazel Bray in Oakland; Michael Scott
in Seattle; and David Smith in Kansas City. Most important was the
enthusiastic response of Rose Slivka, editor-in-chief of *Craft International*
and a respected chronicler of the entire craft movement, who agreed to
act as our primary consultant.

In 1982 we met with the original members of what would become
the curatorial team charged with guiding the project: Bernard Kester, Mary
Jane Jacob, Rose Slivka, Penelope Hunter-Stiebel, and Jonathan L.
Fairbanks. In 1983 the team expanded to include David C. Driskell, George
L. Aguirre, Horace Freeland Judson, Edwin L. Wade, and Ronda Kasl. By
the time the final manuscript for the book had taken shape, we had also

called upon the talents of Lucy R. Lippard and John Perreault. Without the clear thinking and commitment of each of these people the project would have remained only an idea.

The planning stage of the project involved extensive research and development of background material. Information was compiled on the lives and work of more than four hundred artists — a task that required massive cooperation from many sources, including dealers, lenders, collectors, the artists themselves, and the American Craft Council Library. We are grateful to each person who responded when asked for assistance and to Jerri Jones, Marlene Wetzel, Nancy Herman, Ronda Kasl, Sharon Rue, Carlene Larsson, Rickye Dixon, and Tom Young who worked patiently to amass the necessary material.

Throughout, the project has enjoyed valuable support from the past and present chairmen of The Philbrook Board of Trustees, Charles W. Flint, Jr., Kathleen P. Westby, and Robert J. LaFortune as well as other museum trustees, both past and present, especially Sander Davidson, R. Robert Huff, David Browning, Jr., Samuel C. Stone, Joan Seay, and Elizabeth Head. James R. Dodd, a museum trustee, provided very special assistance by helping us make our first contact with our major corporate sponsor, Mobil Oil Corporation. Staff members have also been supportive: we are grateful to Evelyn Washburn, Bea Crites, Raakel Vesanen, Jean Hagman, Michael Sudbury, John A. Mahey, Christine Knop Kallenberger, and Gary F. Moore whose support, though in some cases indirect, has made our undertaking easier. We are deeply indebted to our friends and colleagues Olivia Mariño and Ed Wade, who have been our intellectual sounding boards and whose criticism and guidance continually clarified our ideas, and to Helen G. Sanderson for her encouragement of our missionary spirit. At The University of Tulsa we received welcome assistance in the form of release time for Tom Manhart so that he could pursue the project. Thomas F. Staley, provost, Bradley E. Place, previous chair of the art program, and Susan Resneck Parr, dean of College of Arts and Sciences, are responsible for this generosity.

The editing of *The Eloquent Object* and its design and production have required the commitment of considerable energy. We are deeply grateful to Horace Judson, whose vast encouragement, patience, and editorial expertise made it possible for us to set our thoughts on paper, and who was also of assistance to Ronda Kasl and Mary Jane Jacob. Bernard Kester and Terri Neff read the manuscript in first draft and made useful comments and Linda C. Hults supplied art-historical expertise. Jocelyn Wolfe assisted in compiling the artist index. Carl Brune assisted in board production and both he and Rickye Dixon supplied extremely valuable assistance in preparation of manuscripts for telecommunication typesetting. Rickye gathered photographic images, a lengthy and arduous task. Carol Haralson, chief of publications at Philbrook, copy-edited as necessary, coordinated editing, designed the book, indexed it, and oversaw each detail of its production. With untiring tolerance and patience she met last-minute decisions, repeated delays, and unmet deadlines cheerfully. Carol has shared our vision from the beginning. Her devotion, professionalism, creativeness, care, and love are apparent throughout the pages of this book. To Carol, we are forever grateful, for no one else could have done what she did to make this book an eloquent object.

For major corporate support for this project we are extremely grateful to Mobil Oil Corporation. The National Endowment for the Humanities supplied an initial planning grant and, later, major funding of this book and the exhibition which has been critical to our undertaking and we are grateful for that support, as well as for support from the National Endowment for the Arts and the State Arts Council of Oklahoma. We have been fortunate in receiving assistance in funding also from Ben G. Henneke, Jr., and the Oklahoma Foundation for the Humanities; and extremely valuable in-kind support from The Williams Companies, Tulsa, The Westin Hotel, Tulsa, and Arthur Andersen and Company, New York.

Every thanks comes from the heart, but our last expression of gratitude comes from a deep and special place in our hearts. If we could dedicate this book and the project of which it is part, in some ways the most important professional undertaking of our lives, to anyone, it would be to our daughters, Emily and Mandy. Without their support and love, nothing else would matter. In hopes they will always know this, we thank them for their enormous patience and extraordinary understanding.

Marcia Manhart and Tom Manhart
May, 1987

THE WIDENING ARCS:

A PERSONAL HISTORY OF A REVOLUTION IN THE ARTS

MARCIA MANHART AND TOM MANHART

The early 1960s were supremely rich in images and influences. Impulses in the crafts that had been seeded earlier were coming to fruition in the work of artists in many materials and traditions. Our own tradition was the American studio crafts movement, and our medium was clay (in the early 1960s Tom was teaching ceramics in the art department of The University of Tulsa and Marcia was an undergraduate in fine arts at the university, studying with Tom). Naturally we were first aware of the new objects that were transforming ceramics. As we understood later, the transformation of ceramics did indeed form a vanguard. Soon we realized that comparable changes were taking place in other media within the craft movement — among the jewelers and metalworkers, the weavers, the woodworkers. Later our view would change, and enlarge outward in widening arcs, to embrace what had reached far beyond the studio walls — the powerful currents of diverse American cultures that were applying familiar materials to uses that were alarming, polemical, spiritually satisfying, often wildly unfamiliar. They were eloquent.

In 1963, in a university setting, we could take for granted that our work and that of our colleagues, whatever their media, would find the attention and regard that its aesthetic strength earned for it, object by object. But we also knew that those materials and techniques labeled *crafts* ranked low in the eyes of the high-art world, and in many museums

Patti Warashina
Airstream Turkey, 1969
Earthenware, low-fire glazes and lusters, 9½ x 19¾ x 9½
Seattle Art Museum, Seattle, Washington, Long Term Loan/Promised Gift, The Sidney and Anne Gerber Collection

Margaret De Patta
Pin, 1944
Sterling silver, quartz crystal sphere,
2½ x 2⅛
The Oakland Museum,
Oakland, California
Gift of Eugene Bielawski

The decisive moment in De Patta's artistic development came in 1940 when she attended a summer session taught by Lazlo Moholy-Nagy at Mills College in Oakland. In 1940-1941, at the age of 37, she attended the School of Design in Chicago, founded by Moholy-Nagy two years earlier and employing many artists from the New Bauhaus group among its faculty. From 1940 onward, Bauhaus ideology is the most persistent and emphatic feature of De Patta's work. Characteristically, in 1958 she spoke of the "bursting of restraints" and she enumerated what had been and would continue to be the dominant concerns of her work: "freedom to develop or use new materials — freedom to manipulate materials by newly developed techniques — and the necessity to incorporate in our work the influences of our time." De Patta often compared her work to sculpture or architecture; given her Bauhaus beliefs, it is probably more accurate to state that she perceived no difference at all, save one of scale. (Margaret De Patta, "Vision and Individual Response," transcript of a paper presented at the Second Annual Conference of American Craftsmen, June 22-25, 1958.)

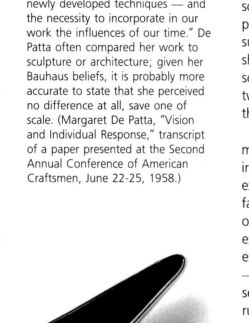

and galleries, especially those in New York and Los Angeles. The Whitney Biennial at the Whitney Museum of American Art in New York claims to be the premier general exhibition space for new art of this country. To this day, objects categorized as crafts by the Whitney have rarely been included in the biennial. Works in craft media, whatever their degree of aesthetic sophistication and provocative content, must be able to be classed as painting or sculpture to be shown. Artists in clay were first given substantial recognition at the Whitney Museum only in 1981, with the show *Ceramic Sculptors: Six Artists.* The Metropolitan Museum of Art still segregates crafts as "decorative arts," set apart in different galleries from twentieth-century painting and sculpture, curated by different curators; the same is true for the Los Angeles County Museum of Art.

The distinction never made sense to us. As we think back on the many developments that led to this schism, we recall one in particular, ironically one that arose in the very period of aesthetic ferment, experiment, and upheaval that was the sixties. This was the American craft fair, an elaboration on the traditional folk event common in the early part of the century, where rural and small-town dwellers could meet and exchange handicrafts and homemade comestibles. In the early 1960s, especially in our region, something new was added to this oldtime event — the university-trained production craftsman was invited to show and sell his wares there. And thus was made the peculiar marriage between a rural folk tradition and a new population of art/craft producers trained in unprecedented numbers in the proliferating art departments of American colleges and universities directly after World War II. The offspring of this marriage are with us today — craft fairs dot the downtown malls of towns throughout the United States in the warm months. In the beginning, the fairs offered young, new artist-craftsmen a chance to show and sell work, but ultimately we believe that the craft fair helped to cause a misapprehension and misevaluation of art in craft media and has become a symbol of that misunderstanding.

The studio craft movement, which traces itself to the 1920s and earlier, was centered in art and design departments of established institutions. Cranbrook Academy of Art in Michigan was perhaps the most important of these. At Cranbrook, architects Eliel and Eero Saarinen, the designer of fine silver and sculptor Harry Bertoia, the sculptor Carl Milles, the ceramist Maija Grotell, and the designers of furniture and interiors Florence Knoll and Charles and Ray Eames taught the ideals of the Bauhaus and International Style. Black Mountain College, in the Blue Ridge mountains of North Carolina, was similarly an artists' community and teaching center. This rooted American tradition was profoundly affected in

Gertrud and Otto Natzler
Bowl, 1965
Stoneware, verdigris crater glaze,
14½ inches in diameter
National Museum of American
History, Smithsonian Institution,
Washington, D.C.

the 1930s by a transatlantic import, the Bauhaus School from Germany, with its rejection of ornamentation and its emphasis on clarity of form in relation to function. The Bauhaus brought with it a classicizing purity and the ideal of the handmade idiom. In the 1930s, many of its practitioners emigrated to the United States. Their influence on American architecture, painting, and design has been direct and, of course, renowned. Less well-known, perhaps, was the Bauhaus influence on American crafts. This was exerted through artists who were teachers — in particular, Anni Albers (who came to this country with her husband, the painter Josef Albers), and Frans and Marguerite Wildenhain. Anni Albers (page 75) was an internationally known artist whose medium happened to be weaving; she taught at Black Mountain College. Marguerite Wildenhain established a producing-teaching cooperative known as the Pond Farm Workshops in Guerneville, California, where she worked and taught hundreds the basics of functional pottery, form, and expression. Frans Wildenhain taught at Pond Farm briefly and became the major influence in ceramics for twenty-five years at the School of the American Craftsman at the Rochester Institute of Technology in New York.

Certain other international influences were strong. Bernard Leach, an English potter, had grown to world standing between the world wars. His studio in Cornwall was a center of the most substantial lineage in an English crafts tradition reaching back to William Morris. Leach's pots and his books were gifted propaganda; for many in this country he epitomized the ethos of studio crafts. In 1952, Leach brought to the United States two Japanese associates. Shoji Hamada, then in his late fifties, was a rare legend among potters and one of those artists designated in the

Toshiko Takaezu
¾ Moon, 1985
Stoneware, matte white glaze with
copper brush design, 18 x 21 x 23
Museum of Fine Arts,
Boston, Massachusetts, Gift of
Mary-Louise Meyer in memory of
Norman Meyer

Takaezu entitled this piece *¾ Moon*
because of its oblate form. Its glaze,
freely dashed and brushed across
the surface, is a rich combination of
matte white and copper, opaque in
parts and elsewhere translucent. The
seemingly random but controlled
handling perfectly matches the
shape and body of the ware, clearly
evoking moon imagery or lunar
landscape.

wonderful Japanese way as a Living National Treasure. Soketsu Yanagi and
Hamada were founders of Japan's *Mingei* (folk craft) movement, and
established folk art museums throughout Japan, elevating the appreciation
of past and present craft traditions. Leach, Hamada, and Yanagi — the
visit of these three had far-reaching importance not only for American
potters but for vast numbers of other craftsmen and artists and, indeed,
for the general public. The time the three men spent at Black Mountain in
October of 1952 had perhaps the greatest long-term significance, even
though it was only the span of a ten-day workshop. There the subtle,
indirectly stated principles of the Zen Buddhist aesthetic and the
paradoxical asymmetrical beauty of the objects created under its influence
broke through the perfectionism of the European-oriented sensibility of
students and faculty alike. Hamada's techniques of throwing at the potter's
wheel, glazing, and firing were in themselves a revelation to potters. Two
years later, Rosanjin, another Japanese potter and philosopher, toured the
country. The Zen spirit, understood well or partially, became a force in the
development of American ceramics in the 1950s and 1960s.

Toshiko Takaezu
Bottle, 1978
Wheel-thrown stoneware, 10½ x 7
Collection of Dr. and Mrs. Leonard
Leight, Glenview, Kentucky

Takaezu lives in a country farmhouse
in New Jersey and teaches at
Princeton University. In the 1950s,
she was one of the first American
potters to close the tops of her
vessels, preferring to deal with pure
form rather than functional issues.
This approach set her apart from
other craftspersons, and marked her
as a pioneer in the exploration of
expressive form. The closed vessel
has become the best known index
of Takaezu's style despite the fact
that she makes a wide variety of
ceramic shapes with an astounding
range of glazes. In recent years she
has also produced handsome bronze
sculpture based upon her pottery
forms.

Ruth Duckworth
Porcelain Drawing on Paper, 1978
Porcelain, graphite, particle board,
40 x 40
Collection of the artist,
Chicago, Illinois

Ruth Duckworth
Bowl (with six dividers), 1977
Porcelain, hand-built, 4⁵⁄₁₆ x 6⅛
Collection of Joan Mannheimer,
Des Moines, Iowa

Influenced by Henry Moore during
her studies in England as a young
German-Jewish refugee during
World War II, Duckworth found clay
to be responsive to the aesthetic
concerns she had as a painter and
sculptor. Inspired by nature, her
sensual porcelain forms are
articulate expressions of the natural
world — the earth, its atmosphere,
and its geological, biological, and
galactic abstractions. This bowl is
layered with thin clay slab dividers
that both articulate and obscure its
roundness. The surfaces are covered
with subtle, colorless crystalline
matte glazes.

Marcia Manhart with sculpture by Daniel Rhodes at the 22nd Ceramic National, 1963, Arkansas Arts Center, Little Rock, Arkansas.

The studio crafts movement was in its own way conservative. In the early 1960s we approached clay, our medium, traditionally, throwing functional forms on the potter's wheel, mastering the skills of surface decoration, glazing, and firing. Other craftsmen, our colleagues in the region working in fiber, clay, wood, metal — even the finest of them — seemed equally tradition-bound. Yet we knew that our deepest interest in clay was stirred by its sculptural nature. In other media, such as painting and sculpture, we could sense parallel possibilities. Change was stirring. We saw change, for an important example, in *Craft Horizons,* published bimonthly in New York and edited by Rose Slivka, who in issue after issue brought to those pages the work of artists exploiting our familiar materials in extraordinary ways. Their images jolted us.

Also in 1963, the 22nd Ceramic National, an annual exhibition organized by the Everson Museum of Art in Syracuse, New York, came to the Arkansas Arts Center in Little Rock. Our encounter with this exhibition is as vivid today as it was then. We both remember it as a dream world in which we were surrounded by images familiar and strange. Here was a lidded casserole, ready for the oven; next to it stood a sculpture tall enough to look one in the eye — disturbing, nonrepresentational, unfathomable. Of the objects that compelled our attention, many were constructed by hand, not thrown on the wheel, and they exhibited new textures, new forms, new combinations of forms and materials.

Three of the objects live indelibly in memory. The first was by a man from California, Conway Pierson, whose work was previously known to us only through photographs. This piece was circular — its form flattened, set on edge — and stood thirty-four inches high. It was distinctly reminiscent of a functional form, somewhat like a bottle; but it violated the rules. The top and bottom of the structure were not of clay but of cast bronze riveted to the body of the form. It was not glazed; the clay was almost naked, with the exception of a heavily textured surface boldly washed at the edge with white engobe, a clay-like surfacing material. This object could have been a container for something. But that was not its purpose. It was to be seen and understood for itself.

The second of these works was by Daniel Rhodes. Rhodes was important to American ceramics as a writer, an artist, and a teacher. In 1957, he had published *Clay and Glazes for the Potter,* which at once became the authoritative text and reference for studio techniques. He was on the faculty of the New York State College of Ceramics at Alfred University, which at that time was one of the focal points for American ceramics. The piece that Rhodes exhibited at Little Rock stood just under four feet tall, which in those days was large for a freestanding ceramic object. Rhodes had formed the bottom on the wheel, but had constructed the top from slabs. He had left the clay exposed, bare of glaze but with unexpected surface embellishments. Though without direct reference to human form, the object was not a container but had a figurative presence. It was physical and immediate. One confronted it.

The third object, and the most seductive, was by William Wyman (pages 54, 265), a potter from Massachusetts, whose work we knew from earlier exhibitions at the Wichita Art Association. Wyman gave it the title *Homage to Robert Frost.* We found it difficult to analyze. It was slightly over two feet high, and looked in every way like a large jar or bottle built of slabs of clay — but its surface had taken over, had suppressed one's awareness of its form. Wyman had incised words of a poem by Frost into the surface of the clay. He left the surface unglazed, but among the words he impressed bits of glass and in the firing these had melted, leaving the form streaming with rivulets of frost. This was a painting rather than a pot.

William Wyman
Homage to Robert Frost, 1962
Glazed stoneware, 27 x 16 x 3½
Everson Museum of Art,
Syracuse, New York

We came home afire with questions that could only be asked of our work, in hours and days and months interrogating the clay, the kiln, and each other.

In 1964, the Third National Sculpture Casting Conference — another annual — convened at the University of Kansas. There we met Peter Voulkos (pages 81, 82), who was already a celebrated artist in clay. In 1955, after his first year as chairman of the ceramics department at Otis Art Institute in Los Angeles, he created a clay revolution by rebelling against the elegant classical pottery forms he had made earlier at the Archie Bray Foundation in Helena, Montana, by stacking pots on pots and making forms that sprouted multiple necks. Voulkos is a robust man, and flamboyantly Greek. The organizers of the conference had not previously invited an artist in clay (prejudices ran deep) but since 1960 Voulkos had become interested in metal and was now casting monumental bronzes. He set the tone of the conference: for one thing, he was doing better sculpture than most of the others there. At Kansas, he gave demonstrations of sculptural techniques and approaches, and for these he used not metal but clay. In one demonstration, he lifted without visible effort a hundred pounds of clay, centered it easily on the moving wheel and, fists inside and outside, opened it, steadily and assuredly raising the walls into a large vessel — an immense vase. He eased the wheel to a stop. Then he stood back, took wads of stiff clay, and threw them like baseballs through the vase, deforming it, holing it, tearing it: this, the act asserted, was now a work of sculpture. Like his work, Voulkos's performances were shrewd and systematic attacks on all preconceived ideas of his medium.

We also held great admiration for three other Californians who were of that founding generation in clay. Henry Takemoto (page 26) had come from Hawaii to work with Voulkos; we have an enduring love for his large, "eggocentric," pinched-top containers, gently and whimsically painted almost in the manner of Miró. Win Ng built clay-slab boxes that he stacked and balanced into compositions similar to some of David Smith's sculptures in stainless steel; these he completed with broad brushstrokes of engobe in a palette of earth tones. Ng's works have the composure, the peace, of a graveyard. Kenneth Price (pages 242, 243, 244) has demonstrated an audacious, restless imagination; at the Ferus Gallery in 1961 he introduced mound and egg forms, organic yet alien, with immaculate surfaces. The first of these we saw was *Silver*, from 1961, a mound with purple finger-like projections, its surface a haunting illusion of depth. On looking closely we realized with shock that he achieved the luminous perfection of his surfaces by a denial of the glazing tradition for the medium. He had coated the surface with acrylic paint.[1]

In the early 1960s some of the most adventurous craftsmen whose work we knew were jewelers. The gem, the noble metal, the discreet setting, the refined preciousness of jewelry — these constraints were shattered. A new aesthetic was accompanied, indeed made possible, by new attitudes and by the rediscovery of ancient techniques.

The taproot and example for these changes was Margaret De Patta

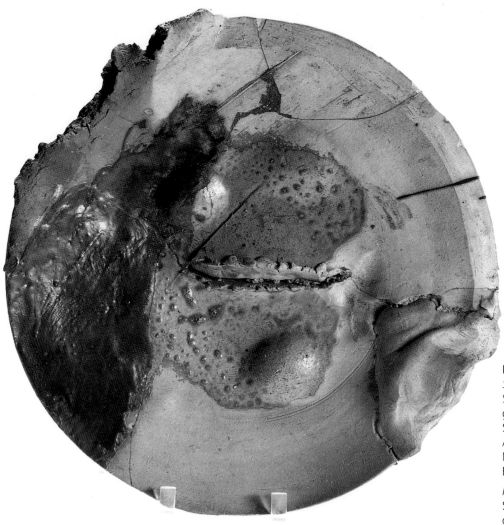

Peter Voulkos
Sevitlanas, 1959 (facing page)
Stoneware with iron slip and clear glaze, 56¾ x 27¼ x 20
San Francisco Museum of Modern Art, San Francisco, California, Albert M. Bender Collection, Albert M. Bender Bequest Fund Purchase

Plate, 1962 (this page)
Stoneware with natural, beige, blue glazes, 3½ x 16¼
The Oakland Museum, Oakland, California, Gift of the Art Guild

(pages 16, 77, 127), whose studio was in the San Francisco Bay area. As early as 1929, she had rebelled against the stolid, unimaginative conventions of jewelry by exploring the reflective, magnifying, and refractory qualities of gemstones, and had created her own free-faceted forms using a synthetic adhesive which allowed the stones to float within the space of their golden skeletal cages. In California, Ruth Radakovich and her husband Svetozar, a Yugoslavian immigrant, demonstrated — no, proved — the present power of certain thousand-year-old techniques of *ciré perdue* (lost-wax casting) and the blacksmith's art of forging. In 1939 Sam Kramer (page 127) opened a studio and shop in Greenwich Village, New York, where he made and displayed his crazy, wild jewels. Kramer demolished conventions with bizarre pendants, brooches, rings, bracelets, and earrings that drew their imagery from science-fiction comics and incorporated everything from glass eyes to bones and children's marbles. John Paul Miller (page 72), who taught at the Cleveland Institute of Art in Ohio, retrieved from craftsmen of the remote past the technique of gold granulation, an Etruscan secret lost for millennia whereby very fine beads

Voulkos's strength and vitality are legendary. He has always been admired for being prolific, producing fifteen pieces to anybody else's one; he once observed of himself that the more quickly he worked, the better he worked. This plate from 1962, Abstract Expressionist in style, is an example of work that belies reports that giving up clay as his major medium affected Voulkos's productivity. At a ratio of fifteen to one, Voulkos could afford to give up several media. In 1962, the man referred to as "Gorilla Man" for his strength, intuition and intelligence, continued producing an amazing body of ceramic art. Although Voulkos's ceramics remained Abstract Expressionist, elements of delicacy and sensitivity are everpresent even

in his toughest work. Voulkos's move to Los Angeles in 1954 signalled the beginning of an upheaval in contemporary ceramics whose reverberations are still strongly felt. Almost immediately, he experimented with unorthodox approaches, constructing large wheel-thrown forms whose subsequent modifications intentionally violated the symmetry and the functional integrity of the traditional vessel. His massive scale was unprecedented, as was his method of constructing. The works are made of separate, usually wheel-thrown, parts which are paddled, compressed and assembled around an inner armature of thrown cylinders — a technique that can sustain size and mass that defy the limitations of the medium. The atmosphere of experimentation at Otis during the mid- to late-1950s encouraged spontaneity and accident, an aesthetic shared and nurtured by the Abstract Expressionist painters who were Voulkos's contemporaries. The possibility of translating the spirit and energy of Abstract Expressionism into three dimensions was a matter of general concern among sculptors by the end of the decade.

Henry Takemoto
First Kumu, 1959
Stoneware, glazed, 21¾ x 22
Scripps College,
Claremont, California,
Collection of Mr. and Mrs. Fred
Marer

Takemoto has acknowledged the influence of Peter Voulkos on his development — an influence which is chiefly seen in his treatment of ceramic form, specifically in his abandonment of conventional shapes and surfaces. Yet Takemoto's sensibility is fundamentally an organic rather than an expressionistic one. His large, handbuilt stoneware forms — moon-shaped jars, long-necked, asymmetrical bottles, tree-shaped vases with narrow bases and bursting, bulging tops — are painted with curlicues, stripes and tendrils suggestive of marine vegetation or of the painted ceramic vessels of Minoan Crete.

— sometimes 1/200th inch in diameter — are organized into patterns fused onto the metal, forming a richly textured surface.[2] Were these objects, made by jewelers, jewelry — or small sculptures?

Still another radical break in the early sixties took place in fibers and textiles. Conventionally, weavers made tapestries and fabrics, all essentially two-dimensional, to hang on the wall or in a window, to lay on the floor or table, or to wear. Classical techniques, like those for double-weave coverlets, were being replaced by painterly approaches, new colors, new compositions, new materials, new uses. Anni Albers and Trude Guermonprez first demonstrated that these limitations could be shattered.

Early and influential were Albers's pictographic woven works which she began in 1933. She was one of the first to use fiber as an idiom for art and her work has proved crucial to all that has come since. Trude Guermonprez (page 74), a colleague of Albers's at Black Mountain College, was influenced by her pictorial weavings. She examined the relationship between tapestry and painting and developed her own textile graphics. Centering her experiments on the loom, Guermonprez used photographs and invented printing techniques with her own stencils and painted abstract images directly on the warp, adding color and texture from the weft.

Soon, weavers began to try neglected techniques from other cultures such as those from Africa, New Guinea, and Mexico. They were examining what could happen when they worked without the loom. The pieces became sculptural, complex, free. The weavings required a new means of display, moving off the wall and into the room. Albers and Guermonprez opened the door for others like Lenore Tawney (page 87), so that a new dimensionality in fiber could be expressed.

Tawney was trained as a weaver of tapestries and had studied drawing and sculpture with Alexander Archipenko. At her studio in New York, she moved away from the traditions and limitations of the loom. In 1955, she exhibited for the first time free-hanging weavings with open constructions — the warp was exposed and the selvages uneven, horrifying other weavers — which were actually beautiful drawings in thread. Her constructions were gossamer. They expanded and contracted; their transparent gauzy layers gave the works form; light and color played through them. Tawney was an experimentalist of exquisite sensitivity.

In 1963, Tawney, along with Alice Adams, Dorian Zachai, and Sheila Hicks (page 224), exhibited their work at the American Craft Museum (then called the Museum of Contemporary Crafts), a few doors from the Museum of Modern Art in New York City. The show was called *Woven Forms* and it was the first major exhibition of the new weaving. Traditional weavers were shocked. Painters and sculptors were exhilarated and inspired.

In wood, the long tradition of handwork was inherited and transmitted by Wharton Esherick (page 30). Esherick is held in veneration for his innate sense of the materials as well as for his rigorous craftsmanship, which never turned to the machine. He understood that wood in its very resistance to the tool is fluid, vital, sculptural even in the

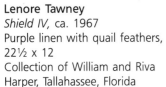

Lenore Tawney
Shield IV, ca. 1967
Purple linen with quail feathers,
22½ x 12
Collection of William and Riva
Harper, Tallahassee, Florida

Shield IV is part of an ongoing series
of small, personal works that
possess the intimate and poetic
quality of Tawney's collages and box
constructions. They are more
textural than her earlier weavings,
becoming three-dimensional by the
incorporation of wrapped elements
rather than the shaping of
applicable surface. In these works
Tawney made extensive use of
knotting, braiding, and fringing, and
added into the fiber collected and
treasured shells and feathers. Called
"shields," their shape relates to
American Indian shields and, more
generally, to the idea of invoked
protection.

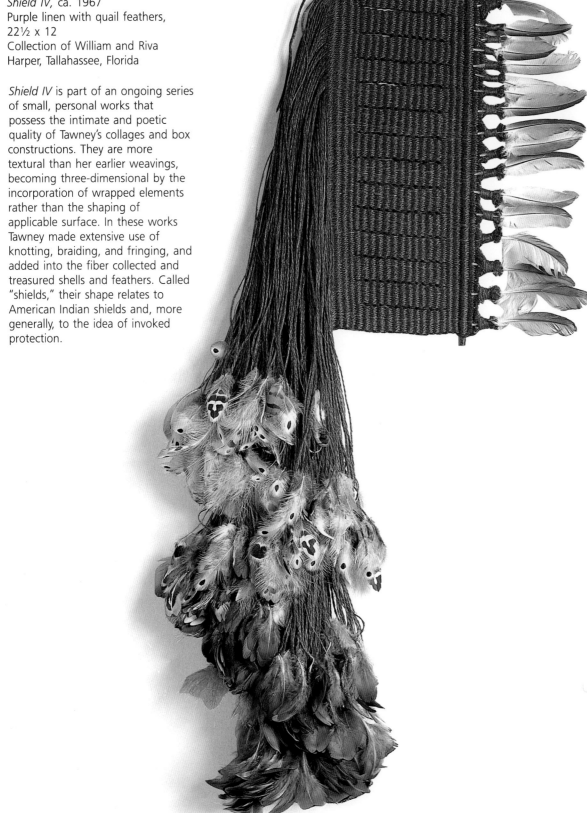

Francoise Grossen
Equilibrium I, 1975
(facing page, right)
Silk, steel, Plexiglas, 33½ x 9 x 3¼
Collection of William and Riva
Harper, Tallahassee, Florida

Equilibrium II, 1975
(facing page, left)
Silk, steel, Plexiglas, 33½ x 9 x 3¼
Collection of Dr. Stephen Mitzner,
Bayport, New York

Equilibrium I and *II* convey physical
and mental tension. A single endless
warp, passed over and over between
anchored stirrups, is bound by
closely wrapped silk filament as if in
a punishment of ultimate
refinement. Each of these exquisitely
disciplined pieces is held taut within
its own Plexiglas cage.

Claire Zeisler
Private Affair II, ca. 1986
Synthetic fiber, 120 x 60 x 60
Rhona Hoffman Gallery,
Chicago, Illinois

In her sixties Zeisler abandoned the
loom on which she had made
functional fabrics for years and
began to make off-loom, free-
standing and free-form fiber
sculptures that helped pave the way
for a revolution in fiber. She was
inspired by ancient weaving
techniques and especially by Native
American baskets she collected.
Knotting and wrapping became her
primary techniques for building
clustered and cascading hanging
forms. These monumental
works find their counterpoint in a
series of more private miniatures
which Zeisler has simultaneously
pursued.

utilitarian object. These qualities resonated in the flowing line of his *Music Rack* of 1953. Another master of materials and of classic techniques in wood, a master furniture maker of understated strength and consummate grace, is Sam Maloof (pages 118, 156, 169). With his *Rocking Chair* series of the early 1960s, he stretched the functional ideal toward a sculptural dignity and scale, transcending style and time.[3]

Not Esherick and not Maloof, however, but Wendell Castle (page 117) is the furniture maker who definitively obliterated the boundary between furniture and sculpture. In 1963, Castle emerged to world renown with his *Music Rack*. A film was shot of his making of the *Music Rack* which allowed the viewer to see the raw material, wood, romantically transformed by the craftsman's hands into a sophisticated and rhythmical form. Castle's objects are inherently dramatic. He invented a stacked lamination of woods, a new method that brought his pieces scale and formal mass, as well as a distinct personal character. By taking conventional furniture making far beyond its original context, Wendell Castle has redefined the art of furniture making and of furniture making as art. Trained as a sculptor, he is a sculptor still.

In June 1964, at Columbia University in New York, Aileen O. Webb, founder and chairman of the organization now called the American Craft Council[4], convened the First World Congress of Craftsmen. The two-week event was intense, both for discussions and demonstrations. Terms flew: folk craft, handicraft, hand craft, decorative arts, applied arts, design, minor arts — and all the other arts. No consensus ruled their use. American scholars and critics who were outside the crafts movement were rarely of help, for they were scarcely aware of the new work and its fecund new imagery.

Craftsmen from Europe or Asia found our arguments baffling and irrelevant, for they rarely thought that the artist's choice of media had much to do with the object's status as a work of art. We found their confidence heartening. Of the numerous demonstrations during the conference, most memorable was one by Harvey Littleton (page 32, 66, 80) on techniques in glass. In 1962, Littleton had established at the University of Wisconsin the first teaching program in glass as a sculptural medium. Previously, at the annual National Decorative Arts and Ceramics Exhibition, held by the Wichita Art Association, we had seen several examples of free-blown glass, bowls and bottles that appeared to be deflated by their tumerous growths. Littleton and his students brought to the conference a portable glass tank, a small box furnace that was heated by a forced-draft propane blowtorch to temperatures of 2000° F so that the Fiberglas marbles in the tank could be melted.[5] With this they presented a series of displays, revealing in both blown and molded forms the medium's inherent brilliance and finesse of flowing form, color, and coruscating light.

Beyond the studio crafts movement we gradually became aware, as the 1960s matured, of objects and artists from other traditions, other American cultures. For us, as potters living in Oklahoma, the work of Native American potters of the twenties through the forties commanded attention from the first — particularly the Pueblo pottery, richly

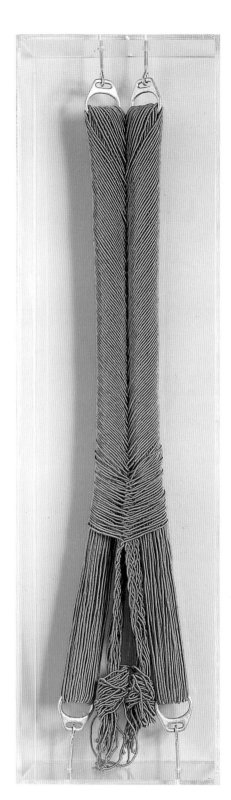

Wharton Esherick
*Library Steps with Elephant and
Donkey Finials,* from the Curtis
Bok House, 1935
Hickory, 35 x 17 x 24
Collection of Rachel Bok Goldman,
Chicago, Illinois

Revered by many contemporary
craftspersons as the spiritual
grandfather of the new crafts
movement in wood, who has
appealed to and influenced a whole
new generation of woodworkers,
from Wendell Castle to Judy McKie,
Esherick was considered an eccentric
in his own time. During years when
fashionable furniture was designed
and manufactured to appoint slick
interiors finished in chrome, steel,
and glass, Esherick affectionately
hand-shaped wood furnishings for
his house (now the Wharton
Esherick Museum, in Paoli,
Pennsylvania). Trained as a painter
and gifted as a sculptor, graphic
artist, and woodworker, he seems to
have been inspired by the Art
Nouveau style of the early twentieth
century. In the early 1930s, Judge
and Mrs. Curtis Bok of Rosemont,
Pennsylvania commissioned Esherick
to furnish a new wing for their
home in Rosemont. The wing
included a circular pine stairway, a
music room framed by solid oak
beams, and a library with both open
and concealed shelves and trays
made of padouk or vermilion wood.
The library also had the easily
movable *Library Steps with Elephant
and Donkey Finials,* made of hickory,
to reach the books in the floor to
ceiling shelves.

Robert Stocksdale
Bowl, 1984 (two views)
Ebony, 4 x 14
Collection of the artist,
Berkeley, California

Stocksdale started turning wood
while imprisoned as a conscientious
objector during World War II. Today
he is the senior figure in American
woodturning producing work that
requires extensive knowledge of
wood anatomy and extremely
precise control of hand-eye
coordination. He is also a
connoisseur of rare woods; like a
jeweler discussing gemstones, he
relishes explaining the peculiar
qualities and origins of each
specimen. The ebony of this bowl is
a light-colored variety from the
Philippines, a species the Japanese
use to build tokonoma. According
to Stocksdale, the Japanese will pay
almost any price for this wood. He
relates with pleasure that he
obtained a piece by sheer luck from
a source near London. The original
piece of ebony, measuring fourteen
inches square and ten feet long,
yielded the example here
representing the best pattern of
grain.

Harvey Littleton
Untitled, (manganese prunted vase)
1964
Glass, 6 x 17
Collection of Jean and Hilbert Sosin,
Bloomfield Hills, Michigan

The passion, talent, and energy of
Harvey Littleton opened the way for
glass as a medium for studio artists.
The son of a Corning physicist,
Littleton was sidetracked by his
independent artistic ambitions which
found an outlet in ceramics.
Graduating from Cranbrook in
1949, he distinguished himself as a
ceramist and teacher at the
University of Wisconsin, but
remained haunted by the desire to
work in glass. In 1962 he headed a
seminar at the Toledo Museum of
Art where artists and professionals
from the glass industry, including
Dominick Labino, developed the
technology for the melting and
blowing of glass on a small scale,
thus ending its dependence on
industry.

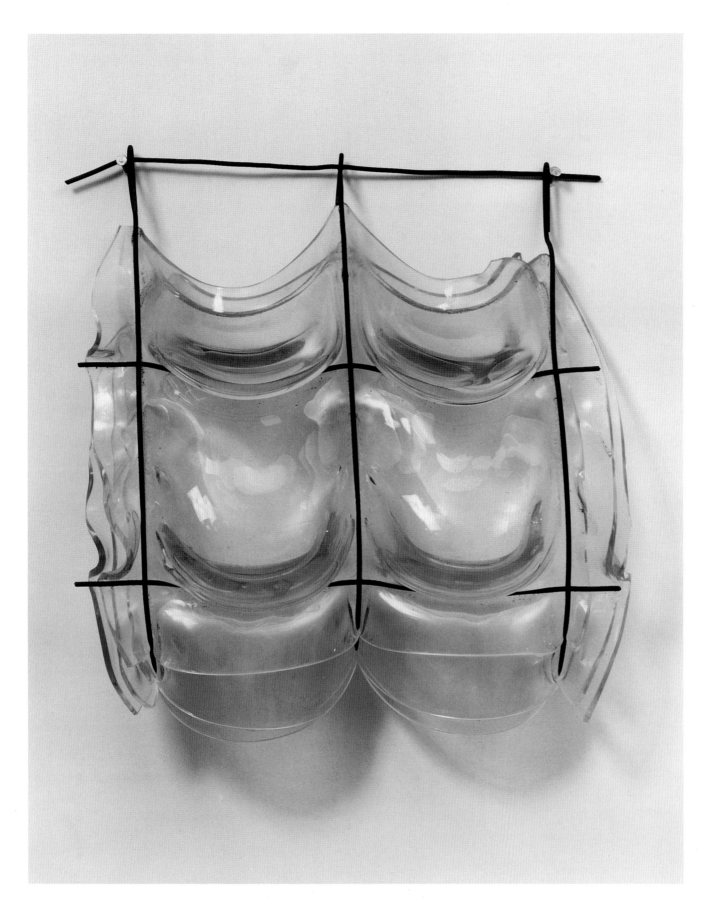

Mary Shaffer
Artemis, 1979
Glass, metal, 17 x 16 x 4
Collection of Ivan and Marilynn
Karp, New York, New York

Mary Shaffer brings two special
qualities to her sculpture, her
rapport with the material of glass
and her womanhood. Plate glass
sheets, large or small, have afforded
her the means of expressing her
ideas. Her works are always
abstract, yet there is a constant
subplot of dominance and
submission with glass as a metaphor
for inferior physical strength. Her
subtle message is most poignantly
conveyed by a series of hanging
pieces where sheets of glass are
suspended in a crude grid of heavy
wire. Heated, the glass slowly
enfolds its bonds, trapping the
restraining metal in a sequence of
gentle ripples and sensuous bulges.
The title of this piece (Artemis was
the virgin goddess of the hunt)
reinforces a feminist interpretation
of Shaffer's abstraction.

represented in collections in Tulsa, Denver, and elsewhere in the region. These pots had evolved strikingly from tribal traditions of the nineteenth century. Even by the twenties, certain Pueblo potters, above all Julian and Maria Martinez of San Ildefonso and Fannie Nampeyo of Hopi, were combining classical Southwest American Indian forms and decorative images with elements of the latest Art Deco style. They were making pots of effortless sophistication. In 1968, we saw and were able to study a film about Maria Martinez. The film, *The Hands of Maria,* traced Maria Martinez through a full potting sequence. The progression was natural at every step, from her digging New Mexico clay through firing the objects with a fuel of dung from local cattle. Primitive-seeming materials, primitive-seeming techniques: we were awed to see the elegant forms and finishes she realized. We were used to mixing clay from sacks delivered once a year, preparing surface agents in laboratory conditions, and firing our pottery in a commercially-built gas kiln. Now we found ourselves digging local clays at roadsides and asking ranchers to let us collect dried manure from their fields. We learned a lot, and our art changed. Much the same thing was happening elsewhere: the use of the simplest tools and of materials found in the immediate environment spread among ceramists across the country, the next development after the Oriental influences of the previous decade.

Lucy M. Lewis
Seed Jar, (Acoma-Pueblo) ca. 1959
Black-on-white painted pottery,
6½ x 10
The Philbrook Museum of Art, Clark Field Collection,
Tulsa, Oklahoma

Lucy Lewis ranks in many minds as the Acoma equivalent to San Ildefonso's brilliant potter Maria Martinez. She is unquestionably a twentieth-century master. Lewis integrated a variety of prehistoric designs into her ceramics, among them the ancient walnut black-on-white, as in this jar, and other western New Mexican and central Arizonan prehistoric pottery motifs. Recently she has concentrated on ancient Mimbres and Zuni designs.

Lolita Concho,
Jar, (Acoma-Pueblo) 1984
Ceramic, polychrome, 8¾ x 12¼
The Philbrook Museum of Art,
Tulsa, Oklahoma,
Gift of Friends of Native American Art

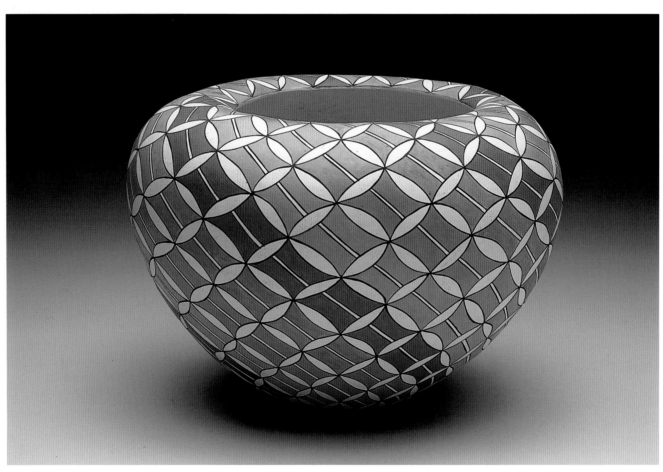

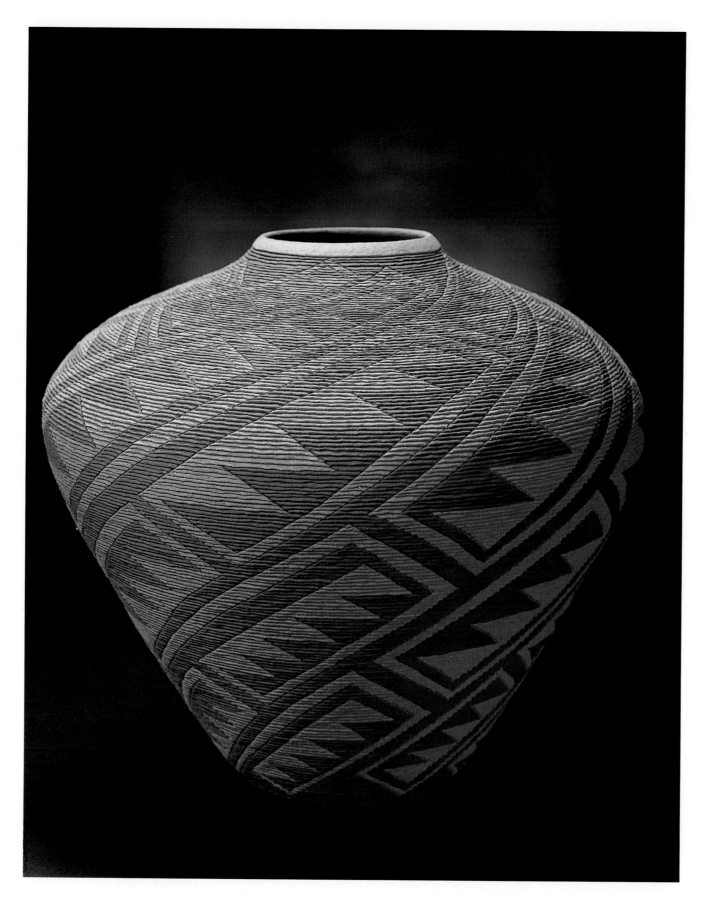

Richard Zane Smith
Vessel, 1987
Ceramic, 19½ x 19
Richard and Barbara Faletti Family
Collection,
Clarendon Hills, Illinois

Smith's work could qualify as
samples of historic expressionism.
Drawing upon the deep aesthetic
and technical tradition of prehistoric
Southwestern potters, he has taken
the ancient culinary ware tradition
of corrugated pottery and has
advanced it to a level of fine art.
Within his relatively short career, he
has evolved through a meticulous
concern for surface, texture, and
painterly abstraction using "fire
clouds" produced during firing to
elaborate step-fret and geometric
compositions indented into the
surface of the vessel, reminiscent of
the Anasazi basket weavers of the
prehistoric American Southwest.

Larry Fuente
Mad Cad, 1980-1984
1960 Cadillac Sedan de Ville, mixed
media set in epoxy resin, lifesize
Collection of the artist,
Mendocino, California

Alfonso Ossorio
Juggler, 1961 (facing page)
Plastic and various materials on
masonite, 52 x 48
Courtesy of Oscarsson Siegeltuch
Galleries,
New York, New York

At an extreme from such cool perfection lies the art of the inner city
and the new ethnic assertiveness — unsubtle, garish, shocking. Often
these objects convey, in the strongest terms, the relationship of an
unassimilated social group to the larger society. Often the artists
accomplish this by combining the most unusual substances, even recycling
the castoff trash of the consumer society: art made of the ignored, the
neglected, the despised, which says, when it works, "This is our
experience."

During the 1960s, Alfonso Ossorio assembled relief constructions
within a rectangular framework, combining found and fabricated objects
— surreal, kitsch, and outrageously imaginative. Ossorio, from the
Philippines, is a graduate of Harvard and of the Rhode Island School of
Design. Always distinctly Hispanic, his works seemed neo-rural, neo-folk,
neo-naive — but they were never innocent. They challenged the canons of

beauty and the conventions of taste by bringing together the throwaway objects of a plastic society — its fantasies and fetishes — in trenchant anti-cultural statements. Ossorio transformed these remnants into assemblages to which he gave gleaming new lacquered surfaces. The objects do not die; they are reclaimed and preserved. These works proved to be precursors to a new wave of Hispanic or Latino art in the United States.

Extraordinary examples of the recycling of the castoffs of industrial society are presented by the Chicano Wagons of southern California. These are old automobiles that have been lovingly rebuilt and decorated — "customized" — to a bizarre extreme that is sometimes undeniably beautiful. A Chicano Wagon begins with a car, often one headed for the scrap yard. It is disassembled, restored, repainted, ornamented, altered, reassembled with all the care, machine-shop skill, and expense that others would devote to an antique. Often the changes made by the artist are so extreme that the make of the original vehicle is virtually impossible to recognize. Whole sections of the bodies are resculptured so drastically as to create forms that suggest completely new intentions. They are ornamented with found objects. Colors are brilliant, high-key, often creating optical effects that visually negate the structure. These objects are tinselly, brassy, expressive. They stand at a crazed intersection of the high-tech and the handmade; they are working class and anti-establishment, they are the last exflorescence of the American cult of the car but transplanted from small-town Midwest to the barrios of Los Angeles and San Diego.

An artist who emerged in Southern California later in the 1970s, Larry Fuente, describes his medium as "light in all its splendor" — and that ringing phrase characterizes many Latino artists. Fuente turns a refrigerator into a reliquary, a splendid and sumptuous container, bejeweled with scraps from a local dump. Fuente's *Angel* is a store-window mannequin covered with found objects. (It was put on the cover of *National Geographic* in April 1983, with the headline "The Fascinating World of Trash.") Fuente's art is as vibrant as the cultural cross-influences that make America.

When we first became aware of the new ethnic art, particularly the Latino art, it was unlike anything we knew; it smashed and brushed aside classical aesthetic standards. Its forms were alien, and intransigently challenged our visual understanding. Yet it compelled attention and commanded respect. And we began to recognize it in the most unlikely places. Even graffiti, defiant and assaulting as they deliberately are, have taken on formal compositional characteristics, with dimensionality, vibrant color, and aggressive social and political messages. Objects that were made primarily as conscious works of art carried with them the same cultural intensity. Their roots may be traced to the Meso-American Indian heritage, to issues of immigrant and barrio life, to the strong religious traditions of *santos* carvings and *retablo* paintings that embellish portable altars. We were startled to discover that some of these works incorporated historical elements reminiscent, for example, of Antonio Gaudí's

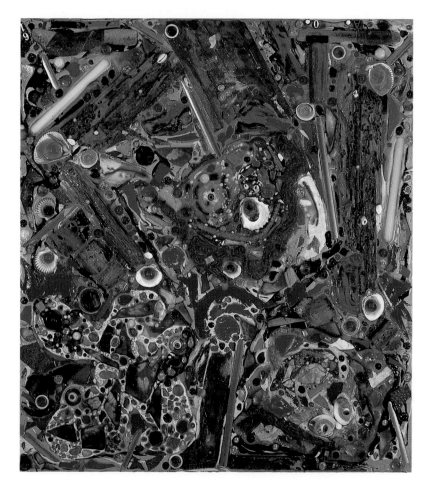

Larry Fuente
Oasis (detail), 1970
Mixed media set in resin,
90 x 43½ x 40½
Collection of Ann Harithas,
Mendocino, California

In *Oasis,* mere plumbing has been transformed into an altar/throne/fountain by a bewildering, glittering array of materials and found objects. These center on the Virgin Mary, flanked by angels and oddly appropriate ceramic swans with fluttering wings. *Oasis* gives Dada an ethnic flair as it expresses Fuente's concern with light — to dazzle and to be dazzled — as well as his unabashed celebration of the gaudiest aspects of barrio culture.

Marcia Keegan
India Truck,
Bodh Gaya, India, 1986.

architecture — flowing, animate, Art Nouveau-like forms, with surfaces covered with potshards and bits of glass inlaid like mosaic. The effect is dazzling in color and reflectivity, with a strong cultural heritage.

When Africans were brought in slavery to America, their memory of their visual heritage was rapidly attenuated if not altogether lost. Their new experience in America was strengthened and powerfully communicated through blues, soul, spirituals, jazz, and rhythmic dance. The Afro-American artists of this century have developed their own artistic traditions in painting, sculpture, and crafts. They have synthesized personal interpretations from the Black experience with reinterpretations of their newly rediscovered ancestral heritage which dramatically resurfaced after World War II.

Martin Puryear
Simple Gift, 1982
Pine, maple, yellow cedar,
64 x 58½ x 1¾
Collection of Mr. and Mrs. John C. Kern, Oak Brook, Illinois

While in the Peace Corps in Sierra Leone, West Africa, Puryear learned the traditional techniques of the local carpenters. This experience and his subsequent study with Swedish furniture makers in Stockholm, Sweden, are important to his art. Sometimes his objects appear to be found; their shapes are so intrinsic to the wood that they seem to have been fashioned by nature itself. In others, where the artist's hand is clearly evident, the joinery is so precise that the constructed forms appear to be wholly carved. In the 1980s Puryear made an extensive series of circles which, in their variation of painted surfaces and details, cover a gamut of associations. To Puryear, they are about lines; like drawing with wood, he creates objects that are at once attached to the wall like paintings and three-dimensional like sculpture. *Simple Gift* is an homage to the unexcelled craftsmanship of the Shaker woodworker, its title adapted from the Shaker song, "The Gift to be Simple."

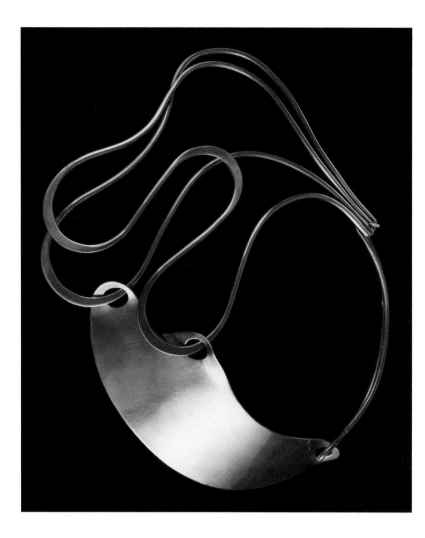

Arthur Smith
Neckpiece, 1948
Copper and brass, 7¾ x 6 x 1⅝
The American Craft Museum,
New York, New York

Smith stressed the necessity for
boldness in jewelry design — a
quality which characterizes his work
better than any other. The most
impressive of his early works are the
large neckpieces and bracelets from
the late 1940s made of forged brass
and copper. These daring works
were conceived specifically as *body*
ornaments, not as dress accessories
or "miniature sculptures." Smith
spoke of them as "an integral part
of the face, arm, or body. . . .
incomplete until it is on, related to
the body. (Lee Nordness, *Objects:
USA,* New York: Viking, 1970, p.
208.)

Art Smith emerged from Harlem and opened a jewelry workshop in
Greenwich Village. He was a maker of body ornaments from non-precious
metals. His philosophy is akin to his ancestral heritage, for he believed that
the large sculptural forms could not take on their full shape and form until
they were integrated with the body. His hammered, raised, and forged
collars and arm bands cross the boundaries of his own experiences as a
professionally trained designer at Cooper Union in New York. However, his
objects are neither neo-African nor Afro-American; they establish Smith's
own distinct language.

Trained in sculpture, a graduate of Yale in the late 1950s, Barbara
Chase-Riboud was one of the first to use fiber in her sculptures, both
monumental and jewel-sized, allowing a transition from the floor or from
the body to cast crumpled forms. As a graduate student, she discovered
the dance masks of New Caledonia and the ceremonial masks of Mali and
Gabon, which served as symbolic references for her work. She used
opposing materials, hard and soft, imbued with a mysterious spirit. Her
fresh aesthetic concepts were woven into her sculpture; the
reinterpretations of their original context is made anew, for she has chosen
to use nontraditional materials — silk, nylon, rayon, aluminum, chrome —
not the materials of her ancestors. A tension is created by these opposites,
but these opposites become a unified whole. Chase-Riboud was
introduced to fiber by a classmate, Sheila Hicks (page 224), another fiber
artist. Hicks taught her the techniques of knotting, wrapping, braiding,
and cording. Her work was revolutionary for both sculpture and craft, a
departure centering on her interest in her cultural roots.

Black roots were strengthened in 1972 when the British potter
Michael Cardeau brought to the United States a Nigerian colleague, Ladi
Kwali. The simplicity and honesty of the traditions of her village, and the
clay vessels she produced were empowered with a spiritual and rhythmical
resonance. That spirit was cast upon the audience who attended her
demonstrations.

We have described these artists and their works in terms of their
abundance, their joy, their life-enhancing exuberance. These qualities grow
more obvious with time. Yet in the middle and late 1960s — after years of
unprecedented social and political crises — these works and others were
expressing protest, anger, and outrage. Visual arts often became a weapon
in the politics of power movements, Black, brown, or Indian. The arts
raised racial and ethnic pride, raised all Americans' awareness of each
race. Those years unleashed horrifying imagery, of an emotional and
intellectual ferocity hardly rivaled since the savage social commentaries of
Hogarth or Goya's last mad paintings. When social activists of the late
sixties made art a platform, the message often overpowered the art. The
harrowing expressions of those moments were often an inseparable part
of the works' lasting vitality. The walls of the ghettos of New York and the
barrios of Los Angeles displayed unknown artists' statements of the
human condition — and while these were direct and transient, other
artists subverted with bitter irony other images of race, in the process
creating unforgettable work. Betye Saar (page 209), in her boxed shrines,

replaced Aunt Jemima's wooden spoon with a rifle to make her a guerrilla warrior. Ron Anderson created a Native American burial rite out of an automobile ready for a salvage yard — a personal interpretation of the Indian's death in modern white society. Rafael Montanez Gritz used ancient religious symbols of death and spirituality in "happenings" he put on in New York to demonstrate his belief that America was dead. Mel Edwards took fragments from torture devices to transform the ritual of a Ku Klux Klan lynching into a sculptural montage about castration and violence. Once unleashed, these strong images have continued and recurred, most notably, perhaps, in Joyce J. Scott's searing emblems (pages 130, 131), executed in jewelry — brooches and pendants made of suckling-pig bones and other found objects — of the Jonestown massacre.

Paralleling the growth of Latino and Black American art has been the emergence of feminist art. It too is rooted in experiences of injustice and inequality that were recognized as intolerable in the 1960s. Many feminist artists, again like many Latinos and Blacks, not only express the themes but also employ the everyday materials that represent social deprivation. Such materials and experiences for women are those that so long characterized women's work and their stereotyped roles.

Most daring and controversial of all feminist artists is Judy Chicago. From the late sixties, she has worked with motifs and images that must be described as organically female. We first met her in 1972, near the beginning of the modern women's movement, when she came to Tulsa and set the intellectual and arts community afire with her displays and discussions of what she called "cunt art." In 1974, during an academic dinner party in Los Angeles, her feminist convictions were outraged by watching the men carry on the discussion while the women, who were no less intelligent, educated, and talented, sat silent. She began thinking about women giving dinner parties: they invited the guests, cleaned the house, shopped for the food, cooked the meal and served it, cleared up afterward — making everyone welcome and animated — but were themselves mere backdrop. From Chicago's determination that able women not be ignored came the idea for *The Dinner Party,* one of the most important if flagrant feminist works. Its scale is as great as its ambitions: some 200 women and men took five years to create it, working in multiple media from porcelain and painting to sewing and embroidery with an industry that recalls the preparations of some ancient royal tomb in Egypt or China. *The Dinner Party* is the luxurious setting of an immensely long table. It portrays thirty-nine women from mythology and history, by means of a place setting for each, while referring also to 999 other women. Embroidered upon runners along the table are significant historical and biographical facts and achievements of the women the work presents. The places are set with porcelain chalices, white earthenware knives and forks, and linen napkins edged with gold. The table begins with a prehistoric goddess and ends with Georgia O'Keeffe. Each of the thirty-nine women is represented, at the center of her place setting, by a fourteen-inch china plate on which is painted the essential image of her femaleness — her vulva.

Arthur Smith
Double Finger Ring, ca. 1972
Silver, opal (set in gold),
½ x 1½ x 1½
Collection of Karen Johnson Boyd,
Racine, Wisconsin

A graduate of Cooper Union, Smith was initially trained in commerical art. His involvement with jewelry design began later when, as craft supervisor for the Children's Aid Society in Harlem, he learned the techniques of jewelry making from a colleague with whom he collaborated. In the late 1940s Smith established his own jewelry workshop on West 4th Street in Greenwich Village, New York.

Judy Chicago
Study for Virginia Woolf Plate, 1978
Glazed porcelain, 12 inches in
diameter
American Contemporary Art
Galleries, New York, New York

One of the figures honored in *The Dinner Party* was Virginia Woolf, the English writer, part of the early twentieth-century Bloomsbury Group. In Chicago's plate honoring Woolf, she used petal or genital forms that open and break away from the plate to symbolize Woolf's fecund genius that broke the historic silence about women's lives. The example here is a test plate made in preparation of the final work.

Patti Warashina
Wash and Wear, 1976
Handbuilt clay slabs, castings,
underglazes, sprayed acrylics,
25 x 16 x 13
Memphis Brooks Museum of Art,
Memphis, Tennessee, Gift of Audrey
Taylor Gonzalez

Miriam Schapiro
Flowerness Fan, 1981
Acrylic, fabric, glitter, 48 x 96
Collection of Ken Goldglit,
Bellmore, New York

Schapiro abandoned paint in the
1970s to take up cloth as her
medium for picture making,
becoming one of the leaders of the
Pattern and Decoration movement.
In 1971 she and Judy Chicago
founded the Feminist Art Program at
the California Institute of Arts,
promoting the making of art out of
women's experiences. Schapiro
began to use fabrics associated with
women in her own art, assembling
them into house, heart, kimono,
and other shapes. Beginning in
1979 she added the format of the
fan to this repertoire.

In 1971, Judy Chicago and Miriam Schapiro (page 176) founded the
Feminist Art Program at the California Institute of Arts in Valencia. The
program soon became one of the most highly vocal and visible
instruments of the movement, shaping the thoughts, works, and destinies
of many women. Schapiro is an initiator of female imagery of a subtler yet
still caustic kind. She incorporates into her paintings remnants of
anonymous domestic handiwork, the activities historically assigned to
women — crocheting, appliquéing, hooking, cutting, sewing, piecing,
embroidering, and quilting. This becomes an iconographic idiom of fabrics
in collage — assembled of materials she has drawn from, literally, the
fabric of the home. Schapiro calls the collages "femmages." One series of
these takes the form of fans. These traditionally have functional,
decorative, and ceremonial values. The woman with a fan cools herself,
yet at the same time the fan is an elegant object of fashion, and it
hides even as it hints at her emotions and sensuality. Schapiro's fans
elaborate patterns, textures, and rhythms into deliberate interpretations of
women's culture and art. They have multiple layers of symbolism.

Patti Warashina, an artist from the Northwest Coast who works in
clay, also makes art that comments socially, politically, and religiously. She

J. Fred Woell

Come Alive, You're In the Pepsi Generation, 1966 (right)
Copper, silver, steel, 4 x 4 x ⁵⁄₁₆
Collection of Kathleen Woell,
Deer Isle, Maine

Class of '78, 1978 (below)
Steel, silicone rubber, 2 x 2¾ x ⅝
Collection of the artist,
Deer Isle, Maine

Woell's choice of found materials was encouraged by the sculptor Frank Gallo to whom he apprenticed in the mid-1960s. He has incorporated common objects such as aluminum can pull tabs, .22 empty cartridge shells, bottle caps, staples, glass, photos, resin, brass, copper, iron casts of animal crackers, Dairy-Creme spoons, and children's toys, combined with other non-precious objects that have no intrinsic value. Woell says that his

work is "anti-jewelry jewelry" for the work has nothing to do with what is normally associated in giving jewelry "value," adornments or gemstones, gold, or silver. *Come Alive, You're in the Pepsi Generation* is mounted like a badge with the connotation of a fetish or icon. The photo of the carefree "Pepsi girl" is a prominent reminder of the easy-come, easy-go of a consumer-good society. *Class of '78* is symbolic of the next generation being "piggish on America." They are all there ready to be spoonfed, and the former work ethic was hogwash. Woell is a remarkable social critic and visual translator — the objects he creates say volumes about the intensity of everyday America with thematic imagery that is direct, powerful, and accessible.

creates feminist icons — or perhaps anti-icons. Her altar series offers small Zen Buddhist household shrines like some she discovered as a child in her Christian, Japanese-American home. Her altars are biographies of domesticity, of women's work. They are disturbing, paradoxical, and angry. In *Wash and Wear* we see a woman who is simultaneously joyous and defiant. She screams hysterically while washing men's clothing, rising to an apotheosis as a laundress.

We think the time has come for the distinction between crafts and the fine arts to be abandoned, put behind us. So varied and vital are the traditions, sources, and themes, the artists and the works themselves that can loosely be grouped as crafts, so undeniably do the works demonstrate these artists' motives and achievements to be rich, complex, and aesthetically demanding, that the debates over the role of crafts that took place endlessly within the crafts movement of the 1960s and 1970s now seem jejune — hardly more than the self-conscious uncertainty of adolescence. The best new works elude categorization altogether — a capacity that, indeed, they share with much other recent art. For in the sixties also, even in the American gallery and museum mainstream, certain younger — or at least freer — sculptors and painters began to break out of the established boundaries of definition by materials. Several American sculptors began the process. After a time of aimlessness and eclecticism, American sculpture emerged in the sixties with startling new themes and unconventional materials and processes — violating all past definitions of the art. The sculptural quality of crushed automobile parts intrigued John Chamberlain; Claes Oldenburg took familiar hard images like toilets, ice bags, electrical plugs, and hand mixers and made oversized soft and stuffed forms; and the landscape became the studio and gallery for Robert Smithson's earthwork sculpture series. Soon, painters were assembling found objects into constructions; sculptors were painting their forms in bright colors; painters gave canvases new shape, new dimensions; sculptors became industrial fabricators; painters became scientists of perceptual illusion; sculptors made figures out of cloth, stuffed and soft, while painters vacuformed hard plastic surfaces. Painters and sculptors alike immersed themselves in popular culture, and both retrenched to the barest essentials of color, form, and surface. The forms of the 1960s dealt with space and scale. They came out of ceilings and walls, engrossed the entire volume of rooms or of buildings — or became conceptually so large that they broke out of enclosed space to run through fields and cover mountains. The boundaries that sculptors and painters had now broken down were the same, in most general terms, that we who still thought of ourselves as in the crafts movement were opening up. Inevitably, we all grew aware of each other's materials, methods, issues, and aims. Above all, the changes have enormously energized American art.

The old limits, old channels for expression having broken down, we need new descriptive categories and new standards: without them, in this world in flux, critical analysis — even simple conversation — is almost impossible. Over the past few years we have worked out several thematic categories for grouping works historically and culturally to make interpretation fruitful. These categories can hardly be sealed off from each other: most of the works easily cross such boundaries. Our intent is to place the objects where they speak most eloquently.

Manuel Neri
Loop #1, 1961
Stoneware, glaze, epoxy,
18 x 22½ x 17½
Collection of Peter H. Voulkos,
Oakland, California

Neri had a strong influence on ceramic artists in California during the early 1960s. His *Loops,* brightly painted and glazed arching forms, were considered Abstract Expressionist ceramics. These gestural organic forms were direct and strongly original. Neri's experiments and developments helped to revolutionize attitudes about ceramic art. The first earthenware *Loop* was painted with acrylics in 1956 and the stoneware *Loop* from 1961 was glazed and epoxied. Neri was a satellite figure around the Voulkos group in Berkeley, which included Archie Bray, Harold Paris, Ron Nagle, James Melchert, and Stephen DeStaebler. This burst of Abstract Expressionist activity was at its peak between 1957 and 1960. Eventually Neri moved on to figurative work, but he is established in the history of American ceramics as part of the first revolution.

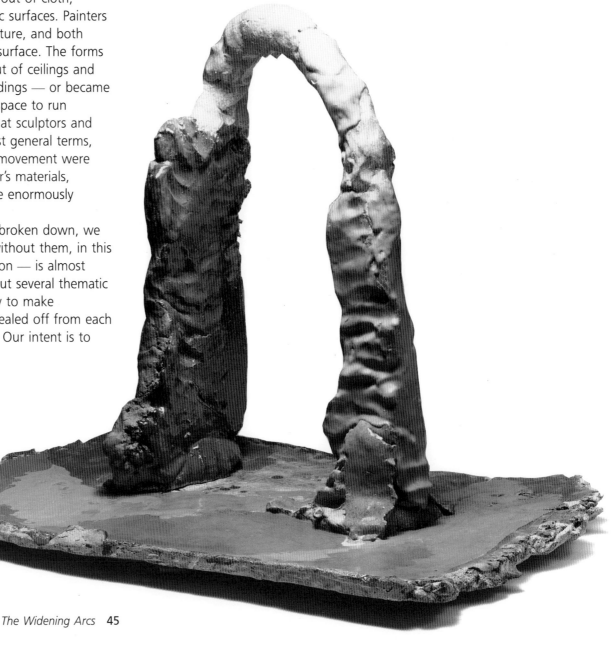

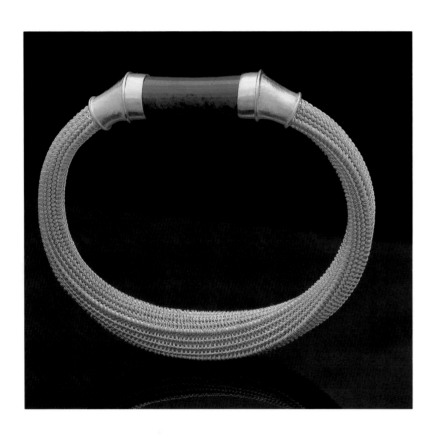

Mary Lee Hu
Bracelet #37, 1986
18k and 22k gold with lapis lazuli,
twined and constructed,
3¼ x 2¾ x ½
Collection of the artist,
Seattle, Washington

Hu's woven gold bracelet represents a penchant for experimentation with classical structures and materials juxtaposed in new combinations. Woven metal thread was not perceived as likely material for artistic statement. However, the use of wire as thread allows free-woven structures to take on dimensionality not usually present with fiber.

IDEA RULES MATERIAL

The mastery of technique that characterizes present-day artists in clay, fiber, leather, metal, wood, and glass has set them free to develop styles and themes that are highly personal and that transcend the materials. Anni Albers's pictographic weavings were enriched by Southwestern tradition and symbolic imagery — notably the cruciform in *La Luz I* (page 75), of 1947. The piece combined linen, strands of silvery metallic thread, and gimp (ornamental cord), establishing the expressiveness of fiber as a painter's medium. *La Luz I* was crucially liberating for artists who followed. A more recent example is Lia Cook's approach to the optical phenomena inherent in fabric structures. Observing Cook's *Translucence*, first shown in 1978, one is immediately taken with the visual deceptions achieved by her use of color and radical technique. Forms appear as undulating waves, yet on a closer look reveal themselves as illusions, created in much the way classical damask weaving creates forms on a flat surface. Cook pushes, pulls, and flattens the warp and weft, creating seductive surfaces as regal as the finest seventeenth-century Flemish tapestries. Ron Nagle (pages 50, 57, 84, 85) developed a series of clay vessels, *Cups,* in the early sixties. The explorations of the cup format executed in the seventies and eighties elicit responses not unlike those one feels upon entering the buildings of modern master architects — Walter Gropius or Richard Neutra. Austerity and a serene beauty emerge from the severity of form and the absence of organic detailing. At the same time, Nagle's *Cups* convey a sensuality created by a colored, textured surface and by the object's unmistakable reference to the vessels from which its otherwise ascetic form derives. David Huchthausen (page 101) creates complex geometrical grids from the glass originally used on the facades of Art Deco buildings — the pieces left by the wrecker's ball. Vitrolite, an opaque and richly colored glass used in those facades, possesses a chromatic density rarely seen in other materials. Huchthausen cuts and assembles the glass into structures reminiscent of video games, broken computer images, or the patterns of our streets. Mary Lee Hu's *Bracelet #37*, of 1986, is woven of 18k and 22k gold wire with lapis lazuli. She imparts exquisite form to the material. The wires twist through space and are gathered into nodes contrasting with the fabric-like structure. Hu uses classical weaving techniques to transform the materials, infusing an ancient tradition with a new sculptural authority.

Sid Garrison
Orchestral Toy, 1983
Leather, acrylic, 22½ x 11½ x 3
Collection of the artist,
Houston, Texas

Garrison did functional custom
leatherwork before beginning to
produce his sculptural vessel forms,
wall pieces, and boxes. The artist
says that one of his continuing goals
is to move the material of leather
past its normal association with
function. His container forms allude
to function, but are not functional
in the usual sense.

Duayne Hatchett
Essex, 1985
Painted steel, 38 x 76 x 18
Collection of the artist,
Buffalo, New York

Of the several trends or schools of twentieth-century European and American sculpture, Hatchett is most associated with Constructivism. His precise, bare works combine Constructivism ideas with basketry techniques of the Pueblo Indians (an area of interest for Hatchett), drawing on the luminous and ethereal qualities of bronze, aluminum, steel, iron, copper and silver. The way he works with these materials is typically hard, rigid, taut. In current work he has released the severe angles into rolling curves, and yet his commitment to hard form persists.

Lia Cook
Translucence, 1978
Rayon, 60 x 36
Collection of Dr. Ruth B. Jamison,
Alexandria, Virginia

49

Ron Nagle
Untitled, 1981
Earthenware, glazed, 6 x 4 x 3¾
Collection of Daniel Jacobs,
New York, New York

By the early 1980s it was becoming difficult to talk about Nagle's *Cups* as cups. Some say his aesthetic concern is outside the ceramic tradition. He has had a reputation for hating pottery, but he says he just hates boring pottery. Certainly Nagle's work has evolved from the vessel format, and his work is still referred to as cups, but he himself says he doesn't think he makes cups anymore. Sometimes they are open but his more recent work is closed, becoming like miniature mountains while retaining the intimacy of cups. His vessels have become volumes and masses; the concept of volume is, as he says, indigenous to ceramics. He was first drawn to clay because with it he could make things directly that he couldn't make in any other media. Nagle speaks with affection of "the old guys" — Voulkos, Melchert, Price, Frimkess. He respects in their work what he refers to as "class" — delivery and clarity — virtues which also mark Nagle's own work.

New techniques, new materials, and combinations of them have driven artist-craftsmen to search for new vocabularies — to produce not functions but ideas and images. These artists have freed themselves from conformity to the consumer's conventional expectations of utility or decoration. Jewelry no longer needs preciousness and noble status. Glass no longer needs to limit itself to the traditional approaches of Lalique or Steuben. Fiber no longer requires the structures and the implied functions imposed by the loom. Clay no longer needs to form a vessel, a device for holding, storing, pouring. Furniture no longer is required to meet a utilitarian demand.

Thus, the small sculptures of Ken Cory (pages 91, 128) explore the use of non-precious metals and of shapes from manmade as well as natural environments. These objects dissociate themselves from the preciousness of body ornament, realizing instead the tactile qualities inherent in the forms. *Pin,* of 1967, is not necessarily to be worn: Cory urges that one hold it, fondle it like a Japanese netsuke. Marvin Lipofsky's *Loops* of 1965-1972 are made of glass yet rebel against the material's glassiness, its inherent austerity. Lipofsky made compound, oozing, "blobular" forms, then painted them and flocked them; he was inspired by a flocked "Fuzz Wagon" he saw at a hotrod show. He was one of the first artists in glass to contradict the reflectivity of glass, one of the first fully to explore its fluidity; he stretched the medium.

Artists working with fiber removed the warp to a free-hanging position, liberating both scale and form. In the monumentally proportioned *The Principal Wife Goes On,* in 1969 (page 224), Sheila Hicks gathered densely hanging linen threads at intervals, wrapping them with colored silks, creating a pattern that evokes the image of bound flaxen locks. Other artists not necessarily active in the women's movement turned to materials that had been part of women's art and domesticity. Elaborate turn-of-the-century quilts are like accidental ancestors to Lucas Samaras's *Reconstructions* (page 170), completed in 1977, which are reminiscent of large-scale, framed paintings. Samaras's glimmering ribbons and their zooming diagonal and zig-zag patterns evoke our high-speed expressways, our mass-communication systems. Kim Levin, a painter and critic who in 1975 wrote a book on Lucas Samaras, later described his work as "narcissistic, radically eclectic," and "irreverent." She added that they "hang on the walls like glorious shrouds from an irretrievable past, ambivalent icons, security blankets for a postmodern future."[6] Like Peter Voulkos, yet largely independent of him, other clay artists took wheel-thrown forms and confuted their functional formality as vessels. Hui Ka Kwong, for example, put thrown forms into new orientations with vibrant surface colors; these are sculptural compositions.

Neda Al Hilali
Richard's Piece, 1974
Paper, dyes, paint, 96 x 60 x 6
Collection of Richard Kaplan,
Beverly Hills, California

One critic called Al Hilali a
Scheherazade with images, which
she sells by the square foot. Of
brickmasons, tile layers, and herself,
she wrote, "we broke miracles into
patterns." Her pieces are energetic,
conceptually assertive, baroque
objects made up of an amazing
complexity of rhythms, crafted with
need, patience, and joy. The
rhythmic actions of the creative
activity are revealed in the
excitement of the three-dimensional
surfaces. The repetition of actions
necessary to accomplish these pieces
become ritual, and ritual usually
accomplishes magic. *Richard's Piece*
is made of rolled paper towels with
the ends dyed. Groups of little girls
(especially trained for this endeavor)
helped Al Hilali plait this material.
The plaited, wadded material was
then run through a press. Al Hilali
painted, stained, and otherwise
worked on the resulting surfaces
until they were rich and sensuous,
sometimes drawing plaited nodules
back out to the surface. As she says,
she has spent a lifetime "braiding
puzzles." (Sandy Ballatore, "Neda Al
Hilali," essay in exhibition catalogue
for Neda Al Hilali, Selected Works:
1968-1985, April 23-May 19,1985,
Los Angeles Municipal Art Gallery, p.
9.)

Lia Cook
Hanging Net, 1984
Rayon, paint, 54 x 20 x 6
Allrich Gallery,
San Francisco, California

Cook's work has always been
concerned with structure and the
potential of fiber to reveal, conceal,
and reflect simultaneously. Unlike
most of Cook's earlier shaped and
woven constructions, *Hanging Net*
seems to have no structure, in spite
of the visible layers of thread
revealed from within its open
network. Most of Cook's other work
has been deliberately formed into
folds, but *Hanging Net* has the soft,
limp, accidental form of a damp
dishcloth draped over a refrigerator
door handle. Its form is mutable.
Cook strives for a particular gesture
frozen in time.

Robert Ebendorf
Set of Nine Brooches (in one wall hanging-unit), 1980
Mixed metals: copper, silver, gold, bronze, 16 x 12¼, each brooch 2¼ x 2¼
Collection of Sue and Malcolm Knapp, New York, New York

A leader in expanding the range of color in metal through the use of heat and chemical solutions, Ebendorf harnessed metallurgical advances to aesthetic purpose in a series of brooches created for a 1980 exhibition. He grouped related brooches and mounted them on wall panels for the installation. Distressed at the dispersion of the work, collectors Malcolm and Sue Knapp commissioned another set of brooches, suggesting a permanent back panel of anodized aluminum be obtained from goldsmith David Tisdale, in order to preserve the impact of Ebendorf's challenge to the limits of jewelry.

Marvin Lipofsky
California Loop, 1970 (below)
Glass, flocked, 15 x 24
Australian National Gallery, Canberra, Australia, Crafts Board of the Australia Council Collection, 1980

From the beginning of his glass experience, Lipofsky thought that the underlying beauty and elegance of the material had to be violated so that personal statements about the form were insured. Never afraid of experimentation, he discovered that the material could be stretched beyond its normal limits and that the surfaces had infinite possibilities. He incorporated sandblasting, mirroring, electroplating, acid etching, lacquering, application of decals, and flocking. All of these surface treatments denied glass the beauty of glass, its glassiness. In fact, the surface applications hid the poor quality of the glass which was disruptive and not characteristic of the purity normally associated with glass. The flocking on portions of the *California Loop* series was inspired by a "Fuzz Wagon" at a hotrod show.

William Wyman
Before You Know There is Love,
1962
Stoneware, 23⅔ x 17 x 3½
Lee Nordness Galleries, Inc.,
Belfair, Washington

Educated at both the Massachusetts
College of Art and Columbia
University, Wyman started work with
clay in 1953. He was intensely
concerned with the resolution of
Abstract Expressionist issues through
the generation of expressive form
and colored surface. Gifted as a
studio potter, Wyman produced
functional wares for which he
became widely known. At the same
time he constructed innovative slab-
built vessels that were freely painted
with rich glazes and scribed with
images of the landscape of
imagination.

ILLUSION IS REDISCOVERED

It's a commonplace that in the last ten years representation —
recognizable subject matter — has returned to painting and sculpture. Yet
representational images raise anew questions about reality and illusion.
Wendell Castle's virtuosity allows him to make trompe l'oeil sculptures
that refer, for example, to a Sheraton card table. The form becomes a
familiar image, sometimes outrageously completed — but is the result a
masterly recreation of an antique or is it sculpture? Wayne Higby (pages
100, 104, 123) paints sculptural landscapes, strong geomorphic forms from
the American Southwest — but these require and yet deny the ceramic
vessels that are his substrate. *Apparition Canyon* is a journey through
landscapes balancing real and illusionistic space. Are Higby's works paintings,
sculptures, or pots? Roy Lichtenstein's *Ceramic Sculpture # 11*, of 1965,
elicits a reflex response, for it refers to common domestic objects — cups
— but at second glance they are not functional cups and saucers at all,
for he has permanently fused them together. The expressiveness of Viola
Frey's earthenware figures is highly subjective and individual. Her
Grandmother Figure (page 200) is an adult memory of a childhood vision
of a brittle but godlike person. But are Frey's works magnified Dresden
figurines or are they sculpture? The personal, story-laden realism of these
artists is inherently illusionistic, allowing them to create an aesthetic
dialectic that wonderfully resists resolution.

Stephen DeStaebler's ceramics are made of mixtures of stoneware, low-
fired clay, and porcelain. They are monumental in form, like the pair of
seated figures illustrated here which are over six feet in height, and they
are enigmatic in meaning. His most characteristic works are assembled
pieces reminiscent of ancient monuments. Human elements seem buried
in the works of clay as if they were imbedded fossiliferous remains found
and broken from the natural landscape. These blocks seem to have been
taken from an imaginary quarry of the mind. Some surfaces are rough and
broken; others are smooth and polished. Wrapped wire marks left on the
sides of the clay seem to reinforce the artist's intent to leave these
evocative works "unfinished."

Stephen DeStaebler
Left: *Seated Figure with Striped
Right Arm,* 1984
Fired clay (in six sections),
73 x 17 x 29
Right: *Seated Figure with Yellow
Flame,* 1985
Fired clay (in six sections),
78 x 14 x 29
Collection of the artist,
Berkeley, California

Roy Lichtenstein
Ceramic Sculpture #11, 1965
Glazed ceramic, 7½ inches in height
Collection of Betty Asher,
Los Angeles, California

In 1965 Lichtenstein began a year-
long collaboration with Hui Ka
Kwong, then his colleague at
Rutgers University. One of their
projects was a series of stacked
restaurant ware sculptures. The
dishes were slip cast, some from
commercially available molds and
others from molds made by Kwong.
The cups, saucers, platters, and
teapots were then assembled in
stacks and painted with glaze
decoration. Technically, the sculpture
is enormously innovative, from the
chemistry of the glazes to the
methods devised for applying them.
The red, yellow, and blue glazes
were formulated by Kwong in order
to reproduce Lichtenstein's palette
exactly. The glazes were applied
either by means of airbrush and
masking tape stencil or by means of
decals of commercially silkscreened
dots of glaze. The ceramic
sculptures are, in a sense, comics
become objects. The ambiguity of
the image/object relationship is
strongly enhanced through the use
of commonplace objects, and by the
analogous relationship between
mass-produced restaurant ware and
a painting technique based on
mechanical printing processes.

56

Ron Nagle
Cup with Box, 1970
Earthenware, china paint, luster glazes, mahogany burl wood box,
4½ x 6¾ x 6¾
The Oakland Museum,
Oakland, California, The Oakland Museum Founders Fund

Nagle (along with Kenneth Price) has been working with the idea of the cup since the 1960s. His treatment of the cup has much to do with his concern about the studio potter in this postindustrial society. In our culture, preoccupied with chic and cool, Nagle held out for tastefulness and style. While other artists were rejecting craftsmanship in the funk protest of ceramic art, Nagle was making cups that he sanded and fired up to twenty times. These tiny cups, around three inches high, were displayed in finely crafted wood and boxes with vacuformed acrylic interiors. Framed in one half of the box was the cup, and in the other half was the negative space that covered the cup if the box were shut.

Marilyn Levine
Herk's Bag, 1980
Ceramic and mixed media,
14 x 18 x 6½
Alpert Family Trust,
Millis, Massachusetts

Levine became interested in art
while pursuing a career as a
research chemist in Canada. Her visit
to California in 1968 was a turning
point. There she met other artists
who were also intent on using clay
as a sculptural medium. At the time
she was making colorful geometric
forms with oozing extrusions. After
James Melchert's ceramics workshop
in Saskatchewan, she began to
experiment with renditions of real
objects. They are not deliberate
copies but have their own
mysterious authenticity; age is
implied, but they have no age; their
origins are unknown. In their
permanent clay form they seem to
have escaped the common fate of
matter — to be constantly aging
and wearing.

As we have already noted, in part, a variety of artists in a range of media has been making strong and persuasive commentaries. Robert Arneson's *Holy War Head* of 1982-83, as its ambiguous title suggests, is an angrily satirical assertion of the hopelessness of nuclear confrontation. It happens to be ceramic. American mass culture provides subjects as in Patti Warashina's *Airstream Turkey* of 1969. Here, Thanksgiving is taken outside by a glistening aluminum Airstream mobile home that itself has drumsticks, while the mountainous landscape is brought inside to the diners. Warashina forces the bitter opposition of our contemporary mobility and our need for family stability. Howard Kottler's *Hustler's Delight* of 1967, again ceramic, is charged with eroticism that has pornographic, perverse, aggressive weight. Betye Saar, in *The Liberation of Aunt Jemima* (page 209) of 1972, transforms the servile black mammy into a gun-toting revolutionary. Karen Breschi, with the rope-bound horrific *Vulture* (page 132) of 1979, cries out for the freeing of women. In these works and others, the confounding of forms and media integrates strong materials into strong statement.

The classical vessel became the dominant format for the art of Frimkess. Using ceramic cultural icons such as the Oriental ginger jar and Greek krater, Frimkess applied contemporary idioms to the classics. The vase provided quiet, timeless canvas for his frenzied chronicle of late twentieth century life. *Covered Jar* from 1968, reflects the political turbulence of the late 1960s. The classical oriental shape is appropriate for displaying those times when America was so deeply involved in Southeast Asia-Vietnam. His subject matter, while whimsical at first glance, is a social commentary on corruption, war, and religious and racial intolerance.

Robert Arneson
Holy War Head, 1982-83
Ceramic, glazed, 72 x 28 x 28
Collection of Rita and Irwin Blitt,
Leawood, Kansas

Howard Kottler
Hustler's Delight, 1967
Ceramic, glazed, 13¼ x 13⅝ x 7⅛
Collection of Daniel Jacobs,
New York, New York

Michael Frimkess
Covered Jar, 1968
Tin glazed earthenware with on-
glaze painting, 28½ x 16
Scripps College,
Claremont, California,
Collection of Mr. and Mrs. Fred
Marer

All cultures have objects of ceremony, ritual, celebration, and spiritual power. Our society — pluralistic and largely secularized — sometimes seems in the process of attenuating these or losing them altogether. Yet as artists have always done, certain of those of the present turn to earlier ritualistic and ceremonial traditions. The difference for many artists, however, is that though these new objects bear multiple references to long traditions, Christian or non-Christian, and though they address the spiritual dilemmas of the end of the second millennium of our era, ordering, protecting, and enhancing life, they are nonetheless displaced from the older established communities, contexts, and purposes. The mixed-media objects made by Dominic Di Mare are excellent examples, for they are poetic and reserved, at once intensely autobiographical and impersonally totemic. In 1976 Di Mare created a series called *Letter Bundles* (page 256), which are visual metaphors for books and libraries. They allude to the very beginnings of written thought, the early libraries of the Middle East, with scrolls bound and placed on racks. Di Mare methodically gathers his materials from the beach; the imagery emerges directly from his life. The messages within the letters in the bundles are sacred, yet they have no words. The letter bundles symbolize evolving family relationships; they are songs. Their making is a spiritual act.

Spiritual content of mystical intensity was the primary and final objective of the artist William Wyman. In his *Temple* series (page 265), Wyman may have resolved a lifelong struggle to relate his visual experiences and responses to his spirituality. Built in clay, these pedestal sculptures refer to Mayan or Egyptian pyramids — places for religious reflection, celebration, and death. They project Wyman's driven search to distinguish inauthentic from authentic meanings. Wyman died in 1980 at the age of fifty-eight. William Harper incorporates numerous unambiguously Christian references. *The Temptation of St. Anthony* (page 154), from 1986, symbolizes self-denial, solitude, and resulting spiritual growth. Harper sees the ascetic hermit, so frequently the subject in Western art since the Middle Ages, as the image of the artist's spiritual growth, thus inspiring him to resist the temptations that distract him from his art, helping him to find the solitude which art demands. In all these works, the intimate relationship of materials, techniques, and cultural associations originating in the crafts is directly evocative of values of simplicity and humanity that spiritual rediscovery must seek.

Arthur González
The French Curve, 1984
Ceramic, glaze, paint, 30 x 28 x 18
Collection of Joan Mannheimer,
Des Moines, Iowa

The figurative tradition has always been a strong element in the work of González, a clay artist who began his career as a photorealist painter. Like paint on canvas, clay is durable, but also fragile. González continues to use the human body as his subject; however, his figures are now depicted from the waist up so that the arm and hand gestures can be seen like a dance ritual. The pose is frozen in time, and the gestures are fully articulated. Colored engobe applied to the face is a metaphor for makeup or for the mud pack some women use, a ritual act of ugliness meant to create what they perceive as beauty.

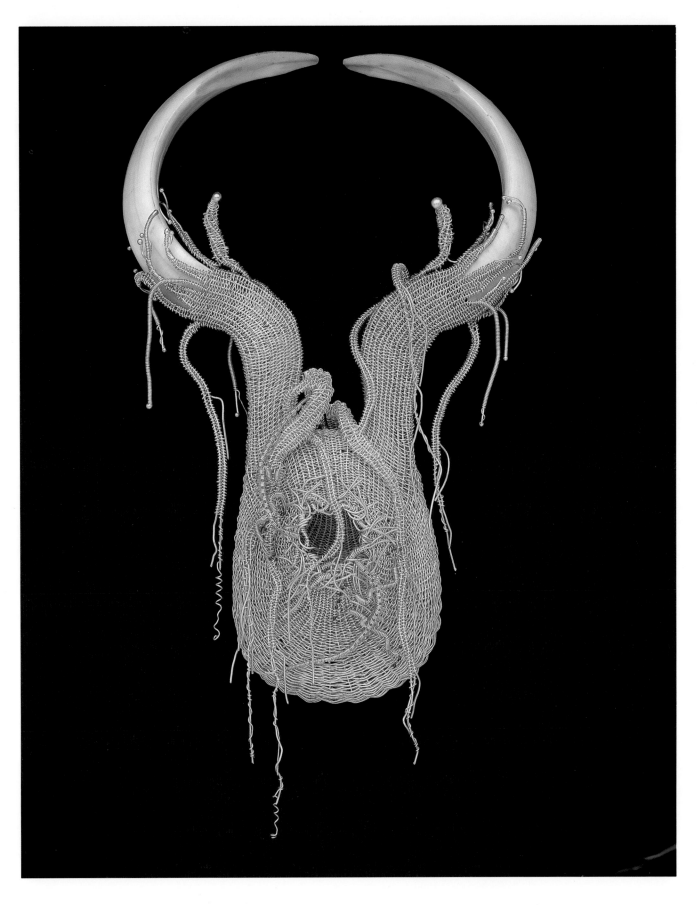

Mary Lee Hu
Neckpiece #8, 1973
Fine silver, gold filled brass, boar's tusks, woven silver wire,
10 x 5½ x 1½
Collection of the artist,
Seattle, Washington

In *Neckpiece #8* Hu uses woven wire to create an organic nestlike structure reminiscent of the weaver birds' nests complete with vine-like overlays. The attaching collar is terminated with boar tusks which provide contrast in both form and material. The piece demonstrates an early and significant exploration into the possibilities of self-supporting fiberlike sculptural forms.

William Harper
Barbarian Bracelet #1, 1980, (above)
Gold and silver cloisonné enamel on
copper, sterling silver with 24k gilt,
copper electroplate, 6 inches in
diameter
Collection of Lois Boardman, South
Pasadena, California
Courtesy Helen Drutt Gallery,
Philadelphia, Pennsylvania

Enclosed Tattoo, 1979, (facing page)
Silver, gold cloisonné on copper, 14k
gold, sterling silver, copper, pearls,
5¹⁵⁄₁₆ x 2¼
Collection of Sydney and Frances
Lewis, Richmond, Virginia

During his graduate study at Case
Western Reserve William Harper
discovered the medium of enamel to
be more compelling for him than oil
on canvas. Turning to wearable
forms and at the same time
broadening his cross-cultural
references, Harper brought
profound innovation to jewelry.
Enclosed Tattoo refers to patterns of
ritual scarification and *Barbarian
Bracelet* owes much to the
inspiration of Celtic and Islamic
metalwork.

Artists now have all but instant access to all the world's cultures, from our own urban Pop to the remotest village. Through quotation and appropriation of images, forms, and methods, artists are assimilating these cultures — though we can expect enormous losses in the original significance in the translation and displacement. Interactions among cultural idioms are proving immensely fertile. We noted earlier, for example, the assimilation of Art Deco motifs beginning in the 1920s and 1930s by Pueblo potters; the sophistication of the work of certain great Pueblo pottery-making families continues to evolve with unflagging vigor, as in Richard Zane Smith's spiraling woven-clay baskets. James Tanner (page 238) makes clay reliefs that recall ceremonial masks of African tribes; their surfaces are as dazzling as their references. Tanner wants to "get past that physical dimension into . . . the psychic or spiritual dimension manifested by the physical."[7] His masks are a metaphor confronting the passage of time. Larry Beck (page 207), an Inuit Indian, gathers commercially-made household utensils, automotive parts, and dental tools, assembling them into masks. Using products and materials that are industrial, urban, and accessible, Beck is nonetheless making bear and walrus masks that reflect his Arctic ancestry. Margaret Wharton's chairs, like *Leopatra* (page 102) from 1982, are fragments from our present civilization. Her interest in the uncanny possibilities of the common object goes back to the Dada and Surrealist movements and to the decade of Pop Art. Her chairs are recognizable, everyday things, yet they incorporate animal references transformed into anthropomorphic shapes; they upset our expectations. Wharton scavenges our past to create new legacies. Salvatore Scarpitta (pages 252, 253) could be accused of being an exploiter — a thief — of someone else's invention. His sleds are about mobility, and are a means of survival, but are not to be used. The materials are recycled from what he finds in the streets; he hunts and he stalks. He says the sleds are about the family — for the family rescues and forms a bond for the wanderer. Sherry Markovitz (page 278) blends the Northwest Coast Native American traditions of beadwork with the images of man and animal. She placed the human head at the throat of *Autumn Buck;* hunting season is over but the radiant trophy lives on.

The arts have become ecumenical. Perhaps at some level they have always been so: artists are impressionable, passionate embracers of the possibilities. Yet at a time when many fear that mainstream Western art has become etiolated and sterile, incapable of renewal from within, the new syncretism of cultures, themes, ideas, images, materials, and techniques that we began to record over a quarter century ago from the limited but strategic viewpoint of the studio crafts movement has grown to be the force irrupting undeniably into everyone's aesthetic awareness. We retain enough of our youthful parochialism to think with great pleasure that crafts have been the transforming principle.

NOTES

1 We have followed the fortunes of that piece: in 1971, at a Sotheby's auction in Los Angeles, *Silver* sold for $2,000 and in 1986 the James Corcoran Gallery, in the same city, offered it for $40,000.

2 The first successful granulations were accomplished by an Englishman, Henry Littledale, in 1933, and in 1950 another procedure was developed by two Americans, Patrick F. Mahler and Donald Tompkins, students at the School for American Craftsmen in Rochester, New York. John Paul Miller created his own secret process in 1948-1949.

3 In the summer of 1985, Maloof was made a Prize Fellow of the John D. and Catherine T. MacArthur Foundation. These prizes amount to approximately $300,000, tax free, over a five-year period; they are given to about twenty Americans a year, and are intended to free the expression of great creative or intellectual capacity. Maloof was the first craftsperson to get a MacArthur Prize fellowship. In 1986, Wendell Castle received similar recognition.

4 Aileen Webb's role in American crafts and the ongoing revolution was pivotal. For an account, we refer to Rose Slivka, "The Art/Craft Connection: A Personal, Critical, and Historical Odyssey," in this volume.

5 The first experiments with studio glassblowers incorporated the use of Johns-Manville industrial Fiberglas marbles as the source for material. These stock marbles were used industrially to produce Fiberglas filaments for the manufacture of Fiberglas boats, automobile body parts, etc. The first experimental studio glass furnaces were designed by Dominick Labino.

6 Kim Levin, "Lucas Samaras: The New Reconstructions," exhibition brochure (New York: The Pace Gallery, 1979). The exhibition was shown at the Pace Gallery, 32 East 57th Street, in New York, from November 29, 1979 - January 5, 1980.

7 Quoted in *Tanner Loftus: Ceramic Wall Reliefs by James Tanner* , exhibition brochure (Minneapolis, Minnesota: Minnesota Artists Exhibition Program, The Minneapolis Institute of Arts, 1985).

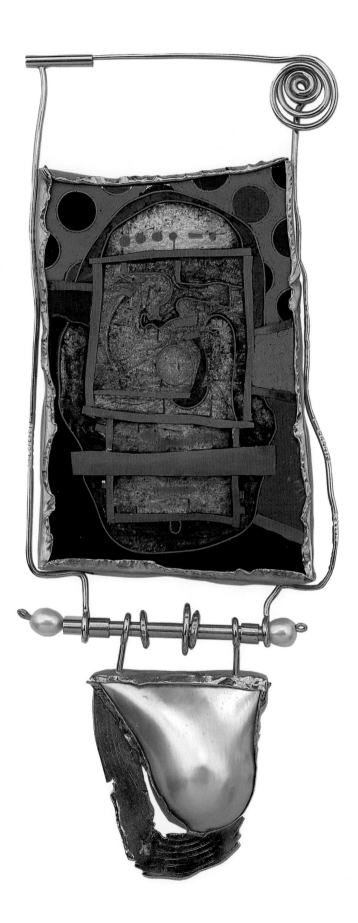

THE ART/CRAFT CONNECTION:

A PERSONAL, CRITICAL, AND HISTORICAL ODYSSEY

ROSE SLIVKA

Harvey Littleton
Red/Blue Twisted Arc, 1985
Glass, 13½ x 13 x 5 (two pieces)
Maurine Littleton Gallery,
Washington, D.C.

In the 1980s Littleton added complexities of color to his bravura manipulation of glass, building up massive tubes of glass in layered hues that are revealed in sliced sections, like the bisected rainbow of *Red/Blue Twisted Arc.* The nobility and power of such sculptures, sustained over a span of two decades, has made Littleton the preeminent exponent as well as founder father of the studio glass movement in America.

I came to the crafts through the New York art world of the 1950s. My experiences in that world allowed me to make a unique contribution to the craft movement as a writer and as editor of *Craft Horizons.* The avant-garde spirit of the time, expressed through painting and sculpture, enriched my vision of craft, its function and aesthetic range. It enlarged my ideas about the energy of materials and forms, the need of each artist to find his or her own way of working with materials, of trusting the events of process, and of recognizing the complex and expanding role of craft as art. In those years we were too involved to know we were making history, but as I look back now I am deeply aware of how significant a history it was.

In 1945, at the close of World War II, there was only a small group of artists in New York City. We had no idea art would become not only a respectable profession but a crowded one. To us it was not a profession, it was a priesthood — a spiritual calling. Most of the artists of my day did not go to college. They went to art schools — the Art Students League in New York, the School of the Art Institute of Chicago, the San Francisco Art Institute (formerly the California School of Fine Arts), to name a few — and they apprenticed to artists they respected who themselves did not expect recognition. To us art was an underground activity frequently practiced only at night or on weekends after working at earning a living. As an artist, you belonged to a secret society of your own kind — your little band of misfits. If you fit, you didn't belong — a necessary

Peter Voulkos and Rose Slivka,
Oakland, California, 1977
Courtesy of Rose Slivka,
New York, New York

Rose Slivka, Louise Nevelson, Willem
de Kooning, Elaine de Kooning, and
Rita Pinehous at de Kooning's studio,
1982
Courtesy of Rose Slivka,
New York, New York

contradiction. The sense of not being part of the outside non-art world
made you uneasy and you wondered if something were wrong with you,
which may well be the beginning of all creative intellect.

The New York City of the 1950s was a place ringing with the great
excitement of the New York School of Action Painting, otherwise known
as Abstract Expressionism, which, through the work of painters Jackson
Pollock, Willem de Kooning, Franz Kline, and others, had declared itself an
American aesthetic. We talked about the nature of art and materials and
sex and politics and everything else that had to do with the making of
things. We talked all the time. No one thought of becoming an artist
because you could make a living at it. (In those days you couldn't anyway.)
It was a way of thinking about life and aspiring to be worthy to engage it
at its highest and most holy place. We were such a small group, too small
at that time to notice whether the men got more than the women. We
were all in the same boat. We were all in it together and we needed each
other.

Everyone did craft. The sculptors made jewelry, the potters painted
and the painters potted. Everyone did everything. An artist called Fred Farr
— now among the dead — originally from Seattle, Washington, had a
pottery (a little storefront with a back room) around the corner from
where I lived. There I took my first pottery lessons and made the tile for
the bathroom of my house. In addition to making his pots, Fred also
painted and made small bronze sculptures in lost wax, casting them in his
centrifugal casting machine, and hammered, soldered, and cast jewelry. He
taught both pottery and painting at the Brooklyn Museum School of Art.

I was born in New York City (it is actually possible to be born there)
to Czechoslovak parents who had come to America. My mother was a
weaver and my father wrote poetry in seven untranslatable languages. My
mother repaired Medieval tapestries at The Metropolitan Museum of Art.
She loved those tapestries and considered her work privileged. Once a
week she took my brother and me to her museum. I grew up deeply
influenced by her love and practice of art and by my father's love of
language. By contrast one block from where we lived was Bond's Bread
factory which every day produced thousands of loaves of virgin, radiantly
white bread (never mind its bleached flour and preservatives) beneath the
proud and famous slogan "Untouched by Human Hands." This slogan
inspired great confidence in Bond's Bread's sanitation, machine perfection,
superiority to bungling, muddling homemade. It expressed the machine
aesthetic of a time in which "made by hand" carried with it the stigma of
the inferior human touch, clumsy and full of mistakes. In New York City of
the 1950s, this would begin to be turned upside down.

Of the three jobs I was offered in 1955, I chose the one at *Craft
Horizons* as having the most news and excitement for me. Although
exploring the sexual revolution as an editor-writer for *Redbook* magazine
was easy for me to turn down when compared with the adventure of the
crafts, I was more conflicted about turning down a job at the Museum of
Modern Art where Edward Steichen was director of the photography
department. (I had previously worked as scriptwriter for the picture

agencies Black Star and Pix, and with the great *Life Magazine* photojournalists Alfred Eisenstaedt and W. Eugene Smith, as well as with the incomparable photo editor Alexey Brodovitch of *Harper's Bazaar*.) Still, the new field of handcraft was where I wanted to be.

At the interview for the job at *Craft Horizons* I met Aileen Osborn Webb, founder and first editor of the magazine, which had begun in 1940 in a mimeographed format and had been transformed in 1948 into a slick quarterly. My encounter with Aileen Webb is as vivid to me now as it was then. She was a large-boned, tall, handsome, gray-haired woman of patrician features and Franklin Delano Roosevelt diction (otherwise known as the hallmark of the New York aristocracy). She began by asking to hear my ideas for the magazine. (At that time I had all the answers; she was old enough to have only questions.) And then she listened with that characteristic focus of attention for which she had such a gift and for which I loved her. After many meetings we finally agreed that I was the one for the job. The remaining applicant, also having been highly recommended by the departing editor Belle Krasne, was Hilton Kramer. He went on to become the chief art critic of the *New York Times,* a position he held for the next twenty years before founding the highly respected new journal *The New Criterion*. In May I went to work under a part-time arrangement which I thought would leave me time for my poems (it didn't) and paid $75 a week, an amount my sculptor husband and I could live on handsomely in those days. I thought it was destiny that I had at last found the perfect job, having avoided it as long as I could.

There were only two of us on the staff of *Craft Horizons* — Conrad Brown as full-time editor and myself as first associate, then managing editor — and we did everything from taking photographs to selling ads. Sidney Butchkes, the well-known painter, designed the magazine from his own studio. Our office was the top floor of a loft building at 601 Fifth Avenue around the corner from Mark Rothko's studio at the time (I took my coffee breaks with him at the corner drugstore). We shared our loft space with a furrier who lent us minks and sables in the winter when there was, too frequently, no heat, and we literally shook from the cold. During those early years at *Craft Horizons* I entered into a Talmudic discussion with the great art critic and philosopher Harold Rosenberg. What is art and what is craft? we asked. What is the importance of material? When does it become metaphor? How does it slip away? The discussion was good for the next twenty-three years. We liked to sharpen our intellectual fangs on the old arguments although we knew what we believed. We believed with Socrates that the act of art is to charge the adornment with speculation. We agreed that speculation is to art what red is to blood.

We danced the jitterbug a lot in those days. And the writers sat around together with the painters and the sculptors in the cafeterias — there was one called Stewart's and another called Bickford's — lingering for hours over the same cup of coffee, relishing our camaraderie and the exclusivity of our hopelessness in ever achieving fame or money. It never occurred to us that some of us would achieve great success and would

Aileen Osborn Webb, founder of the American Craft Council, ca. 1950s. Courtesy of the American Craft Council, New York, New York

The Evolution of the American Craft Council:

1939 Handcraft League of Craftsmen

1942 Merged with American Handcraft Council forming Handcraft Cooperative League of America

1943 Renamed American Craftsmen's Cooperative Council

1951 American Craftsmen's Educational Council

1957 American Craftsmen's Council

1969 American Crafts Council

1979 American Craft Council

Dominic Di Mare
Temple Series, 1979 (four of a series
of six works)
Wood, feathers, paper, beads,
28 x 16 x 8½
Collection of Karen Johnson Boyd,
Racine, Wisconsin

Temple Series is a compilation of Di
Mare's previous works set in a new
format. Here we see a continuation
of his fascination with paper, use of
found materials collected on
morning strolls along the beach and
in the center of the composition the
ever-present flaxen threads which
act as metaphors of his association
with fishing lines and nets from his
youth when he helped on his
father's fishing boat. All of these
elements combine to create an
entrance to a temple. Reference is
made to a gabled architectural
structure through the silhouette of
the composition. One is invited to
penetrate the opening which is
masked by a flaxen curtain. The
doorway is surrounded by magical
objects, a gateway, through which
one passes to the sanctum
sanctorum of one's own thoughts.

graduate from drinking coffee to drinking booze.

The craft world then was as tiny and excited about itself as the art
world, and the making of things by hand was equally an act of faith.
Unlike the New York art world, the craft world of the United States was
scattered throughout the country. People heard about each other without
ever having met and had to bridge great distances to stay in touch with
each other. Not clustered around urban centers, they were more often
attached to universities and professional schools, wherever they happened
to be. To find out about each other, they often took off in pickup trucks
turning up at each other's doorsteps. They traveled from all parts of the
country to meet each other, many for the first time when the American
Craft Council (then the American Craftsmen's Council) held its first
national conference at Asilomar, California in 1957.[1]

And things began to change. Beginning in the early 1950s, practicing
artists without university degrees, especially those from New York City,
were invited to teach in the postwar university explosion. Then came the
history of extraordinary success of American art and extraordinary money
and fame. Young artists were expected to be successful and university art
departments offered clues to the route. The universities began to mass-
manufacture and package artists in unprecedented numbers.

Today there are more artists than there have ever been in the history
of the world. There are the men and there are the women and there are
those who have made it and there are those who have not and there are
the teachers and there are the doers, and frequently they are even the
same. Never before has art been so popular and in such great demand, so
worldwide, so confusing, so diverse. Never before have there been so
many materials of art. At the same time, the meaning of art begins to
escape us. Artists puzzle and elude us with materials for which previous
experiences have not prepared us.

The art world is run, furthermore, by a significant population of non-
artists who even outnumber the artists. There are historians, dealers,
publishers, editors, curators, agents, directors of art associations,
managers, and administrators. The artists who actually create are only a
tiny segment of this population and are getting tinier as the art world's
non-art-making functions enlarge. We have reason to think that if they
could get rid of the real artist but have all the attendant functions
proliferating anyway, they would, and frequently they do. Maybe the real
question for a large population of the art world today is how to look and
act like an artist without having to be one.

It never occurred to us in the 1950s that one day parents would no
longer object to their children practicing art or that art would become a
profession like medicine and law (even better in some ways, because as an
artist you were automatically considered an interesting person and you
would be invited to more parties). We didn't think that in barely ten years
some of us would be experiencing great financial rewards, or that we
would be called an American movement.

The emergence of the American craftsmaker is a phenomenon of the last fifty years.

Modern craft in the United States is the aesthetic paradox of a postindustrial culture. The very technology that almost eliminated the craftsmaker from the culture has freed him to expand his creative scope. Once the useful machine-made product became accessible to everyone, cheaper than you could make at home, craft was no longer required to be useful.

Craft is the expression of the culture's resistance to the depersonalizing forces of technological and corporate power. It asserted itself after World War II and was thereafter stimulated and nurtured by a university system peculiar to the United States. The growth of craft in America is filling a *new* need, responding to a *new* condition, meeting a *new* demand. It is not a nostalgic throwback to old methods and vocations. It is not a "renaissance," as it is frequently referred to by the popular press.

The craftsmaker of the modern world has created an entirely unprecedented situation in which a prolific and vigorous handcraft culture exists within the structure of industrial power. He is the expression of an abundant society's resistance to the homogenizing pressures exerted by mass production, and of its drive to humanize and individualize, accelerated and matured through the internationalizing forces of communication.

From the colonial period through the early twentieth century, agrarian and rural Americans made objects such as quilts, clothing, furniture, and kitchen utensils for their own use. Often these objects were made out of necessity; their manufactured counterparts were unavailable or unaffordable. Much of this production was simply not recorded and that which was tended to be identified with specific communities such as those of the Shakers and the Amish.

In the 1920s and 1930s American craftsmakers were scarce, although it was not uncommon for painters and sculptors to make useful handmade objects as a way of supporting themselves while they practiced their art. A number of studio potters helped keep craft alive in this country. Adelaide Robineau at Syracuse University, influenced by the Arts and Crafts movement, and in the articulation of her own formal style, carved and incised surfaces, and developed glaze tehcnology that made her a memorable figure in the art of ceramics. Charles Harder literally created the ceramics department at Alfred University, developing techniques of reduction firing to produce stoneware with muted, somber

John Paul Miller
Pendant/Brooch, 1975
Gold, enamel, 3 x 3 x ¾
Collection of Dorothy S. Payer,
Moreland Hills, Ohio

Miller is credited with the
reintroduction of a delicate jewelry
making technique used by the
Etruscans which involved the fusing
of minute gold spheres onto a gold
surface. It is a procedure requiring
infinite skill and patience. In
Pendant/Brooch, this "granulation"
technique is combined with vitreous
enamel to create a rich surface
reminiscent of the works of Peter
Carl Fabergé, court jeweler to the
late czars of Imperial Russia.
However, the abstraction of subject
matter and form is definitely
twentieth-century. It is based on
Miller's close observation of nature,
especially pools.

Alma Eikerman
Double-Bulged Bowl with Lid, 1975
Sterling, raised by stretching,
constructed, formed, 5 x 8½ x 12
Indiana University Art Museum,
Bloomington, Indiana

Eikerman has traveled from Oaxaca,
New Mexico, to the mountains of
Tibet to research and study both the
objects of the ancients, such as the
Etruscan jewels of the seventh and
sixth centuries, B.C., and the work
of her time such as the Modernist
canvases of Piet Mondrian. Her
forms have richly absorbed history.
They are characterized by a refined
abstraction that verges on but never
coalesces into geometry. The tension
between this and the qualities of
living forms — growth and
movement — contributes to the
imposing presence of her metal
objects.

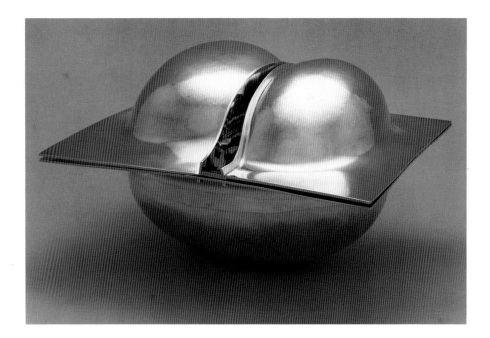

earth colors. This was the ceramic body most popular in production
pottery circles throughout the fifties and until well into the sixties when
brash and bright color, with low-fire techniques, made its appearance.
Arthur Baggs explored the use of salt glazes on stoneware at Ohio State
University. Henry Varnum Poor, who started the California School of Fine
Arts, now the San Francisco Art Institute, came to New York to become
one of the first American painter-potters of human, floral, and animal
imagery on wheel-thrown ceramic forms as well as on murals.

In 1932 the Cranbrook Academy of Art was established in Bloomfield
Hills, Michigan, and the Finnish architect and designer Eliel Saarinen
became its first president. At Cranbrook, Americans got the opportunity to
study with some of Finland's best craftspeople and designers, including
Maija Grotell. Grotell, head of Cranbrook's ceramics department from
1938 to 1966, had a major influence on the development of two new
generations of American potters.

In 1935 the federal government established the Works Progress
Administration Federal Arts Project (after 1939, the Work Projects
Administration), whose purpose was to employ artists, craftsmen, and
photographers. Although the program was created in response to the
Great Depression and its massive unemployment, it gave jobs and
commissions to up to 5,300 artists and craftsmakers annually during its
eight-year span, not only providing a living for many developing artists but
also validating art as worthwhile work in the American social structure.

In 1940, to help her neighbors in the still depressed area of Putnam
County, Aileen Osborn Webb opened a retail outlet in Garrison, New York,
where she lived, for crafts being made in the community by people
working at home. Its purpose was to help the unemployed of the
community and to preserve traditions that might otherwise be
endangered. The shop became America House (relocated in New York City

at 52nd Street and Madison Avenue), the first commercial gallery and shop to promote the work of American craftsmakers. After starting *Craft Horizons,* she established the American Craftsmen's Educational Council, the national organization now known as the American Craft Council.[2]

A major influence on the development of the arts in America in the 1930s and 1940s was the influx of émigré craftsmakers from Germany and Austria. Potters Gertrud and Otto Natzler, the husband and wife team who came to Los Angeles as refugees from Hitler's regime, had no formal training when they began their collaboration. She threw simple, straightforward, elegantly proportioned shapes. He applied glazes of enormous variety and perfection, among them the now famous "crater glaze," a pitted surface of burned, crusted, complex colors. Silversmith and jeweler Margaret De Patta introduced an architecturally designed and constructed jewelry in which pins, rings, and brooches housed stones and gems in a composition of formal integrity and sculptural intention. Marguerite and Frans Wildenhain established the Pond Farm Workshops in Guerneville, California, in 1942, transmitting the Bauhaus aesthetic ideals in the medium of ceramics.

Anni Albers and her husband Josef, the noted painter, participated in the extraordinary interdisciplinary arts and crafts experiment called Black Mountain College during its first fifteen years, he as chairman, she as assistant professor and weaver (along with Trude Guermonprez, who also taught at the San Francisco Art Institute and the California College of Arts and Crafts in Oakland). They came out of the Bauhaus as influential proponents of the rectilinear heritage. Black Mountain, founded in 1933 near Asheville, North Carolina, was a liberal arts college in which studio arts were the central discipline. Throughout its twenty-three-year history, it had no grades, tenure, departments, or accreditation. Instead it had some fifty students and a dozen teachers sharing their creative lives as well as the work necessary to maintain their community. It was owned and governed by the persons present at any one time. And the persons present have become legendary. Buckminster Fuller built one of his first geodesic domes there in 1948. Anaîs Nin came to help set up a print shop with the writing students. John Cage performed Eric Satie's music as well as his own. Bernard Leach brought the Japanese potters Shoji Hamada and Soketsu Yanagi for a workshop. And it was here that Peter Voulkos, Robert Turner, and Karen Karnes met the potter and writer M. C. Richards, then at Black Mountain as a poet married to the composer and pianist David Tudor who was working with composer-poet John Cage and dancer Merce Cunningham. They all worked with composers Edgard Varèse, Stefan Wolpé; the painters Willem and Elaine de Kooning, Franz Kline, Ludwig Sanders, Esteban Vicente, Dan Rice; the poets Charles Olson, Robert Creeley; the novelist Francine du Plessix Gray, to mention a few. It was here that the seeds were planted for the revolution that would occur when Peter Voulkos translated the Abstract Expressionist painting of de Kooning and Kline into his chosen medium, clay.

In 1946 Aileen Osborn Webb made her next contribution to the cause of American craft — she instituted and organized the School for American

America House, 44 West 53rd Street, New York City, prior to its closing in 1971. In 1979, The Museum of Contemporary Crafts, formerly located at 29 West 53rd Street, moved into this location and was renamed the American Craft Museum. Courtesy of the American Craft Council, New York, New York

Trude Guermonprez
Mandy's Motto, 1975
Double weave and inlay technique,
printed fabric and flag strips,
54 x 32
Collection of Eric and Sylvia Elsesser,
Sausalito, California

Guermonprez was a preeminent
figure in the development of the
new aesthetic in fiber art. Her "little
Bauhaus" training at the School of
Fine and Applied Arts, Halle/Saale,
and the School of Textile
Engineering, Berlin; experiences at
Black Mountain College as a student
weaving instructor; association with
Frans and Marguerite Wildenhain at
the Pond Farm Workshops; and
eventual teaching position at the
California College of Arts and Crafts
(CCAC), Oakland, California all
contributed to the development of
her ideas about fiber. While other
textile artists were experimenting
with "off-loom" techniques in an
effort to expand the possibilities of
the fiber aesthetic, Guermonprez
centered her approaches around
classical weaving techniques on the
loom, pushing the classical approach
beyond perceived limitations. Made
one year before the artist's death,
Mandy's Motto represents the
culmination of her deep
understanding of woven structure,
experimental approach to materials,
and ability to express new ideas
within the apparent confines of a
classical tradition. At the center of
the composition is a truncated
American flag surrounded by the
words "The wind don't blow one
way all the time," a reference to the
political unrest of 1975. These and
other elements in the work draw
upon the viewer's knowledge of
history and the American
experience.

Anni Albers
La Luz I, 1947
Linen, metal, gimp, 19 x 32
Collection of Richard Lippold,
Locust Valley, New York

Anni Albers's pictorial weavings of the 1940s were a radical departure from the flat wall hangings of Bauhaus tradition which she made before coming to America in 1933. Smaller in scale, they were conceived as woven pictures, even being "matted" on linen and framed. *La Luz I* is based on the image of a cross, inspired by a visit with her artist-husband Josef to Mexican churches in La Luz, Texas, at Christmas, 1946. Using an ethereal hue, she creates the cruciform shape of silvery metallic threads set against Southwestern earth tones. Pictorial weavings continued to be Albers's direction until she turned exclusively to printmaking in the 1960s.

75

Margaret De Patta
Pendant, 1956 (facing page)
White gold with rhomboid quartz
crystal faceted in opposing courses,
3¾ x 1 x 2½
The Oakland Museum, Oakland,
California, Gift of Eugene Bielawski

Shortly after her return from
Chicago in 1941, De Patta began
her collaboration with the San
Francisco lapidary, Francis J. Sperisen,
Sr.. Traditionally, gemstones had
been cut to reflect rather than to
transmit light; De Patta and
Sperisen, however, experimented
with the optical properties of
alternate cutting and faceting
procedures: transparency, refraction,
reflection, perspective illusion,
distortion through magnification,
multiplication or displacement. The
most innovative of these procedures
was called the "opticut," the effects
of which are exemplified in this
pendant of 1956 in which the cross-
faceting of a quartz crystal displaces
and creates multiple images of the
Y-shaped mounting behind it.

Gertrud and Otto Natzler
Bowl, 1949
Ceramic, flame red matte glaze,
2¼ x 9
Dallas Museum of Art, Dallas, Texas,
Gift of Contemporary House

From thirty years of records, Otto
Natzler estimates that he and his
late wife Gertrud produced some
25,000 pieces of pottery since their
arrival in the United States from
Vienna in 1938. As impressive as
this record is, sheer numbers do not
explain the Natzler's impact in
developing the taste of American
collectors, artists, and the general
public. Each Natzler piece is
experimental in its search for the
perfect match of color and form.
Thoughtful attention to each phase
of the clay's life and the
development of glazes were attained
through the Natzler's systematic
recording of every work. In their
master catalogue they entered the
number of each piece (found on the
bottom of the work) and technical
data concerning the clay and glazes.
Otto observed that by referring to
this prodigious record over time he
"learned from his mistakes," and
perfected his art. His glazes range
from the translucent and smoothly
variegated color comparable to the
iris of a human eye to the deeply
pock-marked surfaces that recall the
lunar landscape.

Craftsmen of the Rochester Institute of Technology. One of the school's
influential forces was Frans Wildenhain, who left the Pond Farm
Workshops to teach there from 1950 until his death in 1978.

Right after World War II in 1946 began a whole new wave in the
American art world, as the returning veterans flooded back into the
universities, their tuition and living expenses funded by the G.I. Bill. It was
a heyday for the arts as the universities and professional schools
established workshops and provided materials on an unprecedented
scale, fostering a whole new generation of artists and teachers of art.
Formerly buried in the home economics or industrial design departments
of universities, crafts were now included in the regular curriculum of art
departments.[3]

American crafts began to come into their own in the early fifties with
the emergence of the first generation of school-produced American
craftsmakers. The cultural atmosphere in a postwar society of abundance
and high curiosity about itself was one of rollicking experimentation.
Knowledge and experience with the tools and materials of craft were
scarce and the first generation made it up as they went along (as did the
painters, sculptors, and printmakers). American artists emerging from the
university system did not make orthodox distinctions among media.

Having been exposed to all disciplines, materials, and techniques in art and craft courses, they made their choices freely, unfettered by traditional craft limits. This explains, for instance, how Peter Voulkos, studying painting at Montana State College, happened to encounter clay in the art department and, thereafter, made it the medium of his art. It was the beginning of what Harold Rosenberg has called the tradition of the new.

In 1956, the American Craft Council (then the American Craftsmen's Council) opened the Museum of Contemporary Crafts in New York City as the major showcase for crafts as creative expression. Then Aileen O. Webb organized the World Crafts Council, which had its first meeting at Columbia University in New York in 1964. I remember watching Harvey Littleton build his glass furnace at 116th Street at the Columbia University campus and blow glass for the whole world and for the street kids from around the corner. He gave his glass as gifts to us, his observers. Craftsmen from forty-six countries throughout the world came to the United States to meet each other for the first time. They came to this country from behind the Iron Curtain, from darkest Africa, from deepest Asia. The population of the American craft world grew from a small group of friends to a large international community of friends, partisans, and strangers.

Francoise Grossen
Metamorphosis II⁴, 1986
Rope, manila, leather, paint,
51½ x 12 x 4
Collection of the artist,
New York, New York

Francoise Grossen discovered fiber through a Bauhaus-style program in the Basel School of Arts and Crafts in her native Switzerland. Her mature work remains rooted in the tactile fascination and intellectual challenge faced by every child manipulating a length of twine, but is taken to an extreme of elaboration and scale that suggests the mythical Gordian knot. Grossen carefully selects her materials for precise effect: coarse heavy-duty rope rife with implications of resistant strength, or shimmering silk or metallic twine hoarded for years to await the genesis of a composition of appropriate preciousness. She wraps, twists, and interweaves the fibers with a regularity so perfect that their arrangement seems to conform to a natural imperative.

James Melchert
Precious a, 1970
Clay with lustres, 6 x 8 x 7
Private collection,
Boston, Massachusetts

Upon reading an English translation
of *Exercises in Style* by Raymond
Queneau, Melchert started a series
of sculptures with the lowercase *a,*
his favorite letter, as subject.
Queneau's book was written in
approximately 100 different literary
styles and the artist appropriated
this concept of theme and variation
to execute the *a* series which was
started in 1969. The series includes
Oldenburg-like soft sculptured *a*'s,
Surrealistic *a*'s and a series of other
interpretations and permutations
based on the subject. Within the
series, several works concern
themselves with the idea of the
precious *a* or the letter presented as
a glorified image. One is elevated on
a plinth and in this case the letter is
placed on a presentation pillow in
the manner of a bride or groom's
wedding ring, recalling a gift of
love.

John Mason
Desert Cross, 1963
Stoneware, glazed, 54 x 43 x 15
Sheppard Gallery, University of
Nevada, Reno, Nevada,
Department of Art

After studying with Susan Peterson
at the Chouinard Art Institute, Los
Angeles, Mason joined a group of
students working with Peter Voulkos
at the Otis Art Institute . From
1955 to 1957 surface design
and innovative handling of clay
engaged his attention as he turned
from clay thrown on a wheel
towards more sculptural,
architectural works in an Abstract
Expressionist style. The imagery of
the large *Desert Cross* of 1963
surfaced early in his pottery and
continued to be used in large totem
pieces as a primal form for exploring
issues related to "how clay fits
together" rather than as a symbol of
spiritual significance.

Harvey Littleton
Gold Ruby Loop with White Lines,
1978
Double overlay inclusions in drawn
and cut glass, 15⅝ x 12½ x 4¼
Oklahoma Art Center Collection,
Oklahoma City, Oklahoma
Jones/Westheimer Fund Purchase

Gold Ruby Loop with White Lines
signals Littleton's emergence as an
artist in his own right as he began
a heroic series of arches based on
the frozen flow of his molten
medium. In thick loops of glass
which appear to climb, thin out,
then plummet back to their glass
pedestals, we see the kinetic drama
of glassmaking.

Peter Voulkos
Plate, 1973
Stoneware and porcelain bits,
3¾ x 19
Henry Art Gallery, University of Washington, Seattle, Washington, purchased with funds from Evelyn Howie, PONCHO and the NEA

In 1976, Rose Slivka asked Peter Voulkos why he still considered himself a potter, and he said that usually it was the last thing on his mind. When asked what got him into thinking that the forms of sculpture, pottery, and painting fed into one another, he replied that it was "bad toilet training." These comments are from the same man who said he got into art because he heard that artists didn't have to get up in the morning. But witnesses say he worked seven days a week and on into many nights,

enthusiastically. Voulkos was still producing a tremendous amount of work in the 1970s, as a mature artist who had evolved from painter to ceramist to sculptor. Often his work in these media was simultaneous. In 1973 he began work on a series of two hundred plates, using Picasso's technique of working on plates that had been thrown for him. He drew vigorously on the surfaces, sometimes pebbling them with white porcelain nuggets, sometimes cutting into them, and sometimes tapping holes into them while they were still green. The series of plates is a masterful collection of Voulkos statements.

In diversity of materials, forms, and concepts, American craftsmakers have extended the traditional confines of craft and pushed into wholly new creative areas, pointing up the difference between submissive, committed labor serving the power of the machine with no responsibility for the end product, and independent work with individual responsibility for making good things. Modern craftsmakers identify work with the process of self-creation: they work for the transformation of life into things and things into life. They recognize fully the liberating power of the machine, but treat the machine as a tool that must serve them, not them it.

Until recently, crafts in the United States were considered by many to be a form of superficial artiness. Those who made crafts, it was implied, had either an insufficiency of talent or a lack of guts; they were afraid to go all the way and be artists. Devoid of the wild and impossible, craft was relegated to knicknackery without even a nook in the ivory tower. Technology had created an atmosphere of contempt for handcraft. Scorned on the one side by the machine culture, which could produce

Peter Voulkos working on a stack, or vase form, Sunday morning workshop, Concord Art Center, Concord, California, 1977

Peter Voulkos
Walking Man, 1956
Stoneware, lowfire glaze, 17 x 12
Scripps College,
Claremont, California,
Collection of Mr. and Mrs. Fred
Marer

The decade of the 1950s was a thrilling time for ceramic artists and observers, and Peter Voulkos was the source of many of those thrills. From 1954 through 1958 he helped run the ceramics department at the Otis Art Institute in Los Angeles. It was a time of extraordinary activity for Voulkos; he was the epitome of the artist as verb. Through clay he expressed his eclectic interests — everything from Zen to Constructivism, from Pollock and Rauschenberg to Picasso and Léger — with unlimited energy and inspired gestures, to produce an unprecedented amount of work. *Walking Man*, a stoneware piece from 1956, is an example of his eclectic work. Expressive action is intrinsic to clay and Peter Voulkos was born to do it, knowing that spontaneity is a flash of expressive precision born of deep familiarity and an instinct for timing.

more rapidly and cheaply, and on the other by the art world, which sanctified the artist and placed his quest above worldly considerations, the American craftsmaker had to establish his complex presence, actually to begin his modern history in the United States.

The craftsmaker's first steps, taken in the 1950s and 1960s, were to free his work from competition with the machine that produces useful commodities for the market. Following Picasso's dictum — if it's good, it's art; if it's not, who cares — modern craftsmakers made an art of materials, skills, and obsession. In doing so, they illuminated the full scope of need and use, showing that the need to make by hand a beautiful functional cup comes from the same impetus as the need to make one that does not function.

The primary media in which American craftsmakers have distinguished themselves are clay, fiber, glass, metal, and wood. The exploration of the structural and spatial qualities of materials started in clay and fiber. In ceramics, a new hybrid arose, combining the painted and textured surface with three-dimensional form. In weaving, the warped loom became the naked armature for a new inside-outside form, for free-hanging or free-standing sculptural construction. The sensational developments in these two crafts — whose practitioners are among the most technically skilled in the world — reveal the complex directions of the artist-craftsmaker.

Jun Kaneko
Sanbon Ashi, 1969 (four pieces)
Glazed stoneware, 19 x 30 x 72
Scripps College, Claremont,
California,
Collection of Mr. and Mrs. Fred
Marer

Untitled Slab, 1985-1986
Stoneware, glazed, 4 x 44 x 22
Klein Gallery, Chicago, Illinois

Kaneko, born in Nagoya, Japan,
shapes clay as linear forms moving
across the environment with highly
colored, articulated surfaces of glaze
and design that both emphasize and
resist the form. His works zigzag,
loop, stack, walk, and occupy the
floor in flat or titled groups. Recently
he has turned out giant disks as his
"canvas" for painting as well as
huge spheres which he glazes and
paints in stripes and pattern.
Kaneko's construction of long bars
in self-supporting stacks, singly and
in combination, are like baskets or
barricades, while his knotted,
crossed, limb-like forms — such as
Sanbon Ashi of 1969 — are like
bodiless, walking legs. He studied
with Paul Soldner at Scripps, where
he got his MFA. From 1981 until
1986 he taught at Cranbrook
Academy of Art, Bloomfield Hills,
Michigan, previously having taught
at the University of New Hampshire
and Rhode Island School of Design.

83

Ron Nagle
Verdeyama, 1978
Earthenware, multi-fired, 4¼ x 3¼
David and Mary Robinson,
Sausalito, California

Nagle, connected with Peter Voulkos
in the 1950s at Berkeley, eventually
became aligned with a cooler strain
of Bay Area ceramics, even though
he adopted the Los Angeles
consciousness that had originated
with Kenneth Price and others in the
Otis circle. In the 1970s his "look"
was generally associated with that
of Price, Melchert, Shaw, and
Frimkess. By the time Nagle
produced *Verdeyama,* he and Price
were sharing the credit for
introducing low-fire clay as a
sculptural medium at a time when
the trend in ceramics was toward
stoneware and toothy clays. Nagle
always considered himself a rebel,
and he said small refined pieces
were his way of being perverse. He
also developed and introduced
techniques of multiple firings and
china painting for low-fire clays,
further challenging the art
community to accept a medium
never considered "aesthetic" enough
for sculpture. In 1961 Nagle and
James Melchert changed the clay
body used at San Francisco Art
Institute to whiteware. Melchert was
already renowned for working in
earthenware. It used to be that only
garage hobbyists laid hands on low-
fire clay — especially whiteware. In
adopting these materials Nagle was
on the fringe of funk, embracing a
"low" common denominator of
taste.

The basic function of craft is implicit in its original Saxon form *kraft,*
meaning power and strength. The craftsman, a man of eminence, made
objects to emanate and invoke power and magic — the amulet, the
talisman, the charm. Not until money replaced objects as the symbol of
and means to power did the craftsman lose his original eminence.

Jewelry is the exception that proves the point. Rooted in the magic of
the amulet and the talisman, it reflects economic and social status. When
power came to mean authority, and authority was associated with money
and artifacts of luxury, objects of jewelry became the emblems of the
authority of the kings and the popes — the ring, the crown, the scepter
— and the social signs of honor, distinction, and wealth. Adornment
continued its ancient powers in a new economic context. Still an art of
symbol today, it imparts a sense of ritual enhancement, an extension of
the reality of the self.

Crafts which functioned in the communal or regional culture of an
agrarian society do not have the same meaning in the internationalized
culture of an industrial society. A decisive change in the nature of craft
production took place when the craftsmaker began to create for an

Ron Nagle
Cup with Silkscreened Photograph of Peter Voulkos, 1963
Stoneware, brown and green luster glazes, 4 inches in height
Collection of Peter H. Voulkos, Oakland, California

Nagle has worked with the cup form since the early 1960s when he began to teach at the San Francisco Art Institute with James Melchert. He says he likes cups because they are intimate. Along with Kenneth Price, he has worked seriously with china paints and low-fired clay since 1961. Nagle's cups, like Price's, are not cups at all, but about cups. Drink only with your eyes, advised the critics. Over the past twenty years the cup has become Nagle's only format and his form has become highly stylized. The *Cup with Silkscreened Photo of Peter Voulkos*, from 1963, refers to Nagle's association with Peter Voulkos, which began in 1959 when Voulkos began teaching at the University of California, Berkeley. Stylistically Nagle owes much to Kenneth Price, but he learned about personal strength and vitality from Voulkos, leader of the "tough-guy" art.

Ruth Asawa
Untitled, 1959
Copper wire, 93 x 18 x 18
The Oakland Museum, Oakland,
California, Gift of the Women's
Board

Asawa's knitted wire Constructivist
forms of the 1950s were pioneering
efforts which superseded the woven
forms of Arline Fisch and Mary Lee
Hu by almost a decade. Asawa has
incorporated many techniques and
structures that were used by the
Vikings and Scythians in making
their fish traps and by the pre-
Columbians in their textiles and gold
work. The delicate openness of the
structure's symmetrical simplicity
projects a beautiful network of
patterns upon the walls and floors
as the large suspended forms
undulate through space. The
aluminum, iron, brass, or copper
wire mesh shapes often enclose
smaller shapes. The pods are
reminiscent of hanging Japanese rice
paper lanterns.

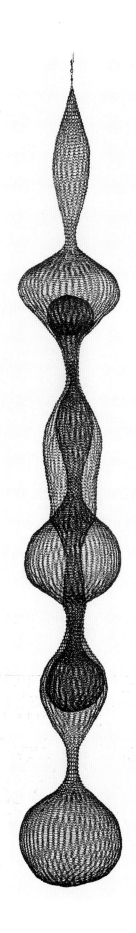

anonymous market, in distinct contrast to his original practice in the intimate and stable community for which he had produced. The village cabinetmaker knew the family for whom he had made a chest. His forebears knew their forebears and his children knew their children. He knew their specific needs and the objects the chest was intended to hold, and he made it to last several lifetimes. But when the craftsmaker was removed from the consumer by distance and from the obligation of satisfying basic functional needs by machine, his choice to be an object maker became a conscious, gratuitous act. This element of choice changed the face of handcraft and signaled the beginning of a whole new creative life. The first purpose of the craftsmaker then was to please himself and to give to the object its intrinsic material self.

In the isolation of his studio or workshop, the craftsmaker began to make objects that related to himself, on a scale that related to his own body in that specific space, and in materials on which he could impose his own reality or be surprised by the imposition of their reality on him. He produced objects that contained his ideas.

The craftsmaker knows the power of objects, their omnipresence in the landscape of man. For the artist-craftsmaker, painting is about painting (the figure or the landscape or the object is a means); so is the pot about pottery and all the pots that have ever been made, glass about glass, weaving about weaving, stitchery about itself, etc.

The machine has given us so many products for every conceivable purpose in every possible material — acetate, vinyl, styrofoam, cardboard, aluminum — with such quick obsolescence that in their unremembered anonymity they make almost no demands on our sensibilities, leaving us free — easy come, easy go — from being possessed by possessions.

Today, the craftsmaker finds himself in the quixotic position of producing objects for a society that already has more objects than it knows what to do with. In a world staggered by the weight and scope of its own material proliferation, we have developed a positive culture of obsolescence. Our aesthetic values have shifted away from permanence, foreverness, stability of materials and subject matter. (The artist himself, in fact, is quite aware of the imminent possiblity of his own quick obsolescence as new ideas, new methods, new actions, and reactions quickly supersede the old.) At the same time, in their challenge to obsolescence and a world crushed by the weight of its own material proliferation, the object makers give value to a toothpick, a chair, an old shoe.

Once obsolescence has given the object the patina of time and isolation from its former life, its actual values are clear, just as the controlled structural life of an air-house may contrast with the eternal life intended for the Great Pyramid. Today, we see the calculable life of a work of art incorporated into itself as an aesthetic. We no longer require ourselves to ascribe lasting values to any object — particularly functional ones. Our functional values too are changing, dictated by the artifacts and extraordinary possiblities of electronic and nuclear energies, new materials, mobility, time.

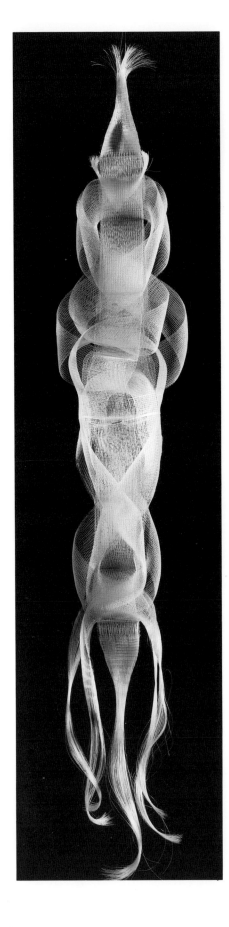

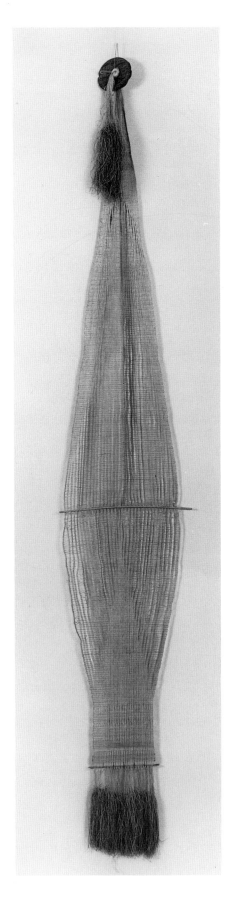

Kay Sekimachi
Amiyose, 1965
Woven nylon monofilament,
60 x 12 x 12
Collection of Kenneth Oberman,
Brooklyn, New York

Sekimachi, who studied with Trude Guermonprez at the California College of Arts and Crafts, became intrigued with the possibilities of making see-through wall dividers from nylon monofilament thread. By weaving four layers of this material on a four-harness loom, Sekimachi was able to open the material for three-dimensional results. She first used this technique in 1963, and for the next twelve years continued expanding this idea. This piece suggested exciting possibilities to many craftspersons, opening up into sculptural format the formal rectilinear grid produced by the weaving process. The complex interpenetration of this construction is heightened by the translucency and transparencies of the monofilament material. Looking into and through this amazingly intricate bundle of clearly articulated elements calls to mind both the microscopic natural world of semi-transparent organisms and the manmade world of complex fishnets and wires.

Lenore Tawney
The Egyptian, 1964
Wet-spun linen, 77 x 13
Collection of Anne Gould Hauberg,
Seattle, Washington

In 1962 Tawney began making long, narrow weavings as hanging sculptures. An acknowledged pioneer of the shift from two-dimensional tapestry to three-dimensional form, she led the way for fiber as a serious medium for sculpture with her shaped constructions first appearing in the 1960s. By using an open, Peruvian-inspired gauze weave technique, she gave these otherwise flat forms dimensionality; by designing a special reed for the loom, she was also able to vary the width of the weaving. In *The Egyptian*, she also gave tangible form to her fascination with things Egyptian by adding an actual ancient wooden object at the top.

Stanley Lechtzin
Torque #31 D, 1972
Cast opal polyester, electroformed
silver gilt, 7½ x 15 x 2
Collection of the artist,
Melrose Park, Pennsylvania

Two of the most difficult problems
facing the jeweler who wishes to
make large-scale wearable objects
are weight and sculptural form.
Casting of metals solves one of the
problems, but not the other. *Ciré
perdue* or lost wax casting gives
great freedom of form, but the
resulting solid mass creates
burdensome objects to wear. Stanley
Lechtzin has pioneered and refined
the use of an electroplating
technique discovered at the
Elkington factory in England in the
1840s. In this process, a base matrix
is covered with metal and then the
matrix is removed, leaving the metal
shell which may be strong, light in
weight, and complex in form.
Lechtzin's interest in recent
technologies and materials has
resulted in stunning works which
take full advantage of the sculptural
possibilities of plastic and metal.
These pieces would have been
impossible to wear as jewelry had
he not chosen this approach to
construction.

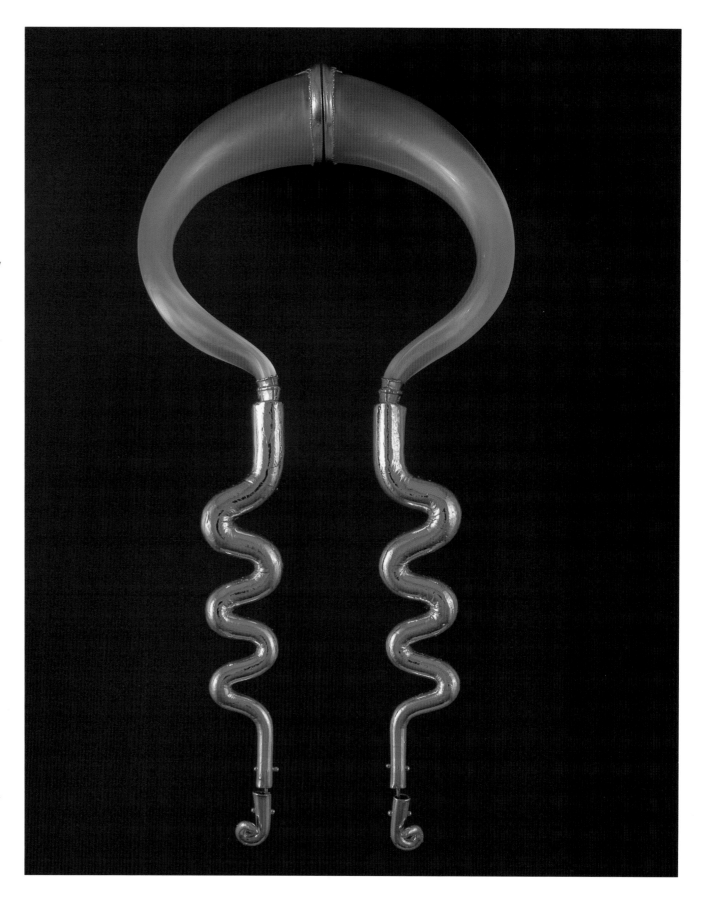

Stanley Lechtzin
Cameo Corsage #83 D, 1979
Electroformed silver, silver gilt, cast
acrylic, photo image, pearls,
6¼ x 3¾ x 3
Collection of the artist,
Melrose Park, Pennsylvania

Cameo Corsage introduces yet
another industrially oriented
technique transformed for use as an
art medium. The viewer will be
more familiar with this process as
the silvered glass he peers into each
morning which we call a mirror.
Here, solid metal is disassociated in
the presence of a vacuum and
deposited on a sensitized matrix
leaving a thin reflective film. The
process is identical to that used in
the manufacture of computer
components where gold vapor is
deposited onto the minute
connectors of the chips. The same
photographic sensitizing is used here
to create figurative images which
seem to float in space within the
structure.

Stanley Lechtzin
Torque #33 D, 1973
Electroformed silver, silver gilt,
purple polyester, 12 inches in width
Yale University Art Gallery, New
Haven, Connecticut, American Arts
Purchase Fund

Marjorie Schick
Neckpiece for the Back, 1986
(facing page)
Wood, paint, rubber hose,
15½ x 22 x 8½
Collection of the artist,
Pittsburg, Kansas

As a graduate student in the 1960s,
Schick was fascinated by David
Smith's sculpture, which she saw
illustrated against a hilly landscape
in an art periodical. She says that
she asked herself what it would feel
like to be a body inside those
precariously but perfectly balanced
forms. Since that time, she has
explored similar compositions in her
wearable sculpture. Her works can
be worn, hung, or placed on a
pedestal, raising once again the
question Is it jewelry or is it
sculpture? Can an object be both?
Schick's refreshing forms are
inventive drawings in three
dimensions.

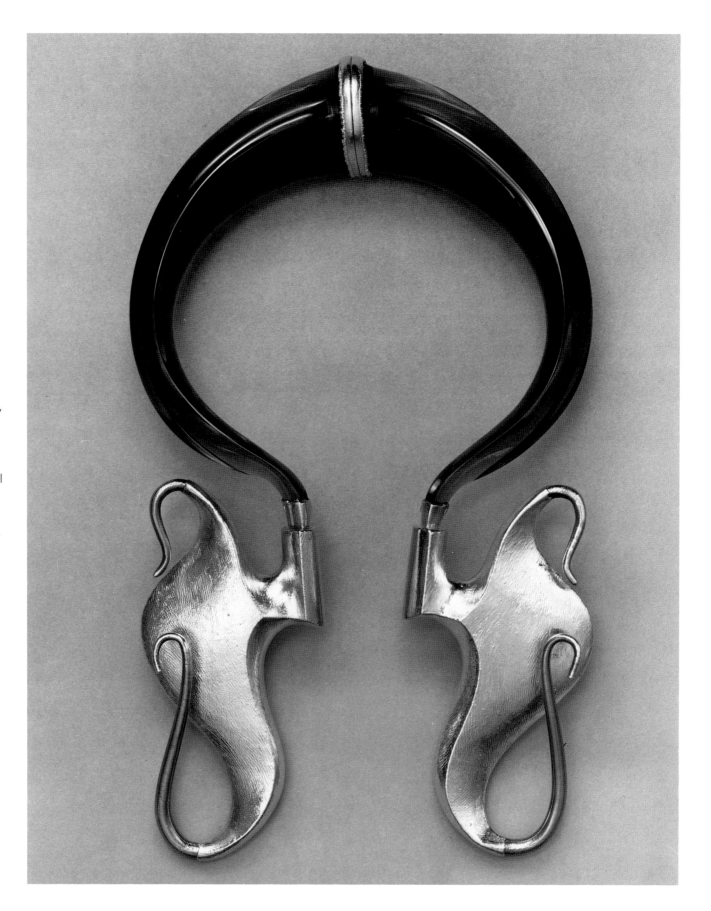

90

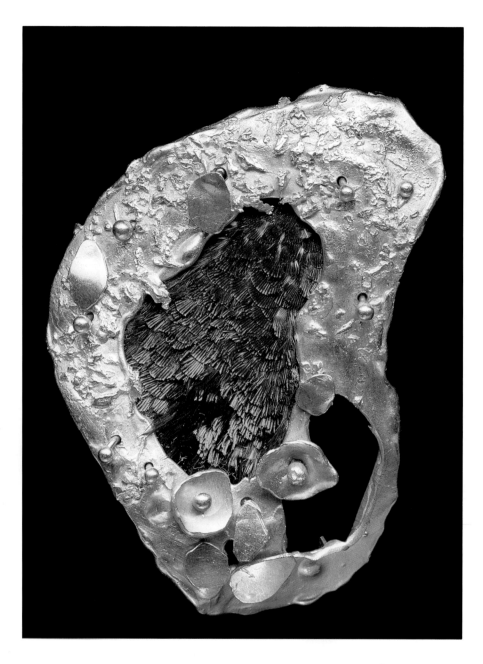

Margret Craver
Eclosion Pin, 1967
En résille enamel, mounted in 18k
gold (fabricated), 2¼ x 2¾
Minnesota Museum of Art,
St. Paul, Minnesota
Gift of the Johnson Wax Company
from *Objects: USA*
Restored in 1985 by Margret Craver
Courtesy Barbara Rockefeller Jewelry
Associates, New York, New York

Craver revitalized an interest in metal
in the United States by reintroducing
hollowware techniques. In 1944, she
went to work for Handy and
Harman, refiners and suppliers of
precious metals, as a consulting
silversmith. There, she developed a
nonprofit program designed to train
professional metalsmiths and
teachers. After leaving Handy and
Harman in 1950, Craver pursued her
own work. She was particularly
interested in en résille enameling, a
process which uses no metal
backing. Her rediscovery and
exploration of this 17th-century
French technique allowed her to
fabricate her own translucent
gemstones, which she frames in
meticulously executed raised and
soldered gold forms.

Velma Dozier
Rain Forest, 1969 (right)
Cast gold, hummingbird feather,
1⅞ x 1⅜ x ⅜
Dallas Museum of Art, Dallas, Texas,
Gift of Otis and Velma Dozier

During the mid-1950s the public
perception of jewelry was that of
Tiffany mounted diamond rings.
However, a storm was brewing
among the studio jewelers of the
time: jewelry was becoming
wearable sculpture. The emphasis
shifted from expensive precious
stones to sculptural form and the
use of material for its intrinsic
character. To Dozier, gold is
important because of its butter-
yellow color, not its monetary value.
Precious stones are valuable because
of their light-catching ability. *Rain
Forest* incorporates the breast of a
hummingbird (killed as it flew into
the artist's patio window). Small
spheres of gold (rather than
gemstones) appoint the form so as
not to compete with the richness of
the ruby breast.

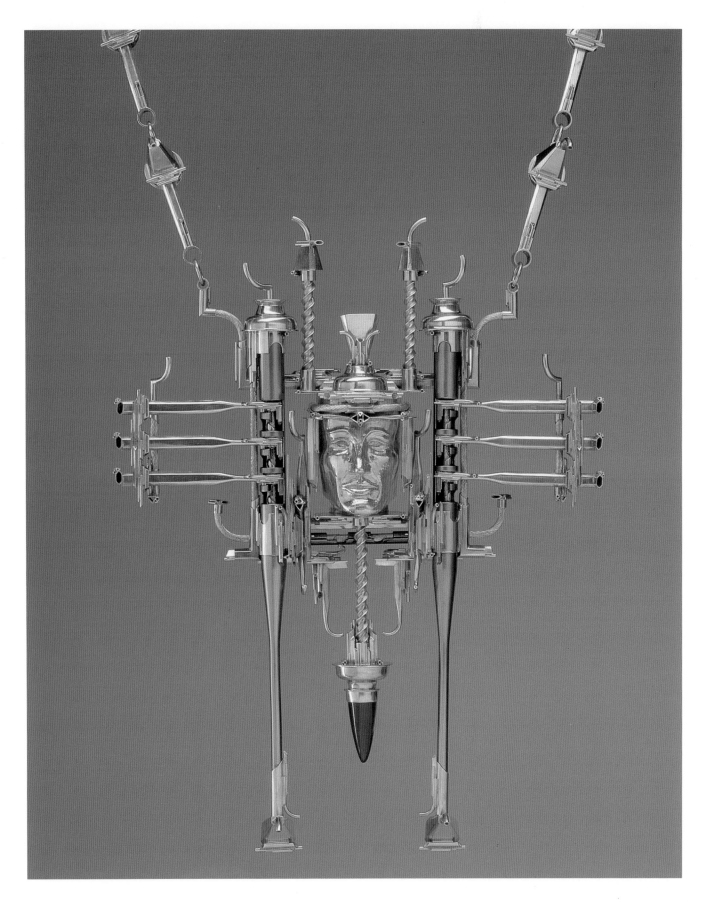

Richard Mawdsley
Headdress #5, 1984
18k gold, titanium, tantalum,
garnet, fabricated, 10½ x 4¾ x ⅞
Collection of the artist,
Carterville, Illinois

Unlike the monochrome austerity of
the *Feast Bracelet,* accomplished by
the use of silver, the *Headdress #5*
employs the color of gold, tantalum,
and fabricated repoussé to augment
and explore the dimensionality of
the work. The headdress series is an
expansion of Mawdsley's earlier
ornaments; its function is an
afterthought. Pieces such as the
Feast Bracelet were conceived
independently of function.
Mawdsley's work persistently refers
to mechanical imagery, however
abstract, organic, or
representational, by way of the
everpresent metal tubing.

Richard Mawdsley
Feast Bracelet, 1974
Sterling silver, jade, pearls,
fabricated, 3¾ x 4½ x 2½
National Museum of American Art,
Smithsonian Institution, Washington,
D.C., Gift of James Renwick
Collectors Alliance

Mawdsley uses his whimsical sense
of humor and a unity of image and
character to create tiny sculptures
that become jewelry. For the silver
Feast Bracelet, at least three years in
the making, Mawdsley adapted his
forms by researching photographs
of historical pieces. Although the
Feast Bracelet is a miniaturized still
life, which he himself calls a genre
scene, it is also a unique personal
vision that transcends its reference
to reality.

The machine proved that even a poorly made thing may function very
well while it lasts; quick obsolescence has nothing to do with the ability
to function. In fact, obsolescence may even reveal its aesthetic quality, like
the graphic stamina of yesterday's newspapers.

Craftsmakers serving purely functional purposes must be specialists of
a many-faceted machine which, after all, is their all-embracing and
consuming tool of production. The skill and knowledge of the mechanical
engineer, the tool and dye maker, the riveter, the auto mechanic, the mold
maker, are formidable. The difference between craft production and mass
production further illustrates this. In craft production you have ten people
each making ten complete objects. In mass production you have ten
people enabling the machine to make one object. The mechanics are as
disassociated from the product which the machine makes as they are from
the consumer who will use it. The difference is between those who serve
the machine for endless production to satisfy manifold functional needs
and those whom the machine serves to satisfy gratuitous needs. As a

Beatrice Wood
Teapot with Figures, n.d.
Earthenware with luster glazes,
18½ inches in height
Garth Clark Gallery,
Los Angeles/New York

Wood's clay objects evoke the
playful delight encountered in the
world of folk art and the exotic
surfaces seen in vessels from distant
lands. Wood's education in art and
theater, her travels to foreign
countries, and her tie to the New
York Bohemian lifestyles of the early
1900s are all sources for her work.
Wood developed an in-glaze luster
technique which is rich in historical
and cultural associations. In
attempting to recapture the method
used in ninth-century Persian luster-
glazed pottery, she developed
colorful surfaces of even greater
depth and complexity.

Robert Arneson
Typewriter, 1965
Earthenware, glazed,
6⅛ x 11⅜ x 12½
University of California Art Museum,
Berkeley, California,
Gift of the artist

Arneson's ordinary objects made of
clay are given skewed meanings
through visual association with other
related objects. His human-fingered
typewriter broke the bounds
established by the new academy of
Abstract Expressionism in ceramics,
led by Peter Voulkos and John
Mason. Arneson's work reflected
modes of expression customary in
literature, such as satire and
punning, even incorporating words
scratched or imprinted onto the
surface of the clay.

heretic against the tyranny of the machine — which requires the creation
of more functions for more products to satisfy its ever-increasing appetite
for more production if only to keep itself going — the artist-craftsmaker is
free to decide whether his object is to function superbly or poorly or not
at all. In so doing, he has invented a fresh new language of craft, and in
probing at the limits of its expression he has expanded the materials of
art.

The United States — compelled by the electrifying idea of personal
freedom that cuts through geographic, social, and economic lines — was
the economic spawn of the Industrial Revolution. In the three hundred
years of our short history, an expanding frontier has kept us absorbed in
the problems of practical function and pressured us to solve them in a
hurry. As a result we have developed a national style based on satisfying
functional needs for the masses in a massive country, with availability an
ideal.

In the United States, by contrast with the rest of the world, the
craftsman never produced for a ruling hierarchy, and only for a very short
time for his immediate agricultural community before he was rendered
unnecessary by the Industrial Revolution.

We are a restless people. A nation of immigrants with a continuing
history of migration, we are obsessed by the need for arrival — a pursuit

whose goal eludes us; so we are always on the go. (Our writers — Walt Whitman, Herman Melville, Thomas Wolfe — have repeatedly explored this theme.) Having solved our need for mobility by mechanical means, we love engineering and performance and the materials and tools by which we have achieved them. If there is any one pervasive element in the Amerian climate it is that of the machine — its energy, its productivity, its violence.

The history of American craft styles parallels that of other art forms — from the frugal handcraft economy of colonial America with products of great formal and functional directness as well as real decorative power to the prosperous industrial economy of the post-Civil War Northeast which looked to the pseudo-classical styles then popular in Europe and the sumptuous artifacts of Oriental palaces to express a growing cultural self-consciousness; then to the boom days of the early twentieth century with Art Nouveau and its flowing organic form for its own lovely sake. With the depressed thirties came a return to the moral purity of form following function.

As far back as 1870, a Shaker spokesman declared that Shaker architectures ignored "beauty of design" because what people called beautiful was "absurd." This had been stated by others before and was restated by many others, including the American architect Raymond M. Hood who called "this beauty stuff" "all the bunk." A typical American attitude, it may well have expressed the beginning of a new American aesthetic rather than a gross lack of appreciation for the old one.

Nothing is needed to last forever, and the rough-and-tumble of American craft, which considers the expressive content most important and takes great liberties with the material, is in distinct contrast to the thrifty, careful, and even cautious practice in other parts of the world where predetermined modes of traditional design guard against waste, where exquisitely exacting and nonwasteful techniques have been invented and evolved with the minimum of materials and tools, where materials are precious and labor is plentiful.

The freedom of the American craftsmaker to experiment, to risk, to make mistakes freely on a creative and quantitative level, has been facilitated to a large extent by the wealth of tools and materials. These give further impetus to the craftsmaker's involvement in total process — in the mastery of technology and the actual making of the object from beginning to end — in marked contrast to the artist-craftsmakers of other countries who do only the designing and finishing and leave the technology and execution to the peasant craftsman. Aside from the fact that there is in the United States no anonymous peasant craftsmaker to do only the technical or preparatory work, the craftsmaker loves his tools too much to leave that part of the fun to someone else. For him the entire process contains creative possibilities. Intimacy with the tools and materials of his craft is a source of the artist's power. Here too, however, lies a contradiction. In the United States, to learn about a craft one must go to an art school or a university where, frequently, the reward of technique is its own virtue. This has been accompanied by rebellion against the tyranny

Paul Soldner
Vase, 1965
Raku fired earthenware,
18 inches in height
Scripps College,
Claremont, California,
Collection of Mr. and Mrs. Fred Marer

Soldner discovered his true vocation in 1954 while working with Peter Voulkos at the Otis Art Institute (now The Otis Art Institute of Parsons School of Design). As an adventurer in the expressive and gestural qualities of clay, Soldner became a leader in developing innovative vessels with distorted shapes and compelling colors. in 1960, Soldner adapted the Japanese concept of raku firing for use in American ceramics, a process that is pervasive today.

Ken Cory
Pin, 1967
Silver, leather, stone, 2 x 1½ x ½
Collection of the artist,
Ellensburg, Washington

Cory makes small sculptures that are
bold, original, and innovative in the
use of multiple materials, often
giving an impression of massiveness
even though they are miniaturized
objects. His pins are examples of the
new direction in jewelry in which
the use of non-precious metals and
materials from natural and manmade environments is explored.

of traditional techniques (after having learned them), deliberate rejection
of customary tools, processes, and materials, by artists who break every
rule. This has also led to a questioning of traditional techniques and to
personal invention of new ways of handling materials, new application of
tools, new materials, and new tools. This ambivalence toward technique is
a characteristic of the modern craftsmaker and artist.

The American craftsmaker, then, is the product of the university
workshop or specialized school with study in painting and sculpture as
well as design and craft techniques. Instead of learning his techniques
from the folk craftsmaker or through heritage or apprenticeship, he does
his research in books, in workshops and university classes, and by traveling
to countries with craft traditions. The craftsmaker of the United States is
the product of international experience. He is, furthermore, a veritable
melting pot of national origins, with the professional artist-craftsmakers
who emigrated from Europe and the Orient as the decisive influences.

All over the Western world the objects of the new objectmakers
provide moral and ethical confrontation with a society that has become
alienated from its objects, that no longer accepts responsibility for them, is
unable to see them, uses them mechanically. The object makers are
commenting on their middle-class culture of mass-produced, standardized
good taste as a domesticated, housebroken, sanitized sensibility. They
make no aesthetic conclusion. The objects are their own comment, their
own mute drama.

Identity induced by words separates things from themselves. Things
lose their power and become illustrations of the word which, when it
ceased to be hieroglyph, or pictographic presentation of the object, ceased
actual connection with the thing and became its own abstract and
powerful object. While seeking the connection between objects, person,
and language, the object makers create a mutual absoluteness for each.

On the other hand, surrounded by a word-filled world dominated by
publication and publicity, our process of education glibly teaches us the
vocabulary and the reproduction before we know the actual object. We
see objects through synthetic media — books, magazines, television,
movies. We see them (maybe) in transition, as we walk from one place to
the next, in the speed of our cars, planes, etc. Actual confrontation in
time and space is rare.

The young artist has also found that he cannot trust the inside of
things — the heart stops beating, the TV tube burns out — which he
cannot see and which, in any case, look quite different from the outside
form and are suspect, therefore, on still another count. In the objects he
makes, everything is externalized, all surface, totally visible all at once. It
does what you see and you see what it does. There is no mystery, no
enigma, no inner life, no conflict. All is cool. It may well have informed
the development of the artist with the sweet rancor of cynicism and
suspicion. By and large, the young American artist today comes from the
very middle class he professes to scorn; he is a product of the eclecticism
of the liberal arts programs of the university system rather than
experienced in the specialized disciplines of the apprenticeship system or

Therman Statom
Untitled, 1981
Cast glass, paint, 11 x 7¼ x 5
Collection of Ron and Kathryn
Glowen, Arlington, Washington

Statom's series of dwellings or
houses, of cast and/or plate glass,
exploit the impurities of the material
to produce a quality of translucence.
Statom, like Marvin Lipofsky, another
pioneer of the studio glass
movement, paints the surfaces of his
glass structures. The impasto texture
and opacity of the vividly colored
paint provides a bold contrast to the
transparency of the material.
Statom's cast houses could easily be
read as blocks of ice. The crystalline
and refractive nature of the
structures that occur in ice intrigue
this artist, and his cast
interpretations of those structures
are an important part of his
permanent "fluid" sculptural forms.

Wayne Higby
Pictorial Lake, 1986
Earthenware, raku technique,
13½ x 34 x 9
Collection of Wayne and Donna
Higby, Alfred Station, New York

Higby's fascination with the aesthetic
achievements of ceramic history did
not lead him to imitation of admired
objects but rather to the adoption
of selected techniques: the vitrified
paste of ancient Egypt, the subtle
crackled glazes of China and the
raku firings of Japan. In his first
works of the late 1960s he searched
for a way to use such devices to a
meaningful end. By the mid-1970s
he had found his vehicle in
landscape vessels.

the concentration of the professional schools. He is an educated man,
thoroughly graced in the arts of articulation and communication. He
knows all about "the power of the press." The young artist has seen the
word supercede the power of the object. He has seen the word become
the object and the real object be denied validity without the word. He has
seen that words, too often, are more interesting to the public and to his
own colleagues, and have more influence on them than the objects they
are supposed to describe. So he knows every book. He has studied the
lives and the words and the acts of his predecessors, not to mention their
work. It has all been published, filmed, and recorded. Based on this
inescapable mass of evidence, he can figure out what works and what
doesn't, write the script of his own life as artist, a known object, and play
its role in a theatrical event of predictable elements. He has seen the
exhibition treated as an area of social status rather than as the arena of
artistic stature. All words are suspect, all objects are suspect — all art is
suspect. Artistic success has never been more vast or international, thanks
to the instantaneous power of modern communication aided and abetted
by the fastidious energies of the public relations industry that so effectively

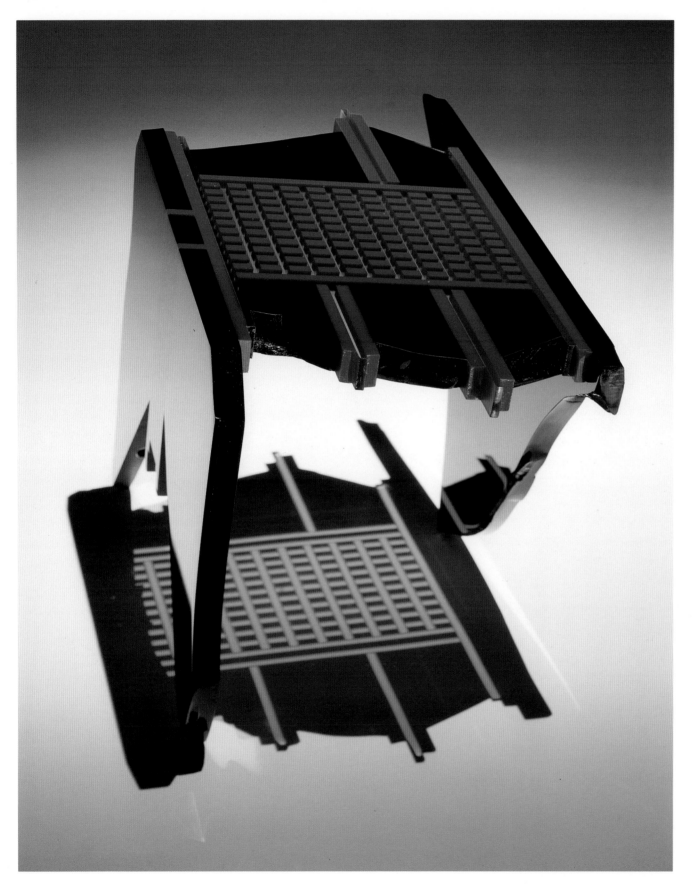

David R. Huchthausen
Leitungs Scherben LSA83, 1983
Cut, fused, laminated and polished
glass, 10½ x 17 x 9
Collection of Jon Kuhn,
Winston-Salem, North Carolina

A dedicated leader of the studio
glass movement, David Huchthausen
began experimenting in the medium
as a student at the University of
Wisconsin at Wausau in 1970 when
he discovered an abandoned glass
furnace. Ironically he struggled for
six months to master the techniques
of glassblowing without knowing of
the program Harvey Littleton had
established only 150 miles away on
the Madison campus of the same
university. He eventually transferred
there and served as Littleton's
assistant. The cool, majestic *Leitungs
Scherben,* Huchthausen's recent
work, are harshly irregular (*Scherben*
is the German word for shards)
constructions that incorporate the
effects of shadow and transmitted
light (*Leitung* means guidance,
direction or transmission).

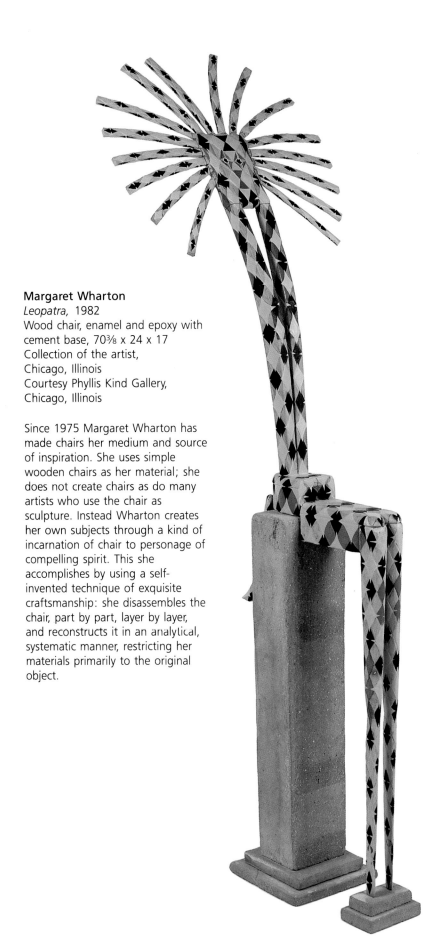

Margaret Wharton
Leopatra, 1982
Wood chair, enamel and epoxy with
cement base, 70⅜ x 24 x 17
Collection of the artist,
Chicago, Illinois
Courtesy Phyllis Kind Gallery,
Chicago, Illinois

Since 1975 Margaret Wharton has
made chairs her medium and source
of inspiration. She uses simple
wooden chairs as her material; she
does not create chairs as do many
artists who use the chair as
sculpture. Instead Wharton creates
her own subjects through a kind of
incarnation of chair to personage of
compelling spirit. This she
accomplishes by using a self-
invented technique of exquisite
craftsmanship: she disassembles the
chair, part by part, layer by layer,
and reconstructs it in an analytical,
systematic manner, restricting her
materials primarily to the original
object.

modulates the spectaculars of museum and gallery show biz. In one eye
and out the other.

Craftsmakers everywhere, including the humble, anonymous
member of a cottage industry whose work is known for its traditional
national mode, are members of the modern, international milieu into
which each artist reaches out to expand his own unique and individual
gamut. While Americans use the old motifs of Nigeria, the colors of India,
the textures of Japan, Nigerian craftsmakers are in turn using such modern
motifs of industrial society as cement intaglio reliefs of bulldozers, planes,
and cranes on their buildings. The craftsmakers of San Blas Islands produce
exquisitely appliquéd blouses decorated with images of Superman and
Donald Duck. And so it goes.

All this has made craftsmakers susceptible and responsive to the
startling achievements of contemporary American painting and sculpture.
For better or worse, they have allied themselves with an expression that
comes from their own culture and their own time, and from an attitude
towards work and its processes with which they can identify. Today, with
their knowledge about themselves, their craft and their art — historically
and contemporaneously — cumulatively greater than ever before, the
United States craftsmakers are eagerly in search of their own identities.

United States culture emerges from those irresistible and galvanizing
catalysts mobility and the machine. Mobility has enabled people all over
the world to shift, to emigrate and populate, to impose and develop new
cultures; through it the crafts and the craftsmaker continue to exercise an
ever increasing influence for change. Work is as varied and multi-
directed as its makers and contrasts sharply to that of the craftsmakers
from communities and cultures whose skills were passed from parent to
child in the same village and whose objects refer to the religious and
functional life of the community they serve.

Today the handcrafts and the fine arts of this country enjoy a
relationship of energies in the arts unique to the United States. The new
creative sensibility of our time is infused with the spirit of handcraft. It is
not, as we have previously said, a renaissance; it is not a revival; it is not a
rebirth. It is a brand-new phenomenon, a handcraft culture feeding into
and fed by industrial freedoms, along with modern painting (also a
handcraft) and modern sculpture (also a handcraft).

Modern handcraft would not have been possible without the
machine, without the accessibility to the mobilized cultures of the world,
without the presence of modern painting. Modern folk craft would not
have been possible without the nostalgia, the hungers, the heightened
consciousness, the conscience and the guilt of the industrialized West.

Hands are our most revolutionary tools, the most flexible, the
cheapest, the best suited to reach new solutions. The object of craft is
encased in metaphors and meanings and opposites like a poem, a
wordless poem. The handcraftsmakers, utterly surrounded by the
magnitude of an automated technology that can not only destroy the
world they live in but create another at the push of a button, living in a
world whose most powerful forces — electronic and atomic, inner and

outer space, speed — are invisible to the naked eye; a world which like a diminutive ping pong ball bounces around with other little planets and under one of many possible suns, are expressing the dilemma of all men of our time. The aspect of man is no longer the center of things and his eyes are only accessories of his own growing sense of displacement. In the face of all this, the survival of the handcraftsmaker — enemy of mechanical mindlessness and carrier of the weight of humanism with all its objects of art and utility that define a culture — testifies to the persistence of man's exuberant reverence for himself, of man the artist, the lover of life, its own best reason for being.

NOTES

[1] At the first national conference at Asilomar, California, I met Peter Voulkos, a meeting that resulted in 1961 in the publication of my essay "The New Ceramic Presence" in *Craft Horizons,* which caused a brouhaha with letters to the editor coming by the bundle for at least two years after its publication. Many subscribers cancelled their subscriptions as a result of the essay but many more hailed it as the new wave of thinking about art and craft. Twenty years later it resulted in my book *Peter Voulkos: A Dialogue in Clay.* The art/craft connection has been the theme of at least two major exhibitions I have curated, *The Object as Poet,* in 1976, at the Renwick Gallery of The National Museum of Art (then the National Museum of American Art), Smithsonian Institution; and *Ordinary and Extraordinary Uses: Objects by Artists* in 1984 at the Guild Hall Museum, East Hampton, New York; as well as many of my articles for *Craft Horizons* and other magazines.

[2] The American Craftsmen's Educational Council was later called the American Craftsmen's Council and then the American Crafts Council. In June/July of 1979 it became known as the American Craft Council. The independent magazine *Craft Horizons* flourished with its own readership unrelated to American Craft Council members until 1959, when it was incorporated into the American Craft Council. The January/February 1960 issue (vol. xx, No. 1) was the first issue copyrighted by the American Craft Council.

[3] Among the major centers of such work today are the Rhode Island School of Design, Alfred University in New York, University of Wisconsin, Southern Illinois University, the University of California at Berkeley, Davis, Irvine, and Los Angeles, and the College of Arts and Crafts in Oakland. In addition, the summer workshop at Haystack Mountain School of Crafts at Deer Island, Maine, has been a significant influence, while the Penland School of Crafts in Penland, North Carolina, which provides a year-round working program for craftsmakers and their students, has been a focal point for emerging craftsmakers.

BREAKING THE FRAMES

HORACE FREELAND JUDSON

Wayne Higby
Apparition Canyon, 1982
Earthenware, raku technique, wheel-thrown and corrected,
11 x 18½ x 16¼
Roberson Center for the Arts and Sciences, Binghamton, New York

Higby's preferred shape is the deep wheel-thrown bowl whose unassuming familiarity provides the perfect foil for the decoration he applies to both interior and exterior. In a feat of lyric legerdemain he creates landscapes which read continuously from exterior to interior. More extraordinary still, variant configurations are offered by every possible viewpoint. The intrigue of the improbable all-around inside-outside continuity engages the viewer only after he has begun a deeper exploration of the obvious visual delights of pieces like *Apparition Canyon,* where turquoise glaze indicates waters glimpsed between gray cliffs of raku-fired clay and snowy mesas of crackled white glaze.

In London one blustery Saturday morning in the fall of 1968, an informal collective of young artists took over a large, vacant building site on the wrong side of the borough of Hammersmith, to mount a day of what were then called happenings. Imagine bulldozed brick rubble and red earth, here and there a stub of old foundation wall. Imagine denims or fatigues, Jesus sandals or military hightops, ponytails and considerable bustling cheerfulness, all indifferent of gender. Imagine a couple near the middle of the space setting up big-headed puppets and a black cloth backdrop. Three bearded men over on that side erecting a crazy half-sized shantytown, mined, they pointed out, with pyrotechnics, all of which they intended later to set alight. A photographer taking close-ups, in a pier glass, of the backs of people's heads. A robust young woman in evening dress bashing a red sports car with a sledgehammer, the sounds amplified like a pop singer's guitar. A lad digging a hole. A trumpeter being wrapped in white bandages. Imagine — if it wasn't exactly these things, it was like that. In point of fact, this was the fringe of the fringe of the self-conscious London avant-garde; yet in 1968 new art in England had been lively for a decade, and some interesting people had come up from previous stages of this same milieu. And then walking briskly along the street came a young, compact fellow in blue jeans and jacket. He bounded down the three rough steps into the site. At their foot he halted in a half-crouch, splayed his hands before him, looked about with widened eyes at all that was going on, and called out, "*Where do I sign it?!*"

The question was more than amusing; it reduced a main line of the century's art momentarily to a one-line parody. Memory fails: was it Duchamp at a sidewalk cafe in Juan-les-Pins or Picasso at the cafe around

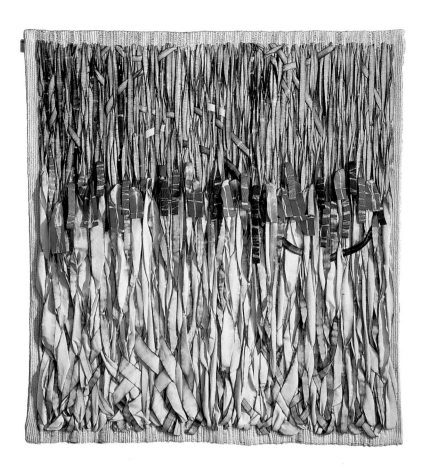

Cynthia Schira
Winter Wheat, 1975
Wool, nylon, 56 x 54
Museum Bellerive,
Zürich, Switzerland

Amplified by *ikat* dying, Schira's
palette allows the woven fibers to
establish a mood while the
"eccentric" lines suggest the subject.
Works in which broken trails of
color float on a background of
modulated cool hues evoke
reflections in still waters. Warmer
tones with brilliant trails evoke a
sunlit day. *Winter Wheat* offers the
most literal extreme of Schira's
imagery. With pared-down
pictorialism she closes in on a tall
stand of grain, massing the luxuriant
golden stalks and sturdy amber
heads against a shimmering blue
sky. References to the plains of
Kansas where Schira makes her
home are obvious in this gentle
work that hovers between landscape
and abstraction.

the corner in Arcachon who, pestered by a collector, picked up an ashtray
and signed it — and by the gesture asserted that this object was to be
looked at with a new order of response, as a work of art? The anonymous
London artist's joke encapsulated an entirely serious question: What, in
the most general way, does an artist do? The other half of that is: To what
and whom does he do it? Which is also to ask: How do we, his audience,
assimilate the new? These have always, of course, been central problems
of criticism. They have been exhaustively fought out; one is uneasily aware
that to offer to say something new about them risks embarrassment —
except that criticism is an empirical business, and certain new kinds of
works are now forcing these questions afresh.

Start with the fact that in America today an extraordinary variety of
objects are being made that develop from traditions and employ materials
and techniques long associated with what we conventionally call crafts,
but have the force and independence, the full aesthetic self-sufficiency,
that we demand of the high arts. When most delicately poised between
genesis and achievement, such an object is perceptually paradoxical: it is
beautiful in the unnerving manner of the thousand-ton boulder that eons
of erosion have left balanced on one corner — shimmering with
consequence. The objects are often three-dimensional, of a scale to be
held in the hand, or walked around, or moved through, while even those
that hang on the wall cast deep shadows. Thus many of them can be
called sculptural; they are less frequently pictorial. Often their substance is
unexpected — fabrics and fibers woven, sewn, or tied; crumpled paper;
leather and plastic; feathers; rope and yarn and hanks of string;
gemstones; glass, ceramics, sheet metal and shredded metal. Often these
substances are used in strange ways and combinations. The works' origins
are as diverse as the things themselves. They have emerged from
American Indian traditions; black traditions and Latino ones so multiple
that they defy ethnic classification; peasant methods and motifs from
Scandinavia, Russia, French Canada; the familiar American arts-and-crafts
roots that run back to the Great Depression and further. These lineages
are even now being transformed by a new generation. The extremes are
suggested by, say, harsh images made up of fetish-like materials, which
appear in certain Afro-American and Caribbean pieces, and, in contrast,
wooden objects from furniture makers' workshops that stretch the ideal of
chair or table so far that we acknowledge them as sculptures in the same
act of perception with which we recognize their function.

This is not a movement. Nobody could have written a manifesto. Yet
such dual or multiple perceptions, simultaneous and conflicting, lie at the
source of the aesthetic power of all the best of these objects — and this
points to the secret unity behind their extravagant disparity. These
remarkable objects are not always and never simply pleasing. Even the
most exquisite are aesthetically disturbing in a peculiar and original way.
They are deeply incongruous, and therefore tense, the cognitive equivalent
of optical illusions: What is form, what is function — which follows, which
leads? Which is figure, which is ground? They bring into awareness and
then into doubt our preconceptions about art.[1]

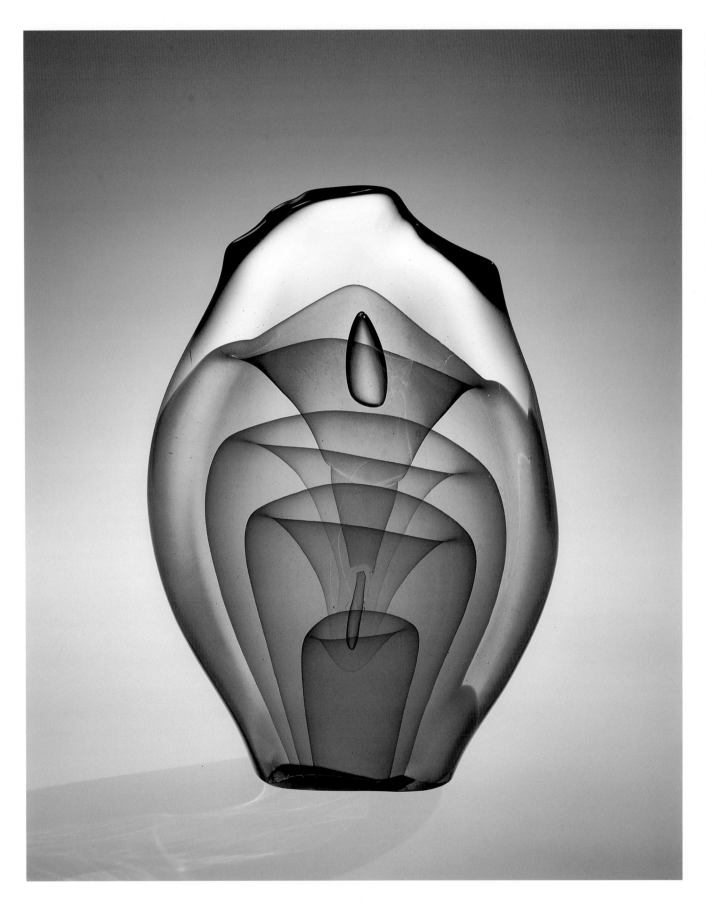

Dominick Labino
Emergence Four-Stage, 1975
Colorless and pink transparent glass
with amber tints, 8⅘ x 6¼ x 2⅓
The Corning Museum of Glass,
Corning, New York, purchased with
the aid of funds from the National
Endowment for the Arts

As head of the Glass Fibers Division
of Johns-Manville Corporation,
Labino was called upon to lend
expertise to the 1962 seminar at the
Toledo Museum of Art which
opened the way for the studio glass
movement. Providing a glass
formula with a lower melting point,
he solved a key problem in making
glass available to the individual artist
working outside the industry and
studio glass blowing so fired his
enthusiasm that he took an early
retirement to pursue the medium. In
the series titled *Emergence* Labino
used the traditional glass
paperweight as his point of
departure. His gather of glass takes
the form of a solid teardrop
enclosing delicately tinted veils and
a languid air bubble. The special
magic of the work lies in the
dichroic properties of the veils which
appear pink or violet with
transmitted light but in direct light
turn to shimmering gold.

Richard Shaw
Couch, 1965
Earthenware, painted with acrylics,
11 x 27 x 12
The Oakland Museum, Oakland,
California, Gift of Rena Bransten

Shaw's work is allied to a long
tradition in American art which
culminates in Magic Realism. At a
second, and perhaps deeper, level
are messages about the mutability
of the material world. Ideas
concerning the transformation of
substance to thought are evoked by
these mysteriously compelling
works.

The dilemma of the new springs from the fact that inescapably we
approach the object, the instance of new work, with expectations. To
begin with, whatever the thing is and whatever else we may find to say
about it, it cannot seem to us wholly new. (One may note in passing that
this is as much the case in the experimental sciences as in the arts.) The
psychology of the work of art — if you prefer, of the maker or presenter
of the work — plays upon expectations. The work if strong is invested
with a conflict that compels our attention: not necessarily our agreement,
but our respect. Good work has a special quality, a strength and balance
of tensions that amounts to a perceptual aura. Great work has an aura
that is not only strong but sufficiently ambiguous — flexible, stretchable,
multiple — to last. The sources of perceptual tension, the aura, invite
scrutiny; they can perhaps best be identified if we trace them from the
time when the pleasures we expect the poet or musician or artificer to
provide began to be considered systematically. The earliest critical
discussions we know of are laden with self-awareness, reflexivity.
Expectations, though sometimes fresher than ours, are never in truth
naive. We think we have come a long way from Aristotle's robust assertion
that art imitates nature. Yet that assertion offers three terms for our
consideration, each gravid with meaning — and the first, which we
translate art, was in Aristotle's Greek *techne.* The implications of that
word, its present-day resonances, are several.

Greeks of the classical era took for granted a unity that we have broken. Aristotle knew a variety of arts that imitate nature, the art of the painter or of the poet but also of the dancer, the singer, the flutist, and so on, and other arts that do not, such as those of the saddler or the cobbler or, for that matter, the art of the military commander (the *strategos*: he has given his name to his art) or of the physician. Each was particular, the *techne* of this or of that. Thus in an essential sense arts were always practical. Aristotle held that the unifying characteristic of all the arts is that they apply systematic bodies of knowledge by special skills to particular cases. He and his time had no general word for what we mean by "artist."[2]

The burgher of fourth-century Athens, when told that Praxiteles had completed a new statue of the god Hermes, now on public view, or when invited by a friend to see the wine cup he'd just acquired, carried certain expectations with him. Those expectations will have been different from our own. They are not beyond tactful conjecture. The classical critics offer scant help: epic, drama, history, and the interest of the state were their concern, to which visual arts were ancillary. We cannot be sure how aware the connoisseurs in that golden afternoon became of what to our eyes — to our expectations — is the extreme stylization of the visual art that was all around them, of the previous centuries' sculpture, say, or of the figures on the vases they admired and collected. More than likely, the cultivated Athenian saw visual styles much as he heard the language he spoke and wrote: not I but other people, barbarians or Boeotians, have accents. But that's a digression. We do know that the technical and stylistic fluency of sculpture and painting had been in rapid development for a century or more. We know that the new was welcomed with excitement — an excitement that strikes us as modern, comparable to responses the arts have repeatedly evoked from the Renaissance to the present day. The sinuous expressiveness of Praxiteles' figures, the glow of living flesh that his modeling brought to marble surfaces — these were wonders. The painters at that time were discovering comparable marvels, shading, foreshortening, perspective. Not insignificantly, we learn this from the vases, which were miniatures of some of the painters' evolving techniques and are about all that survive.

Expectations of the visual arts were in flux and critically undefined. (No doubt that's necessarily true in interesting times: wig askew and shoelaces undone, critical theory is forever hobbling and gesticulating after the arts.) The sculptor or the painter invested the thing he made with a special quality. One looked to and as it were *through* the thing, to — But tact suggests that the best we can do is suggest what the expectations may not have been. Surely for some, for the young if not for their pious grandparents, the specifically sacral quality of sculpture or painting had lost much of its force. The gods and heroes were becoming conventional vehicles for a new particularity of the thing shown — not Hermes in general but this live youth here. The sense of the numinous was for a while diluted. If that was a distinction relaxed, another, which to us is second nature, had not yet grown up. The ceramics confirm what we saw

Richard Shaw
Two Figures on a Stand, 1984
Porcelain with decal overglaze,
26½ x 17½ x 9
Braunstein/Quay Gallery,
San Francisco, California

Shaw, a teacher at the San Francisco Art Institute, is best known for his trompe l'oeil assemblages in porcelain that stimulate the viewer to study common objects and then compare them with Shaw's facsimiles. The viewer discovers that Shaw's appropriations only appear random. They are, in fact, vigorously structured both in idea and representation, demonstrating the artist's extraordinary facility to create illusions of reality and to make porcelain take on the appearance of other materials.

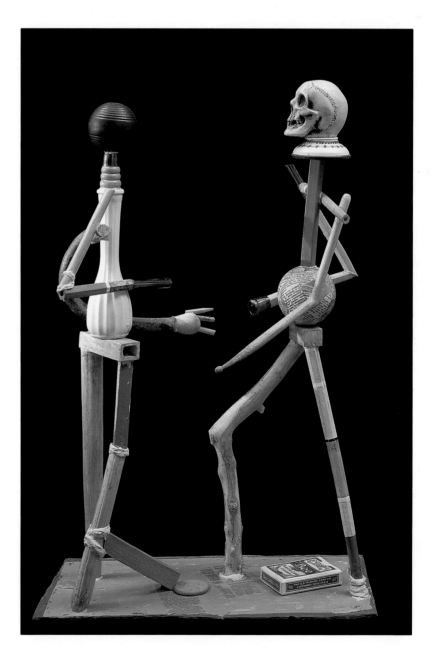

Peter Gourfain
Untitled, Ohio Pot Series, 1980
Ceramic, paint, 40 x 32
Collection of Sidney Singer,
Mamaroneck, New York

Although Gourfain's pots depart from his Minimalist work, they have a similar robustness and refuse to be defined by style or medium. The size, shape, and decoration of the *Ohio* pots bear comparison to ancient pottery — the huge *pithoi* of Mycenae, the geometric grave kraters of Greece, or Minoan pots with their vigorous, organic designs. Like ancient potters, Gourfain unifies surface design and volume: figures form rhythmic patterns or become

handles, and their contours echo those of the vessel. But Gourfain transforms these influences by a brutal, satirical expressionism. His primitivistic figures participate in a modern universe characterized by greed, racism, economic and political exploitation, suffering, and impotent silence. The Christlike handle-figures, the Archimedean screw from the mouth, the observing throng, and grasping hand are only some of the motifs contributing to the grotesque human comedy of the *Ohio* pots.

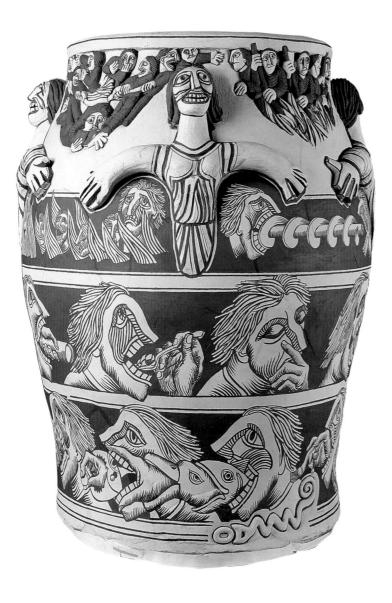

from the critical vocabulary of the time, that art and crafts were not felt to be separate. In a further contrast with the modern day, the individuality of the artist, his excellence and his distinctive manner, though of course recognized was not taken as an end in itself. In a time when painters and sculptors appeared to be perfecting their means for achieving visual realism, the doctrine that the arts imitate nature could hardly be disputed, and the drive of that realism must have seemed the principal source of the special power of the thing made by art.

At other periods, expectations have been estranged from realism — and more radically by far than in our self-importantly abstract century. The fullest saturation of the numinous in Western visual arts was attested in a set of orations, now unjustly neglected, written about the year 730 by St. John of Damascus, his three *Apologies against Those Who Attack the Divine Images*.[3] One may be pardoned for not recalling that at that time and indeed for more than a century in the Eastern Christian church within the empire the iconoclasts were ascendant: they searched out and destroyed all visual representations of Christ, saints, the cross; they hunted down as idolators and killed or exiled those who worshiped the pictures. (We note the homage that all this implies to the power — the extreme dangerousness — of art.) From the safety of Moslem Asia Minor — the ironies are complex — John wrote to demonstrate that veneration of images of Christ and the saints was not merely permissible but sanctioned and commanded by God. John's tracts were crucial to fixing iconoclasm as a heresy. Critically they are startling, for they aligned the direction of imitation along a new axis, explicitly orthogonal to the Euclidean and temporal dimensions in which one supposes that imitation could be attempted. The divine images were an art that imitated a nature otherwise insubstantial, literally unimaginable. In the expectations of painter and worshiper the aura took its extreme significance: it was depicted as the halo.

Tensions of expectation grew self-conscious and many-layered as painters and sculptors, in the first pangs of the Renaissance, deliberately reached back in order as they thought to move forward. Once more the drive was felt as the expansion of technical means — the mastery of perspective, shadowing, coloration, anatomy, forms of nature, modeling of flesh, the freezing of the transient. Beneath that, though, the aim of imitation was shifting again. From High Renaissance to Baroque, historians note, painters adjusted their attention from the object out there to the object as perceived, from detail to impression, from outlines to areas — from the delineated, the draughtsmanly, to the surface, the painterly. Portraits provide the canonical examples — Botticelli or Dürer, say, contrasted to Velázquez. With all that, the quality of light became paramount: the light of Rembrandt, the light of Vermeer, was a more considerable change than anything further Renoir or Seurat achieved. As part of the Baroque transition, historians also note, compositions were no longer likely to be contained by frames. Action swirled through the painting, not bounded by the surface of the edges; the statue moved out of the niche. In sum, imitation had matured and become subtler: surface,

light, ambiguity, not the copy but the illusion — and for the first time the breaking of the frames.

Pause to observe that the unity of what we today distinguish as art and craft persisted rather well. How does one account for Cellini? A stonemason's son, draughtsman as a boy and goldsmith by training, Cellini made his living by a variety of arts of which few authenticated objects survive: two seals, three medals, seven coins, one large object of goldsmith's work, and seven complete sculptures. The goldsmith's piece is the great saltcellar he made for François I of France (page 146), an exquisite object that is tableware only, yet crucially, in its function as a social marker. Then several years later, commissioned by Cosimo de' Medici, Cellini made and cast in bronze the *Perseus*, which established his fame. The unity of this virtuosity is attested by his masterly *Treatise on Goldsmithing and Sculpture* — even in its title. Yet Cellini is equivocal. He wrote; he took sculptural subjects (the figures of the saltcellar as well as the *Perseus*) from the classics; one can argue that as the visual arts and artists clasped hands with literary humanism they began to edge away from the crafts.[4]

Within the Renaissance was rising, meanwhile, the most momentous transformation that human intellect and power have known: the scientific revolution. Science in the sense we've been taking the word for nearly four centuries, and the technologies the sciences spin off, have become the dominant single influence on all of Western (and by now of world) culture — albeit an influence that some find repellent. In the earliest stages of the scientific revolution, certain artisans made objects of a special purpose and signification. These were the instrument makers. Their origins are not well studied. The things they made have not been included among the fine arts or the decorative. Early instruments — take the brass astrolabes, or the ivory setting of the eyepiece of a telescope of Galileo's

The Virgin and Child with Saints (Virgin Hodegetria), Byzantine, late 10th century,
Ivory, 4¾ x 4⁹⁄₁₆; wings 4¼ x 2³⁄₁₆
The Walters Art Gallery, Baltimore, Maryland

The subjects and the poses of the icons of the Eastern Christian churches were wonderfully diverse yet each for the most part fixed by tradition; the materials and techniques employed by their makers were varied and rich. Haloed heads painted on wooden panels, which the mention of icons brings to mind, were themselves frequently overlaid with sheets of beaten gold or encrusted with gems — the jeweler's craft called in to protect the holy image itself, to deepen its mystery, to embody its tran cendent preciousness. Icons were often carved of precious materials, notably ivory: here is an ivory triptych, Byzantine, from the second half of the tenth century, of the Virgin and Child shown full face, the Child making a gesture that represents teaching — a pose and action called the Virgin Hodegetria. The wings of the triptych show saints, possibly Saint Demetrios at the left with Saint Prokopius above him, and on the right Saint George with Saint Nicholas above. The simplicity of the figures is in tension with the delicacy of the miniaturist's technique and the sensuousness of the ivory.

Pablo Picasso
The Chair, 1961
Metal cutout, folded and painted,
43⅞ x 45⅛ x 35
Musée Picasso, Paris, France

perceived as coexisting"; these are "likeness and unlikeness, or sameness and difference." He went on, "In respect to a work of genuine imitation, you begin with an acknowledged total difference, and then every touch of nature gives you the pleasure of an approximation to truth."[6] The point is easily generalized beyond realism: the tensions of expectation are present from the first because the work and its significance are radically dissimilar. We look to the work and through it — and, in the Zen warning, the finger pointing at the moon is not the moon.

Thus, even for the classical painter or sculptor, the work commands our attention because the block of marble, say, cannot be flesh, yet Praxiteles' skill allows us to sustain simultaneously a poignant sense of the flesh: we actively enter into the creation of the perceptual tension. In the veneration of icons the believer who is not idolatrous does not confuse the image with what it portrays but holds the two in an exactly similar if more excruciating suspense. Although these days we do not often build the tools of science as though they were works of art, yet we cannot help but perceive a thrilling significance in, say, an array of radio-telescope dishes marching across the desert, and we respond in imaginative sympathy to the way in which, for the early instrument maker, the astrolabe in his hand signified a new order of the universe. From the Baroque through the Impressionists, the means of illusion become more skillful and more daring precisely in the increasing intensity they demand of our participation.

Considered in this way, the twentieth century's breaking of the frames turns out to be a conjurer's trick, though of bold import. The found object — surely at its most vulgar and unadorned, the ashtray with a signature — subverts the idea we all have that the work of art is something the artist has uniquely made. Yet that ashtray, the original one with the original signature, had gained the tension that persuades us, despite our palpable sense of being hoodwinked, that this thing before us is more and other than what it is. We discover that our perceptions are so constituted that even in the moment of breaking, the frames are touched with the magician's rod and reconstitute themselves stronger. Most generally, in fact, what the artist does is to put frames around things and thus say, "*Look!*" And we look anew.

Consider two chairs and two tables. We may arrange them in a line. At left stands *The Chair,* which Picasso made in 1961. He cut it out of a single sheet of metal which he then folded and painted; not quite four feet tall, it stands on a wooden base he built for it. But it is a crazed chair, with an oval tongue sticking forward at the center of the back and a slant seat; not even a cat could sit on it. Next in line we place *Table with Gloves and Keys,* made by Wendell Castle in 1981. This is a semicircular table built of wood in canonical eighteenth-century form, intended to stand in well-bred silence against the wall in a gentleman's entrance hall. But the wood is mahogany, superbly finished in glowing red-brown, and on the table sit a red-brown key case and a pair of red-brown gloves half hanging off, perfectly realistic, yet in fact integrally part of the table top — carved, without joint, from the same slab of wood. Next in the lineup,

Wendell Castle
Serpent Table, 1967
Laminated oak, 18 ½ x 72 x 18
Collection of the artist,
Scottsville, New York

Table with Gloves and Keys, 1981
Mahogany, 33 x 40 x 16
The *Forbes Magazine* Collection,
New York, New York

As imitators of his organic designs multiplied in the mid-1970s, Castle plunged in a direction so technically demanding that none could follow. He created replicas of traditional furniture coupled with still life elements in the form of highly realistic wood carvings depicting just the items one would expect to find in use: a coat thrown over the back of a chair, an umbrella in its stand, or keys and a pair of gloves left casually on a hall table. Reviewing an exhibition of Castle's trompe l'oeil work John Russell wrote: "The pieces are triumphs of ingenuity on the level of craftsmanship, but they also have a secret poetry that steals up on us." (*New York Times*, January 9, 1981).

Sam Maloof
Rocking Chair, 1975
Walnut, 45 x 27¾ x 45¾
Museum of Fine Arts, Boston,
Massachusetts, purchased through
Funds from the
National Endowment for the Arts
and the Gillette Corporation

In 1949 Maloof made a decision to leave the field of graphic design to pursue furniture making. Now, after more than thirty-seven productive years as a woodworker, he is recognized as a major figure in American woodworking. Because his shop is not production-oriented with many specialists working in assembly-line fashion, Maloof works on every piece, thereby maintaining superb quality control. Each piece is signed, dated and serially numbered. Each year, he adds two or three new forms to his working program, all the while continuing to perfect earlier models with a consistency of vision unusual in twentieth-century art.

another table, built by Castle in 1967. It is six feet long, made of piled-up thick layers of oak, with a massive base at one end from which the top, progressively thinner, is cantilevered — *Serpent Table,* the overall effect indeed distinctly cobra-like. And at the right stands a rocking chair, made in 1975 by Sam Maloof, of walnut. It is lean, startlingly graceful, just understated enough.

These four objects comprise a spectrum of dissonant expectations. Picasso's *Chair* is nothing but an object of art, and indeed a minor one except that it is clever in construction and is witty because it has so obviously just escaped from a Picasso painting. Castle's antique with gloves and keys gets its effect by a standard Surrealist tactic, enhanced, however, by an unnerving use of color and by the fact that the joinery is classic: this is such a nice table that one half-way resents the trompe l'oeil. This Castle table is functional if not quite practical. Maloof's rocking chair is just what it appears — except that it insinuates itself into memory by its quintessential elegance. The four objects in a row exert a curious pull on each other. Where's the sculpture, where's the craft? All four are, in fact, craftsmanly; other Picasso constructions confirm that he was a bravura performer with tinsnips. In the context created by the other three, the Picasso chair sounds a new overtone, perhaps an enhancing one. Castle's two tables are on opposite sides of a perfect balance between the conventional expectations of craft and fine art, and as we regard them each tugs the other closer to that balance. The effect of the other three objects on our perception of Maloof's chair is subtlest. This object is patrician, youthful, and so poised — it's important that it is indeed a rocking chair — that it raises expectations of imminent movement. By not setting out to be sculpture, it becomes a rare demonstration of form in perfect harmony with function.

"Arts and crafts" has a dismissive connotation, and of all the craft media, ceramics — with certain foreign exceptions, like the Grecian urn and the Ming vase — are the most plebeian. The potters of the pueblos of the American Southwest, however, come to the construction, finishing, and firing of pots from a tradition that remembers their ritual significance even as it imposes a conservatism of form and decoration. The milieu offers a potential for transformation. A test of the tensions possible in clay can begin with an exquisite object, an earthenware bowl made in 1981 by Effie Garcia, who is one of a lineage of potters from the Santa Clara pueblo in New Mexico. The bowl is of a form that in times past was used domestically. It is deeply incised in a bold, simple geometric pattern that is not, in fact, strictly traditional. The cultural interchanges here defy stereotypes. The fact is that in the 1920s and 1930s, Pueblo potters incorporated elements of patterning from the then-contemporary Art Deco, which was of course a design fashion of the Anglo cities. Far from corrupting the naive purity of the Indian craftswomen, the result has been a fusion of twentieth-century American visual styles that then and to this day achieves unparalleled elegance. Effie Garcia burnished the surface of this bowl, then fired it in a carbon-rich atmosphere produced by smothering the fire of her open hearth with wet organic material. The carbon was driven into the vessel's surface, transforming it to a brilliant saturated black. The pot glows like a gemstone. Its perfection is the ceramic equivalent of Maloof's rocking chair. The bowl stands three inches tall.

To get a further sense of the transformation Garcia has made, contrast this bowl with the earthenware olla, fifteen and one-fourth inches in height, black on black, made by Maria and Julian Martinez, working at the San Ildefonso pueblo in the 1940s. Then move forward again in time, to the jars made in the 1960s and 1970s by Fannie Nampeyo and by Dextra Quotsquyva, members of a family of celebrated Hopi pottters. These objects have a perfection and serenity of line that makes every nuance significant; they open slowly to the eye.

Effie Garcia
Bowl, (Santa Clara) 1981
Earthenware, burnished, carbon impregnated, 3 x 4½
Private collection, Tulsa, Oklahoma

Although non-Western arts are often stereotyped as unchanging, conservative, and tradition-bound, in fact, experimentation and individual artistic expression have always been part of the creation of these arts. Southwest American Pueblo pottery provides a cogent example. To the untrained Western eye, burnished blackware pottery is tied to a static tradition. However, this general style which arose in the late 1920s is characterized by extreme tribal and personal variations including matte paint on polish black, polished paint on matte surface, incising, deep carving, etching, paint outlining of recessed planes, and hundreds of distinctive shapes and forms to complement surface treatments. Effie Garcia, a member of the youngest generation of Santa Clara potters, has masterfully impressed her style upon this tradition of pottery-making. Her designs range from the naturalistic to highly abstract Puebloan adaptations of Art Deco geometrics and severely classical vase forms arising from European design tradition.

Dextra Quotsquyva
Jar, (Hopi) ca. 1980
Ceramic, painted with clay slip,
5¼ x 8
The Philbrook Museum of Art, Tulsa,
Oklahoma, Museum Purchase, Clark
Field Acquisition Fund

The Hopi potter Nampeyo and her
uniquely personal ceramic style
fundamentally altered the course of
twentieth-century Pueblo pottery.
The fluidity and compositional
inventiveness of her pottery,
perfectly complemented by
meticulous craftsmanship, created an
artistic legacy which continues to
grow through the brilliance of her
artist descendents. Dextra
Quotsquyva carries forward this
spirit of experimentation with
ancient and personal design as well
as elevating technical expertise to an
unparalled plateau.

Maria and Julian Martinez
Olla, (San Ildefonso) ca. 1940
Black-on-black pottery, 15¼ x 9⅞
The Thomas Gilcrease Institute of
American History and Art,
Tulsa, Oklahoma

During their long, innovative careers,
members of the Martinez family of
San Ildefonso have experimented
more widely with ceramic firing
techniques than have any other
known group of potters. Around the
turn of the century, Maria first
perfected the then-traditional
polychrome-on-cream-slipped style
she had learned from her maternal
aunt, Nicolosa. Her husband Julian's
inadvertent burning of a firing of
pottery resulted in the now-famous
black-on-black ware. Though this
style has changed considerably since
its inception in the 1920s, in its
basic form it still remains the
mainstay of both San Ildefonso and
Santa Clara pottery-making.

Few objects can stand near the modern Pueblo pots without appearing crude. Christina Bertoni's earthenware *Io*, though, has a paradoxical quality that derives from an effective yet minimal visual echo of astronomical orbits, rings, and inclinations. A table sculpture from 1983, six inches tall and twice that in diameter, *Io* begins as a flared, shallow bowl, light and mottled gray within; in this is canted a glazed, darker ring and, askew in that, a pale disk. The scientific reference is glancing, literary, yet sufficient. Wayne Higby made a similar reference — geological rather than astronomical — in *Apparition Canyon,* from 1982.

Christina Bertoni
Io, 1983
Earthenware, 6 x 15 x 19
Collection of Beth and Peter Rabinowitz, Concord, Massachusetts

Io calls to mind the cosmology of space. The work of Bertoni represents an important sector in the art of the 1970s and 1980s

when the advent of the space age and high technology fascinated so many Americans. The imagery of planetary bodies and rings within Bertoni's heavenly bowl evokes mankind's fascination with representation of the universe, whether by the dome of a church or that of a planetarium.

Wayne Higby
Yellow Rock Falls, 1975
Raku fired, glazed earthenware,
14 x 29 x 7½
Collection of Robert L. Pfannebecker,
Lancaster, Pennsylvania

There is a sympathetic accessibility in groups like *Yellow Rock Falls* of 1975 where covered containers, which seem derived from kitchen canisters, nestle together. Their decorated exteriors are meant to be read from two sides. Pure pictorial landscape is presented on one side, while the other suggests geologic section. The imagery is defined by incising the clay; contrasting features are indicated by different glazes and accented with inlays like those that depict the rushing waters of *Yellow Rock Falls.*

This is a bowl, just under a foot tall. Higby drew landscape forms deeply into its clay surface, then painted the surfaces inside and out in glazes of white, sky blue, and earth and water tones to create the effect of landforms implied by the title of the piece. The illusion would not have worked in any century before the airplane and the aerial photograph. One sees through the object to an ideal, simplified, grand landscape.

Some present-day potters get their tensions with the aid of a deliberate denial of elegance. Vast buttocks, face into pillow, heavy thigh, rumpled bed, knee crook'd and arse raised high: *Big Ellie, Prostitute Pot* is a picture of a woman, painted and glazed in beiges, ochers and browns on a stoneware jar nearly three feet tall. Rudy Autio, who made it, is chiefly a ceramicist but also a sculptor in bronze and steel. He was born sixty years ago in Montana and has spent most of his life there; yet he has come up through the main line of American crafts, the studio and academic crafts movement, and is now head of ceramics in the School of Fine Arts of the University of Montana. *Big Ellie, Prostitute Pot* in its technical vigor displays not exactly crudity so much as the directness of the western frontier; but the thing itself is far from unschooled, for it must, after all, be taken as an instance of a revival of the 2,500-year-old tradition of painting vases with genre scenes. Seemingly, image comports with object: the coarseness of Autio's picture, in both subject and expression, agrees with the plainness of his pottery. Yet this rough concord distracts attention from the deeper stress. Here is a handmade object of utility, a container. But what it contains is on its outside.

Other present-day potters, in comparable ways, are breaking through the anonymity of clay, the meek domesticity of the utensil. Michael Frimkess has recovered what he believes were the techniques of classical Greek potters, and works close to the forms of the Grecian urn and the Chinese jar — but then paints and glazes them with an exuberant California imagery, political, racial, cultural, upbeat. He said several years ago, "I want to complete the pun and put together all my research into a melting pot."[7] His *Ecology Krater II,* made in 1976 (page 138), stands more than two feet tall. The krater is stringently classical in shape and in its red-figure painting, but the subject of the painting is something else — around the top is a frieze of pairs of small animals, and on the body, where the Greeks showed sportsmen, warriors, or lovers, Frimkess has placed conservation-minded bicyclists, and, centrally, four adults pedaling a four-seater tandem bicycle with a baby waving from a carrier seat at the back. The piece is friendly and funny.

With Frimkess as with Autio, the container and the thing contained (and that's a metonymy beloved of a more rhetorical age) are of a different order of significance. We are closer than was obvious to Castle's tables, Garcia's jewel of a pot, St. John's icons.

For many years, American craftsmen have labored under the curse of an uncertainty that has often risen to acute self-doubt about the relationship of their work to the fine arts. Their distress has seemed to them simultaneously a truism and a condition of life. Yet artists from Europe or the Orient who become aware of their American colleagues'

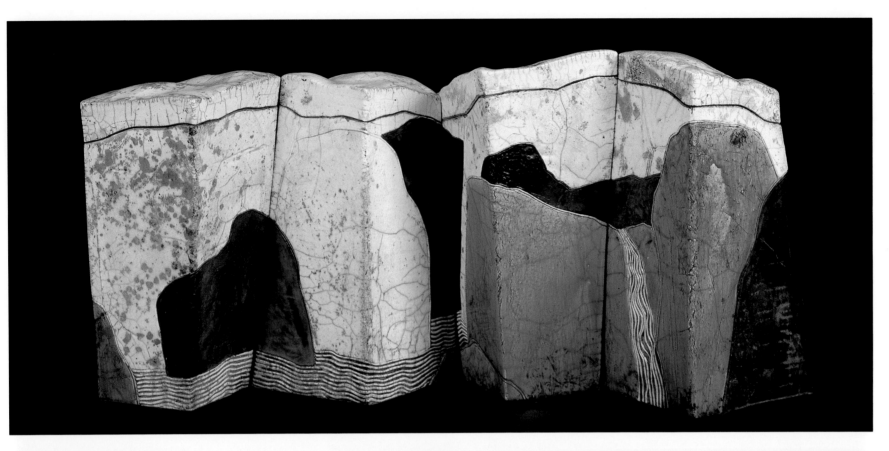

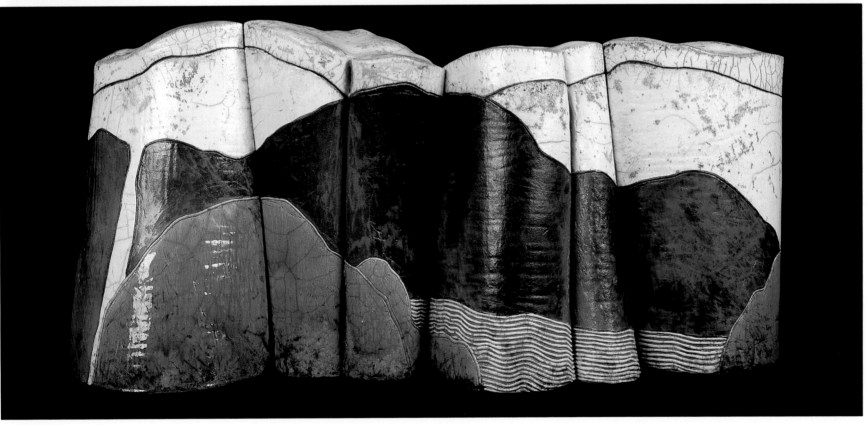

Rudy Autio
Big Ellie, Prostitute Pot, 1976
(above)
Stoneware, glazed,
32 inches in height
Lannan Foundation,
Venice, California

Double Lady Vessel, 1964 (right)
Stoneware, black and white slips,
28¼ x 10½
Everson Museum of Art, Syracuse,
New York, 25th Ceramic National
Exhibition

Head of the ceramics department at
the University of Montana, Autio is
recognized for his large-scale
architectural works as well as his
slab-constructed vessels lyrically
inscribed or painted with figural
imagery. Autio worked with Peter
Voulkos at the Archie Bray
Foundation in Helena, Montana,
from 1952 to 1957. In the fifties
and early sixties he was deeply
immersed in the pioneering work of
releasing ceramic arts from the
vessel tradition and introducing
principles of Abstract Expressionism
to ceramics.

Michael Frimkess
Platter, 1960
Stoneware, 18¾ inches in diameter
Scripps College,
Claremont, California,
Collection of Mr. and Mrs. Fred
Marer

Sam Kramer

Roc Pendant, 1958 (facing page)
Sterling silver, gold, ivory, horn, taxidermy eye, coral, tourmaline, garnet, 4¾ x 2¼ x ¾
The American Craft Museum, New York, New York

Instead of aiming at the realization of a predetermined design, Kramer advocates allowing ideas to develop spontaneously out of and in response to the materials and processes of jewelry making. Although Kramer was master of a variety of metalworking techniques, he is probably best known for his development of a "direct-metal" method in which scraps of metal, usually silver, are fused together using a blowtorch. Each piece of metal is fused separately and the composition is built up gradually in a manner that is not entirely predictable. If there are accidents, so much the better. He occasionally fused other metals, or even enamels, into the silver to enhance the texture and enrich the coloration of the surface. Because the method is an additive one with potential "jumping-off places" for further exploration and improvisation at nearly every stage, it is particularly well suited to Kramer's attitudes toward materials and processes. Kramer's disquieting imagery obviously owes much to Surrealism, as does the spontaneity of his approach to materials and tools, his allegiance to the emotional and the accidental and his allusions to the unconscious.

Alexander Calder

Bracelet, ca. 1930s or 1940s
Hammered silver, 4¾ x 4 x 2
The Museum of Modern Art, New York, New York, Purchase, 1967

Calder is surely best known for his development of hanging, movable sculptures — Duchamp was the first to call them "mobiles" — and for the vigorous assimilation in his work of diverse aspects of European Modernism, from Miróesque Surrealism to Constructivism. In addition to his well-known sculpture, Calder also created an astonishing variety of objects intended primarily for personal use and enjoyment: toys, kitchen utensils, jewelry. Calder made jewelry for friends and family throughout the course of his career but, with the exception of exhibitions at Willard Gallery in 1940 and 1941, and at Perls Gallery in 1966, he rarely offered it for sale. Comparatively few pieces were executed on commission, most of them around 1940, when Calder seems to have been unusually preoccupied with the idea of making jewelry.

dilemma respond with raised eyebrows. The uncertainty appears self-imposed — and tedious. At the extreme, it is the jewelers who are likely to find their relationship to other arts most constrained, the self-consciousness many times compounded. Jewelry is precious in several senses. It is finely wrought of the finest materials. It is elegant, or must at least be gorgeous. It is miniature, and only rarely in Western history has work at a comparable scale — one thinks of medieval manuscript illumination or of Tudor and Stuart miniature portraiture — been accepted as high art. Yet jewelry is the antithesis of the functional or of the plebeian. From its prehistoric origins, it has always served a deep but narrow social function, the assertion, blatant or subtle, of wealth, status, and power. It is decorative but not informed with significance, or, rather, it's rich with the significances of that narrowly conspicuous display of standing. It is silently elite. Except in the one way, jewelry for thousands of years has asserted nothing, told nothing.

Consider another sequence of objects, this time in a temporal order — jewelry by five makers, created over a span of half a century at intervals of about a decade. In 1940 or thereabouts, Alexander Calder, who for ten years had been building steel sheet and rod into monumental mobiles, made a piece of jewelry, a bracelet cut, then hammered, out of sheet silver. It's a thing of coils — a band bent back on itself to cuff the arm thrice, and from the band a dozen or so double spirals hung to move and jangle. The spirals have a family resemblance to paintings Calder has made on paper. He worked the silver roughly; he treated the sheet metal as though he were cutting shapes to amuse a child. The effect is reminiscent of some object from a Mycenaean tomb. The piece radiates the robust

and careless energy that Calder brought to all his work. Because it
occupies a space four inches by four-and-three-quarters, two inches wide,
one is not likely to recognize the maker at once, yet when he is identified
the response must be, "Of course!" Calder imposed himself on the
medium. In 1950, Margaret De Patta, a jeweler who worked from 1929
until she died in 1969, made a pin, two inches by three and one-fourth,
out of silver bars, a square of white gold, a square of black onyx, a piece
of malachite, a bit of coral, a disk of agate and another of amber. The
arrangement is rectilinear, balanced, syncopated — a frozen rhythm.
De Patta is revered as the precursor and progenetrix of much of the most
unconventional modern jewelry in the United States. Yet anyone having
seen the Calder bracelet and then coming to this pin without knowing its
maker would be likely to guess it to be by Piet Mondrian. The pin is
beautiful; its derivation, deliberate or unconscious, is unmistakable. Again,
in 1958 Sam Kramer made a pin, four-and-three-quarter inches tall and
two-and-one-fourth inches wide, of silver, oxidized in places, and gemstones,
in the form of a cartoon bird sporting a monocle. The piece has gaiety, a
promise of bumbling savoir faire. If De Patta's pin recalls paintings by
Mondrian, like the familiar *Broadway Boogie-woogie,* from 1942-1943,
Kramer's evokes the cheerful lunacy of a painting by the young Miró —
say, *Person Throwing a Stone at a Bird,* from 1926.

These three pieces of jewelry command a kind and closeness of
attention that conventional jewelry cannot; they make a claim to be
miniature sculptures. They reach across the contentious border into
modern art. Yet they do so in part by reference; they have not integrated
medium, form, and content fully; they do not stand independently. In this
respect they are, after all, less than fully satisfying. Set against these a pin
by Ken Cory, a metalsmith from the Pacific Northwest who when he made
the piece — in 1968 — was immersed in the time's rebelliousness. This
object, a bare two inches tall by two-and-a-half wide, is composed of a
pyramidal block of copper hanging point down, its texture roughcast, with

a bit of copper tube projecting upwards from which emerges a plume of clear Plexiglas that undulates like smoke — or toothpaste — down across the front of the object. The pin is cool and precise, but neither in materials nor in design nor in workmanship is it refined or merely decorative. It is as enigmatic as a Minimalist sculpture. It is not literary, which is to say, it refers to nothing outside itself.

In 1979 and 1980, Joyce Jane Scott fashioned four objects out of raw anxiety and anger. They are all about the same size, ten inches by five. She assembled them from various materials including beads, stones, pieces of pig bone, plastic coating, pins, razor blades, hair, hide, and photographs. They can be worn, but Scott said recently that she thinks of them not as

Ken Cory
Pin, 1968
Copper, Plexiglas, 2 x 2½
The American Craft Museum, New York, New York, Gift of the Johnson Wax Company from *Objects: USA*

Cory's pins, cast in brass, copper, or silver, have impure pitted and fissured surfaces that are deliberate. The artist fabricates "gemstones" of material such as leather, Plexiglas, and resin that protrude or wriggle from their metal forms. The pins are not necessarily meant to be worn, but held like Japanese netsuke.

Albert Paley
Pin, 1970
Silver, gold, tourmaline, moonstone and pearls, 8 x 7½ x 1¾
Collection of the artist,
Rochester, New York

As a student of Stanley Lechtzin, Paley delved beyond technology to tackle the design problems of jewelry. Banishing commercial fixtures in favor of organic functional construction, he fashioned necklaces as torques and brooches as fibulae. By his graduation in 1969 he was creating wearable sculptures charged with the energy of precious metals forged in whiplash lines as if impelled by their own dynamism.

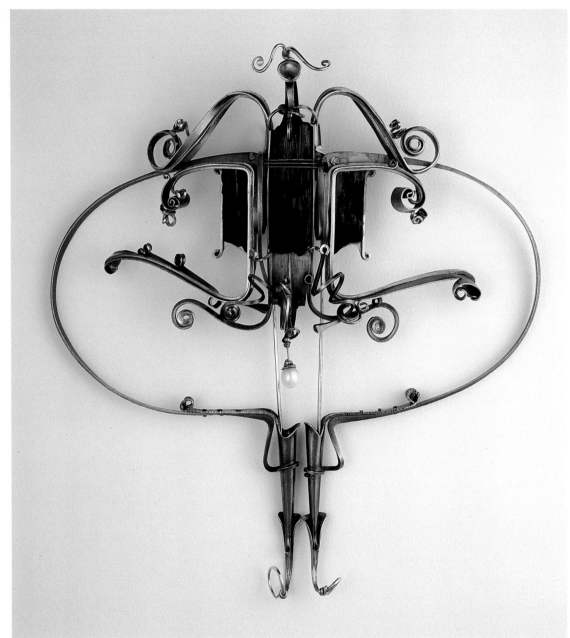

jewelry but as sculpture. "They are wearable art. And if they are not on the body they should be on the wall." Their references are strident. She calls them *The Jonestown Series.* She made them to work out, to exorcise, the outrage and despair she felt on reading of the Jonestown massacre, in which, just before Thanksgiving of 1978, in a settlement in the rain forest of Guyana, first an investigating United States congressman, Leo J. Ryan, was murdered, and then 912 men, women, and children, mostly poor and ignorant American black followers of a messianic white cult leader, Jim Jones, on his orders killed each other and themselves, chiefly by cyanide swallowed in a fruit-flavored drink. Scott was born in Baltimore and lives there still. The women in her family, her mother in particular, have been quiltmakers for generations. In the late 1970s, Scott was weaving and working with fiber in other ways, making clothing and jewelry; she was also using these kinds of materials in performances. More recently, she has been working chiefly with beads, making elaborate beaded collars. "These are abstract pieces of wearable art." She identifies herself as African-American and comes, she said, "from a Pentecostal, apostolic background"; she is acutely aware of the survivals in this hemisphere of elements of African animist religion.

The four objects in the Jonestown series "are a quartet," Scott said. "They occupy the four corners of the experience." One, *Kool-Aide Kocktail,* is a brooch. Its shape is defined by a photograph of one of the metal tubs, like garbage cans or wash boilers, in which the poisoned punch was mixed. On this she superimposed a cut-out second photo, of a dead person in fetal position, as though floating in the tub, tied up with crisscrossed threads. The whole is coated in clear plastic as if preserved in amber, then rimmed with 131 tiny bright-red beads and fringed with stiff, straight, dark-brown hair. *For the Souls* is three lumps of black stone encased in shiny plastic dangling from a larger piece on which are mounted, pinned, framed in tiny beads — enshrined — photographs of babies of the massacre. "They are souls floating over Guyana," she said. "Because when you die of violence your soul cannot rest." *The Double Cross* takes the form of a Byzantine pectoral cross, but a grotesque, travesty cross, the figure hanged on it wired together from white pig-knuckle bones, its head a photo of a person crying out, the whole thing elaborately, gaudily beaded. *The White Boy's Gone Crazy,* the fourth in the series, is a human figure made of tree bark with bone extremities, its head Jim Jones's with the photograph haloed in beading, while a picture of Congressman Ryan is crudely cross-stitched to the chest, and over the belly is a single-edged razor blade. "The genitalia are photos of the cups they drank from," Scott said. The figure is pierced by innumerable stickpins with beaded heads. The violence of the piece explicitly recalls macumba, a blend of Christianity and voodoo widespread in northern Brazil. "Razor blades are important in macumba ceremonies to separate the soul from its ties to earth."[8]

Tensions of expectation arise also from putting the immense range of craft materials and techniques to the service of what seem at first inspection to be straightforward artistic ends. The best examples are

Joyce J. Scott
Overleaf:
Kool-Aide Kocktail, 1980 (from *The Jonestown Series*)
Mixed media, 5½ x 4½ x ¼

For The Souls, 1980 (from *The Jonestown Series*)
Mixed media, 10 x 5 x 1

The Double Cross, 1980 (from *The Jonestown Series*)
Mixed media, 10 x 5 x 1

The White Boy's Gone Crazy, 1980 (from *The Jonestown Series*)
Mixed media, 10 x 3 x 1
Collection of the artist,
Baltimore, Maryland

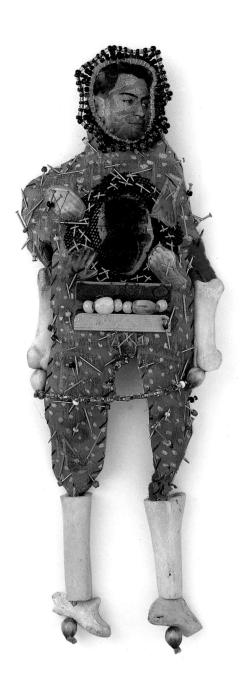

Karen Breschi
Vulture, 1979
Clay, acrylic, rope, cloth, resin,
36 x 21 x 12
San Francisco Museum of Modern
Art, San Francisco, California,
Anonymous Gift

sculptures. Of clay, cloth, resin, acrylic paints, and rope, Karen Breschi made the torso of a man, three feet tall from the cutoff at mid-thigh, wearing blue jeans, leather belt, tight black leather shirt, with his arms tied at his sides, his hands bloodied talons, and his head a bird's with hooked beak and baleful glare: *Vulture,* she called the statue, and it is vividly polychrome and brutal. Out of wood, leather stitched and nailed, and metal buckles and rings, Nancy Grossman made a head, thirteen inches tall, all in black, strapped with many straps into a close-fitting helmet and tight high leather collar: *A.M.X.* is sadomasochist, intense, and svelte. These pieces make their points — and exhaust them — swiftly. Each is overstated to a degree that momentarily may distract one from its maker's extreme technical proficiency. But put aside the violent symbolism: in each piece, the materials are entirely subordinate to a clear and controlled sculptural intent — which total subordination is precisely the origin of the perceptual paradox, the aura. For the materials and the ways they are used make the statues what they are, the materials and methods themselves create the disturbing symbolism and subvert the pieces' seeming continuity with sculpture of times past.

Susan Lyman built a frame of cane, intricately laced with reed and raffia left in their natural colors, curved and tapered, nearly a yard long, then covered it almost completely with a heavy, soft, hand-laid paper of pale green. The result, *Eel Hive,* is shapely and poignant as some gentle Chopin nocturne. This is abstract sculpture with the strength and grace that abstraction at this level sometimes offers. Fragile in materials, its visual and tactile resonances finesse stone. As does Dominic Di Mare's *Mask.* Di Mare is the son of a Sicilian fisherman, born in 1932 in San Francisco, where he still lives. His pieces combine various substances — wood, paper, fibers, beads, feathers. *Mask* began with a thrown ceramic bottomless bowl, its shape flaring like the bell of a horn. Before firing the bell, Di Mare pierced it with a row of holes, close together and evenly spaced, around half the rim, and a corresponding row of holes halfway around farther down. That same hemisphere of the inside of the bell bears concentric bands of glaze in sand and earth colors. After taking the piece from the kiln, he laced the holes with linen thread, creating a radiant pattern of flax and shadow. He then turned the object on its side: it mounts on the wall, the bell like a megaphone, the decorated and woven hemisphere at the top. Then from the horizontal midline threading he hung more and heavier flaxen fibers, longer than the bowl is wide, and to many of these, just at the low point of the bell's rim, he laced feathers, large, striped in black on white and tipped in scarlet. The symmetry of the object is the more exquisite for being modulated by the natural variance of the materials. The fusion is complete: once more, form, sculptural intent, and materials are indistinguishable. The resultant symbolism is self-contained, and the more powerful for that. Di Mare's sculpture is a musical cadence, a vehicle for meditation, balm to eye and spirit, a resolution of perceptual and cognitive tensions. Its aura cannot tarnish.

Ours is a time, not the first time, when responsible critics are anxious and with reason that the arts have lost direction and vigor. For a decade at

Terry Rosenberg
Untitled, 1982 (left)
Leather (painted cowhide),
81 x 25 x 31
Collection of Daniel Jacobs,
New York, New York

Rosenberg's leather sculptures
suggest the inner life of the animal.
His earlier works were mounted like
hunting trophies, sometimes bearing
actual horns or fur. The more recent
works often have cloaks and hoods;
their size is slightly larger than
human life-size, suggesting both the
powerful wild fauna of dreams and
also the evolved human self of the
future — also perhaps of dreams.
His work has been said to combine
the executioner's song with the
transcendental music of the spheres.

Nancy Grossman
A.M.X., 1969-70 (below)
Wood, nailed and stitched leather,
13 inches in height
The Art Museum, Princeton
University, Princeton, New Jersey,
Museum purchase, John Maclean
Magie and Gertrude Magie Fund

Grossman's white plaster male heads
armored in soft black leather, nail
heads showing, mouth, eyes and/or
nose vulnerably exposed through
the mask, are striking, shocking.
This man's eyes and mouth are
closed — perhaps by force, perhaps
voluntarily, so as not to see and
speak the evil that surrounds him,
perhaps to dream. Though bound,
the man can breathe, and his
dignified, solemn look suggests that
his inaccessibility is perhaps his own
choice.

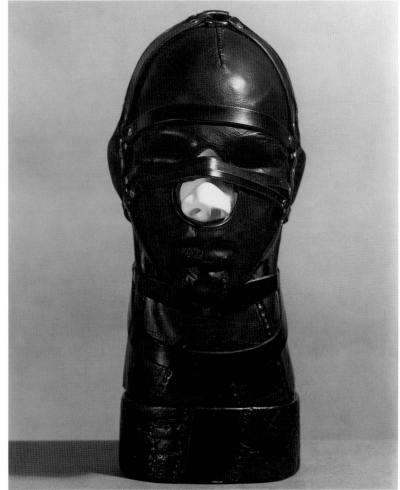

Susan Lyman
Eel Hive, 1979
Reed, cane, raffia, handmade paper,
20 x 33 x 11
Collection of Gayle and Andrew,
Camden, Detroit, Michigan

Eel Hive is a skeletal vessel covered
with a paper skin. Like Lyman's
other works of the late 1970s, it is
organic, referring to nests, cocoons,
and hives, in part belying its
underlying geometric structure. In
1978, Lyman began using flexible
fiber materials to allow more
movement and gesture in her work.
Adding the translucent paper
covering to her complex structures
both reveals and conceals them,
setting up a tension that is repeated
by the delicacy and power of the
image. The structures of the late
1970s were carefully engineered.
Lyman's more recent work
incorporates the same gestural
quality, but the forms have been
freed to move randomly into space.

Dominic Di Mare
Domus #5 - Harbor Lights, 1983
(facing page)
Mixed media, 43 x 14 x 6
Braunstein/Quay Gallery,
San Francisco, California

One of a series of eight works
executed over a period of two years,
this piece is reminiscent of Medieval
or Renaissance portable altarpieces.
Di Mare's title *Domus* refers to the
word domicile or place where
special precious objects are kept. In
this case the outer wings, like side
panels on an altarpiece, are opened,
revealing tresses of horsehair. When
the hair is brushed aside the viewer
sees a photograph of the artist at
one year of age. The pieces in this
series are reliquaries for personal
memories as embodied in the
photographs of family members
which are obscured and enshrined
within them.

134

least, the arts of the West have been recognized to be at a standstill — lacking new problems, increasingly syncretic in style, increasingly alienated from the art-conscious public, increasingly self-referential. Signs of malaise are everywhere. Architecture had become postmodern, which appears for the most part to mean aimlessly decorative. Even films — and the movies are the art unique to the twentieth century — have become self-consciously laden with cannibalistic references to great films of the past. In particular, the program of abstract art appears to have been fulfilled, and in all its variants. The stylistic excitement of the 1940s through the early seventies, from Expressionism to Minimalism and conceptual art, has played out. Frank Stella, the painter who more than any other in the 1960s seemed to personify the abstract movement, indeed the most influential and successful of the latest generation of mainstream artists, said recently, "Many defenders of contemporary art look backward for sanctions of value and quality." He added, "The tendency that developed in American abstract painting after 1970 is antithetical to everything that the great painting of the past stands for," and went on, "The point is that abstraction today seems bound by an innate niggardliness of vision."[9] Stella himself has recently all but abandoned painting for sculpture. Hilton Kramer, editor of *The New Criterion,* sometimes chief art critic for *The New York Times,* and the leading as well as the most fastidious of conservative critics, wrote recently, "Even among the most dedicated partisans of abstract art, . . . there is a discernible sense of crisis in regard to its present and future course." He went on:

> From what ideas or impulses abstract art may now draw fresh inspiration, and in what spirit and toward what end it is now to pursue new achievement — these are questions that, for serious artists, have to do less with changes in cultural fashion than with the most fundamental aesthetic problems of their art. It is precisely with aesthetic problems at this most basic level that the exponents of abstract art are more than ever haunted as they make their way through the last years of the century that saw its emergence.[10]

The point is, of course, more general: for "abstract art" one can read "the gallery and museum art that artists, dealers, curators, and critics have conceived to be the mainstream."

Over the past hundred years or more, the most vigorous new cultural phenomena of all sorts have appeared at the intersection, the cross-reaction, of influences and lines of development not previously understood to be intimately related. This is true of individual writers as diverse as Henry James, Joseph Conrad, Samuel Beckett, or Günter Grass. It is the case in sciences — like, say, molecular biology, which fused disciplines as disparate as biochemistry and crystallography. It has been true of several previous movements in the arts of this century. It is true of the works we consider here. These new objects come not from within the recognized

community of artists — as did the Surrealists or the Abstract Expressionists or the Minimalists, however revolutionary they once seemed — but rather from underground, from what may be called popular sources. These objects, the best of them, brush aside that question, "You mean, anything goes?" From Maloof's rocking chair to Scott's *The Double Cross* to Di Mare's *Mask,* these are objects of great power. Breaking and resetting the frames, they say, once more, *"Look!"*

Dominic Di Mare
Mask, 1968
Clay, linen thread, feathers,
8¼ inches in width
Collection of Daniel Goldstine,
Berkeley, California

NOTES

1 The notion of a tension of expectations about a work of art obviously relates to the argument — the program — of E. H. Gombrich, particularly in *Art and Illusion,* fourth edition; (London: Phaidon Press, 1972). Gombrich, though, is more directly concerned with the psychology of perception of pictorial representations, and with the role of conventions in that.

2 No classicist I: the realization that classical Greeks lacked a generic word for *artist* and that their word for *art* is ancestor to our *technology* arose in the course of discussions with Lowell Edmunds, professor and chairman of classics at Johns Hopkins University, during which he kindly helped me check nuances of meaning and the adequacy of standard translations of certain passages and terms of Aristotle's having to do with critical theory and with the relationship of the sciences to the arts.

3 Joannes, of Damascus, *On the Divine Images: Three Apologies against Those Who Attack the Divine Image,* translated by David Anderson (Crestwood, New York: St. Vladimir's Seminary Press, 1980).

4 Michelangelo, poet, is the better instance. Jonathan Brown, in his recent biography of Velázquez, distinguishes the position of the painters of Italy from those of the generation before Velázquez in Spain; Brown's observation is relevant to the status of crafts then and since. "Unlike in Italy, where by 1600 the connection between the arts and letters had become well established, in Spain the two had never been joined," Brown writes, and goes on, "It was through the identification of painting with poetry that the former gained the status of a liberal art, as opposed to a craft" (*Velázquez: Painter and Courtier*, New Haven and London: Yale University Press, 1986, page 2). But the situation is complex: for example, well into the enlightened eighteenth century, the French, like the classical Greeks, lacked a generic term for "artist" in our present sense: *les arts* included the mechanic arts, an *artisan* was a craftsman, while an *artiste* was a performer, an actor, juggler, musician. Our modern obsession with what Arthur Koestler called "the act of creation" and the veneration we give to those thought to perform it may be aberrant.

5 An initial observation that provoked this passage I owe to a conversation with the late Derek da Solla Price, historian of science.

6 S. T. Coleridge, "On Poesy or Art," reprinted in *Biographia Literaria,* vol.2, J. Shawcross, ed., (Oxford: Oxford University Press, 1907), p. 256.

7 Quoted by Garth Clark, *American Potters* (New York: Watson-Guptill Publications, 1981), p. 41.

8 Conversation with Joyce J. Scott, December 1, 1986.

9 Frank Stella, *Working Space* (Cambridge, Massachusetts: Harvard University Press, 1986), pp. 1, 43-46.

10 Hilton Kramer, "The Crisis in Abstract Art," *The Atlantic* (October 1986), p. 94.

THE CRAFT OBJECT

IN WESTERN CULTURE

PENELOPE HUNTER-STIEBEL

Michael Frimkess
Ecology Krater II, 1976
Stoneware, 26 x 26 x 19½
Collection of Daniel Jacobs,
New York, New York

Ecology Krater is more consistent in technique with its Greek cultural past than other Frimkess vessels. Hydras and kraters were decorated with contemporary myths and events. Frimkess continued that tradition on the black body, red-figured krater. An upper frieze of sympathetically portrayed endangered animals includes an eagle, chimpanzee, whale and rhinoceros. Below, stylized Greek decorative bands are interjected with the main story, a four-person bicycle: the twentieth-century bike-riding Californians have made ecology into a circus act.

Distinctions between fine and minor arts are treated as a momentous issue in today's art world, yet they appear a fiction when we examine our artistic heritage. The work of past ages does not obligingly conform to the categories and values of the nineteenth and twentieth centuries of Western art despite the efforts of art historians.

One of the primary components in our latter-day category of fine arts is painting, yet painting as we think of it today, visual images on a portable flat surface, only came into existence in the Renaissance. In all other societies, and even in the West before the Renaissance, artistic expression has been made through what are now thought of as alternate media. Before the advent of fuel-driven mechanization, manual labor was the foundation of society. It was not prestigious, however, and the distance the individual could place between such activities and himself often marked the level of his rise in his community. Despite these aspirations, which often found reflection in literature, the objects most highly prized in every community represent the fusion of the work of the mind and the skill of the hand.

The notion that function somehow denigrates the aesthetic merit of an object falls apart in a historic context where art for art's sake never existed. Function, of course, did not necessarily have to be literal: a fibula may have served to hold a cloak closed against winter winds but it just as importantly served to indicate the wearer's wealth. Only the emphasis has changed in the modern world where a collector of abstract art may refuse to acknowledge anything representational, much less functional, as worthy

Egyptian Mask, XVIII Dynasty
Tomb of Tut-ankh-amun, Thebes:
Valley of the Kings
Photography by Egyptian Expedition,
The Metropolitan Museum of Art,
New York, New York

of interest. Yet the collection displayed on the walls of a home or office announces the collector's intellectual attitude and the niche in society that he or she wishes to occupy. In both cases, the creator of the object has imbued it with quality that goes beyond the fulfillment of function to afford pleasure and distinguish the work even when it ceases to perform its original role.

An overview of Western civilization's evolving attitudes toward craft can begin with the culture of ancient Egypt. From the biographical inscriptions on tombs of those who ascended to the very top echelon of society, we know that, although the hierarchy was rigid, it allowed for some mobility. Government was the avenue of ascent and literacy was the means. An often-quoted inscription from the Middle Kingdom has been taken to demonstrate the lack of respect for the arts in Egyptian society.[1] The sculptor, goldsmith, potter, and weaver were classed with the farmer, barber, and such, and denigrated for their manual labor. The bias is only natural if the purpose of this so-called Satire of the Trades is taken into consideration: it was an admonition from a father to his son to study well at the school for scribes as this would prepare him for the best of careers. Direct knowledge of the crafts must have been an asset even in the upper ranks of administration, if we can judge from the tomb paintings of Rekh-mi-rē in Thebes, where the vizier is shown setting forth the program and supervising various aspects of production including what we would now regard as art.[2]

Excavations of a community of professional craftsmen at Deir el-Medina, Egypt,[3] reveals that they lived very comfortably. Employed in the royal workshops, they earned supplementary income by making funerary equipment for private individuals. Royal patronage extended beyond the preparation of tombs; the remains of a glass factory within the palace precincts of Akhenaten and Nefertiti indicate interest in a field that was brought to a high level during their reign.[4] Appreciation of aesthetic quality was not limited to the upper class as can be seen by the fragments of faience tile, painted with graceful reeds, which were found in the remains of the poorest slum dwellings, presumably culled from the castoffs of wealthy households.[5] From the treasure hoards of royal tombs and the supplementary evidence of archaeology, we can piece together the picture of a world where beautiful objects of all sorts were valued whether they were used in this life or set aside for the next. There, they magically served the spirit of the deceased, ensuring that life would go on and evoking the beauty of nature that the ancient Egyptian, even in death, refused to relinquish.

The response of the public to Egyptian art is based on excavated artifacts. Yet such portable objects are considered lesser stuff in the discipline of Egyptology where architecture, monumental sculpture, and wall painting are classed as major art. However, the finely crafted object played as significant a part in the rituals of worship and death as did sculpture, fresco, or tombs and temples themselves. The fluidity of the mystical view of the universe, in which all things have the capacity for spiritual significance, invites no necessary hierarchical distinctions among art forms. It might well be claimed that the single most charismatic art object of our generation has been the gold mask of Tutankhamen, focal point of one of the most popular art exhibitions ever held. Throngs in Europe and America were moved by this powerful object which so eloquently conveys the message of a youth empowered, and imprisoned, by a sophisticated civilization. They might be surprised to learn that this idealized portrait, hammered in the golden armor of death, could be categorized as a lesser form of art.

From classical Greece come Western civilization's standards of excellence and abstract values of formal beauty. Although most craftsmen's names are not known to us, there is contemporary record of tremendous respect for objects made with great skill and imagination. No distinction appears to have been made according to the nature of the object. Just as Myron, the sculptor, was widely praised for his full-size bronze cow, so realistic it was repeatedly mistaken for a living animal, so was the metalworker Glaukos of Chios for his iron krater stand. This remained a star attraction among the votives at Delphi for some seven centuries after its presentation by a Lydian king of the sixth century B.C.[6] Admirers rhapsodized not only about the technique of welding iron, which Glaukos was credited with inventing, but also about the krater stand's decoration of small figures, animals, and plants. They had no problem with the clearly functional nature of the object because in Greek society every product was made for a specific use. Even sculptures like Myron's cow were created for dedication to a god, then considered a very real function.

Greek vases, often regarded as the quintessential form of classic art, were collaborative efforts of potter and painter. In the new democratic system the potter was a private entrepreneur owning a workshop and employing assistants. The profession could lead to wealth, as we know from the presence on the Acropolis of a marble relief dedicated to a potter, for only those who had achieved considerable financial success were so represented. Painters came to work for potters on a freelance basis, some establishing a long-term relationship. Although failing eyesight is the accepted explanation of why the famed painter Euphronios later became a potter, the prospect of greater financial security may have played its part.

In 1972 the news media proclaimed that modern appreciation of classic art was alive and well when The Metropolitan Museum of Art purchased a calyx krater at a cost rivaling that of exceptional Impressionist or Old Master paintings. Ironically, the sensationalism surrounding the acquisition introduced a broad audience never before exposed to Greek vases to this sophisticated aesthetic. By means of a theatrical installation, uninitiated eyes were focused on Euphronios' virtuoso painting and the harmonious shape given the vessel by the potter Euxitheous. In a masterfully controlled design, the position of the handles is used to separate two pictorial fields framed by palmettes. Euphronios' advances in the accurate rendering of anatomy are demonstrated in a scene from the death of Sarpedon. All elements of human tragedy are expunged from the

Calyx Krater, VI century B.C., ca. 515 by Euxitheos and Euphronios
18 x 21¹¹⁄₁₆
Side A: Dead Sarpedon carried by Thanatos and Hypnos
Side B: Warriors Arming
The Metropolitan Museum of Art, New York, New York, Purchase, Bequest of Joseph H. Durkee, Gift of Darius Ogden Mills and Gift of C. Ruxton Love, by exchange, 1972

The March of the Christian Army, from the First Crusade Window, Choir, Ambulatory Chapel, Saint-Denis, about 1150
Pot metal glass with grisaille paint, 19¾ inches in diameter
The Glencairn Museum, The Academy of the New Church, Bryn Athyn, Pennsylvania

Richard Posner
Another Look at My Beef with the Government, 1976
Colored glass, photographic transparency, sandblasted, leaded, 26 x 31
Collection of the artist, Seattle, Washington

Although few in number, Posner's early self-contained stained glass pictures, rooted in the symbolic tradition of figurative windows of Medieval Europe, established him as a wry social critic. The subject of this window is Posner's situation when he was drafted out of the domestic Peace Corps for military duty in the Vietnam War. Claiming conscientious objector status, he was assigned forty-four months alternative service unloading a hospital dishwashing machine in the course of which he suffered severe back injury. We see the artist peering in at a figure in pelvic traction, helpless against the advance of mechanized cows, one of which conceals two hunters in the manner of the Trojan horse. In the foreground a book etched in mirror glass reflects the viewer's own image. Every detail has relevance, even to the patterning of the wallpaper with hinds of beef divided into cuts, the coverlet on the bed figured with meteorological maps of the United States similarly dissected, and the trademark figures of Dutch Cleanser.

subject. Euphronios has depicted the lifeless body of the son of Zeus as a sublime object supported by elegant winged warriors representing Sleep and Death. Together, painter and potter created an object in which no contour, volume, or surface mark could be changed without disturbing the absolute functionality and harmony of the whole. Despite its necessary physicality, the krater comes as close as possible to a purely abstract ideal — the perfect form for its vessel-type. A paragon of formalism, this ceramic embodies the Platonic striving for a perfection that transcends the sensible world.

After the collapse of the Roman empire, art and culture were kept alive in Europe by the monasteries. Ongoing contempt for manual labor was mitigated by the moral value of work and self-sufficiency within the monastic way of life. Theophilus, a monk of the tenth century, offers his *Essay Upon Various Arts* "to all wishing to overcome or avoid sloth of the mind or wandering of the soul by useful manual occupation."[7] In what is considered the most important art book of the early Middle Ages, Theophilus provided instruction on the full range of techniques practiced at the time, from metalwork to stained glass. The religious justifications he described for each endeavor leave no doubt that each is of equal value in creating a "likeness of the paradise of God."[8]

From the few names that have come down to us, it is clear that monastic artists had an extraordinary breadth of abilities and could achieve high rank. The authorship of the ivory altar cross from the English abbey of Bury St. Edmunds, now among the most prized treasures of the Cloisters of The Metropolitan Museum of Art,[9] is ascribed to Master Hugo on the basis of the intensely energized figures which can be recognized in the Bury Bible illustrated by him around 1135. Hugo is also believed to have been a master of printmaking and bronze casting, for he made both the abbey's silver seal and its bells. In addition he is thought to have been responsible for its mural paintings. Matthew Paris, the thirteenth-century abbot of St. Alban's, England's most important Benedictine monastery, is remembered for his chronicles. But he was also a painter, miniaturist, goldsmith and sculptor. A tenth-century Benedictine monk named Dunstan, both an illuminator and goldsmith, ascended via a number of key monastic posts to the archbishopric of Canterbury and subsequently to sainthood. It would appear that his involvement in these "minor" arts was no hindrance to his elevated status, but actually contributed to his reputation for piety and holiness.

Stained glass became the special focus of artistic endeavor as the vehicle for the illustration of Church teachings which took on otherwordly conviction when beams of light animated a window. The art form was launched through the building program of Suger, Abbot of Saint-Denis from 1122 to 1151. Windows were particularly appropriate to his church because the abbey's founder, Saint Denis, had been wishfully identified by the monks as the author of a treatise on light. Otherwise known as Pseudo-Dionysius the Argeopagite, this sixth-century philosopher had postulated light as the source of faith and the truth of God. The window of glass allowed its passage into the church while shielding the faithful

The Hunt of the Unicorn, second tapestry, the Unicorn at the Fountain, late XV century
Wool and silk with metal threads
from the Chateau of Verteuil
The Metropolitan Museum of Art, New York, New York, The Cloisters Collection, Gift of John D. Rockefeller, Jr., 1937

The mixing of religious and secular symbolism in a single work was not unusual during the late Middle Ages, when people did not consider the god of heaven and the god of love incompatible. This combination is manifest not only in the unicorn himself and in the flora throughout the Cloisters series, but also in the many remarkably lifelike birds and beasts assembled before the fountain.

within from all else. To create the windows for Saint-Denis, Suger declared that he had enlisted the "exquisite hands of many masters from different regions."[10] It has been suggested on stylistic grounds that some of those masters were illuminators and others were goldsmiths.

The principal subject matter of the stained glass in the choir of Saint-Denis was the illustration of concordances between the Old and New Testaments. One window in the choir was, however, devoted to the first Crusade. A historical concordance could be extrapolated here, as Suger was instrumental in organizing a second campaign to free the Holy Land, during which he served as regent of France. One of the few surviving panels from Suger's stained glass program depicts the march of the Christian army in the first Crusade. The inexorable nature of the Crusaders' advance is conveyed by their tight formation and the fixed focus of each soldier and steed. Central to the composition is their king. We are convinced that his faith and determination provide the motivating force by the determination of his strongly delineated features and his position in the midst of his men rather than at their head. Illuminated by what was thought to be the light of divine truth, this type of imagery must have been powerful propaganda for the second Crusade.

The rise of towns, an economy based on trade, and a new merchant class, generated a private market for art objects. Instead of living much like their Egyptian counterparts in large teams near the construction sites, staying in place for generations or moving on when one building program ceased and another began, professional artists settled in towns. There they assumed the role of independent capitalists, setting up workshops and selling their products. From the thirteenth century, they entrenched themselves in the community, exerting collective strength through guilds. These professional organizations, comprised of independent masters, maintained standards and protected the established members from the competition of new arrivals in the community. Although the professions were interdependent in many aspects of production, constant rivalry was played out as bickering among the guilds.

At the beginning of the sixteenth century, Brussels became a great center of tapestry weaving. The guild of painters, jealously guarding the prerogatives of the profession, initiated a skirmish with the recently established guild of tapestry weavers, many of whom were designing their own works. By a ruling of 1476, the weavers were forced under threat of fine to apply to professional painters for their cartoons, but they retained the right to design for themselves "textiles, trees, boats, animals, and grasses for their verdures" and to complete and correct the cartoons supplied to them by the painters "with charcoal, chalk, or pen." [11]

It was probably from the intense and stormy marriage of painters and weavers in Brussels that the great tapestry cycle of the Hunt of the Unicorn was born around 1500. The set was designed as one of the portable amenities with which peripatetic nobles transformed the forbidding stone chambers of the castles they visited into habitable rooms, in this case most likely an inviting bedroom. Patterned with beguiling flora and fauna and alive with vignettes of human interest, these weavings set forth the most profound and original iconographic program of the late Middle Ages. The unicorn, which appeals so directly in its beauty and vulnerability and which was thought to purify with the mere touch of its horn, is the product of a wealth of classical references and bears theological interpretation as a symbol of the Incarnation of Christ in the Virgin's womb. Each element is fraught with meaning, even details in the second tapestry such as pheasants drinking from the fountain — an allegory of human love — and rabbits, representing fertility. These, together with many other references, suggest that the ambitious cycle was commissioned for a wedding. Such tapestries, with their usefulness, visual appeal, and intellectual payload, were rated the most valuable items in the inventories of princes and noblemen in this new age of personal possessions.

The Italian Renaissance engendered new interest in the individual and values by which a man could achieve social status on the basis of intellectual achievement without wealth or pedigree. A cult of great men developed, along with a literature of biography transforming local celebrities into popular heroes and sources of civic pride. Such distinction held great appeal for painters and sculptors as an alternative to the guild system, whose protection no longer seemed worth the restriction to one locality, one type of work, and sometimes even one medium. To gain acceptance along with men of letters in this humanist elite, painters in particular waged a battle of the pen. The volumes of rhetoric arguing the special nature and virtues of the painters' profession were adopted as the foundation on which the modern discipline of art history has been structured. According to Sir Anthony Blunt:

> Painting, sculpture, and architecture were accepted as liberal arts, and are now [by the sixteenth century] grouped together as activities closely allied to each other and all differing fundamentally from the manual crafts. The idea of the "Fine Arts" comes into existence this way . . .[12]

Sir John Pope-Hennessy offers a differing view. To his mind, "Paintings are *aspirant* works of art." Although the painters may have claimed higher calling, their products "were actually objects made for specific purposes like any others. It was only in the nineteenth century that they were turned into works of art" and divorced from the rest of production. [13]

Because of the overwhelming abundance of literature supporting painters and sculptors, it is generally overlooked that they were equaled in all but their press by goldsmiths of the time. Although Vasari, foremost of the polemicists on the arts, dropped goldsmiths from the second edition (1568) of his compendium of artists' biographies, he had included them in his first publication (1550). The influx of precious metal from the New World coupled with the recently legitimized sumptuous cravings of society, brought the art form to new heights of inspired invention and technical perfection.

Benvenuto Cellini
Saltcellar
Gold, silver, enamel, 10¼ x 13½
Kunsthistorischmuseum, Vienna

Benvenuto Cellini stands out among a number of virtuoso goldsmiths as one of the stellar figures of the Renaissance by virtue of his powers of self-promotion. With uncanny perception of the import of the written word, he engraved his name in history with a treatise on his craft and, most important, a colorful autobiography relating the particulars of his career as an international celebrity. A stylistic innovator in the forefront of Mannerism, he was sought after by popes and princes. After seeing just one of Cellini's works, Francois I was so eager to engage his services that he secured the goldsmith's release from papal prison (where he had been incarcerated on a trumped-up charge of stealing some of the jewels entrusted to him by Pope Clement VII). Released from prison, Cellini arrived in France in 1540. Francois's personal interest was such that years after his return to Italy Cellini (with uncharacteristic modesty) was to write, "All that I am, whatever of good and beautiful quality I have produced, all this must be ascribed to that extraordinary monarch."[14]

Only one object by Cellini escaped the usual fate of goldsmiths' work whose constituent precious materials were regularly recycled to meet their owners' financial exigencies. The saltcellar now in the *Kunsthistorisches-museum* of Vienna does indeed support Cellini's claim to fame. Although it was completed for Francois I, it was originally commissioned by a Florentine cardinal as the consummate product of High Renaissance Italy. Cellini rejected the design suggestions offered by two leading Florentine humanists in favor of his own sophisticated scheme of a reclining couple representing Earth and Sea. The fully realized nudes, sculpted in the round, owe much to Michelangelo, the only artist Cellini admitted to be his superior, and yet they have a lithe sensuousness all Cellini's own. Function was not forgotten amid the profusion of enamel and gold animals, sea life, and figures of Night, Day, Twilight, Dawn and the Four Winds that crowd the object. Beside his personification of the sea, Cellini, in his own words, "placed a ship, elaborately wrought in all its details, and well adapted to hold a quantity of salt"; and by his figure of Earth, "a richly decorated temple firmly based upon the ground. . . . intended to receive the pepper." Yet the impact of the piece lies not just in its "luxuriant ornamentation" but also in the dynamics of the two majestic long-limbed figures, "considerably taller than a palm in height" leaning

Visit of Louis XIV to the Gobelins (October 15, 1667)
Woven in the Le Blond Studio, 1729-1734
Wool, silk, and gold, 20 threads per inch (8 per cm.), 147⅝ x 228⅜
The Mobilier National, Paris, France

This fine example is from the fourteen-piece suite called "The History of the King." It is a low-warp tapestry and is the fourteenth piece of the sixth weaving of the series. In the upper border are the arms of France; there are fleur-de-lis in the corners and the king's monogram in the cartouches of the side borders. The inscription in the cartouche of the lower border may be translated as: The King Louis XIII Visting the Manufactory of the Gobelins where the Lord Colbert Superintendent of his Works Conducts him in All the Studios in Order to Show him the Diverse Works Which are Made There.

Robert Ebendorf
Portable Souls, 1970
Silver, glass, beads, brass, corpus,
coke top, three pieces, each
3¾ x 3¼ x ¼
Collection of Carol Anthony,
Bridgewater, Connecticut

An all-American nostalgia is evoked
by assemblages like *Portable Souls.*
The daguerreotype case fitted with a
crucifix (unearthed from the sands
of a playground), set between
buttons emblazoned with the
American flag stands at once as a
personal treasure, and a cultural
relic.

out from the oval base at such an angle that they seem held in place only by the magnetism of mutual attraction suggested by their erotically entwined legs.[15]

Cellini's special relationship with Francois I was not unique: the goldsmith Friedrich Sustris so won the admiration and confidence of Wilhelm V of Bavaria that in 1587 the duke decreed that all work of painters, sculptors, and handworkers for the Munich court should henceforth be planned, designed, and distributed by Sustris.[16] Such organization of art production became the trend. In 1588 the Medici formalized the group of virtuosi they had attracted to Florence appointing a superintendent of the workshop where the artists worked, the *Opificio delle Pietre Dure* (or "Hard Stone Workshop," although the name is misleading) to avoid "ourselves always being disturbed" in the effort to direct the activities of "jewellers, inlay workers, cosmographers, goldsmiths, gardiner, turners, distillers, porcelain makers, sculptors, painters, and those concerned with the crystal furnace, the chapel and music both of voices and all sorts of instruments."[17]

In the next century Louis XIV was to follow the Medici model, establishing in 1663 the *Manufacture royale des meubles de la Couronne* (The Royal Manufactury of Crown Furnishings) at the Gobelins where the existing tapestry workshops were expanded to include studios for embroidery, gold and silver work, cabinetmaking, and lapidary work. The endeavor had a twofold function: to enhance the monarch's prestige by providing the accoutrements of glory to his residences, and to produce

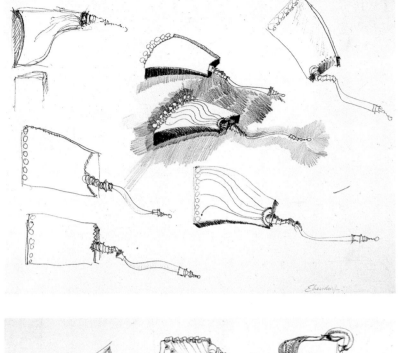

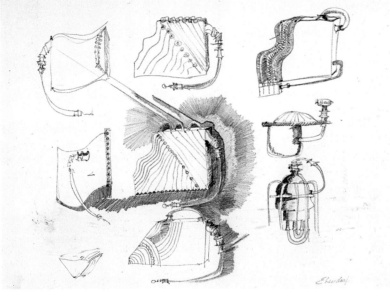

Robert Ebendorf
The Colored Smoke Machine, 1974
Metals, copper, Plexiglas, pearls,
5⅛ x 1⅝ x ½
Nordenfjeldske
Kunstindustrimuseum,
Trondheim, Norge

Drawings from The Colored Smoke Machine Series, ca. 1973-74
Graphite colored pencil and pen on paper, 8 x 10
Collection of the artist,
Highland, New York

Ebendorf begins with what he calls idea drawings, or sometimes with paper models, when starting to work on a piece.

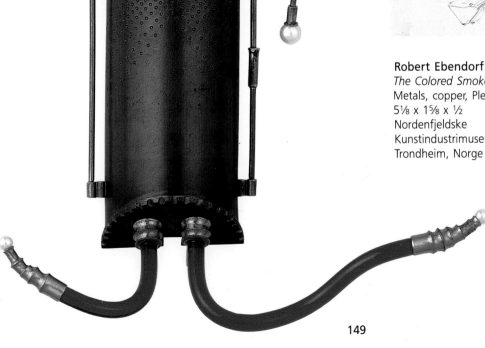

149

William Harper
Rain Rattle, 1972
Enamel, copper-electroforming with
deer antler, 10 x 5 x 2
Collection of Dr. and Mrs. Matthew
Cohen, Tallahassee, Florida

The resolution of a highly individual
style, playing the irregularity of
found objects against the discipline
of enamel compositions, can be
seen in *Rain Rattle.* Although its
antler handle and rattling pebbles
suggest use in an Indian rain dance,
the piece belongs equally to the
European tradition of dressing table
accoutrements.

luxury goods for sale abroad. Since this was the key to his mercantile policy, Louis XIV had his great minister Colbert take direct charge of the organization, and he appointed the first painter to the king, Charles Le Brun, to the post of resident director. As a result, the Baroque pomp and splendor associated with the Sun King was fostered in every aspect of production. So important was the enterprise in the *grand politique* of the monarchy that one of the fourteen tapestries of the great series conceived by Le Brun to illustrate the main events of the reign of Louis XIV was devoted to his visit to the Gobelins in 1667 (page 147). Presented for the inspection of the king (in the plumed hat) and Colbert (on his left) by Le Brun (hat in hand below them) are massive pieces of cast silver, tapestries, and elaborate furniture. Directing the unveiling of a monumental cabinet with "four large twisted columns in imitation lapis and vine scrolls of copper gilt"[18] was its author, Domenico Cucci. The multimedia showpieces created by this Italian-born master, which he encrusted with marbles, mosaics, and metal mounts and set on sumptuously carved bases, mark the start of the development of furniture into one of the primary arts of France under the Bourbon monarchy.

Louis XIV continued the practice established by Henri IV of awarding lodging in the palace of the Louvre, and exemption from guild supervision, to artists and artisans of exceptional merit. Here painters lived and worked on an equal basis with clockmakers, cabinetmakers, and such. In 1672 the king awarded André-Charles Boulle accommodation in the Louvre on the basis of Colbert's recommendations that Boulle was "the most skillful in Paris in his profession."[19] The cabinetmaker had been admitted to the guild of Saint Luke on the basis of his skills in sculpture and drawing before his admission to the guild of furniture makers. Boulle's development of furniture along sculptural lines won the admiration and personal friendship as well as the patronage of the king. The nature of his art can be seen in the novel pair of cabinets he created for Louis XIV's bedroom at the Grand Trianon in 1708-1709. No longer merely boxes enriched by surface ornament, their shapes have become a curving essay in Baroque volume. Projections are sheathed in bronze cast with imposing figural imagery but integrated in the overall design. Their surfaces of intricately patterned brass and tortoise shell marquetry represent an original technique that became known as boullework. The form, soon named the "commode," became the vehicle for the display of mastery of the succeeding Rococo and Neoclassical styles by French cabinetmakers who regard Boulle as the founding father of their art.

Art and science combined with patriotism and mercantile theory in the matter of porcelain. Since the late Middle Ages, Chinese porcelains had been known and treasured in the West. With the establishment of regular trade with China in the seventeenth century, the popularity of the imported ware reached fever pitch. It became the ambition of every prince to discover the secrets of its technique and set up his own porcelain factory, both as a point of pride and in the interest of developing an export industry. Success was finally achieved through the joint efforts of a high-born physicist, Ehrenfried Walter von Tschirrnhausen, and a scalawag alchemist, Johann Friedrich Böttger, in the employ of Augustus the Strong, and in 1710 the Royal Saxon Porcelain Manufactory was founded at Meissen.[20] Other factories soon followed but Meissen remained preeminent for half a century.

Early Meissen products were technological essays which followed Oriental prototypes, but in 1720 a new director initiated the use of the material as a field for painting, and soon hired several sculptors to create models for the factory. Among the recruits was Johann Joachim Kandler, a young sculptor who was to become Meissen's great interpreter of the new medium, as he translated the existing German tradition of small sculpture in ivory and wood into ceramic. He added a new dimension by playing on porcelain's preciousness and aristocratic context to create an idiom of social satire with caricatures of recognizable courtiers. The most ambitious of these was the large portrait bust of the court jester "Baron" Schmiedel, dating from 1739. The conventional Rococo composition is invaded by rodents, one dangling from the subject's mouth, in obscene contrast to his elaborate finery. Beneath the ribald humor is pathos: Schmiedel's well-known fear of mice made him an easy mark, and Kaendler's colorless depiction of Schmiedel's sullen resignation presents a silent indictment of the society that cast him as its butt.

With Neoclassicism came a newly analytic attitude toward art. Not only were media and subjects, even individual artists, ranked and categorized, but works of art also began to be systematically classified and studied, with an eye toward their value as tools of education and moral edification. Even the earliest collections of antiquities formed in the eighteenth century were studied, organized, and published by a new profession of scholars such as Johann Joachim Winckelmann, who worked on the gems, coins, and sculptures acquired by his friend and patron Cardinal Albani. The approach was disseminated through Winckelmann's personal proselytizing and publications such as his 1764 *History of Ancient Art.* With didactic purpose supplanting delectation as the motive for amassing art, private collections became museums. The mid-eighteenth century excavations of Herculaneum were undertaken by Charles de Bourbon, King of Naples, with the specific aim of creating a museum in Naples, and the Vatican opened its rapidly growing holdings of antiquities to the public in 1772 as the *Museo Clementino.*[21] In a concomitant reassessment of values in 1781, the porcelain collection of Augustus the Strong that had been the pride of the Saxon court was none too carefully removed from display in Dresden's Japanese Palace and replaced with antiquities, a coin collection, and a library. This denoted the transition to an educational institution in which decorative arts were of secondary importance.[22]

At the same time, Europe was gearing up for the industrial revolution. Mass production and the assembly line, with their resulting separation of individual worker from finished product, were to become the norm in meeting society's needs for functional or decorative items. The finely crafted object would become a rarity. A broadened consumer class cared more about the quantity of goods than their quality, an attitude

Portrait Bust, Meissen, about 1740
Modeled by J. J. Kandler
Porcelain, approximately 28 inches in height
Royal Saxon Porcelain Manufactory, Meissen
Courtesy of The Trustees of the Museum of Applied Arts and Sciences, Sydney, Australia

This is a caricature of "Baron" Schmiedel, the royal postmaster, who was famous for his morbid fear of mice.

Robert Ebendorf
The Colored Smoke Machine, 1974
Metals, copper, Plexiglas, pearls,
5⅛ x 1⅝ x ½
Collection of the artist,
Highland, New York

In the *Colored Smoke Machines* of
1974, minutely detailed structures of
base metal and colored Plexiglas
demonstrate the influence of the
German goldsmith Claus Bury on
American jewelry. The inspiration for
these pieces was a drawing made by
Bury on a visit to Ebendorf's home.
In the drawing Ebendorf's home
emits a stream of colored smoke as
a token of the human warmth it
contained.

illustrated especially by the Victorian middle-class parlor, overstuffed with
knickknacks and Rococo-revival furniture. An increasingly affluent
bourgeoisie wanted the reassurance and connotations of economic status
inherent in familiar appearances. They favored the recapitulation of
historical styles — associated in the past with the aristocracy but now
obtainable more cheaply in manufactured form — over original design.
Painters and sculptors retreated to high ground, concerning themselves
with noble subjects of virtue, religion, and patriotism, and clinging to the
Academy, whose structure protected their position.

During most of the nineteenth century, theory was of considerably
more interest than product in the decorative arts. A continuous parade of
reformers decried the divorce between art and industry. Pugin, Ruskin, and
Morris cast their diatribes in terms of morality, taking the level to which
design had sunk as a symptom of the ills of society. The official reaction
was to offer education as a panacea. Princely treasure hoards were
marshaled to this end, their contents programmatically classified by a
newly created cadre of curatorial civil servants for presentation in
museums constructed for the purpose.

The Victoria and Albert Museum in London was the prototype "effort
to improve public taste and promote popular Art teaching." Evolving out
of the government School of Design, founded in 1837, it took on the
dimensions of a museum in 1851 with the allocation of funds for the
purchase of objects "notable for excellence of their Art or Workmanship,"
and opened to the public in South Kensington in 1857 as the Museum of
Ornamental Art.[23] After the foundation of the Museum for Art and
Industry in Vienna in 1864, German governments rapidly followed suit.[24]
Paintings and sculpture were housed in separate edifices with separate
curatorial staffs. Their mandate was one of spiritual uplift while the
decorative arts museums were expected to produce direct improvements
in industry.

Seeing little result, artists rebelled against the establishment. William
Morris followed a Utopian course. As an early socialist and design
reformer, he preached rejection of the machine and the revival of
handcrafts in a medievalizing style. Painters focused on the Academy,
rejecting its authority and forming alternate associations and exhibition
societies.

Mending the breach between the fine and applied arts was one of
the goals of the Vienna Secession, formed in 1897 with Gustav Klimt as
its president. The poet and spokesman for the movement, Hermann Bahr,
proclaimed, "Painting is not enough. We shall not have a truly Austrian art
until it becomes a living force in our daily lives."[25] Architects and
designers were influential members of the group, and applied arts were
presented on the same footing as painting and sculpture in the Secession
exhibitions.

The ideal of the *Gesamtkunstwerk,* a total multimedia art statement
espoused by architect Josef Hoffmann (member of the Secession and
cofounder of the Wiener Werkstaette which designed and produced a full
range of applied arts), represented the end of hierarchy in artistic values.

Few know how fully he realized his goal. Hoffmann was commissioned by industrialist Adolphe Stoclet in 1905 to build a residence in Brussels. The Palais Stoclet stands unchanged as the private, closely guarded preserve of the Stoclet family. Its dining room offers the climactic experience of Hoffmann's architectural masterpiece. The austere furniture and array of silver serving pieces, all specially made by the Wiener Werkstaette, are set in a long narrow room. Lining the walls are mosaics designed by Klimt: a complex abstract composition defines the axis of the room; a frieze with a taut figure of a solitary, anxious woman set against the spiraling branches of a spreading tree runs the length of one side; and a couple locked in rapturous embrace before a similar tree covers the opposite wall.

If these sublime mosaics were better known they might go far towards laying to rest the argument of fine versus minor arts. Unfortunately only the cartoons now in Vienna's Museum fur Angewandtekunst have been widely published and they convey nothing of the impact of the room of which the mosaics were an integral part. The designs in isolation cannot evoke the dramatic tension created by their interrelation. For their execution Klimt called on the skills of the

Dining Room of the Palais Stoclet
Bild-Archiv der Oesterreichischen
National-bibliothek, Wien

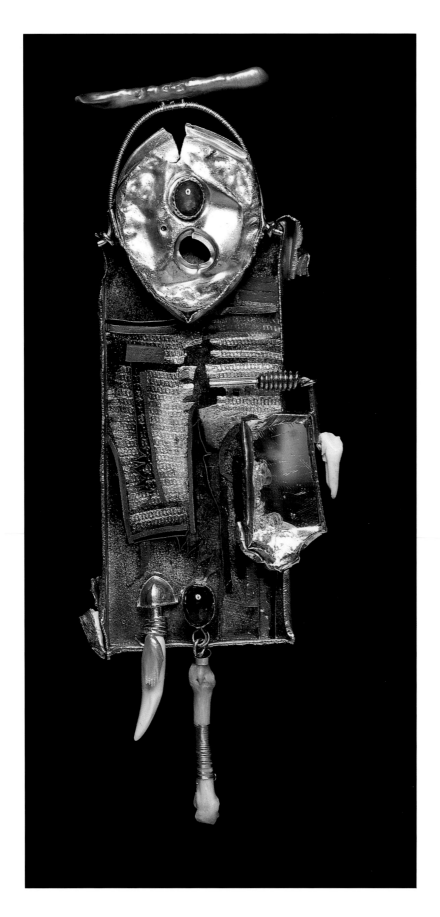

goldsmith's studio of the Wiener Werkstaette, the enamel studio of the School of Applied Arts, the Wiener Keramik pottery, and Leopold Forstner's Mosaikwerkstaette as well as the marble workshop of Orestre A. Basteri.[26] The delicate graphics of the cartoons, however, convey no sense of the tactile richness of the mosaic of stone, glass, ceramic, metal, enamel, and mother-of-pearl for which they were destined.

Klimt was among the first of modern masters from Picasso to Calder to reject the conventional distinction between high and low art. Although the professions of art history and criticism keep alive the segregation of the arts as if the ninteenth century were yet with us, artists have long been working to make whole the aesthetic fabric rent by the Industrial Revolution. As the twentieth century draws to a close, so does the polarity between art and daily life that marked only one circumscribed period in fifty centuries of civilization.

NOTES

[1] Miriam Lichtheim, *Ancient Egyptian Literature, A Book of Readings,* vol. 1, *The Old and Middle Kingdoms* (Berkeley: 1975), p. 185-191.

[2] Norman de G. Davies, *The Tomb of Rekh-mi-rē at Thebes* (New York: Metropolitan Museum of Art, 1944).

[3] Morris Bierbrier, *The Tomb-Builders of the Pharaohs* (London: British Museum, 1982), passim.

[4] Cyril Aldred, *Akhenaten and Nefertiti,* exhibition catalogue, (New York: Brooklyn Museum, 1973), p. 212.

[5] Aldred, p. 157.

[6] Writings of Herodotus (485-425 B.C.), Pausanias (middle and late second century A.D.), and Athenaeus (circa 200 A.D.), excerpted by J. J. Pollitt, *Sources and Documents: The Art of Greece* (Englewood Cliffs: 1965), p. 44.

[7] Translation of Robert Hendrie London, 1847, reprinted in *A Documentary History of Art,* vol. 1, Elizabeth Gilmore Holt, ed. (New York: Doubleday, 1957), p. 2.

[8] Holt, p. 8.

[9] Thomas P. F. Hoving, "The Bury St. Edmunds Cross," *The Metropolitan Museum of Art Bulletin* (June 1964).

[10] Jane Hayward, "Stained Glass at Saint-Denis in the Time of Abbot Suger (1122-1151)," *The Royal Abbey of Saint-Denis,* exhibition catalogue (New York: The Metropolitan Museum of Art, 1981), p. 65.

11 Margaret B. Freeman, *The Unicorn Tapestries* (New York: The Metropolitan Museum of Art, 1976), pp. 208, 218.

12 Anthony Blunt, *Artistic Theory in Italy 1450-1600* (Oxford: Oxford University Press, 1966), p. 55.

13 Conversation with Sir John Pope-Hennessy, September 9, 1985.

14 J. F. Hayward, *Virtuoso Goldsmiths and the Triumph of Mannerism, 1540-1620* (London: Sotheby Park Bernet, 1976), p. 172.

15 Hayward, p. 148.

16 Hayward pp. 37-38.

17 Annapaula Pampaloni Martelli, *The Opificio delle Pietre Dure Museum of Florence* (Florence: 1974), p. 8.

18 Identified in the inventory of Louis XIV by Pierre Verlet, *French Royal Furniture* (London: Barrie and Rockliff, 1963), p. 5.

19 Comte de Salverte, *Les Ébénistes du XVIII Siecle* (Paris: F. de Nobele, 1962), p. 34.

20 William B. Honey, *Dresden China* (New York: Tudor, 1946), pp. 25-32.

21 Carlo Pietrangeli, "Archaelogical Excavations in Italy 1750-1850," *The Age of Neo-Classicism,* exhibition catalogue (London: Arts Council of Great Britain, 1972), pp. xvi-xviii.

22 Joachim Menzhausen, "Five Centuries of Art Collecting in Dresden," *The Splendor of Dresden,* exhibition catalogue (New York: The Metropolitan Museum of Art, 1978), p. 26.

23 Gilbert Redgrave, editorial, *The Art Journal,* 1887, p. 221.

24 Barbara Mundt, *Die Deutschen Kustoewerbemuseum im 19 Jahrhundert* (Munich: 1974), pp. 22-24.

25 Quoted in Werner Hofmann, *Gustav Klimt* (Greenwich, Connecticut: 1971), p. 11.

26 Cited by Werner J. Schweiger, *Wiener Werkstaette, Kunst and Handwerk 1903-1932* (Vienna: Christian Brandstätter, 1982), p. 160.

William Harper
The Temptation of St. Anthony,
1986
Gold cloisonné enamel on fine silver with 14k and 24k gold, sterling silver, aluminum, opal, tourmaline, mirror, freshwater pearl, ivory, bone,
6½ x 2½ x ¾
Collection of the artist,
Tallahassee, Florida

The most intensely personal product of Harper's fascination with the imagery of various religions is *The Temptation of St. Anthony.* Inspired by paintings by Hieronymous Bosch (died 1516) and an engraving by Martin Schongauer (1430-1491), Harper identifies the saint's struggle between aesthetic impulse and worldly attractions as his own plight. A discarded flip top from an aluminum can provided him a tortured visage to set on an enameled body dangling vestigial limbs. With a device borrowed from fetishes of the Congo Songye tribe, the amulet engages the viewer through the flashing reflections of a broken mirror.

I would like to thank Christine Lilyquist, Dietrich von Bothmer, Joan Mertens, Charles Little, Edith Standen, William Rieder, and Olga Raggio of The Metropolitan Museum of Art, Colin Eisler and Gert Schiff of the Institute of Fine Arts of New York University, Kathryn Hiesinger of the Philadelphia Museum of Art, and Sir John Pope-Hennessy, from whom I received guidance in the investigation of my subject in the fields of their profound expertise.

CRAFTS AND AMERICAN ART MUSEUMS

JONATHAN L. FAIRBANKS

Sam Maloof
Settee, 1986
Fiddleback maple, 30 x 36 x 24
Collection of the artist,
Alta Loma, California

Maloof's furniture asserts forceful presence. This settee made in 1986 is among the most eloquent of contemporary American furniture. It exhibits a classic balance between voids and solids. The interplay of hard and soft edges that undulate across the seat and are echoed in the crest rail provide a rich rhythm that recalls the texture of windswept sand dunes or snowdrifts. Like all Maloof furniture, this comfortable sculptural seating was finished with a smooth, polished surface. The use of fiddleback maple, however, is exceptional as Maloof is more famous for his black walnut furniture.

No special boundaries separate art from craft, nor is one sort of creative work more important than another. Artists and craftspersons may use different materials and have diverse technical objectives, but they share the goal of transforming raw material into expressive, spiritually moving work. Although recognizable differences exist between painting, sculpture, ceramics, woodworking, metalwork, fiber constructions, and glass, all media involve the shaping of planes, envelopes, colors, tones, line, and other plastic elements. The essential unity of these arts implies the interchangeability of the terms *art and craft, artist* and *craftsperson.*

The utilitarian nature of manmade objects is often cited as the determinant for whether a work is craft or art; such a distinction is folly. It descends from seventeenth-century academic notions which elevated painting and sculpture (because they were "useless" in a practical sense), ignored architecture, and demeaned other manmade works as non-art (because they were "useful"). In contrast, most informed critics today acknowledge art in simple functional works. A prehistoric stone celt may be useful and yet fulfill all the requirements of art. Similarly, few would dismiss the high artistic qualities obvious in as humble an object as a well-cut, expressive tombstone made in coastal Massachusetts during the seventeenth century.

John Foster Headstone, attributed to the Charlestown Stonecutter, probably Charlestown, Massachusetts, 1681
Slate, 28⅝ x 23⅜ x 2³⁄₁₆
Boston Parks and Recreation Commission, on loan to the Museum of Fine Arts, Boston

Augustus Elianers, Boston
Library Chair, ca. 1845-60 (two views)
Oak with mahogany stain,
40 x 24½ x 22
Museum of Fine Arts, Boston, Massachusetts

Judgements about the aesthetic content of objects are subject to revision, depending, in part, on what museums collect and art historians publish. There are at least two sorts of art: temporal expression (music, talk, ritual, dance, theater, etc.) and art which incorporates physical materials in space (works traditionally displayed by museums). Boundaries between these two activities blur when temporal arts are collected through audiovisual means and are thereby translated into tangible substance. The fallacy of classification by substance becomes clear with the realization that art is easily transmutable. The artist adapts familiar forms and incorporates existing knowledge as often as he discovers new alternatives through various media. Aesthetic invention changes and enlarges human awareness through the senses.

Since the writing and analysis of history are always unfinished, boundaries in art and history will continue to change, as will the meanings of words. Certain works, popular during specific eras, offer some insights. The use (and abuse) of the term *abstract,* for example, has plagued thoughtful people over the past few decades. All art is abstract, even the most intensely representational work. For centuries many of the crafts have been nonrepresentational, but now there is a vigorous infusion of figural traditions from painting and sculpture; conversely, the widespread pursuit of non-figural or decorative effects in painting and sculpture may ultimately derive from ideas generated by historic crafts.

Three hundred years ago hybridization in the arts seemed of little concern. All human improvements on nature were identified with art as part of a grand "divine plan." By 1800, upwardly mobile Americans expressed a more self-conscious concern for style and "good taste." The buzzwords of that era, "in the best taste," suggested the latest fashion in art imported from major cities abroad. By the 1850s, crafts were identified as "domestic arts." Some artisans called themselves "domestic engineers," as did Augustus Elianers of Boston, who designed, built, and patented a library step-chair. Within a generation the approved term for crafts shifted to "applied arts." By the turn of the century, "other arts," "minor arts," "arts and crafts," "home arts," and even "articraft" were common appellations. The twenties awakened a fresh interest in the crafts, which were renamed "decorative arts." Out of fashion for another generation, the term *craft* gained status and popularity shortly after World War II and came to flower in the sixties and seventies. Now the terms *craftsman, artist,* and *designer* seem freely intermixed. Craftspersons, however, usually identify themselves with their medium (woodworker, metalsmith, or glassblower).

The tensions implicit in such polarities of language are worth tracking. Words that shift meaning over time offer a chance to glimpse patterns of thought shared by many individuals in the past. The issue is not so much what is written or said but *how* things are said or perceived. Beauty pertains to cognition — to understanding and appreciation. Classification attempts to order seemingly unrelated parts; it alters perceptions in ways quite similar to those of poetry or art.

Prejudices seem to be self-perpetuating. They often infiltrate

Jack Earl
*I Met Marsha in a Bowling Alley
. . .*, 1969-1970
Porcelain bas-relief with burned
wood frame,
40½ x 34 x 5½
Collection of Thomas and Geraldine
Kerrigan, Bisbee, Arizona

Inscription (left panel)
"I met Marsha in a bowling alley
over in Belle Center about two years
ago. I don't remember how we
really first met but anyhow she
showed me a few pointers about
bowling and we had a couple of
beers. She asked if I wanted to take
her home and I asked her where she
lived because I didn't have much gas
and I didn't have a dollar left to buy
any. She said she lived over on 51
and I thought I ought to have
enough for that so I said okay. She
set real close to me all the way and
she put her hand inside my shirt.
That felt real good and I kept
thinking about whether I'd have
enough gas to make the trip . . ."

Inscription (right panel)
"I got her home and she asked if I
wanted to sit in the car for awhile
and I said I'd like to but I had to get
back before the bowling alley closed
and pick up Tim and take him
home. She took her hand out, gave
me a pretty long kiss, thanked me a
lot and went in the house. After I
saw her at the allies a couple more
times and we started dating and
after a couple months I figured we
ought to get married and we live in
a house trailer now and I still got
my same job. She is going to have a
baby in three months and after we
get the trailer paid off we are going
to use it for a down payment on a
nice house. Until then we store the
stuff we don't have room for in her
dad's barn." (from Lee Nordness,
*Jack Earl: The Genesis and
Triumphant Survival of an
Underground Ohio Artist,* Racine:
Perimeter Press, 1985, p. 79-80.)

159

institutions such as museums and universities, which then sustain them. While most college curricula today place a strong emphasis on the fine arts, rarely do they offer developed courses in the crafts and even more infrequently in the history of decorative arts. Despite such neglect, most people realize that the old-fashioned notion of fine arts versus crafts was an intellectually dead issue over a hundred years ago. The English social reformer and craftsman/designer William Morris made it clear in the nineteenth century that a contemplative worker who produced excellently crafted work was also an artist.

Dividing the world of fine arts from that of craft is as impossible as separating the functional from the spiritual worlds. Just as in life, the physical and metaphysical aspects of art are inseparable. Virtuoso artists in the Renaissance promoted the belief that genius distinguishes fine artists from other human beings. This self-serving rhetoric, aimed at breaking the restrictions of the guild system, ignored the fact that all mankind has genius to be expressed. Genius is not the exclusive domain of "fine artists." Despite Morris's well-reasoned thesis which blew apart the myth of differentiated status in the arts, even today some individuals continue to cling to these outmoded notions. The critical issue in determining artistic merit is whether the maker effectively manipulates his materials to evoke the viewer's emotions, thoughts, attitudes, or sensory responses.

A recent example illustrates the kind of perversion in the arts that is generated by the "fine arts versus crafts" notion. While mounting an exhibition, a curator requested the reframing of a work which had been done in a careless way that distracted from the finished product. The artist refused, however, claiming that he was not into that "craft thing." He pompously inferred that his painting was so superior that the framing defect was not only irrelevant but appropriate, since it expressed his belief in the superiority of one art form over what he considered an insignificance. The cult of the virtuoso thus continues even though such folly is a vestige from the past with no purpose other than self-aggrandizement. Many painters today self-consciously deny the craft aspects of their work and omit the use of frames, strainers, and other methods and materials which seasoned practice recommends. Ironically, this disdain comes at a time when accurate knowledge of the nature of materials and the promotion of quality in workmanship have become growing concerns among younger artists who are appalled by the aesthetics of throwaway material culture. The craftsperson has not forgotten that knowing his or her materials is essential to realizing the expressive power of the work. For the potter, the clay and its processing through shaping, glazing, and firing are a physical recapitulation of inner thoughts. Similar feelings are invariably articulated by many craftspersons who work in wood, fiber, glass, metals and other materials. A curator who has the privilege of working with living craftspersons can learn about these artistic intentions; such thoughts about materials or accomplishments rarely surface in the records concerning historic craftsmen.

The ordering of collections in large public art museums demands

William Morris, ca. 1880
Courtesy of the National Portrait Gallery, London, England

William Morris (1834-1896), an English writer, designer, and craftsman, began his career at Oxford, then settled in London as a painter and a member of Dante Gabriel Rossetti's Pre-Raphaelite circle. The project of furnishing Red House, his new home in Kent, led to his founding a firm which eventually produced textiles, stained glass, furniture, wallpaper, and carpets. Later he established the Kelmscott Press, designing type and decoration for a series of fine books. Morris's ideas about the decorative arts in relation to society and his popular writings and lectures had an enormous impact on his contemporaries. His insistence on simplicity, honesty, and respect for materials and processes, and on the joy of handwork, became the basis for humanistic functionalism in generations that followed. Morris's famous dictum, "Have nothing in your home that you do not know to be useful or believe to be beautiful," became the foundation of a modern aesthetic.

Harrison McIntosh
Bowl, 1950
Green engobe, ivory matte glaze,
sgraffito design, 4¼ x 7⅜
Los Angeles County Museum of Art,
Los Angeles, California,
Gift of Catherine McIntosh

Over thirty years ago McIntosh
chose a stoneware body, single-firing
system, basic engobe and glaze
surface treatment, and vocabulary of
robust forms. Thus he set up his
own boundaries within which
seemingly limitless variations are
possible. McIntosh was aware of the
American explorations of Japanese,
Abstract Expressionist, Pop, and funk
art applications to clay developing
around him in California during the
1950s and 1960s, yet he maintained
his commitment to classical objects
with clarity of shape and design in
the tradition of the Bauhaus. His
forms, both the earlier vessels and
the more recent completely enclosed
shapes, display clean contours,
generous volumes, and precise
geometrical surface patterns.

specialized divisions which maintain the prejudices of previous generations
and reflect current taste. Museums divide collections in several ways: by
material (paper, textiles, paintings, woodwork); by time (ancient,
Medieval, and contemporary); or by cultural group (Asiatic, Egyptian,
tribal, classical, American). Crafts and craftsmanship permeate each
category. In the 1920s, many urban museums formed a new department
for "the other arts" or "minor arts." Such demeaning nomenclature
became passé in 1925 when the *Exposition Internationale des Arts
Décoratifs et Industriels Modernes* took place in Paris.[1] This exposition and
its publications established a new level of respect for fine craftsmanship as
art. Soon many major art museums established departments of decorative
arts, developed according to the interests of respective curators .

   Although there is no simple explanation for how museum collections
grow, the present trend seems to favor the addition of contemporary
crafts to art museums. During the 1930s and 1940s the traditional view
was quite different. Although he was an ardent advocate for crafts,
Ananda K. Coomaraswamy, Keeper of Indian and Islamic art at the

Dale Chihuly
Cylinder, 1984
Glass, 16¾ x 9¾
Collection of Elmerina and Paul
Parkman, Kensington, Maryland

In a period when the studio craft
movement centered around the
ethos of a single artist conceiving
and executing a work, Chihuly
adapted the traditional Venetian
team system in which he now casts
himself in the role of a cinema
director. His first cylinders of 1975

announced his achievements as a
colorist. Their direction was inspired
by Navaho blankets, and the
compositions were laid out in glass
rods by a member of the team, first
Kate Elliott and later Flora Mace.
The hot glass cylinder was rolled
over them, picking up the design
and fusing it into the glass with
reheating. No matter how many
hands were involved, however,
concept and the succulent coloristic
values were unmistakably Chihuly's.

Museum of Fine Arts, Boston, wrote, "the modern artist's ambition to be
represented in a museum is his vanity, and betrays a complete
misunderstanding of the function of art . . . it is not the business of a
museum to exhibit contemporary works."[2] Many curators before the
1950s believed that the sole function of an art museum was to preserve
and present masterworks of the past. Attitudes regarding contemporary
art have changed in different ways within individual art museums. This
shift responds partly to the marketplace, partly to public expectations, and
partly to an increase in the quality and variety of works being made. Today
contemporary arts and crafts enter museum collections through many
routes, including patrons, dealers, and curators. A museum collection
ultimately grows or stagnates according to the curator's breadth of
interests, knowledge, and activities.

The historical record concerning contemporary crafts at the Museum
of Fine Arts, Boston (hereafter MFA) is instructive. In 1870 the MFA was
founded with a mission to improve public taste and the arts of industry
(i.e., crafts) through collections and education; the model for the MFA
was London's Victoria and Albert Museum The first crafted American
work, a contemporary silver pitcher made by Tiffany & Co., entered the
MFA's collection in 1877. It was purchased by the donor one year earlier
at the Centennial Exhibition in Philadelphia. Although modest in size, the
piece is a superb example of the work of its era.

Following this initial accession, the collection of American crafts grew
gradually. Most objects came through donations and were historic or
antique. During this time, the museum was a vigorous exhibitor of works
produced by members of the Society of Arts and Crafts, Boston (1897-
present), the most important organization of its type in the United States.
By World War I, the initial energy of the arts and crafts movement had
begun to wane as popular nationalistic fervor moved fashionable taste
towards revival of America's colonial arts. During the 1920s and 1930s,
the MFA was committed to collecting early American decorative arts and
only occasionally acquired contemporary pieces through donations. New
directions began to form in response to the new crafts movement
following World War II.

This passive phase of collecting contemporary crafts changed in 1970
with the founding of the Department of American Decorative Arts and
Sculpture. Staff members today believe that each decade of American
crafts should be richly represented at the MFA, showing the visitor that all
generations have produced works worthy of recognition. Since the
founding of the department, more than seventy-five examples of
contemporary crafted wooden objects have been acquired, including
turned and carved works and pieces of furniture. Under grants from the
National Endowment for the Arts matched by private corporations, many
of the latter were commissioned to be made, both for the permanent
collection and to offer public seating in the galleries. Enthusiastically
received, the program has acquainted thousands of visitors with works by
living craftspeople. Contemporary ceramics is another area of collecting in
which the MFA has obtained distinguished works. Since 1970, more than

100 examples of contemporary American ceramics have been acquired, largely through the generosity of patrons. Despite these efforts, a vast number of materials has yet to be collected at the MFA.

Art museums, like all public institutions, are looked upon in many different ways by the general public. Few visitors concern themselves with philosophic questions regarding the basis of crafts in fine art museums nor do they seem much concerned with aesthetic issues. More frequently the general visitor sees the art museum as an art form in itself — both a work of civic pride and a stage for temporal events. It provides a place to meet friends, dine, shop, and experience art as a part of social ritual.

The craftsperson may experience the art museum in this way but also sees collections from a different perspective. He may use objects as a standard against which to measure personal work; alternatively, the artist may view the museum as a facility for potential display. Dealers and collectors may similarly desire to use the museum to confirm their judgment and taste. A well-regulated institution provides checks and balances to prevent exploitation or commercial gain while offering reasonable expression to all. One of a curator's functions is to encourage patrons to collect works, which over time may be carefully studied and considered for donation. This is a slow process and one which complements the more active role of accessioning the work of recognized craftspersons either directly or through dealers. Conversely, a curator must also gather works of art which have fallen into undeserved obscurity. Such rescue work affirms undervalued work by living or dead artists. Like the attention given by environmentalists to endangered species, this effort usually brings little credit at the time to the curator.

Craftspeople, dealers, agents, and collectors sometimes look upon museums as a means to promote a particular artist's work. This is a sensitive area for curators. Without interest and help from dealers, collectors, and artists, few great collections would come into museums. While a curator may encourage artists or craftspersons in their work, ethically, he or she is not supposed to act as an agent or personal promoter. The purpose of museums is to reflect culture rather than form it. "Museumification" of contemporary work is a kind of transformation but it does not necessarily help mold a career for an artist.

Most of the older museums in America have limited display space, which requires rotating works of art from storage to public view. Such recycling may involve different generations of curators and innumerable loans to other institutions. Storage is not, however, a dead and useless entombment. Staff and researchers can critically examine and compare stored works in ways not possible when the same pieces are on public view. Storage also assists with preservation, since perpetual display subjects the art to physical deterioration while submitting visitors to visual boredom. New display involves the discovery of fresh relationships with other works of art. Allowing objects to regenerate their physical structure and visual impact through storage/display rotation is sound museum management.

Choice is a major ingredient of any artistic enterprise. Choices made

Pitcher, by Tiffany & Co., New York, 1876
Silver with copper, 8 x 4 x 2⅝
Museum of Fine Arts, Boston, Massachusetts

James Hampton with *The Throne of the Third Heaven of the Nations' Millennium General Assembly,* ca. 1950-64 in his garage
Photo courtesy of the National Museum of American Art, Smithsonian Institution, Washington, D.C.

James Hampton
The Throne of the Third Heaven of the Nations' Millennium General Assembly, ca. 1950-64
Gold and silver tinfoil over furniture
National Museum of American Art, Smithsonian Institution, Washington, D.C., Gift of Anonymous Donor

by an artist may differ from those of a curator, but both decisions are based on impulse generated by experience, intuition, and thought. Such parallel tracks sometimes converge and present problems. For example, when a curator is installing the works of several living artists he or she may disagree with the maker regarding a particular wall color or special placement. Craftspersons sometimes forget that museum display entails compromise based on the resources of the institution, space or shape of the gallery, proximity of other objects, and the constraints imposed by designers and administrations. Public display is not the same as display in a private gallery. Objects inevitably change in nature when they are absorbed into museum collections and exhibited in new contexts. Collectors and artists often prefer to see their pieces displayed together. This seldom makes art-historical sense.

Curators endeavor to present works in ways that explain their original intention. If a weathervane is fixed to a wall in a gallery of folk art, however, its original function is definitely changed. Instead of the viewer seeing the object at a great distance, moving in the wind and reflecting light, it is seen at close range where it takes on wholly different aesthetic values. James Hampton's elaborate *Throne,* made in a rented garage from discarded objects covered with gold and silver foil, takes on meanings quite different from its original religious intent when displayed in a museum setting.

Objects once used together in the domestic setting usually become dissociated and are displayed separately when they enter museum collections. Rarely do curators have the opportunity to reassemble historic artifacts into the period rooms which originally contained them. At the MFA, the Oak Hill rooms represent a recent effort to recreate rooms from the Derby/West House, about 1800.[3] Visitors confronted with refurbished period rooms seem to enjoy the experience but are generally unaware of the philosophical and practical problems (e.g., historical honesty and object security) that such rooms present. Despite this the period room or diorama method of display has become so pervasive that it has influenced a number of craftsmen/artists whose works depend on the built environment — the arrangement of many parts affecting the whole artistic statement. The conceptual issues addressed in contemporary environmental displays (e.g., the work of Duane Hanson and George Segal) parallel those of period rooms. While such groupings involve a variety of crafted materials, the separate parts are not as important as the overall effect the composition creates.

Ironically, art museums usually display objects as isolated scientific specimens dissociated from context; science museums, by contrast, display works of art according to use or meaning. It is amazing that in the field of large urban art museum management, relatively little important philosophical progress has been made in display concepts since 1904, when three methods of arrangement — technical, historical, and aesthetic — were described in a report to the trustees of the Museum of Fine Arts, Boston.[4] By contrast, there has been much subsequent change in the museum field. The Smithsonian Institution now has at least three major display areas concerned with crafts. The National Museum of American History exhibits American crafts thematically and didactically. The Cooper-Hewitt Museum deals with international decorative arts and design. The Renwick Gallery hosts loan exhibitions of contemporary crafts, while the American Craft Museum recently commemorated its thirtieth anniversary with the opening of new permanent galleries.

The popularity of early American arts in historic houses, villages, and decorative arts museums is also growing. Old Sturbridge Village, the Winterthur Museum, and Colonial Williamsburg are only three of the relatively new museum complexes which reveal the popularity of historic American arts and crafts. The collecting and study of early American art emerged from the arts and crafts revival of the late nineteenth century and from the search for a national identity following World War I. Scholars today who study the arts of colonial and federal America examine everyday life. They are concerned with the work of printmakers, carvers, goldsmiths, and potters, furniture makers, glassblowers, provincial sign painters, and makers of hatchments and portraits as well as many other

Parlor of Oak Hill (Danvers, Massachusetts, 1800), Museum of Fine Arts, Boston. Installed 1980.

Robert Arneson
Frontal, 1980 (left)
Gouache, acrylic, conte and mixed media on paper,
41½ x 29⅝
The Whitney Museum of American Art, New York, New York, Gift of Nancy M. O'Boyle in honor of Flora Miller Irving

Huddle, 1973 (right)
Terra cotta, slip glazes,
16¾ x 13½ x 13½
Collection of Ben Short,
New York, New York

Although Arneson's early career involved cartooning, his initial work in ceramics under the influence of Abstract Expressionism was not figural. With the Pop Art and funk movements of the 1960s, figural motifs emerged in his work.

crafts. The abundance of surviving works and their manifest robustness argue that early Americans enjoyed a rich artistic climate, despite the rhetoric adopted by early American artists John Singleton Copley, John Vanderlyn, John Trumbull and a relatively small number of others caught up in Renaissance notions about art. These prominent people complained profusely about the cultural desert and artistic backwardness they found in the United States. Copley's complaint to Benjamin West that "in this country . . . there are not examples of Art" indicates his perception of what constitutes art rather than the actual condition.[5] Copley's perspective introduces the idea of elevated art versus the so-called "mere crafts" — crafts that built America and produced spectacular crafted silver and other objects for domestic use.[6]

Most serious art critics and historians understand that the issue which separates fine arts from crafts is an illusion of nomenclature. Most craftspeople today have extensive artistic training through apprenticeship in a fine arts studio or through formal study of drawing, painting, sculpture, or design at college. Relationships between various works by master craftsmen are grounded in more than the material out of which they are made; basic design gestures unify their art forms. The preparatory drawings of Albert Paley are sensitive works of art in their own right; those of Sam Maloof, like his furniture, are solid, sculptural, bold, and surely formed. Drawings by Robert Arneson are integral partners with his ceramic sculpture. Stephen DeStaebler is a vigorous painter and draughtsman as well as a sculptor of bronze and ceramic objects.

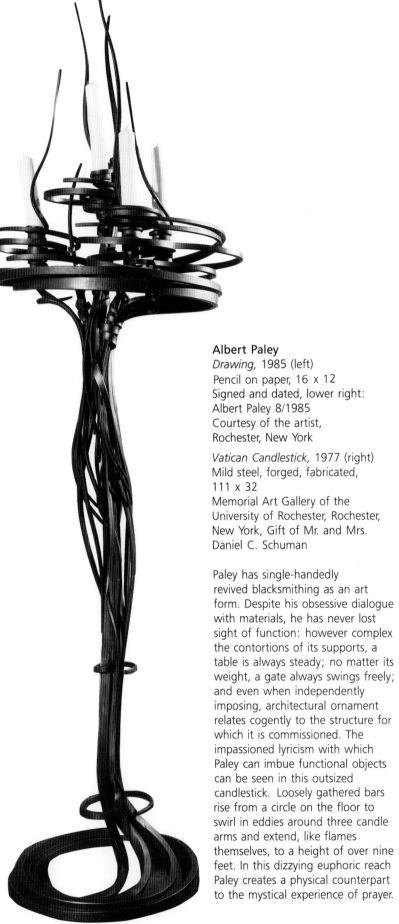

Albert Paley
Drawing, 1985 (left)
Pencil on paper, 16 x 12
Signed and dated, lower right:
Albert Paley 8/1985
Courtesy of the artist,
Rochester, New York

Vatican Candlestick, 1977 (right)
Mild steel, forged, fabricated,
111 x 32
Memorial Art Gallery of the
University of Rochester, Rochester,
New York, Gift of Mr. and Mrs.
Daniel C. Schuman

Paley has single-handedly revived blacksmithing as an art form. Despite his obsessive dialogue with materials, he has never lost sight of function: however complex the contortions of its supports, a table is always steady; no matter its weight, a gate always swings freely; and even when independently imposing, architectural ornament relates cogently to the structure for which it is commissioned. The impassioned lyricism with which Paley can imbue functional objects can be seen in this outsized candlestick. Loosely gathered bars rise from a circle on the floor to swirl in eddies around three candle arms and extend, like flames themselves, to a height of over nine feet. In this dizzying euphoric reach Paley creates a physical counterpart to the mystical experience of prayer.

Dale Chihuly
*Pink Sea Form Group with Gold
Braun Wraps,* 1984
Hand blown glass, 9½ x 21 x 18
Collection of the artist,
Seattle, Washington

The baskets that Chihuly first made
in 1977 at the Pilchuck Glass Center
in Washington of which he was cofounder are fragile vessels whose
distended glass membrane
suggests impending collapse. With
Robert Morris as his principal
glassblower since 1979, Chihuly has
developed his basket theme in a
completely different mode, moving
from delicacy to sheer bravura. In
Sea Forms, pastel hues and
groupings of shapes that allude to
shells, rippling water, and aquatic
flora create a tone of lyric transport.

Historical references and convergences are inevitable in contemporary crafts. Paley's curvilinear ironwork invites comparison to the sweeping lines of the late nineteenth-century Art Nouveau, as do the organic forms of Dale Chihuly's glass shells. Both artists reflect the taste of a generation that dramatically rejected the rectilinear designs popular in the 1930s and 1940s. Chihuly's work also recalls the artist's interest in Navajo rugs, which he saw exhibited at the MFA in 1976. Inspired by these designs, Chihuly produced glass cylinders with complex imbedded patterns. This interest preceded the attention given to decorative surfaces and ornamentalism by craftspersons in the early eighties.

To explain the nature of culture, the curator must search for the movements or ideas that change the shape of art. Specialization tends to make curators advocates of particular movements, themes, materials, or styles. If connections rather than differences are explored, fundamental relationships between all the arts emerge. Museums with art from different cultures and eras provide the opportunity to establish these links. Use of an object implies action, and whether that action is strictly visual or requires touch is not important. New or old, a superb object cannot help but evoke memories and comparisons. These two issues — time and taste — are the intangibles which concern art museums and curators. In the commodity-filled world of twentieth-century America, eloquent objects are highly useful and often essential for those who are contemplative.

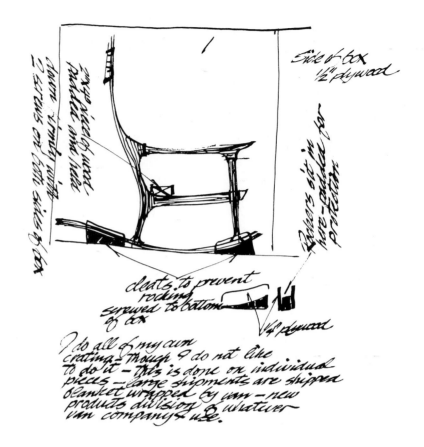

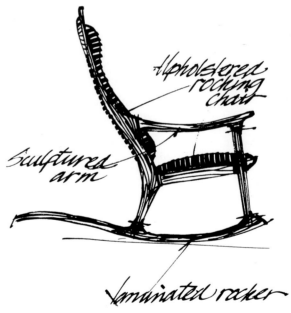

Sam Maloof
Drawing of Shipping Box, n.d.
Upholstered Rocking Chair, n.d.
Pencil on paper
Courtesy of the artist,
Alta Loma, California

NOTES

[1] See Léon Deshair, ed., *Exposition Internationale des Arts Décoratifs et Industriels Modernes* (Paris, France: Imprimerie nationale, Office central d'éditions et de librairie [1927?]).

[2] Ananda K. Coomaraswamy, *Christian and Oriental Philosophy of Art* (formerly titled *Why Exhibit Works of Art*) (New York: Dover Publications, Inc., 1956), p. 7.

[3] See Jonathan Fairbanks, "Recent Renovations to the Oak Hill Rooms at the Museum," and Wendy Kaplan, "The Reinstallation of the Oak Hill Rooms," *Bulletin* (Boston: Museum of Fine Arts, Boston), vol. 81 (1983), pp. 5-14, 46-59.

[4] Hans Dedekam and J. Folnesicz, "The Three Methods of Museum Arrangement: Technical, Historical, and Aesthetic," *Communications to the Trustees, II* (Boston: Museum of Fine Arts, Boston, 1904), pp. 49-53.

[5] Alan Gowans, *The Unchanging Arts: New Forms for the Traditional Functions of Art in Society* (New York: J. B. Lippincott Company, 1971), p. 43.

[6] Gowans, pp. 43-46.

THE IDEA OF CRAFTS

IN RECENT AMERICAN ART

MARY JANE JACOB

History's course in twentieth-century art, usually viewed as a sequence of movements and styles, has also been characterized by a series of shifts in the definition of high art, low art, and craft. Marcel Duchamp, a primary exponent of Dada early in the century, dramatically effected this discourse with his "ready-mades." His *Bottle Rack* of 1914 — a common piece of restaurant equipment in France which Duchamp designated as art solely by artistic fiat — set off a revolution. Duchamp in particular (and Modernism more generally) led to diverse explorations that deposed the choices of medium and technique from their standing as the defining criteria for what was looked at and judged as art.

Heir to Duchamp in the contemporary era were the Pop artists who in the mid-1950s used banal objects of everyday life to create deadpan, cheerful, ironical reflections of middle-class America. Reversing Duchamp's impulse, however, the Pop artists did not use actual found objects but created images of them — sometimes making them by hand, as did Claes Oldenburg, other times producing them as though commercially, as did Andy Warhol who had apprentices turn out his silkscreens in his studio workshop "The Factories." The objects of Pop Art were never functional but took their form and, on occasion, their materials and techniques from the vernacular.

By the late 1960s, artists were working with unprecedented freedom. They seized the power to decree what art could be, and art and the real world, to a remarkable degree unrestricted by traditions, came closer together. Pervasive experimentation — in lifestyles and in art — led to an explosion of new art forms: conceptual art; artists' books; earth art;

Lucas Samaras
Reconstruction #12, 1977
Sewn fabrics, 103 x 120
Collection of Whitney Museum of American Art. Gift of the Wilfred P. Cohen Foundation

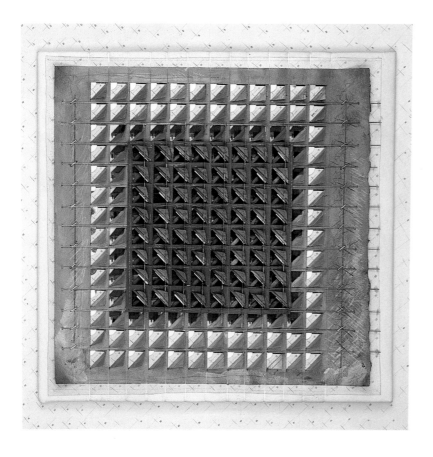

Jody Klein
Square on Square, 1983
Paper, fabric, paint, pencil, thread,
23 x 23 x 3
Museum of Fine Arts,
Boston, Massachusetts

In 1974 Klein began to develop a
system of making stitched quilts
composed of paper squares and
stamped with a variety of popular
images including stars, balloons,
cows, motorcycle riders, and dolls.
Accepted as a quilt maker, she
successfully entered many
exhibitions and collaborated with
seven other artists in a project
entitled "Object as Poet" displayed
at the Renwick Gallery of the
National Museum of American Art
(Smithsonian Institution,
Washington, D.C.) and the American
Craft Museum (New York). Later
she began to replace recognizable

imagery with rigorously geometric
grid pattern constructions such as
Square on Square. Cut-out and
folded triangles in each square of
this and similar works by Klein were
inspired by the simple act of turning
back the curtain of a window. Each
square is a miniature window
through which the viewer sees
various layers of shimmering
materials. As the viewer moves his
or her head these layers shift,
creating a sense of optical
disorientation reminiscent of the
effect given by eighteenth-century
American quillwork sconces,
especially those seen under the
flickering light of a candle.

installations and other defiantly ephemeral projects; and the temporally
organized arts of video and performance. In all this, artists' voracious
appetite for alternative media — conspicuously and necessarily including
media long associated with crafts — brought forth new hybrids. Thus the
arts of the 1980s have to a considerable degree absorbed the materials,
techniques, utilitarian forms, and decorative styles once associated only
with crafts.

Still other forces have also become powerful in today's art world.
Most important is the force of money. The boom in the art market that
began a quarter-century ago and gathered enormous momentum by the
end of the 1970s has inescapably affected artists working today. Private
buyers and collectors are once more asking for works they can enjoy and
show off, and artists have turned, or returned, to fabricating them. These
artists make their work available to as large an audience as they can reach
— but not in the programmatic populist way of the artists of the 1970s
who made conceptual pieces, installations, street art, performances, and
events. Instead they are making objects that people can buy. Yet this is not
the simple swing of the pendulum that it might seem, not exactly a
counter-revolution. Inescapably an art for the 1980s, a consumer's art, this
is nonetheless an art for the people. Many of the stylistic references for
the newest work are drawn from middle-class, popular culture — bearing
a sense of nostalgia that increases their accessibility. To restate the point:
where many of the most interesting artists of the late 1960s and 1970s
attempted to reach beyond the elite, creating an art of the streets in order
to further social or political aims, this work of the 1980s is a populism of
accessibility, a populism, as it were, of the shopping malls, made to serve
aesthetic interests but pragmatic ones as well. Using notions associated
with crafts, artists have been better able to make works that serve both
ends. This new direction exhibits itself perhaps most dramatically in the
proliferation of artists and galleries in the past few years in the East Village
of New York — which declared that money's back in style. But how do we
arrive at a new understanding of the relative position of art and craft
today? Issues of style, issues of function, questions of materials and
methods, questions of aesthetics and utility — these will yield only to
detailed examination of key figures, of the artists and their work.

In the late 1950s, H. C. Westermann, began to construct boxes,
houses, ships, and figural forms using the tools and materials of a master
woodworker. In these works, he told compassionately of his painful
observations on humanity. After military service in World War II,
Westermann went to art school on the G. I. Bill. At the same time, he
worked as a carpenter. He came to use the skills he learned as a
tradesman to make artistic statements. Drawing directly from his wartime
experiences, Westermann explored, throughout his career, themes of
senseless destruction and the individual's helplessness in the face of death.
For example, in a series of works based on the house — a form both
archetypal and closely identified with the carpenter — he spoke of human
relationships. His *Mad House* of 1958, looks like a carnival fun house; but
its decorative style is deceptive, for the amusing forms tell of threatening

experiences as the protective shell of the building is transformed into a house of horrors. (Westermann built *Mad House* at the time of his divorce.) Essential to all Westermann's pieces is the evidence of handwork — and its refined precision. His materials, most often wood, and his technique, which conveys a sense of perfection reached through great skill and meticulous labor, add fathomless depth of meaning to his subjects.

Work of a notably decorative style has long been dismissed as "low art" because decoration was considered to be conceptually shallow, a matter of beautifying utilitarian objects or architecture, and incapable of dealing significantly with ideas. Several artists in the 1970s set out to prove that decoration is aesthetically strong, and some used it to address issues in contemporary society. The Pattern and Decoration painting style was begun around 1975 by artists who took the motifs of past decorative arts and architecture and recycled them, applying them to the painted canvas. They acknowledged historical sources in mainstream art, most importantly Matisse, as well as Oriental influences, particularly Eastern folk and decorative arts. A leader of the movement who still works vigorously in this manner is Robert Kushner, for whom the use of decoration is a way to reinfuse imagery into the bland aesthetic he feels was created by Minimalism. Kushner was previously doing performances, for which he made costumes; then, studying Near Eastern color and design motifs, he turned to painting. His works were made rich through an additive process, with colors and patterns juxtaposed to approximate the opulence of the Near East. The Pattern and Decoration artists also adopted the utilitarian forms of traditional decorative arts. Kushner made kimono-shaped paintings, Kim MacConnel refurbished furniture by covering it with cloth he painted, Cynthia Carson decorated wall surfaces, Ned Smyth made fountains, and Joyce Kozloff executed wall tiles for public projects. Such works — such artists — seized upon the decorative from the province of crafts and proclaimed it to be art as well.

Lucas Samaras uses decorative materials and patterns for their emotional potency. His obsessive technique and his overflowing abundance of materials first appeared in the 1960s, in the form of boxes bursting with accumulated pins, yarns, dinnerware, and other vernacular objects he combined into intricate patterns with an indisputably decorative quality. They were distinctly threatening, however, thus alienated from our usual comfortable associations with such objects and with the decorative generally. Samaras continued this manner of working in his *Reconstructions,* sewn fabric collages from the mid-1970s. He began this series at about the same time that Pattern and Decoration art emerged, and though Samaras had no direct connection with that school, his works have been linked to it critically and in exhibitions. With the *Reconstructions* Samaras broke formal boundaries: cloth was his material, sewing his technical means, decoration the style. Yet, like all of Samaras's art, they also carry with them autobiographical associations — in this case, with the women in his family who sewed, and with his father who was a furrier. And so here, as throughout his career, Samaras has sought out materials and methods from which he can create emblems that connote a

H.C. Westermann
Mad House, 1958
Glass, metal, enamel, wood,
39½ x 17½ x 29
Museum of Contemporary Art,
Chicago, Illinois, Gift of Joseph and
Jory Shapiro

ritual intensification of being.

Miriam Schapiro, an early proponent of the feminist movement in art, has also used decoration to invest her art with symbolic and metaphoric meaning. Dissatisfied with the expressive limitations of painting, she turned in 1972 to incorporating handicraft objects made and decorated by women — handkerchiefs, aprons, doilies, napkins, tablecloths, quilts — into collages which she termed "femmage." Appropriating these everyday objects as her medium was important in creating art about women's lives. She told an interviewer in 1980: "I choose to use fabric in the decorative arts as tangible symbols for my connection to domesticity and to express my belief that art resides in domesticity. For me, the fabric of my art and the fabric of my life neatly equate each other."[1] In her art, Schapiro monumentalizes these small, intimate items; she glorifies the anonymous women who were the makers; she brings their decorative patterns

Joyce Kozloff
Vestibule, Wilmington, Delaware, 1984,
Glazed ceramic tile,
360 x 240 x 180
Architects: Skidmore, Owings & Merrill, Restoration of Frank Furness 1908 Building
Courtesy of Joyce Pomery Schwartz, New York, New York

H.C. Westermann
Defoliated, 1967
Wood, swamp alder, string, mirror,
59 x 39½ x 11¾
Collection of Mrs. E.A. Bergman, Chicago, Illinois

Westermann's very personal brand of art springs from his service in Korea during World War II and his subsequent employment as a handyman/carpenter while studying fine art. His themes — senseless destruction, human mortality, and the irony of life — are expressed through the craftsmanship of an expert woodworker whose durable, solid, and built-right objects become metaphors for the ethical rightness of the values they incorporate. *Defoliated,* made during the period of protest against American involvement in the Vietnam War, embodies the dualism of ironic humor and profound social commentary characteristic of Westermann's art. In it a wooden tree house is set amid branches that are stripped bare of foliage, as if by the chemical defoliants of war.

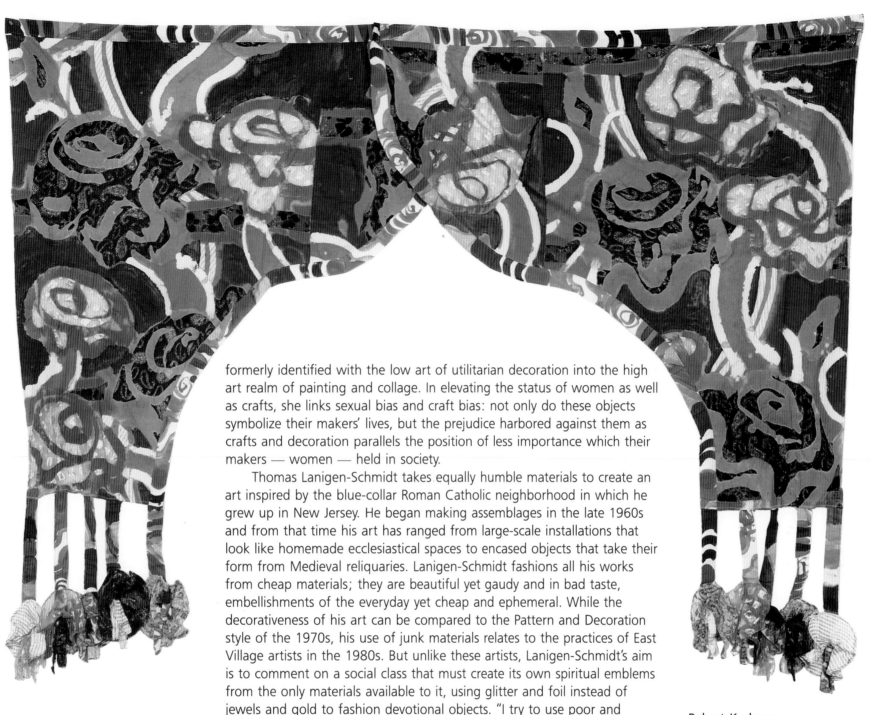

formerly identified with the low art of utilitarian decoration into the high art realm of painting and collage. In elevating the status of women as well as crafts, she links sexual bias and craft bias: not only do these objects symbolize their makers' lives, but the prejudice harbored against them as crafts and decoration parallels the position of less importance which their makers — women — held in society.

Thomas Lanigen-Schmidt takes equally humble materials to create an art inspired by the blue-collar Roman Catholic neighborhood in which he grew up in New Jersey. He began making assemblages in the late 1960s and from that time his art has ranged from large-scale installations that look like homemade ecclesiastical spaces to encased objects that take their form from Medieval reliquaries. Lanigen-Schmidt fashions all his works from cheap materials; they are beautiful yet gaudy and in bad taste, embellishments of the everyday yet cheap and ephemeral. While the decorativeness of his art can be compared to the Pattern and Decoration style of the 1970s, his use of junk materials relates to the practices of East Village artists in the 1980s. But unlike these artists, Lanigen-Schmidt's aim is to comment on a social class that must create its own spiritual emblems from the only materials available to it, using glitter and foil instead of jewels and gold to fashion devotional objects. "I try to use poor and inexpensive materials, aluminum foils, plastic wraps, cellophane tape, staples, and felt-tip markers. With these materials, 'knick-knacks' are constructed and used as metaphors to dramatize the clash in value systems among the different social classes," Lanigen-Schmidt said in 1983. "To survive, those on the bottom must transform these materials into one art form or another to express self-worth in the society that considers them almost worthless."[2] Inspired by this vernacular, homecrafted tradition, Lanigen-Schmidt's installations, icons, and reliquaries reflect the simultaneous profundity and tackiness of this struggling class that endeavors through its objects to maintain hope.

Robert Kushner
Rose Gate, 1980
Acrylic on mixed fabric, 89 x 111
Courtesy of Holly Solomon Gallery,
New York, New York

Miriam Schapiro
Mexican Memory, 1981
Acrylic and fabric on canvas,
48 x 96
Collection of Lynn and Jeffrey
Slutsky, Ellenville, New York

Lucas Samaras
Book, 1968
Wood, paper, paint, collage,
10 x 10 x 2
Collection of George M. Irwin,
Quincy, Illinois

In adopting the functional form of crafts to shape art, several artists have turned to making furniture, sometimes endowing these art objects with a practical purpose as well; one of the earliest is Richard Artschwager, who since the early 1960s had made furniture objects for aesthetic and not practical purposes. His methods, materials, and subject — that is, furniture — reveal an indebtedness to crafts. Painstakingly fabricating these sculptures, Artschwager developed his work out of both his occupation as a furniture maker and his study of art. *Portrait II* of 1964, for example, appears virtually identical to a real chest of drawers. Artschwager reminds us, however, that it is a sculpture made in the image of a piece of furniture by rendering the object functionless in any conventional, practical sense. The drawers do not open. The mirror, where one's image would normally appear, is not glass but white Formica — preventing the beholders, in spite of the title, from seeing their own portraits. The spatial ambiguity of the work's design allows it to be read both two- and three-dimensionally as it shifts between painterly illusion and sculptural presence. The material Artschwager uses enhances his illusions. The "wood" is not wood but wood-grained Formica — a photographic image of wood, not reality but its representation. Artschwager also contructs illusion into these objects. Flawlessly fabricated

Samaras has always worked with the stuff of everyday life to create his art and yet his works have both a decorative and a threatening side. These qualities appear in *Book.* At first it seems to be a fanciful children's book. It is made of fat thick squares of cardboard like books for young children, the ten pages of ten-inch squares pierced by whimsically shaped cutouts. The pages are all highly decorated with dots that grow larger and paler as they progress through the book, and there are many flaps to unfold and parts to otherwise manipulate in order to make secret compartments accessible for viewing. Yet the stories told in small print in these hidden areas are of erotic fantasies and perversions.

Richard Artschwager
Portrait II, 1964
Formica on wood base,
68⅝ x 26⅜ x 12¾
Courtesy of Leo Castelli Gallery,
New York, New York

of industrial materials, appearing surely to be factory productions, they are actually handmade by the artist; seemingly reproducible, they remain unique.

Vito Acconci brings into question the societal and sexual structures of our culture. During the 1970s, he worked in autobiographical performance art, a movement of which he was a leader. Toward the end of the decade, he turned to the making of furniture. The arms, legs, and overall shape of the furniture form have an animate quality, a necessary human reference, that Acconci exploits in a manner not unlike his former use of the human body. Replacing the artist-performer with the viewer-participant, he creates sculptural furniture that, while nonfunctional in a conventional sense, is participatory and can be sat on or otherwise occupied. Acconci views furniture as a container for people; it shapes and restricts our movement, regulating how we interact, while also maintaining certain artificial social relationships. *Stretched Facade,* of 1984, is a facelike structure incorporating seating units. These individual nooks, resembling an eye, nose, and mouth, offer places of rest, comfort, and security, but also separate the occupants, barring conversation and social contact. This work simultaneously protects, fostering a sense of privacy, and isolates, creating a feeling of confinement. The following year Acconci made an experimental mazelike configuration of glass tables and seats on a glass floor. It was originally conceived for the visually impaired, but can also be used by the sighted. Made completely of glass, *Maze Table* is captivatingly brilliant and beautiful, hospitable and inviting, yet also threatening because of the narrow space between elements and the potential danger of physical injury that its fragile material implies. The confined movement and disorienting distortion of space causes the sighted, as well as the blind, to feel their way along. The cold orderliness of the forms is also, to Acconci, a metaphor for the precision of computer technology and, in the state of uneasiness produced by this piece, Acconci wants us to ask, "How am I victimized by these things?"[3]

Many artists since the late 1970s have ventured into the field of furniture. Rather than using it symbolically or metaphorically like Artschwager or Acconci, they have adopted the form of furniture, as well as its practical function, and have linked their art further to crafts or the decorative arts. Artists working in this way today do so in a variety of styles.

Some Minimal artists have recently turned the purity of the simple, geometric forms they developed for their art in the 1960s to useful ends. For some it is an adjunct activity; for others, furniture and furnishings have become their primary focus. A leading figure of Minimalism has been the sculptor and theoretician Donald Judd, whose multiple boxlike forms of the sixties have strongly directed the movement. Judd first made functional works in 1978, when he conceived of "site-specific furniture" in order to give a consistent aesthetic look to the interior of his home and studio in Marfa, Texas. Whereas previously he hired workmen to fabricate his industrial steel box sculptures, here he employed craftsmen Jim Cooper and Ichiro Kato to give to his ideas the precision of form and skillful sense

Sol Lewitt
Dinnerware, 1984
Designed by Sol Lewitt in 1984,
handpainted by Sandro
Weschini in Deruta, Italy
Courtesy of the artist and Rhona
Hoffman Gallery, Chicago, Illinois

of perfection that had characterized his sleek sculptures. Since 1982 Judd has made limited editions of chairs, benches, stools/tables, desks, and bookshelves available in choices of woods. Sol Lewitt has adapted his open gridlike cube sculptures and systematized design formulas most often used to produce wall drawings to the service of functional objects. His glass-topped coffee table sits atop a gridded, open, white structure which closely resembles his sculptures. His serial method of using shape, color, and/or line has also been applied to a set of glazed ceramic dinnerware. Combining and rearranging several shapes and colors, LeWitt produced a wide range of interrelated pieces and had each design variant fabricated in an edition of 500. Larry Bell, known best for glass cubes of the 1960s, has also crossed into the realm of crafts by designing furniture. A set of table and chairs by the artist was based on an ellipse, a shape inspired by a 1930s-style second-hand chair he had purchased. Complementing these forms, he created elliptical arcs, plate-glass corner lamps, putting all these works together into an ensemble-cum-art installation in 1981.

Scott Burton is perhaps the most important artist emerging in the 1970s to use furniture forms, sometimes functional, sometimes not. Burton came to the use of the crafts or vernacular idiom of furniture early in the decade when he made photographs of actual furniture installed outdoors in roomlike settings. From 1972 to 1980 he created sculpture-theater works, which he called *Behavior Tableaux* in which furniture stood in for people. Here furniture forms carried psychological as well as formal

Donald Judd
Two Library Chairs and One Library Stool/Table, 1984
Brown elm with oil finish,
15¾ x 15¾ x 17¾ (stool/table)
15¾ x 15¾ x 29½ (chairs)
Courtesy of the artist and Rhona
Hoffman Gallery, Chicago, Illinois

Vito Acconci
Maze Table, 1985
Glass, 162 x 162 x 30
Courtesy of Joyce Pomeroy
Schwartz, New York, New York

Scott Burton
Equitable Center Atrium, New York,
New York, 1984-86 (right)
Marble, granite, onyx, bronze and
plantings
Courtesy of Max Protetch Gallery,
New York, New York

Rock Chair, 1980-1982 (below)
Gneiss, 40 x 40 x 48
Collection of Eileen Rosenau, Bryn
Mawr, Pennsylvania
Courtesy of Max Protetch Gallery,
New York, New York

meaning: their relationships served as investigations of behavorial patterns
and their various stylistic motifs signified different cultural backgrounds
and values that told, as Burton noted, a kind of "social history." By 1975,
Burton began to make his own furniture in order to explore a wider range
of materials and identifying styles — from high-tech plastic to natural cut
boulders. Today Burton's work exists as objects that are simultaneously
sculptural and functional. Taking on commissions for spaces of public use,
he finds the aesthetic and practical ends of his work to be complementary,
especially in making his art more accessible to a greater number of
people. He sees these works as capable of carrying the social aim with
which he hopes to invest his art: "I feel the world is now in such shape
that the individual liberty of the artist is a pretty trivial area. Communal
and social values are now more important. What office workers do in their
lunch hour is more important than my pushing the limits of my self-
expression."[4] To achieve this, an idiom from the vernacular, an object
common to everyone's life, a work with which the viewer can interact —
furniture — is to Burton the most significant form to bring his art and
ideas to his audience.

Recently the production of furniture by artists has so increased that
one might say there has been an art furniture movement, bringing onto
the scene unique pieces or limited editions by artists, designers, and
architects. Profiting from the thriving art market of this decade, art
furniture has become identified with its maker, like the products associated
with the current designer craze, a phenomenon observed by the *Wall
Street Journal*: "At its most simplistic level, art furniture is a limited-edition
functional object designed by a well-known painter, sculptor, architect, or
craftsperson — the aesthetic equivalent, say, of bedspreads by Ralph

Alphonse Mattia
Hors d'Oeuvre Table, 1985
Ebonized walnut, dyed sycamore,
paint, 68 x 22 x 18
The Saxe Collection,
Menlo Park, California

Mattia is one of a number of artists
today who have turned to furniture
as an art form. In addition to his
more conventional-looking pieces,
he also makes works which take
their shape from functional furniture
objects, but serve aesthetic
purposes, such as the recent tables
and valets. These are made of
various woods which Mattia carves
and paints, and each is endowed
with an individualized, fantastic
head and animated legs.

R. M. Fischer
Front: *Scribe,* 1985 Mixed media
Back: *Age of Triumph,* 1985
Mixed media
Courtesy of Daniel Weinberg Gallery,
Los Angeles, California

Lauren or towels by Perry Ellis."[5] Among the work being produced in this field today, one major stylistic trend is based on the 1950s design and that period's vision of the future. The style adopts the new industrial plastics, Formica, and other materials developed in the 1950s and the corresponding design aesthetics of curved, biomorphic shapes evoking Scandinavian design and Sputniklike orbs; the fantasy and sense of the incredible of science fiction; and the zaniness and humor of television's futuristic cartoons, notably "The Jetsons." By and large, the artists making this furniture and furnishings were born during the 1950s and early 1960s, and so draw directly from childhood nostalgia and the banal, popular culture they experienced. They evoke the past through a post-modern recycling of images.

A leader in this revival style is R. M. Fischer, a New York sculptor who makes lamps. In 1980, while employed as an artist by the city, Fischer began working in a functional way, making fountains and birdbaths for a park on Staten Island. Lamps, however, became his signature works — bizarre hybrids of diverse materials, industrial components or pieces of decades-old home appliances, combined into single structures — sculptures that are also sources of light. The parts from which Fischer constructs his lamps originated in an earlier, more hopeful era of middle-class prosperity. He told an interviewer in 1985, "The lights have this kind of optimistic emphasis; I'm trying to replace that in many cases now with just the thrust of the finial, to create some kind of futuristic, gothic, celebratory or religious thing."[6] Fischer formally describes his work as "abstract objects in a representational mode;"[7] he uses lighting to make his sculptural abstractions accessible to a broader public. Fischer also

Tommy Simpson
Rabbit Chairs, n.d. (facing page)
Wood, painted, 10½ x 7
One chair, Collection of Ruth and
John Raible, Hastings-on-Hudson,
New York; the other,
Collection of the artist, Washington,
Connecticut

Is it painting? Is is furniture? Is it
sculpture? Simpson first introduced
his colorful furniture in the mid-
sixties when other furniture makers
were still concerned with function
and the beauty of natural materials.
His chairs eschewed the orthodox.
These were new statements for
furniture as sculpture — they are
useful and not useful, real and
unreal, familiar and unfamiliar,
humorous and serious.

makes his art more accessible by breaking through the established world
of studio and gallery and showing his work in effective commercial
venues. In 1979, with a friend in the advertising business, Fischer set up a
firm called Ronell Productions to distribute and market his work beyond
the gallery system. His first shows were held at Artists Space, Art et
Industrie, (a fashionable gallery-store in New York's SoHo) and Fiorucci. In
sum, concerned with the functional and the aesthetic, Fischer makes
objects that are art and that sell.[8]

Furnishings have been both subject and medium since about 1983 to
a new group of young artists — who are associated not so much with a
school or a movement as with a location. In the early 1980s, a number of
new galleries opened in what had been one of the more unpleasantly
bedraggled and bedrugged districts of central Manhattan, the eastern
fringe of Greenwich Village around St. Mark's Place. These new galleries
were primed by and promoted the work of certain young, enthusiastic,
and soon-to-be-known artists. Money was resurgent in the art world —
or, more precisely, now it was okay to acknowledge that money had never
really been absent — and these artists made an art that could be bought.
The work was decorative, useful, available, relatively low in price —
attractive to a new generation of collectors eager to move up. To be sure,

Rhonda Zwillinger
*Give Me Liberty or Give Me
Romance,* 1983
Mixed media,
Installation View — Gracie Mansion
Gallery, November, 1983
Courtesy Gracie Mansion Gallery,
New York, New York

Rodney Alan Greenblat
Tiki Chair, 1985
Painted wood, 40 x 35 x 25
Private Collection, Courtesy of Rosa
Esman Gallery, New York, New York

Kenny Scharf
Van Chrome Television, 1981-83
Customized Sony Trinatron
television, acrylic and found
objects, 10 inch screen
Private Collection, California
Courtesy of Tony Shafrazi Gallery,
New York, New York

hardly ten years earlier the artists of the Pattern and Decoration movement had supplied a precedent, conceptually as well as stylistically, when from time to time they designed practical and even commercial items. But they proclaimed that decoration was itself content. The East Village group took a leap farther and put aside notions of content, making pleasure their purpose. In 1981, the first gallery to open in the East Village called itself Fun, and its name was its aim. Arch Connelly, one of the artists emerging at that instant, said, "I want my work to be the most beautiful thing I can create at the moment I do it, using all the things I have. My work is purged of ideas."[9] Taking furniture, Connelly paints colorful, floral motifs and encrusts the forms and designs with fake jewels and beads to further decorate them. Others who worked similarly and began showing around this time included Rodney Alan Greenblat and Rhonda Zwillinger. Whether unique or existing in multiple, the works' style and execution of decoration render them unquestionably handmade.

Kenny Scharf and Keith Haring, also associated with the East Village galleries, hold a position somewhere between populist and popular. Scharf

is a native of the Los Angeles area; influenced by the vernacular tradition of customizing cars in California, he customizes manufactured objects, such as televisions, by adding other objects and decoration to them. Scharf has also executed entire decorative ensembles, of considerable if transient substance. In one of the most visited of these, *Closet Symbol #7*, created for the Whitney Biennial of 1985, he painted a corridor and restrooms in riotous patterns and Dayglo colors, transforming all objects in his path — telephones, coat racks, water fountains, doors and door handles, sinks, basins, and toilets, and then illuminated them with ultraviolet light, so that they glowed, creating an installation of the eighties with the nostalgic feel of student rooms and hippie pads of the sixties. Scharf has not had trouble finding commissions: he held his first New York exhibition at Fiorucci, a fashionable boutique on the upper East Side, and more recently decorated a nightclub, the Paladium, somewhat farther downtown. He now aspires to work in the entertainment field. Of his aims he told an interviewer recently, "I like to have fun. I think everyone wants to have fun. I think that having fun is being happy. I know it's not all fun, but maybe fun helps with the bad. I mean, you definitely cannot have too much fun. Okay, it's like I want to have fun when I'm painting. And I want people to have fun looking at the paintings."[10]

Keith Haring, native to New York and influenced by its indigenous graffiti, seeks to bring his art not only to galleries and museums but also to people in subways, in the street, and on school playgrounds. Making art for general consumption is for him an important corollary to painting pictures for the elite. Haring asserts that his public projects and affordable art can "break down this supposed barrier between low and high art."[11] One way to achieve this is through his store, The Pop Shop. Located in SoHo, it is filled with T-shirts, knickknacks and other things by Haring and other artists. To Haring, The Pop Shop demonstrates that art can have a practical or decorative function, taking notions formerly only associated with craft and assigning them to art. "Hopefully what I'm doing," Haring told an interviewer recently, "is forcing all those definitions of art to be reconsidered, forcing people to have to sort them out. . . . By being in a museum and in a subway at the same time, to me the best thing about it is that it strips all the myths away from what gives value to art objects."[12]

Perhaps art has gone too far. Perhaps it has crossed the line, moved out of the realm of art, first adopting notions of crafts, and finally moving into commercial design ventures. The blurring of art/craft distinctions today was predicted by Robert Morris when speaking of current art in 1981 he noted, "Refusing to leave its functionalism at the door of the gallery, such work occupies two places at once and the distinction between fine and applied art gets further breached. The last few years have also seen a great deal of work which does not raise the issues of category so much as it draws on the decorative as thematic material for painting, sculpture and installation work. Upbeat with a vengeance and seriously mindless, such work is now pervasive enough to threaten us with what might be termed a new 'boutique' style."[13] Kim Levin, in a 1985 review of the paintings and decorated objects of the East Village, termed

Keith Haring
Swatch Watch Advertisement, 1985
Limited edition of Swatch Watches
designed by Haring
Courtesy Swatch Watch U.S.A.,
New York, New York

Fumio Yoshimura
Bicycle with Parking Meter, 1978
Lindenwood, 68 x 53½ x 16½
The Albuquerque Museum,
Albuquerque, New Mexico, Gift of
Frederick Weisman Company

Yoshimura sometimes draws for
three or four months before starting
to work with wood. His
understanding of the forms he
sculpts develops from studying and
using the forms, but Yoshimura
believes the finished sculpture is
quite different from the "real" thing.
Yoshimura does not work in metal
or stone, preferring the
biodegradability and fragility of
wood, whose innate properties —
grain, texture, color — he uses to
emphasize the geometric abstraction
of form.

this new direction "the Aesthetic of Cute" — a style which uncritically
finds its imagery in novelty items accessible to the masses.[14]

As we look at art today, we see that the long dialogue with craft has
shifted. Once we had hoped that crafts — through the assimilation of clay,
fiber, glass, and so on — could influence the media of art; but craft has
contributed in another direction, by giving to art the craftsman's precision,
decorative styles, and practical function or functional form. Notions —
utility or decoration — once associated with crafts and considered the
drawbacks which relegated crafts to a position of low art have now been
taken over by art. Yet today, even though utility and decoration are part of
art and the art object and craft object may be ostensibly the same, the
former earns its status by being proclaimed art by its creator, the artist:
the law of Duchamp is still operative. In other words, works of equal
stature may not earn the title of art if the maker by training or association
is identified with the crafts rather than with the art world. There is not the
same "artistic" license; a prejudice against crafts endures, even while art
has come closer to crafts through an active exchange of ideas. In our
campaign to earn the status of artist for those who have excelled in their
use of crafts materials, we have but to look at the changes in
contemporary art to see that the former criteria for defining art and craft
are no longer applicable, and to acknowledge the indebtedness of today's
art to the ideas of crafts.

NOTES

[1] Ruth A. Appelhof and Miriam Schapiro, "Interview," in Thalia Gouma-Peterson, *Miriam Schapiro: A Retrospective, 1953-1980,* exhibition catalogue (Wooster, Ohio: The College of Wooster, 1980), p. 48.

[2] Martin James Boyce, "Thomas Lanigen-Schmidt: Joy of Life, Predestinationism and Class-Clash Realism," *Flash Art* 114 (November 1983): 60.

[3] Andrea Miller-Keller, *Vito Acconci/MATRIX 87,* exhibition brochure (Hartford, Connecticut: Wadsworth Atheneum, 1985), p. 2.

[4] Douglas C. McGill, "Sculpture Goes Public," *The New York Times Magazine,* 27 April 1986, p. 67.

[5] Barbara Jepson, "Art Furniture: 'Sculpture That Invites Use,'" *Wall Street Journal,* 12 January 1986.

[6] Wade Saunders, "Talking Objects: Interviews with Ten Sculptors," *Art in America* 73, no. 11 (November 1985): 115.

[7] Nancy Princenthal, "Art with Designs on the Public Domain," *Industrial Design* 31, no. 2 (March-April 1984): 49.

[8] For additional exemplars of this direction, see *Future Furniture*, exhibition catalogue (Newport Beach, California: Newport Harbor Art Museum, 1985). Among those expressing a sense of optimism like Fischer's in their work is Harry Anderson, who also makes lights. Anderson says, "I salvage the past for the sake of the future . . . the lamps I construct draw on the idealism of the past while anticipating a new humanism of the future" (p. 6). Similarly, Jim Isermann, who uses mass-produced items of 1960s design, views his work both as an exploitation of style and of a "lost optimism." By employing these discarded ideals, he feels he "points the way to a brighter tomorrow." (p. 22).

[9] Arch Connelly in *New York/New Work: Glittering Art,* exhibition catalogue (Miami: Barcardi Art Gallery, 1986), p. 8.

[10] Gerald Mazorati, "Kenny Scharf's Fun-House Big Bang," *Artnews* 84, no. 7 (September 1985): 77.

[11] Alan Jones, "Keith Haring: Art or Industry?," *NY Talk* (June 1986): 45.

[12] Jones, p. 45.

[13] Robert Morris, "American Quartet," *Art in America* 69, no. 10 (December 1981): 101.

[14] Kim Levin, "The Aesthetic of Cute," *Village Voice* 30, no. 7, 12 February 1985.

CRAFTS IS ART:

NOTES ON CRAFTS, ON ART, ON CRITICISM

JOHN PERREAULT

Jack Earl
Sy, Book of Psalms I, Zachariah Chapter 10, Verses 1 and 2, 1984 (two views)
Ceramic, oil, 39 x 21 x 31
Collection of Sy and Theo Portnoy, Scarsdale, New York

The upright shape of *Sy* is like a gravestone, or stela memorializing a great event or marking a boundary. Its monolithic quality contrasts to the animated realism of the portrait, which recalls the common family snapshot, and the spaciousness of the flat landscape. The combining of an evocative shape with a surface imagery rich in potential narrative meaning allows Earl to probe the viewer's own relationship with the land, understood not simply as landscape, but as "home." The biblical reference in the title makes clear that the soldier defends not just the territory, but home in this larger sense. The emphatic centrality of the single tree offers an allusion to the "rootedness" of the soldier.

Crafts should be approached with caution, for the terrain is full of pitfalls and booby traps. As a critic conversant with what might be called avant-garde art for the last twenty years or so and as a partisan of art that was perceived as at "the cutting edge," I now find myself at a slightly different edge, but one that is no less cutting.

Although I retain my passion for paint-on-canvas art and noncraft sculpture, these forms presently seem tired, uninspired, and strangely commercial. More challenging to me is the analysis and defense of ceramic art, fiber art, glass art, even metalwork and woodwork, *as art*. It is here that the art spirit is still in force, and not yet totally compromised.

The following sections — chunks, blocks — represent a continuous attempt, presented discontinuously, to grapple with crafts-generated issues. Although interrelated, these thoughts do not pretend to present a seamless argument. That they are contradictory, that they are unashamedly present tense, that they refrain from mentioning particular artists or craft objects is intentional. The use of the plural *crafts* with the singular verb *is* is likewise intentional and meant to call attention to the way in which we address such categories. We are working here at a level of abstraction scarce in crafts criticism. Logic is at the service of insight, as is taste.

We will gain no intellectual or aesthetic advance if we back away yet again from the confrontation just beneath the surface of the art/crafts interface or exchange; world-ordering philosophies are at stake. Thus severe anxiety — often expressed by wit — surfaces at every turning. To tamper with categories, even if the categories are painfully inadequate, is to tamper with power.

THE STATUS OF CRAFTS

Coming into a new consciousness about the time of Abstract Expressionism, continuing through Pop Art and Minimalism, persisting throughout the pluralist period, and now rising above the instant neo- and post-*x* "style" clusters (*x* equals anything in the history books) that clutter up the art world, a radical change has occurred: crafts is art. It is accurate to use the word *radical* to describe this development, for the crafts are probably the root of art, historically and spiritually. In the crafts the practical is magical. In some senses, the foundations for this remarkable shift were laid in the last century. But we are not talking about an Arts and Crafts revival (or even something as logical as a Bauhaus ideal). Since the 1950s there has been a seepage, an interchange, an interface between once mutually exclusive realms of art production, or, more fashionably, a series of appropriations — some achieved by stealth, some accomplished by bravado. Slowly but surely the dividing line between so-called fine art and crafts has become a dotted line.

Although insights can be gained by cataloguing instances of crossover — some of them irritating, some of them spectacular — what once could be seen as a dialectic between art and crafts has dissolved into the bewilderment that signals a change of paradigm. There is no need here to list examples of artists trained in painting and sculpture suddenly using crafts media or crafts artists quickly assimilating fine art strategies and styles. These were scouting actions or forays into the unknown territory ahead.

The time-tested categories have broken down. One way of understanding this is to proclaim that significant differences between fine art and crafts no longer exist. One could also adjust one's stance by deeming most visual production "art" and then creating a subcategory called "art in crafts media." Some have proposed "alternative media" as a new rubric for crafts. This has the virtue of eliminating the odious term *crafts*, but implies that these media — clay, glass, fiber, etc. — are inferior or secondary to the main business of art, which many still believe to be paint-on-canvas art and noncraft sculpture.

What I propose is something more flamboyant. It is not that crafts (as traditionally understood) and art (i.e., fine art) are blurred, are overlapping, have merged. These concepts represent an easy way out of the dilemma and fail to dramatize serious aesthetic issues. Everyone is relieved of responsibility; we are one big happy family. People working in clay, as well as those dabbing in oil on canvas, are all making Art, and the world is a better place for it. Go tell that to a painter.

Rudolf Staffel

Vessel, 1973 (below right)
Porcelain, handbuilt, 5¾ x 8½

Vase, 1972 (facing page)
Porcelain, handbuilt, 9⅝ x 6⅝
Collection of Dr. and Mrs. Perry
Ottenberg, Philadelphia,
Pennsylvania

Staffel studied with painter Hans Hofmann, whose push-and-pull theory of modern painting posits that visual tension results from the contrast between the illusion of infinite space and the recognition of an actual flat picture plane. As the critic Sid Sacs has observed, Staffel's thin porcelain vessels play the same trick. Their translucency, which functions like deep space, is contradicted by their surface decoration which brings the viewer back to the reality of the clay. Through his study of Zen Buddhist philosophy the artist has explored the idea of the harmony of opposites, here expressed in an asymmetrical thrown and handbuilt vessel form. Staffel became fascinated with translucency when he saw an exhibition of German blown glass in the early 1930s. His interest in ceramics evolved from painting during his studies with painters Jose Arpa and Hans Hofmann. Early in Staffel's development as an artist he said, "I always had the notion that I could be a painter and a potter or rather be a painter who was a potter or eventually be a potter who was a painter and then eventually be a potter." Staffel's interest in glass and his studies with Hofmann led to the creation of his porcelain "light gatherers." (Interview with the artist by Paula and Robert Winokur, "The Light of Rudolf Staffel," *Craft Horizons* [April 1977], p. 26).

Nor do I wish merely to propose that crafts and fine art have switched places. This in itself might be mind-boggling enough to be productive — productive of satire. Surely all the derogatory things said of the crafts, in part helping to define them as second-class pursuits, can now be said with more truth about paint-on-canvas art and noncraft sculpture. New art of the East Village sort prides itself on lack of originality and on quotation, repetition, appropriation. It is made to please a specific market; it is made to sell. It is usually portable, always "decorative" — that is, it can be placed over a sofa or on a coffee table — and it certainly eschews ideas.

Furthermore, productionware has long been the downfall of attempts to conceptualize craft-as-art, art-for-the-people idealism notwithstanding. But what about fine art productionware, those dreary photolithographs or even offset prints cranked out by the thousands to pad the coffers of both the dealers and the "artists" involved? By comparison, craft art is involved with sincerity of expression, originality, and formal values.

Judy Moonelis
The Man, 1984 (two views)
Earthenware, 21 x 25 x 14
Collection of Jane and Robert
Saltonstall, Jr.,
Concord, Massachusetts

The Man is a small example of Moonelis's work, which ranges as high as six feet. Despite its size, Moonelis favors this piece because of its combination of strength, simplicity, and sadness; intensity of emotional moods is an issue which preoccupies Moonelis. One side of *The Man* has a single face convex in form. The other side, formed by interconnecting transitions between head and other shapes, takes on altogether different personalities as three concave faces. Such contrasts and ambiguous form and imagery are characteristic of Moonelis, who has staked her aesthetic territory among "opposing elements and their subtle connections." (Judith Stein, "Judy Moonelis," *American Ceramics,* [Summer 1980]: 61.)

To summarize: 1) Crafts and fine art are one; it is only quality that makes a difference. There is no such thing as a good craft object, for a good craft object is an art object. 2) Crafts and fine art have switched places; it is paint-on-canvas art that is the middle-class mode, not pottery. It is "fine art" that is kitsch.

Some insights may be gained by adopting either of these views of our current predicament, but both delay a more difficult insight. Crafts — meaning art in crafts media, in other words, ceramics, glass art, fiber art, *et al.* — can now be caught in the act of *replacing* "fine art" in art media, that is, paint-on-canvas art and noncraft sculpture.

Of course, it all depends on one's priorities for art or what one expects or hopes art can accomplish (or at least stand for). Here I am a traditionalist. I expect art to address, express, and add to human experience through material or conceptual forms that embody the spirit. This can be done with love, with wit, and even with fury, but it cannot be done with both eyes on the cash register. Hemmed in by the distribution context and by the economics of living and working, artists must nevertheless follow their own lights. It is in the craft art area that I see these principles expressed, and less and less in the high-power, high-money art world *per se.* Craft art is replacing art; crafts is art, and perhaps no other art exists.

Ken Little
Red Bird, 1982
Leather, paint, shoes, mixed media,
76 x 53 x 16
Contemporary Arts Center,
Honolulu, Hawaii

Prior to 1981, Little used trophy
forms from the taxidermist. Now he
prefers to work with the image of
the animal in a way that is symbolic
and no longer associated with
trophies and their "big game
connotations." His interest in
sculpture began when he was a
graduate student working in clay;
he was inspired by the spontaneity
of the California approach and the
work of Peter Voulkos, John Mason,
Robert Arneson, Clayton Bailey, and
Ken Price and also by his association
with Rudy Autio at Missoula,
Montana. Works like *Red Bird* are
personal (symbolic) and they are
conscious (communicative). The deer
is lifesize and its form is embellished
with a coat of shoes: shoes that
suggest family footgear, adult men's
and women's shoes as if from a
mother and a father, and baby
shoes. The deer is in mid-leap, as if
across the headlights of an
oncoming car containing a family
who will see, swerve, and save the
life of the animal.

CRITICISMS

An examination of crafts criticism is not difficult. After stating that most of it is puffery, description, biography, or technical tips, little is left to say. But to proclaim that something is wrong with crafts criticism, and this has ever been the case, is not enough. In fact, something is wrong with criticism in general: it has not been thought through. I am referring to criticism of the visual arts.

Art criticism itself — where attempts have indeed been made to blend description, evaluation, and philosophy — is not in a very creative period. Here too what we have is puffery, description, biography, and *marketing* tips. Confined to the promotional mode by commercial interests, burdened by uninspired language conventions that are reinforced by mediocre editors, weighed down by sloppy thinking, and compromised by the rush to embrace the latest French ruffle, art criticism currently has little to offer as a model for evaluative writings about craft art.

Like the crafts criticism that it always prided itself on being above and beyond, art criticism has now excluded the negative. Criticism cannot be defined as negation, ordinary usage of the term notwithstanding.

L. Brent Kington
Air Machine #19, 1967
Cast sterling,
6½ x 12½ x 8
Collection of the artist,
Makanda, Illinois

The birth of his first child gave Kington a new direction for his silversmithing. Acknowledging a fascination with antique toys and miniature sculpture, he began creating new heirlooms for the next generation. The rattles and whistles gave way to pull toys, then push toys. While maintaining a whimsical quality, the machines and vehicles are sophisticated enough to attract adults as well. *Air Machine #19* combines the memories of childhood homemade go-carts with anthropormorphic birds.

Tony Hepburn
Chicago Analog, 1983
Clay, wood, slate, canvas, hydrocal,
96 x 60 x 36
Collection of the artist, Courtesy of
Ree Schonlau, Omaha, Nebraska

Hepburn came to Alfred University
to teach ceramics in 1975. Though
first influenced by English pottery
traditions (he was born in England),
he was deeply affected by the
Abstract Expressionism of Peter
Voulkos. *Chicago Analog* is a
combination of materials on a large
scale — clay sheets, wooden beams,
branches and fragments, slate slabs
and cast forms, with a backdrop of
painted canvas depicting aspects of
the multi-media constructions
themselves.

Nevertheless, positive reinforcement as a critical tactic be damned, criticism without the threat of negation is criticism without impact. The critic must smile, but carry a whip.

Criticism, of course, does not exist in a vacuum. Criticism is written (or spoken) by persons for other persons — or at least is so addressed — about the art production of other persons. Where criticism is published is another factor, for the print media involve still other persons: publishers, editors, copy editors, and, above all, advertisers. Money is involved, but before we assume venality and greed it should be known that most critics are paid a pittance for their labors. It is glory that oils the machine. Money in larger amounts does come into the picture, however. Criticism is exposure for the artist. Even an attack is of commercial value. Existence in print is historical existence and often it leads to the artist earning more money or some money, along with the larger amounts usually earned by dealers and collectors who have a stake in the art and the career.

Criticism, as now practiced, is largely composed of a series of hidden agendas, even when — particularly when? — the critic is trying to focus on specific objects. Sometimes the critic is not influenced by envy, unexamined prejudices, historical knowledge or its lack, a bad stomach (or an empty one), but there are always people involved, looking over the critic's shoulder. Criticisms, like artworks, are mainly social. This can be a debilitating truth, for it is impossible to parse all vectors of the social

Kreg Kallenberger
Titanic Series #268, 1986 (right)
Cast optical crystal, cut, polished,
6¾ x 17 x 4¼
Philbrook Museum of Art, Tulsa, Oklahoma, Museum Purchase with funds donated by: Telex Computer Products, Inc.; Mr. and Mrs. Donald R. Feagin; and Mr. and Mrs. David R. Guthery

Titanic Series #268 is a conjurer's tool for focusing perception. The references made to the great ship disaster seem less important than the lens-like ability of the piece to allow perception of another dimension. Comparison might be made to the act of peering into a crystal ball and observing real time and space, distorted, inverted, and extended infinitely. Eyes and mind are confronted by the seen and unseen, the bound and unbound, led into crystalline spaces which exist only in the mind's eye. One is allowed to float in, not on, this fathomless visual sea, catching fleeting glimpses of reality as it floats by on the outside.

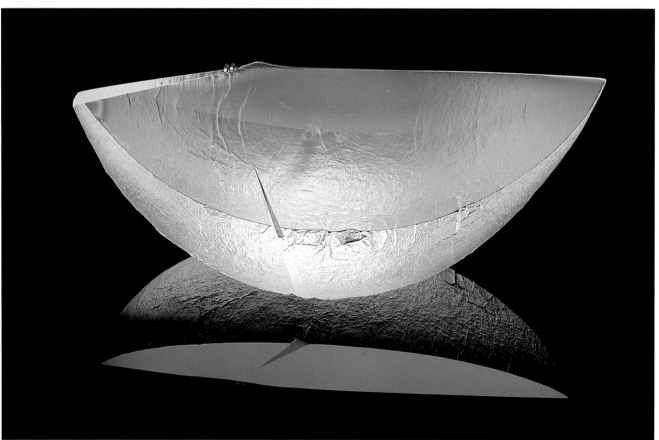

dynamic. If criticism in its highest form has something to do with analyzing, discovering, and creating values, then what we are really dealing with is a triangulation: aesthetic value, economic value, and social value interact.

Perhaps if art criticism itself were not in such a bad state, it would be easier to claim that crafts criticism need not differ significantly. Values and methodology should be the same. Crafts criticism is merely art criticism applied to craft objects. Surely both kinds of writing share the difficulties presented by language. Language is linear; art or craft objects are not.

Writing about craft art, however, is more difficult than writing about paint-on-canvas or noncraft sculpture. Beyond what can be adapted from established critical vocabularies, the proper discourse for crafts criticism is still being formed. We are dealing with uncharted areas of visual production, usually confined to the cataloguing mode of the decorative arts template or to oral culture. We must also factor in the understanding that crafts objects present experiences that more effectively balance, play with, or set in contradiction optic and haptic forms of perception than either paint-on-canvas art or noncraft sculpture.

In the meantime, there is the enormous task of straightening things out, for confusion reigns. What we call crafts now is different from what used to be called crafts. Craftspeople as well as outsiders are confused, causing enormous difficulties for all concerned. Many who find crafts anathema have never really looked at craft art with open eyes and are in reality thinking of the horrors perpetuated by well-meaning high school teachers and handmade-ashtray vendors.

What we call crafts now in the United States are artworks, or, if one prefers, art propositions made with some reference to nearly extinct, preindustrial craft traditions, even if only by virtue of the materials, forms, and techniques employed. Most of these artworks are not made by humble, untutored folk, but by people who have studied their métier in universities and art schools, having taken studio classes in ceramics, fiber art, glass art, papermaking, metalsmithing, *et al.* That they have had to set themselves upon an academic track to learn their craft is telling.

Ideally craftworks, like all artworks, are made to express the unexpressible or to discover new forms and new thoughts. Craftworks factor into the aesthetic mix particular material and technical traditions along with function and/or decoration. On the practical level, however, craftworks, unlike artworks, are earmarked for several market contexts. First is the populist marketplace of studio sales, craft fairs, and craft shops; this area, with luck, offers some artisans a chance at making a living. Second is the craft gallery network, featuring unique items, higher prices, and more prestige. Finally there is the fine art market, previously reserved for paint-on-canvas art, works on paper, and noncraft sculpture. This market, now slowly being infiltrated by craft art, offers even more financial reward but only to a small number of artists. However it is probably the chance of being included in art history that makes the fine art market so desirable, for the two other markets offer this not at all. Immortality is seductive.

Kreg Kallenberger
Interlock System³ #287, 1986
(facing page)
Glass, blown, cut, polished,
8½ x 9 x 8
Collection of the artist,
Tulsa, Oklahoma

Kallenberger works by blowing a number of "blanks" at one time, then taking those into the cold-work studio, where he dissects them and experiments with their formal possiblities: this way of working results in series which may often reveal different facets of a central idea or pursuit.

Thomas Patti
Solar Riser Series #LH4, 1978
Transparent light green and gray architectural glass; laminated and blown, 5½ x 3 x 2¼
The Corning Museum of Glass,
Corning, New York

A 1970 course in glassblowing at the Penland School of Crafts introduced Patti to the medium that would give performance to his purpose. With glass Patti could manipulate expansion and compression on a small scale with full control and lasting effect. From that point Patti followed a path all his own, creating an evolving series of vessels, which, although unlike those of any other glass artist, have won him international recognition as a leader of the studio glass movement.

CRAFT ISSUES ARE THE REAL ART ISSUES

Why have we separated art and use? Is there a valid distinction to be made between art and crafts? Since, as I have already pointed out, the material criteria for art no longer applies, why is a stigma attached to media historically associated with crafts? How does art, through the eyes, affect the hands and the body? Can these effects happen the other way around? Is there a perceptible effective difference between a handmade object and a machine-made one? If two objects, one handmade and one machine-made, were visually identical, could we still somehow feel the difference? If so, how?

Although the crafts field has been weighed down with decades of romanticism, anti-intellectualism, anti-Modernism, and anti-industrialism, the notion of the artist as important and perhaps crucial to human life has been held to with a steadfastness that flies in the face of normal evidence. When this idealism is not sentimentality, it is a powerful creative force. This idealism has been lost in the fine art field, one hopes only temporarily. Perhaps crafts, because they are rooted in some kind of physical exertion, are less susceptible to self-deception. Skill and patience are required.

Yet crafts are looked down upon because they are associated with manual labor, and thus with poverty. The general tendency in modern Western civilizations has been to consider physical labor demeaning. Those who work with their gray matter are thought of as better (and better off) than those who actually touch and lift the awful stuff of matter.

There is too a minor tradition — perpetuated by the genteel — that physical work is purity itself and spiritually transformative. I think we should not romanticize physical work; only if it is approached with the correct attitude is it spiritually nourishing, and it should not be debilitating as it often is in peasant societies. We must also remember that mental work can be boring and debilitating too. Craft fairs and department store boutiques notwithstanding, the handmade may be acknowledged as having some charm, but it is almost universally thought of as being for those who cannot afford the mass produced.

As the world of work becomes universally computer dominated, forcing upon one's mental life a space that is no space, a space that is without hue, substance, texture or poetic resonance, art has two choices. It can capitulate to the no-space, exploiting the speed, efficiency, and boredom of bits and bytes or it can balance the no-space with the intense tactility that art in crafts media alone can provide. When one is working with a computer, even if it is only for word processing — as I am now doing — the body disappears.

MORE QUESTIONS

How may a work, an art object, or art proposal, be placed in either a crafts category or a fine art category? Why do we want to categorize this work? Convenience? Salesmanship? Illumination of particular qualities? Honor? Purposes of comparison? Toward what end? Why can't an object be in two or more categories at the same time? Why can't an object be a craft object and an art object simultaneously? Is the distinction between art and craft object relevant, productive, useful? Why are the categories maintained against all evidence? Who has gained? Who will continue to gain? Why do some of us want to abolish the categories?

Changing what things are called can be successful only if this reassignment functions as an acknowledgement of a shift of meaning that has already taken place. Calling a kettle white when, as the pot knows, the kettle is entirely black, does not make the kettle white. If the kettle is gray, calling it white might emphasize its difference from the pot. However, if the kettle is indeed gray, calling it so may be difficult but is proper and just, and helps avoid false conclusions.

But before we begin changing the names of things — if that is indeed what we must do — we should give some thought to what art objects are usually called, and, more importantly, why they undergo categorization. In a world that is governed rather than illuminated by classifications, taxonomy is destiny. It is tempting to think of groupings and labels as merely instrumental, but ease of reference is also ease of manipulation. Efficiency disguises control.

The area of visual production usually called crafts has changed enormously. The old precepts and concepts do not apply. A preponderance of conundrums, mishaps, misunderstandings, and general messiness prevails. Nevertheless the shift from crafts as pre-art or sub-art to art in crafts media has already taken place. It has not been adequately acknowledged. The old definitions and prejudices linger because they are comfortable. A change in definition is a change in thought; new thought is painful.

Should we abolish the word *craft?* Would that we could. Old words die hard. They usually survive by adopting new meanings.

Great numbers of people still make things by hand and sell them or try to sell them: uninspired scarves, belts, candles, wooden boxes, wallets, cups and saucers, ashtrays, teapots, vases, and costume jewelry. Most of these products are either inept or dull. They are generally inferior to mass-produced counterparts of a similar price and have as little aesthetic value. They are almost always dusty rose, powder blue, or violet when they are

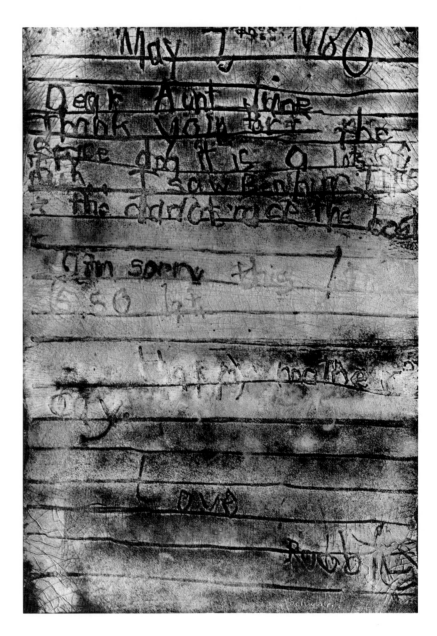

June Schwarcz
A Letter from Robbie, ca. 1960
Enamel on copper, 13 x 8⅜ (unframed)
Collection of the artist,
Sausalito, California

A Letter from Robbie results from the artist's experiments with calligraphy and abstract forms and from an actual letter to the artist from her nephew which she decided to preserve in enamel on copper. By using many processes in the making of a single object, Schwarcz challenges the limitations of her medium, searching for the sensuous, tactile and reflective qualities inherent to the material. She believes that there is no technique that isn't permissible if it works visually. Distinguished as one of the leaders in experimental enameling during the early 1950s, Schwarcz has focused on the surface enrichment, not the function of the piece. Her early work incorporated etching techniques and in 1963, after several years of research, she invented her own electroplating and electroforming processes.

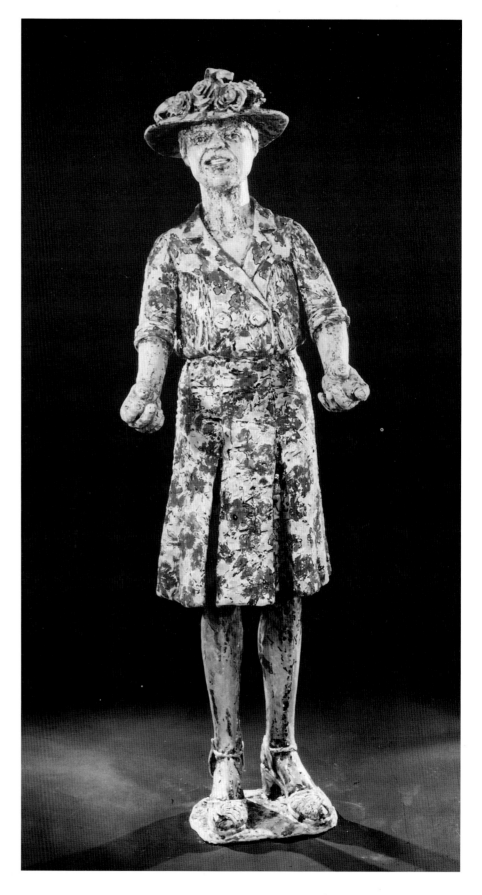

Hank Murta Adams
Dem, ca. 1985
Blown glass, cast glass and copper,
28 x 17 x 18
Collection of John McCall,
Austin, Texas

Sometimes Adams approaches glass
as if it were bronze; sometimes he
allows it to crack, working against
the old association of glass with
preciousness. His technique and
imagery are important to glass art
as his work reflects the interests of
some new glass artists in freedom
and spontaneity.

Viola Frey
Grandmother Figure, 1978-80
Ceramic, glaze, 72 x 24 x 18
Collection of Daniel Jacobs,
New York, New York

Frey is best known for her low-fired
earthenware polychrome sculpture.
She is a painter as well as a ceramic
artist whose lifesize and over-lifesize
human figures in clay have earned
her an international reputation. The
figures, covered with thick unctuous
glazes, teeter in a startling way
between allusion to reality and
illusion of reality.

not overwhelmingly brown. True artists and artisans sometimes appear at the craft fairs where these wares are peddled, but they are soon squashed by the rigors of the marketplace. Craft fair crafts make hippie crafts, therapy crafts, and hobby crafts seem artistic by comparison.

What we look at when we gaze at the photographic reproductions in the crafts magazines and books is something very different: it is art. Should we stop calling it craft? Or is it the craft fair items that we should stop calling craft, reserving the term for the better things? It won't work. *Crafts* as a term draws customers at the high end of the market as well as the low. Most craft artists have decided for convenience to take advantage of the already existing craft system until the larger art system can absorb their work. They play both ends against the middle.

In the meantime the artification of crafts continues — preserving and sometimes enlarging endangered craft disciplines and forms; helping artists to earn their livings; encouraging the more talented by virtue of the potentially greater feedback, honor, and financial reward. But there are drawbacks. The art market, because it is so commercial, may inhibit freedom of creativity and force compromises of media-specific traditions and techniques. The process of aiming one's work for the fine art context may co-opt the non-art energy of crafts and corrupt the true art spirit.

For the art world, there are positive aspects of the crafts invasion. Markets and audiences will expand. Art critics, as the demands of the markets force them to deal with art in crafts media, will find that dealing with these strange objects creates a remedial dislocation of language.

The artification of the crafts tends to involve the elimination of the utilitarian and a downplay of the decorative. But divorcing craft objects from use — putting them on a pedestal, as it were — is dangerous. Use factors often control key aspects of form and meaning. If the craft object has not been made for actual use, this lack of intention will show. Viewers will know that the spout or the handle will fall off the teapot, the vase will leak, the colors of the fabric will bleed or transfer to the skin. The work in question will then become merely an image that stands for or refers to craft objects of one or another kind.

Eliminating use makes form symbolic, denying the full force of the chief aesthetic virtue of craft objects: their perceptual and conceptual complexity. Most craft objects have a more balanced relationship between their haptic and their optic qualities than paint-on-canvas art or noncraft sculpture, thus allowing a doubleness of being. Seeing and touching merge or contradict each other. This is the purest art quality of objects made in the craft tradition and the one unique to them. It is such a strong quality that objects that look like or represent craft objects partake of it through association.

Experiencing craft art that retains and celebrates utilitarian forms requires the ability to receive, perceive, and process more than one constellation of sense data at a time. By extension this means that one must also be able to think more than one thought at a time. If we can simultaneously manage seeing and touching *and* using, we have accomplished something quite miraculous. Only craft art allows us this.

Italo Scanga
Fear of Drinking, 1980
Oil on wood, glass bottle,
47 x 24 x 13½
Collection of the artist, Courtesy of
Karen Amiel, New York, New York

Scanga, a teacher at the University of California, San Diego, works in a variety of materials. He often incorporates branches and other parts of trees into his works, giving them a figurative aspect. He then paints them and adds whatever material and forms are required to express his theme or idea. *Fear of Drinking*, in which the configurated tree section holds a ready-made bottle, is part of a series on human fears. Scanga's works embody a strong narrative and pictorial tradition of moral and human dilemmas.

Alison Saar
La Rosa Negra, 1985
Tin and found objects on wood,
14½ x 10 x ½
Collection of Daniel Jacobs,
New York, New York

Saar's *Black Rose* offers an
interesting juxtaposition of
contemporary collage form with
symbolic archaism. Visually it is a
good Pop image, yet it incorporates
floral metal ceiling tiles, a
Romanesque lion effigy head and
decorative architectural elements
surrounding a portrait which has a
tantalizing similarity to Medieval and
Spanish colonial *retablos.* This
feeling of a sacred portrait is even
more enhanced by the Black
Madonna surrounded by a pseudo-
nimbus. Although her worldly, aloof
sensuality tells us this clearly is a
street-wise Madonna, one is
tempted to draw an analogy with
the classical Lady of Sorrows and
her symbolic rose. Alison Saar is the
daughter of the artist Betye Saar.

GIVE AND TAKEOUT:

TOWARD A CROSS-CULTURAL CONSCIOUSNESS

LUCY R. LIPPARD

The real humanity of people is understood through cultural differences rather than cultural similarities . . . . Children of the dominant society are rarely given the opportunity to know the world as others know it. Therefore they come to believe that there is only one world, one reality, one truth — the one they personally know; and they are inclined to dismiss all other worlds as illusions.

JAMAKE HIGHWATER[1]

Today we know better than ever that no single cultural group or tradition has a monopoly on wisdom. Our survival in the twentieth century is largely dependent on our ability to respond to the challenge that is implicit in that fact. For citizens of the United States, the challenge is double: America is a plural society whose diversity is a precious resource.

JEWELL GRAHAM[2]

The struggle to maintain culture is in itself a revolutionary struggle. . . . We have never claimed to be perfect or to have the "secret of life." We <u>demand</u>, though, an end to romanticism, paternalism, and racism. . . . We must demand to be taken seriously as the people we are, by the world, and especially by other peoples on this continent.

JIMMIE DURHAM, CHEROKEE[3]

Is cowboy art ethnic?

JIM COVARRUBIAS[4]

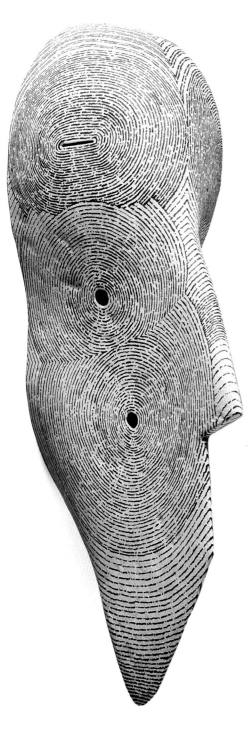

Slowly, over the last decade, something potentially exciting has been happening in the so-called art world. While the art market (the true identity of that world) remains a small, incestuous, ethnocentric domain, it has expanded geographically from New York City to Los Angeles, Houston, Chicago, Atlanta, and other cities. This expansion has been paralleled by the general blurring of boundaries between crafts, folk art, and high art. At the same time, the educational and political legacy of the sixties, spreading through the grass roots of peripheral, underground, and community arts during the seventies, has helped to re-identify the makers of and participants in the dominant culture to include those for whom European culture is alien.

It would be difficult to say which of these events are causes and which effects. However, skimming the art magazines and catalogues of the seventies, it is hard to avoid the fact that the pluralism which made that decade so stylistically confusing had a broader base than the perennial avant-garde search for novelty/marketability. One way to celebrate the immense diversity of cultural expression emerging from our multiethnic society, to develop a true cultural democracy, is to perceive cross-culturally. The term suggests an equal exchange between cultures, the liberal transcendence of differences instead of the standardizing "universal" or melting-pot concept that has obscured "other" cultures in favor of the dominant Euro-American culture. Cross-cultural means cross-class as well. Classes exist within cultures within countries. And each class views the role of culture and that of the cultural worker differently. These differing viewpoints provide mirrors, or windows, with which we may see into our own and others' lives. For instance, in contemporary Japanese-American culture, creative activity is still "viewed as an integral part of life and is not set apart as 'art.'"[5]

In the early seventies, some white male artists in the United States began to respond to the demands for inclusion of women and non-white artists in their hitherto exclusive domain. At the same time, excluded groups took things into their own hands and founded alternative galleries, publications, presses, film and video co-ops, and even museums. If the most powerful and most influential makers and consumers of art today remain Euro-American males, the seventies at least saw the entry into the high-art scene of a large number of white women and an unprecedented, if small, number of Black, Hispanic, Native American, and Asian-American artists. A few is more than before.

The very existence of a mini-movement of so-called primitivists in the seventies was an acknowledgement that Western Modernism needed new blood. The avant-garde had run through some five centuries of Western art history (and superficial borrowings from other cultures) with such a strip-mining approach that it began to look as though there were no new veins left to tap. Individual artists had long turned to non-Western cultures for inspiration — Claude Monet to Japan, Pablo Picasso to Africa, Henry Moore to Meso-America, to name a few. Wholesale invasion came, however, only with the intellectualization of the mid-sixties, when conceptual art opened up to anthropology, sociology, and other

Robert Brady
Untitled, 1982 (two views)
Ceramic, 25 x 8 x 11¾
Collection of Daniel Jacobs,
New York, New York

Brady's tomb-like death masks are an amalgam of conflicting sensibilities — they have no identity, no past, no future — yet they are mortal. They are sometimes theatrical like the Japanese Noh masks, but they are also ritualistic and spiritual like those of the Mexican Day of the Dead. Masks traditionally provide a new identity or a place to hide. Brady's fascination with archaeological remains is reflected in his work. The broken concentric circles on this mask might be compared to patterns engraved into the surfaces of conch shells uncovered at Spiro Mounds, a repository of Mississippian artifacts dating to around AD 1200.

sociocultural disciplines. (Before that, a number of geometric abstractionists had almost surreptitiously been influenced by Navaho women's geometric art, via rugs they owned.) Where the Cubists had appropriated the *forms* of traditional cultures and the Surrealists had used their dream-like *images* to fantasize from, many artists in the seventies became educated about and fascinated with the religious and cultural *meanings* of architecture, sacred landscapes, shrines, objects, and rituals.[6]

This is not to say, unfortunately, that many of the mainstream artists who use elements such as stones, earth, feathers, branches, woven reeds, bones, spirals, and sun signs in their works have felt any particular responsibility to their origins. James Clifford has pointed out that our notion of the primitive is "an incoherent cluster of qualities that, at different times, have been used to construct a source, origin, or alter-ego confirming some new 'discovery' within the territory of the Western self."[7] Art, like anthropology, he says, "assumes a primitive world in need of preservation, redemption, and representation."[8] This situation of course infuriates Native American artists, who try to combat the paternalist romanticism in which, for example, Indians are discussed in the past tense rather than as members of living cultures. It is presumed that tradition means "*things* we used to *do,* such as 'roaming the Plains,' or making arrow-heads," says Cherokee sculptor and poet Jimmie Durham. However, "the traditions that we mean are not the exterior manifestations that are easily identified as 'Indian,' not the 'artifacts' and objects of our culture, but what we call our 'vision' — the value system that makes our culture."[9]

All cross-cultural work is made up of many complex parts. A great deal of the art being made today is *un*consciously cross-cultural. Native American artists do not relate just to Modernism and to the white mainstream, but also to the many other Native American nations outside their own, now coming together for mutual political and spiritual support. As Tuscarora photographer Jolene Rickard observes, Indians in the East "didn't wear bright-colored clothing with pink feathers and act stoic . . . . There is no one Native American . . . . There is no one headband or one style of dress or one hairdo that would signify the same thing for all of us."[10] In visual art, then, an Iroquois artist will not use feathers in the same way a Plains or Pueblo artist will, and a Plains or Pueblo artist will not use them the same way a descendant of the Mayans will, who will not use them the same way an Eastern European-American in New York's garment district will . . . and so on and on. Yet there is a tendency to meet feathers in an artwork (whether by a native or a white artist) with a reflexive stereotype such as "voodoo" or "drumbeat" or "back to nature."

Similarly, every "ethnic" group in the United States has its own subcultures and each subculture has a different set of histories, beliefs, and customs. Asian-Americans, although usually perceived as Chinese or Japanese, include some fifty other nationalities, each with different religions and experiences of cultural dominance and oppression. (And even Chinese-Americans come from different ethnic groups within China and Taiwan, and speak entirely different languages.) Afro-Americans — although they have the longest common history and the strongest

Larry Beck
Punk Walrus Inua (Poonk Aiverk Inua), (Inuit) 1986 (facing page)
Mixed media, 16 x 12 x 12
Collection of the artist,
Seattle, Washington

Though still relatively unknown, in the past five years Beck has moved to the forefront of Native American avant-garde sculptors with his surprising Eskimo mask forms that incorporate found materials. Says Beck, "I am an Eskimo, but I'm also a twentieth century American. I live in a modern city where my found materials come from junk yards, trash cans, and industrial waste facilities, since the ancient beaches where my ancestors found driftwood and washed-up debris from shipwrecks are no longer available to me. But my visions are mine and even though I use Baby Moon hubcaps, pop rivets, snow tires, Teflon spatulas, dental pick mirrors, and stuff, to make my spirits, this is a process to which the old artists could relate. Because, below these relics of your world, reside the old forces familiar to the Inua." (Personal conversation with the artist. December, 1985)

Charles Loloma
Bracelet, (Hopi) ca. 1970
Silver with ebony wood, ironwood, nara wood, mastodon ivory, walrus ivory, lapis, turquoise, and coral, 3 x 3 x 1
Collection of the artist,
Hotevilla, Arizona

Drawing from the rich aesthetic traditions of his Hopi heritage, Loloma brought a new vibrance to sculptural jewelry. Apparent contradictions (stone as a kinetic force or turquoise symbolizing the sonorous effect of flowing water) blend into dynamic intellectual and sensory puzzles in Loloma's work. He uses Hopi myths and theology in a Native American approach to the inherent animism of earth and life.

interpolitical ties of any minority in the United States — also came originally from different nations, and they are now joined as American Blacks by Haitians, West Indians, Cubans, and Brazilians whose African roots have borne many different blossoms.

Though more and more people in North America come from "mixed ancestry," we have no English equivalent word for the Latin American words *mestizo* or *ladino* or the Hawaiian *hapa haole,* except the unaccepted "mulatto" and the unacceptable "half-breed." Yet each culture is a melting pot in itself. Hispanic Americans are in the unique position of having already made the synthesis North Americans are now confronting. Latino-Americans from this hemisphere — Chicanos, Mexicans, first- and second-generation Puerto Ricans and Cubans, refugees from Central America, middle-class Latin American exiles — have roots in Spain, Africa, Europe, and possess a variety of indigenous traditions. The extraordinary diversity within each of these groups defies the stereotypes most white Americans cherish. Cuban art critic Gerardo Mosquera has written of the Caribbean that it "was a kind of time machine that united in the same environment people belonging to primitive communities, from the so-called Asian mode of production, from feudalism, and from the beginnings of capitalism. There they mixed. Each one brought not only the race and the mores associated with his or her ethnocultural identity, but the inherent consciousness belonging to his or her moment in historical evolution."[11]

Aunt Jemima
Pancake and Waffle Mix, ca. 1986
Courtesy The Quaker Oats Company,
Chicago, Illinois

The arts are the most powerful vehicles with which to open cracks into other worlds. They are apparently unthreatening, often pleasurable and entertaining, but they have a tremendous educational and emotional power. All through the seventies, while mainstream primitivists, mostly white, admiringly pillaged non-Western cultures, Third World communities all over the United States were asserting their own cultural identities and making their own peace with Modernism. At the end of the decade, in New York and other urban centers, young artists disillusioned with the commercialism of the art world began to make rebellious alliances with their contemporaries on the Lower East Side, in the South Bronx, through graffiti and public art. They tended to have more friends from other backgrounds, other races, than the previous generation — thanks partly to pre-Reagan open admissions — and tended to be more sensitive to the cultures of the Black, Latino and Asian urban underclasses. For example, Jenny Holzer and Lady Pink have collaborated on paintings; John Ahearn and Rigoberto Torres have formed a permanent partnership.

In the early eighties, an interesting crossover between popular arts, the mass-media culture, folk art, and primitivizing high art began to appear on the peripheries of the art world. After the Civil Rights movement and the Black Power consciousness-raising of the sixties, the Afro-American community was newly involved with Southern folk arts and with African culture — its rituals and textiles and the inspired fetishism of its traditional religious arts, the stories and tales of its oral history. Betye Saar's *Aunt Jemima* and her autobiographical collages and Faith Ringgold's stuffed-figure sculptures (which she also activates in performance) were among the talismans of the time. From the Hispanic community — especially in the Southwest and California — came a new militant cultural pride in the past of *La Raza,* or Latinism, and a new appreciation of the Mexican muralists and pre-Columbian cultures which resulted in an impressive array of bold, brilliantly colored public murals. The Asian community, traditionally more reserved, its arts more conventionally accepted and admired, also began to reject imprisonment in the white culture's image and expectations of orientalism. One Asian artist observes, "We are expected to be artists, so it isn't hard to get into the mainstream, but the stereotypes are very limited, and we've accepted and regenerated them. Our art doesn't reflect our social realities."[12]

Yet all this is happening beyond the confines of the art world, which is usually blind to the positive ideas and images arising from the interstices of invisible and alien cultures, even those in our own communities. While folk art has recently been welcomed into the vestibule of high art (and has thus provided a field of respectability in which even the lowly hobby arts can be seen with fresh eyes),[13] folk art objects are typically of more interest to the market than the artists and their motives. Grass-roots folk

Betye Saar
The Liberation of Aunt Jemima,
1972
Mixed media, 11¾ x 8 x 2¾
University Art Museum, University of
California, Berkeley, California,
Purchased with the aid of funds
from the National Endowment for
the Arts (Selected by The Committee
for the Acquisition of Afro-American
Art).

The stereotyped racist figure of the
smiling maid, Aunt Jemima, is
liberated by the fist of Black Power.
Her broom on one side is her gun
on the other. The piece is a
statement against racism and
sexism. It recalls an old image, one
with which we are all familiar, and
juxtaposes it with the rage of the
modern-day Black Power Movement.
At the same time, Saar uses the
overall form of an altarpiece as her
continued reference to the
spirituality so important in
maintaining the positive life force.

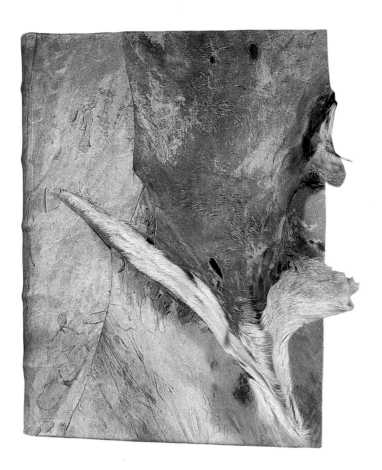

art is the stream flowing beneath everyone's feet. Susan Hankla has described it as "a lesson in what the have-nots have.... Folk art, indigenous and strange, is not concerned with issues in art — rather its concerns are with the human condition.... In its use of found materials, and because much of it shoulders current political and spiritual issues, modern folk art does not exist in isolation from its culture and times. In fact, it is the folk artists who are the most tuned into popular culture, translating and expanding it."[14]

Because there are few well-known Black or Latino artists, and none with the direct influence of, say, Frank Stella or Claes Oldenburg, cross-cultural impact comes from the past or from underneath. There is a terrible reluctance to consider solutions other than those dictated by upper-class Western tradition. Most artists from working-class or non-Western backgrounds are concerned with maintaining their own aesthetic heritages while simultaneously maintaining their right to take their share of the dominant North American culture, in which they and their ancestors have also lived. Most Western artists feel the same way, but ethnocentrism and capitalism have conditioned them to feel that they can take whatever they want, whenever they want, and they don't even need to say please or thank you. "Vanishing" cultures are fair game, public domain. The colonizing culture now owns them and can borrow, imitate, destroy, or exhibit their artifacts as it chooses. No art form is free of the politics of domination. For instance, Maori militant Titewhai Harawira, protesting the exhibition *Te Maori: Maori Art from New Zealand*

Richard Minsky and Barton Lidicé Beneš

The Dog Bite, book by Beneš, 1970 — binding by Minsky, 1977 (above)
Book, bound in skin of unknown origin, 13¼ x 11¼ x 2⅛
Collection of Barton Lidicé Beneš, New York, New York

Master bookbinder and maker of books as art, Minsky rented a storefront in 1973 in a low-rent area of the Bowery in New York City; there, a year later, he founded The Center for Book Arts whose classes and exhibition program have been responsible for stimulating the movement to restore the art of the book in America.

Bruce Schnabel and Timothy Colohan

Cha Cha, 1981 (two views)
Blind-tooled goatskin, color foils, Arches paper, gouache, 9½ x 11 x ¾
Tony Zwicker Contemporary Bookworks, New York, New York

The traditional art of bookbinding demands both disciplined craft and a sensitivity for collaboration, since the artist must produce a mechanically sound binding which is aesthetically appropriate to material inside. The festive quality of Timothy Colohan's gouache paintings is introduced by the bright color-foil patches and blind-stamped squiggles suggesting confetti and streamers, of Schnabel's cover. At the same time, the cover stands as a work of art in its own right.

Collections, organized by the American Federation of Arts and shown at The Metropolitan Museum of Art in 1985, denied that the Maori people as a whole had been consulted about its export:

> The Maori people have been used by Multinationals, New Zealand's government, and the U.S. government to promote trade and tourism through the display of Maori artifacts at the Metropolitan Museum. Our artifacts are not "art." They represent us, the Maori people, yesterday, today, and tomorrow. The Maori people are angry because we are being used by a [monocultural] country that does not recognize us as a people.[15]

Even the *New York Times* reported that Mobil sponsored the show to grease the way for construction of a natural gas conversion plant in New Zealand.[16]

Consciousness is a crucial ingredient in all art, but especially in that which comes not from one's own daily experience or even one's own history, but from a past that can only be acknowledged with shame. I certainly don't mean that every Euro-American artist influenced by the power of other cultures should be overwhelmed with guilt at every touch. But a certain *humility* wouldn't hurt. Well-meaning white artists who think

Faith Ringgold
Three in a Bed
Mixed media, life size
Bernice Steinbaum Gallery,
New York, New York

Mary Frank
Walking Figure, 1977
Ceramic, 22 x 18 x 12
Collection of Martin Sklar,
New York, New York

Frank, born in Zurich, Switzerland, came to the United States in 1947. Working in clay as an intermediary material to be cast into bronze, she was one of the few sculptors in the 1960s who made the transition from lost wax casting to firing clay after studying with ceramicist Jeff Schlanger and others. She works with sheets of clay to achieve draped and fragmented limbs, heads, and torsolike forms. Keeping them hollow, she achieves a surface and tactility only available through the direct manipulation of the medium.

they are ultrasensitive often identify with other cultures. It is difficult not to be moved by the spirituality, anti-materialism, formal successes, and principled communal values of much international indigenous art; there is no proper or politically correct response. But there is a difference between homage and robbery, between mutual exchange and rape.

All artists have a perfect right to use what they see, what they respond to. Modernism itself has had the positive effect of opening up all materials and techniques to the artist (including postmodernist appropriation, relevant to this discussion, but too complex to address here). Nevertheless, knowledge of one's sources and respect for the symbols, acts, or materials sacred to others cannot be separated from the artistic process. The superficiality of so much contemporary Western art that borrows from other cultures may be partly because the artist's eye is on the goal rather than on the source — on the product's destination (the art market) rather than on its efficacy as spiritual communication, as evocation of history, or as a new experience of mutual understanding. Such humility is uncommon among Western artists educated to express *themselves.* It includes a realization that they/we are the beneficiaries of something we/they have neither experienced nor worked for, something our forebears did their best to destroy. A major component of such an enlightened attitude would be the heightened awareness of the *contemporary* arts being made within the cultures whose pasts now appear to be common property.

A classic example worth mentioning because it has received so much publicity (much of it adverse) is The Museum of Modern Art's controversial *"Primitivism" in 20th-Century Art: Affinity of the Tribal and the Modern.*[17] The exhibition included *no* current art by Native Americans, Africans, or Melanesians. (Pre-Columbian art was designated "court" rather than "tribal" art, and therefore omitted.) But it did include a section of recent Western art influenced by other cultures, as well as such utter irrelevancies as a Kenneth Noland target painting of 1961, absurdly juxtaposed against a New Guinea sculpture that incidentally bears concentric circles.

Also almost entirely absent from this huge show were cross-cultural or transitional objects bearing witness to the effects (often powerfully integrated) of contact with the invaders, this being considered "impure." As James Clifford has pointed out in regard to both the MOMA show and the newly installed Hall of Pacific Peoples at the American Museum of National History, these "historical contacts and impurities . . . may signal the life, not death of societies."[18] Durham says it is a "very Indian activity" to take new ideas that are useful: "We took glass beads, horses, wool blankets, wheat flour for fry-bread, etc., very early, and immediately made them identifiably 'Indian' things. We are able to do that because of our cultural integrity and because our societies are dynamic and able to take in new ideas."[19] (Ironically, the same can be said of the history of the United States.)

Flathead, French-Cree, and Shoshone painter Jaune Quick-to-See Smith combats the notion found in both Indian and Western scholarship that native peoples incorporating Modernism into their art become, in the process, "inauthentic." Contending instead that they are simply acknowledging the reality that they live in two cultures, she says, "Dying cultures do not make art. Cultures that do not change with the times will die."[20]

The notion that art by non-white peoples relating directly to the dominant culture in which we all live is "derivative" throws up another major obstacle to cross-cultural understanding and synthesis. As Peter Jemison, Seneca artist and former director of the American Indian Community House Gallery in New York, has said:

> You now have a lot of situations coexisting at the same time. You have the person like Joe David, a Kwakiutl artist who makes masks on the Northwest Coast. He is college-educated, but his father is quite traditional in his thinking, and I think that even after Joe's experience as a designer in the design world, there was a recognition on his part that the thing that was probably the closest to the bone was to go back and do those masks — not to repeat the imagery that had been created by the previous generations, but in effect to create his own sense of aesthetic within that particular tradition of mask carving on the Northwest coast.[21]

Jemison went on to say that "What is usually missing in a discussion like this is all of the white people who have taken things from Indians and reflected off us as though they were their own ideas, i.e., Jackson Pollock, Max Ernst, Andy Warhol. . . . You know, it's okay for Picasso to take African masks, so it's okay for us too."

There are two sides to cultural crossing over — the one-way trip in which TV, Donald Duck, and Coca-Cola replace ancient customs; and the return trip where abducted remnants of ancient customs are carried triumphantly home to the West, to rest in splendor in elaborate museum installations (or in basement storage with no public access). Both trips also have some positive stopovers, yet ironically and sadly, access to information about other cultures is more available to the educated and well-traveled, usually white, artist than to the deracinated heirs of those dehistoricized cultures. This constitutes a dilemma for the non-white or non-Western artist whose work may even be called derivative because its authentic sources have already been skimmed by white artists. For instance, in regard to the massive absorption of native imagery in primitivist art, Quick-to-See Smith said it makes her "feel sad, because it's material we could be using. White artists can be objective about it, where Indians are subjective and not exactly sure how to draw on their backgrounds, because they are so much closer."[22] On the other hand,

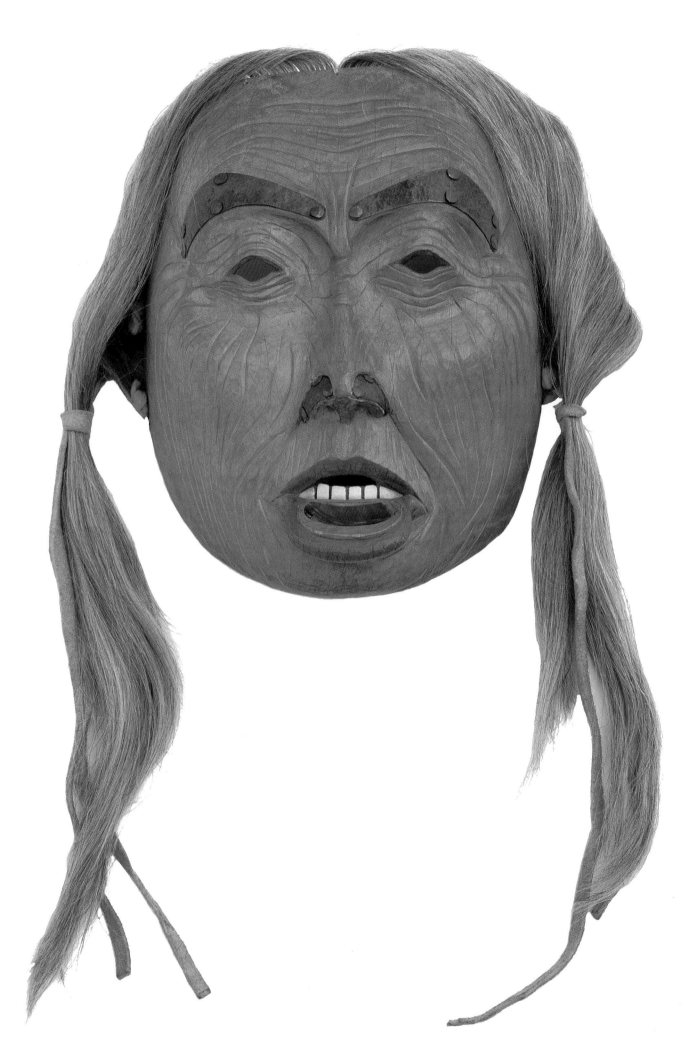

Dempsey Bob
Old Woman Face Mask (Tahltan-Tlingit), 1974
Alder wood, copper, hair, abalone shell, moose horn, 9 x 7 x 7
Collection of the artist, Prince Rupert, British Columbia, Canada

Among the Northwest Coast peoples of North America wood is considered the most eloquent medium for communicating artistic as well as social messages. Though a contemporary work, *Old Woman Face Mask* illustrates the fine art of mask portraiture acclaimed throughout the traditional Northwest Coast cultures. Actual individuals are the subject matter of such works and this realism is enhanced through the incorporation of actual hair, mobile skin eyelids, wooden articulated jaws, and a sophisticated anatomical rendering of facial planes that, in the context of a fire-lit dance performance, creates the illusion of flesh and bone.

Hopi tapestry artist Ramona Sakiestewa says, "I take anything from anywhere myself, so I can't really complain . . . Borrowing can be sort of good now, when everybody wants to sign their individual work in blood . . . so long as it's not blatant plagiarism." Both, however, like many of their colleagues, express anger and disgust at the generalized exploitation of an Indian mystique that distorts their heritage.[23]

Student: Is it art or craft?

Teacher: What difference does it make if you enjoy doing it?

Student: If it's not art, I'm not going to keep doing it.[24]

Because art in modern Western culture is not recognized as something experienced communally, an exchange, there is a sense that the artist is a superior being, coming with great gifts from Somewhere Else. There is little awareness that the audience, other artists, and other cultures have something to give in return. This lack of understanding of art's function is at the core of the false dichotomies between different art forms and art for different audiences.

As distinctions dissolve, we have greater respect for the needlework and quilts our mothers and grandmothers may make in the great tradition of women's useful arts; for the objects that our fathers and grandfathers may make under the guise of inventions or hobby arts; for posters and demonstrations and comic books and movies as valid and imaginative ways to get ideas and images across. I don't mean that we should drag these things into museums and sacrifice them to the avant-garde, but that we should respect them for what they *already* are in their own contexts.

Michael Aschenbrenner
Airborne Repair Kit, 1980
Glass, wire, cloth, bone, acrylic paint, 13 x 46 x 7
Collection of the artist,
New York, New York

Aschenbrenner works with glass, which has the strength, beauty, and fragility of human bone and is thus a material metaphor for his imagery of war and death, from Vietnam to El Salvador to nuclear winter. *Airborne Repair Kit* is autobiographical as well. As a nineteen-year-old volunteer in Vietnam, Aschenbrenner was injured during the Tet Offensive in 1968 near Laos. Almost abandoned, but rescued and sent to an army hospital in Japan, he watched his own leg heal while a friend's was amputated. The glass bone, also resembling a helicopter propeller, is

the dominant form in *Airborne Repair Kit* — a horizontal lying like a horizon, and also "in" the earth, where glass comes from. Aschenbrenner's use of the bone resembles the Medieval symbolic device of *pars pro toto* — a part representing the whole, and also the dismembered bones found in prehistoric graves, separated from each other for ritual reasons to seed another life. The leg bones here are not just the artist's, but those of the people of the Republic of Vietnam (as he made clear in another work) and, by extension, those of all the victims of war.

John Cederquist
Jungle Dresser, 1982
Pecan, East Indian rosewood inlay,
glass, mirror, pencil, dye,
59 x 38 x 14
Workbench, Inc.,
New York, New York

Cederquist, who worked as a
graphic designer before turning to
woodworking in 1968, is interested
in optical illusion. This dresser
demonstrates his use of optical
imagery to appropriate conventional
forms for nontraditional ends. Such
skewing of reality places Cederquist
in the vanguard of the new wave
craftsmen who seem more
interested in perception than
function. Yet Cederquist's furniture
does function according to its own
set of special rules. The *Jungle
Dresser* was inspired by a Dover
reprint of a 1904 Thonet catalogue
which contained a plate illustrating
pseudo-bamboo turning. Cederquist
took this turning style a step
further: the apparent roundness of
the bamboo is actually drawn and
stained on flat surfaces and the
caning of the top is stenciled and
stained and placed under glass to
complete the illusion.

Ferne Jacobs
Container for a Wind, 1974-75
Waxed linen, coiled, 44 x 11 x 4
Lannan Foundation,
Venice, California

Only in Western culture are all these things separated from each
other, because many traditional cultures emphasize process over
production while Western capitalism emphasizes the commodity produced.
Though for very different reasons, ephemerality and process were the base
of so-called process art or *arte povera* in the United States and Europe in
the late sixties. A similar focus on process, but based on the daily activities
of women's lives, was integral to feminist art of the early seventies, when
women discovered their own traditional arts and consciously denied the

gap between high and low arts, revivifying china painting, quilting, and needlework, especially in relation to the repetitive, modular, rhythmic power consciously drawn from the history of women's work in general.[25]

It was this new consciousness, which spread to male artists as well, that engendered the Pattern and Decoration movement of the late seventies. The revival of some of the ideas of British socialist William Morris, (page 160) combined with feminism's new awareness, suggested many new functions for the high and low arts combined. Fine artists made clothes, jewelry, furniture, architectural decoration, parks, and playgrounds. Ceramist Betty Woodman collaborated with painter Joyce Kozloff, (page174) who had begun to work with ceramic tiles, having been influenced by Mexican and Islamic decoration. Scott Burton (page180) made furniture-sculpture, and these overlapped with the work of artist-designers like John Cederquist and Wendell Castle.

Ferne Jacobs, a fiber artist, collects rugs woven, braided, and hooked by women and is moved by the "soul" in folk art. "I want to talk about small things," she says, "things that people tend to overlook, about the connection in time of women." The ancient coiling technique she uses refers to early fertility goddesses, and to the human body as a container.[26]

Michelle Stuart
Galesteo Book II, 1978
Earth, great horned owl feather, and string from Galesteo, New Mexico, muslin mounted rag paper
13½ x 9½ x 3
Collection of the artist, Courtesy of Max Protetch Gallery,
New York, New York

Stuart's art was influenced by her experiences growing up in Southern California where she came to know about geology, deserts, water reserves (she traveled often into the interior of California with her father who was a water rights engineer), and the upheavals caused by earthquakes. Her art brings together this sense of geological history and time. In the early 1970s Stuart began making earth drawings using graphite on paper to create homogeneous yet subtly varied surfaces. In 1972 she began a series of hanging scroll-like panels of paper into which she ground pulverized rock and earth. Her *Rockbooks,* begun at the same time, were fashioned using paper or soft cloth, impregnated with natural materials; often, as in *Galesteo Book II* they were also covered with strings, stones, feathers or other objects found at the site. In their reference to a site they became documents of the place.

Cynthia Schira likes fiber work because "the commonality and accessibility of fabric with its direct connections to time and place, to history and daily life, symbolize for me things that I value."²⁷

These attitudes are identical to those of artists such as Michelle Stuart, whose rubbed earth-on-paper works also refer to the repetitive rhythms of women's traditional work, to the conjunctions of earth, corn, bread in other cultures. Yet reading Barbaralee Diamonstein's interviews with craftspeople, I was struck by the emphasis on technique and by the lack of conceptualizing about their non-Western sources. Native American, Peruvian, and particularly Japanese arts were constantly acknowledged but rarely analyzed. There was little consideration of the cross-cultural roles of secular and sacred pots, for example, or of weaving as process in society and religion. Lack of thinking through to the sources suggests a lack of interest in the aesthetics (as opposed to the appearance) of such work. In fact Neda Al Hilali is scathing about those "who think they have made something beautiful just because they use beautiful materials," and fiber artists who take the "short route to status" by going after "the look of art."[28]

On the other hand, fine artists have cavalierly appropriated craft materials and techniques to their own ends and much negligible fine art is inflated by a frame of elaborate ideas borrowed from current academic fashion. The blame may lie with critics as much as with artists. Both crafts critics and art critics are imprisoned in their own subcultures, the former elaborating on technique, the latter on form and theory, neither spending much time on content, or on the social analysis which is an integral part of art making as well as art meaning.

This is also the source of the split between minor and major arts, which Naomi W. Towner traces to the Middle Ages and the "demise of the European guild system."[29] During the Industrial Revolution, although women were among the first textile factory workers (on the power looms still considered their domain), they were soon relegated to ephemeral piecework done at home which no longer included production, but was devoted to reproduction. This process of deskilling (whereby women bought factory-made rugs produced by their sisters or themselves under conditions of low pay, no aesthetic choice, and minimal satisfaction) was only reexamined when middle-class women in the homebound fifties began to make things again — this time for pleasure rather than necessity — and also out of fear of making art that would compete with men's work. In the interim, personal control was replaced by imposed homogeneity, the homemade had been devalued and replaced by no new cultural activity. Today, women whose grandmothers were grand mistresses of quilting or needlework, producing objects for both physical and emotional warmth, are having to learn all over again how to sew.

The reclamation of skilled handwork should have produced a mainstream sympathy to tribal arts such as those of the Igbo, of which Nigerian writer Chinua Achebe has written: "Visitors to Igboland are shocked to see that artifacts are rarely accorded any particular value on the basis of age alone . . . . When the product is preserved or venerated, the impulse to repeat the process is compromised."[30] (This statement might have been made by a conceptual artist in the late sixties, protesting the commodification of the "precious object" and advocating ephemeral art.) Similarly, Barre Tolken points out that the work of folk artists represents "the expression of the aesthetic factors central to their everyday lives . . . . It is in turn directed back at everyday life . . . . One does not expect to live forever; neither does one expect a saddle to last forever . . . . Quilts end up on beds, pies get eaten, beaded bags are used and worn out."[31]

Daniel Crowley has written that in other African societies, "new masks were preferred to old because they have the stronger power that

Cynthia Schira
Midland Winter, 1985
(facing page)
Cotton, rayon, linen, 43 x 62½
Collection of the artist,
Lawrence, Kansas

Technical innovation won Schira a place in the 1969 landmark exhibition *Objects: USA* where her weft-twined jute hanging was indicative of the general desire among avant-garde fiber artists to break away from the confines of the loom. In the years that followed Schira returned to the loom but in a manner all her own. She has described it as "expanded brocade or supplementary weft technique" in which "eccentric lines are put in by hand after the piece has been removed from the loom." The technique has allowed her to develop a highly personal, impressionistic, pictorial style that emphasizes color rather than line, often using ribbons as a painter would use bold brushstrokes to create images.

Neda Al Hilali
Santa Monica/Atlantis, 1984
Detail of room installation, canvas,
paper lamination, mixed
media collage, approximately
180 x 180 x 120
Collection of the artist,
Santa Monica, California

Born in Czechoslovakia, Al Hilali was trained in Europe, India, and the Middle East before moving to the United States in 1961. Her early memories of the complex rhythms and repetitions that make up India's cultural fabric have acted as a conduit for her artistic expressions, her fiber structures, and pattern paintings. In the early 1980s Al Hilali became interested in how her forms could become more rigid, but still communicate a crumpled fluidity when mounted on the wall or from the ceiling. She wanted to freeze their gestures. Fascinated by spontaneous palm frond forms and specifically the plumed serpent from pre-Columbian mythology (a symbol for fecundity, nature, and divine power), she began using metal to capture the large gestures created by the growth of fronds. The metal (tin, aluminum, and copper) provides a crisp and stable material for large-scale gestures that appear to be growing and swaying.

comes with youth."[32] Igbo scholar Chike C. Aniakor denies the static Western view of African art history: "It is illusory to think that which we comfortably label 'traditional' art was in an earlier time immune to changes in style and form; it is thus unproductive to lament changes that reflect current realities. Continuity with earlier forms will always be found" perpetuated by the inherited values of family and community.[33] This attitude is what Ad Reinhardt, painter of an "endless" series of black square canvases, admired about traditional fine arts, especially those of China and India — the slow respectful pace with which aesthetic change came about, as opposed to the rat race of the current art market.

Artists working within a crafts context today may be in a better position to understand some of these values than are fine artists, because, so far, their pace is slower. Craftspeople might be said not to pillage or compete with traditional works so much as to continue them, albeit outside of a traditional or even a single-culture context. Weaving done on a Guatemalan hand loom, a reconstructed Jacquard, or on a high-tech machine is still weaving, no matter how multicultural its sources. Within the high-art world this is a mixed blessing. Neda Al Hilali says, "It is this physicality, the texture, that is always seen first in a fiber piece. It will shout 'fiber' before any other message can get across. Texture is like loud static, the drone of a sensual material. Through this 'fiber noise' it is very difficult to make audible the ring of illusion or the clear sound of spirituality."[34]

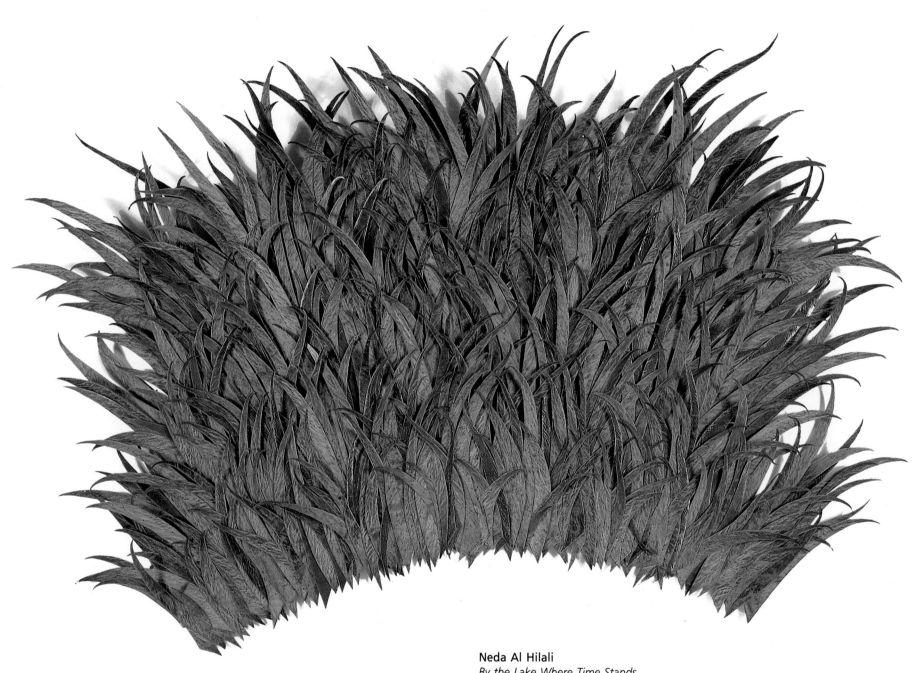

Neda Al Hilali
*By the Lake Where Time Stands
Still*, 1986
Copper, 40 x 60
Collection of the artist,
Santa Monica, California

221

John McQueen
Untitled Basket, 1985
Sticks and twigs — red osier, ash,
maple, wax, 16 x 19 x 22½
Collection of Daniel Jacobs,
New York, New York

Fiber sculptor Claire Zeisler in her
Chicago apartment with her
collection of American Indian
baskets and other contemporary art,
1985.
Courtesy of *Fiberarts Magazine,*
Asheville, North Carolina

John McQueen, a basketmaker trained as a sculptor, says that the
difference between a basket and a sculpture is that the basket is first and
foremost a *container,* that "in baskets, there's nothing new. Sculpture can
be all different kinds of things, but baskets are always the same . . . .
Eventually you want to find out what a basket is and what it isn't."[35] He
has contradicted himself by expanding the definition of baskets, weaving
them with a wide variety of woods and grasses. They may be armored
with bark, or loosely constructed of sticks like a bird's nest. Despite the
basic fact of regularity — the weave — his baskets can be asymmetrical
and wonderfully wobbly as well as precisely elegant. Containers or not, I
would call them sculptures . . . if there were any reason not to call them
what they are — baskets.

Claire Zeisler, a fiber artist who collects baskets, says she might have
made them but she "couldn't compete with the Indians."[36] Feminist artist
Harmony Hammond made both baskets and fiber sandals in the mid-
seventies and exhibited them with her paintings and sculptures as homage
to women's experience in other cultures. Her 1974 *Floor Pieces* (painted
and hooked rugs) challenged the novelty of flat formalist sculptures such
as Carl Andre's metal modules. Sheila Hicks studied art at Yale University in
the fifties but was alienated by the "big, macho Abstract Expressionist
routine" then prevalent in the art world. She is best known (with Zeisler
and Lenore Tawney) as one of a female "triumgynate" that revolutionized
the fiber arts. She makes imaginative installations aimed at de-isolating art,
using local materials, especially ones that have already been used. In

Claire Zeisler
Page I, 1975
Natural chamois with red cotton
stitching, 4 x 10¼ x 5⅜
Collection of Derek Mason and
Daniel Jacobs, New York, New York,
In Memory of Nicolas Rodriguez

Page I is part of a series based on
book imagery. It is made of chamois,
a soft flexible material that can be
shaped simply by cutting, pinking,
or as here, folding. Zeisler
machined-stitched the edges with
red cotton thread, enlivening and
curling the "pages."

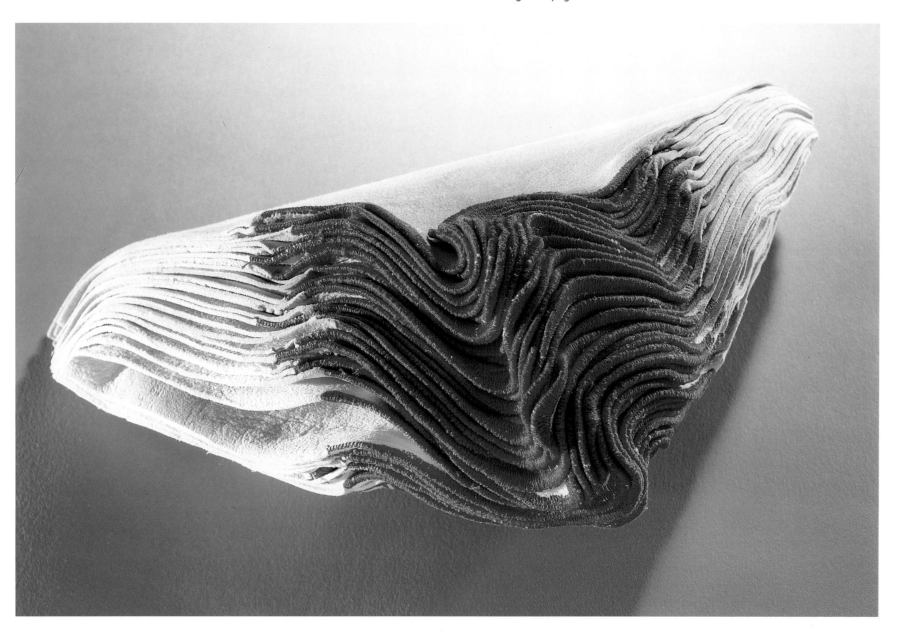

Sheila Hicks
The Principal Wife Goes On, 1969
(Detail)
Linen, silk, wool, synthetic fibers,
180 inches long
National Museum of American Art,
Smithsonian Institution, Washington,
D.C., Gift of S.C. Johnson & Son,
Inc.

Adelaide, Australia, she made her sculpture out of water bags for trips into the bush; in Lund, Sweden, people lent her their bedsheets for her work, and in Israel, *Back From the Front* was made of knotted soldiers' uniforms.

Hicks, who did graduate work in Chile researching the textiles of pre-Incan cultures, also lived in Mexico, has been influenced by Peruvian tapestry and Mitla macrame, and has worked with Malabar craftsmen in a textile factory in India. She wants to "live within the context of all civilizations," to "tame the thread, become part of its nature." Interested in anthropology, she likes to "parachute into ethnological gatherings and listen to how people talk about culture." Hicks is clearly respectful of the non-Western cultures from which she has learned so much. "Once you've discovered something, or think you have, you look at it and realize that it has already been done by some tribe in Africa or Indonesia." Yet by virtue of her own background, she is able to "parachute into" a broad variety of situations.[37]

At this point, with fine artists crossing into crafts territory and vice versa, there is far less contact between the two worlds than might have been expected. Craftspeople, equally isolated from other contemporary cultures, continue to resent their exclusion from fine art, while simultaneously maintaining their own highly successful network of museums, galleries, magazines, and markets. Like The Museum of Modern Art, fine artists remain primarily interested in the antique or exotic crafts rather than in their peers in the crafts sector. What seemed like breakthroughs for the primitivists (the use of rope, reeds, bark, thread) and functionalists (the use of tile, fabric, glass) was hardly news to craftspeople. Yet most seem hesitant to violate the canons of their own fields, in spite of all the innovations made in the sixties and seventies in terms of technique, scale, and altered surfaces. A double taboo still operates, maintaining the divisions between the arts; and an involuntary racism and classism still operate throughout both the craft and the art worlds, often riding on the issue of so-called quality or professionalism.

Cultural authenticity is at the heart of all good art. Cultural authenticity can endow a less skilled art with more force than a highly skilled but culturally inauthentic art. But endless contradictions cloud the issue. Authentic for whom? Who's to say? Minority artists who remain in the women's or Latino or Black or Asian cultural ghettos may have the satisfaction of reaching audiences who understand them, but sooner or later they want to communicate to a larger and admittedly more powerful art world. At that point things get complicated. Take, for example, the following exchange: In 1985, black artist Claude Ardrey wrote to *Arts Magazine* reviewer Gerrit Henry to protest his statement on Sam Gilliam — a Black artist from Washington, D.C., who paints on loosely hanging or arranged fabric. Henry had characterized Gilliam as "a kind of living monument to his own persistence and tenacity, a latterday representative of Sartre's 'existential man' who, having no traditions, no high-art past to draw on, must create his own past, his own present, and his own art-historical future." Ardrey indignantly replied:

> Whether you may know it or not, Black or African people have a very "high-art" past to draw from and many creative traditions. Sam Gilliam draws from his heritage of African art . . . . from the carved stone churches of Ethiopia to the masterpieces in wood carvings, weaving and bronze sculpture. Maybe your "no high-art past" remark means that you believe that functional and utilitarian art doesn't qualify? But be assured that just because Western civilization has decided on a certain set of rules to judge art, it doesn't mean that those rules or ideas are universally true. . . . The hypocrisy that comes out strongly in light of the fact that the Western "world" is constantly borrowing or co-opting ideas, styles, and creativity from non-Western people and countries, and giving little or no credit where credit is overdue.[38]

So long as the dignity offered the objects is denied to the people who made or inspired them, cross-cultural consciousness will be an uphill battle. On the hopeful side, in 1984, thousands of North American artists banded together to form Artists Call Against U.S. Intervention in Central America, under the motto: "If you can simply witness the destruction of another culture, you are sacrificing your own right to make culture." This statement is the product of consciousness, recognizing the massacres of indigenous people in El Salvador (in the 1930s) and in Guatemala (today) and the disastrous results of cross-cultural misunderstanding between the Nicaraguan government and the Miskito, Rama, and Sura Indians.

Respect for other cultures brings interdisciplinary respect. Exhibitions that mix these sectors expose the false dichotomies between art and crafts and the "folk art" of diverse cultures. Artists become acquainted with each others' work across the boundaries, and audiences (including curators, critics, collectors) get their categories jolted. Alas, such situations are all too frequently denied those artists who deserve them most — contemporary non-white or non-Western artists whose pasts are respected and whose presents are ignored.

A subversive aesthetic is simmering among disenfranchised artists today, recalling the gentle but bitter sarcasm of Indian art, the tragically exuberant songs and dances of Black slavery, the richness of colonial quilts made in economic and psychological poverty. As we Westerners learn to read the unfamiliar symbols and images buried in the experiences of others, we have a chance to share the development of a fresh outlook (or an "inlook," a vision). Those who do not choose to look through these cracks in the walls we have built are condemned to dangerous isolation from most of the human race. For now, the eloquence of these objects rests on the silence of others.

NOTES

[1] Jamake Highwater, *The Primal Mind: Vision and Reality in Indian America* (New York: New York American Library, 1981).

[2] Jewell Graham, introduction to course on cross-cultural studies at Antioch College, Yellow Springs, Ohio, 1985.

[3] Jimmie Durham, *American Indian Culture: Traditionalism and Spiritualism in a Revolutionary Struggle* (1974), p.7; reprinted 1984. Reprints are available from the Cooperative Distribution Service, Room 1222-93, 17 N. State St., Chicago, IL 60602.

[4] Jim Covarrubias, paper read at Cultural Apartheid Panel, April 24-27, 1985, NAAO Conference, Houston, Texas. (Reprinted in newsletter of CEPA, Buffalo, 1985.)

[5] Sheila Pinkel, introduction, *Multicultural Focus: A Photography Exhibition for the Los Angeles Bicentennial* (Los Angeles: Los Angeles Municipal Art Gallery, 1981), p. 7.

[6] This is the subject of my book, *Overlay: Contemporary Art and the Art of Prehistory* (New York: Pantheon, 1983).

[7] James Clifford, "Histories of the Tribal and the Modern," *Art in America* (April 1985), p. 176.

[8] Clifford, p. 171.

[9] Durham, p.7.

[10] Jolene Rickard, in transcription of a panel, "Out of Sight, Out of Mind (I): Native American, Black, and White Artists in search of Cultural Democracy," *Upfront* 6-7 (Summer 1983): 20. (Published by Political Art Documentation/Distribution. A transcript of "Out of Sight, Out of Mind (II): Asian and Hispanic Artists" was published in *Upfront* 9 [Fall 1984]. The publication is available from PADD, 339 Lafayette St., NYC 10012).

[11] Gerardo Mosquera, introduction, *New Art from Cuba* (Old Westbury, New York: State University of New York, 1985), p. 1.

[12] Robert Lee, at panel on Asian-American art, Asian Arts Institute, New York, June 1983.

[13] See "The Pink Glass Swan" and "Making Something From Nothing," in Lucy R. Lippard, *Get the Message? A Decade of Art for Social Change* (New York: E.P. Dutton, 1984).

[14] Susan Hankla, in *Retrieval — Art in the South,* (Richmond, Virginia: 1708 East Main Gallery, 1983).

[15] Titewhai Harawira, spokeswoman for Mana Wahine, leaflet distributed in New York, 1984.

[16] *New York Times,* 5 February 1985, p. 27.

[17] The addition of quotation marks to the word *primitivism* (though not to the word *tribal*) did not pacify the people to whose cultures the term is applied. See Durham.

[18] Clifford, p. 171.

[19] Durham, p. 7.

[20] Jaune Quick-to-See Smith, in *Women of Sweetgrass, Cedar, and Sage* (New York: Gallery of the American Indian Community House, June 1985), unpaginated. Quick-to-See Smith was co-curator of this unique national show of contemporary art by Native American women.

[21] Peter Jemison, *Upfront* 6-7 (Summer 1983): 20.

[22] Jaune Quick-to-See Smith, conversation with Lucy R. Lippard, Santa Fe, New Mexico, January 1985.

[23] Sakiestewa.

[24] From Ed Rossbach, "Answers Without Questions," in *Matter-Memory-Meaning* (Honolulu, Hawaii: Honolulu Academy of Arts, 1981).

[25] See Judy Chicago's two books on *The Dinner Party* and one on *The Birth Project* (New York: Anchor/Doubleday, 1979, 1980, 1985); and Charlotte Robinson, ed., *The Artist and The Quilt* (New York: Alfred Knopf, 1984).

[26] Ferne Jacobs, in Janice Raithel, "Encompassing Space," *American Craft* (April/May 1983), p. 8.

[27] Cynthia Schira, unpublished statement, November 1984.

[28] Neda Al Hilali, an interview by Betty Park, *Fiberarts* 6 (July-August 1979): p. 41.

[29] Naomi W. Towner, in *Filaments of the Imagination* (Honolulu: 1982), p. 6.

[30] Chinua Achebe, quoted in Clifford, p. 175.

[31] Barre Tolken, quoted in press release about exhibition of Oregon folk art at the Renwick Gallery, Smithsonian Institute, Washington, D.C., September 1980. Eva Hesse had a similar point of view about her latex sculptures which would not last.

[32] Daniel Crowley in "An African Aesthetic," essay quoted by Thomas McEvilley in "Letters," *Artforum* (May 1985), p. 67.

[33] Chike C. Aniakor, quoted in Clifford, p. 175.

[34] Neda Al Hilali, p. 40.

[35] Interview with John McQueen, in Barbaralee Diamonstein, *Handmade in America: Conversations with Fourteen Craftmasters* (New York: Harry N. Abrams Inc., 1983), p. 154.

[36] Claire Zeisler, conversation with Janet Koplos, *Fiberarts* (July-August 1983), p. 28.

[37] Interview with Sheila Hicks, in Barbaralee Diamonstein, *Handmade in America: Conversations with Fourteen Craftmasters* (New York: Harry N. Abrams, Inc., 1983), pp. 93-103.

[38] Claude Ardrey, unpublished letter to *Arts Magazine*; Gerrit Henry's review was in the February 1985 issue.

Since I wrote this essay in summer 1985, I've read a wonderful book I would have quoted *ad infinitum* and want to recommend as required reading for those interested in these issues: Guy Brett, *Through Our Own Eyes: Popular Art and Modern History* (Philadelphia: New Society, 1986).

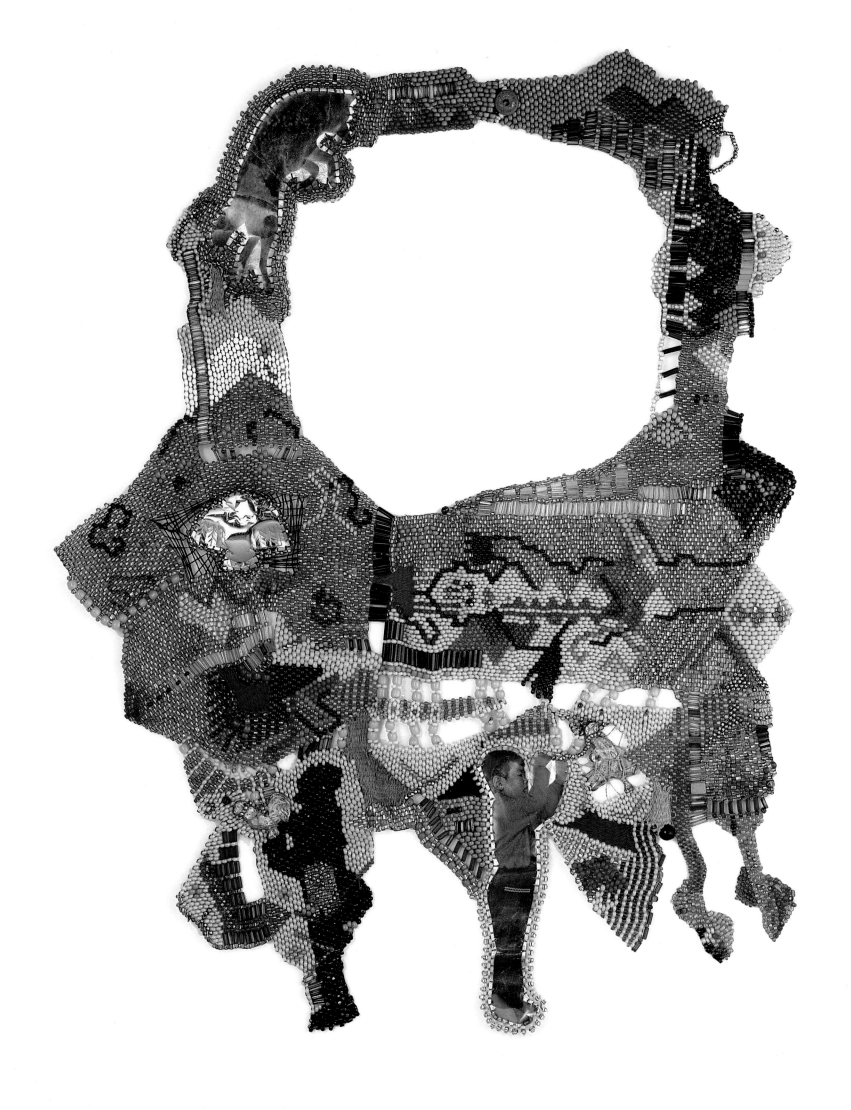

CULTURAL PLURALISM

AND THE AMERICAN CRAFT MOVEMENT

GEORGE L. AGUIRRE

What sets worlds in motion is the interplay of differences, their attractions and repulsions. Life is plurality, death is uniformity. By suppressing differences and peculiarities, by eliminating different civilizations and cultures, progress weakens life and favors death. The ideal of a single civilization for everyone, implicit in the cult of progress and technique, impoverishes and mutilates us. Every view of the world that becomes extinct, every culture that disappears, diminishes a possibility of life.

OCTAVIO PAZ[1]

Joyce J. Scott
Bird Trapped In Shadows, 1981
Beadwork, 12 x 12 x ½
Collection of the artist,
Baltimore, Maryland

Scott's talismanic neckpieces in beadwork, such as *Bird Trapped in Shadows,* are ritual objects at once rich with historical legacy and dream images, and also charged with a vigorous emotional life. It is this sense of celebration and vitality, mystery and passion that conjoins the process of beadwork and the beaded image. The process becomes the image, on more than the literal level. Beadwork is committed, single-minded, obsessed activity — the indomitable will set to beaded patterns. The life force that poured hours of tedium into this art form is robust and alive in the sparkling, vital image that results.

A friend of mine, on an anthropological study in Tanzania, was invited to afternoon tea with the elders of a neighboring village. Sitting in a circle with a dozen old men and women under an acacia tree, my friend exclaimed, "What a beautiful day!" An elder, who did not speak English, asked his son, a graduate of Nairobi College, to translate what the *mzungu,* the white man, had said.

There ensued an animated argument, lasting nearly fifteen minutes. Finally, the graduate turned to the anthropologist and explained that his father had not understood the word *beautiful* and that they had been discussing how one would use that word appropriately in their native language.

The graduate pointed to the sky. It was one of those elemental African days. The earth was flat and dry like a dusty piece of cardboard and the sky was a globe, not just above but all around them, under the piece of cardboard, too, and the sun was a round fire. There was nothing else but the people kneeling and squatting on the piece of cardboard,

drinking tea. The graduate pointed to the sky and asked, "Do you see that cloud?"

The anthropologist shaded his eyes and squinted. Near the horizon in the west, he saw a tiny cloud.

"Yes," said the anthropologist, "I see it."

"That is how we say beautiful," said the graduate, "How that cloud is in the sky there is how we say beautiful."

American. Craft. Movement. Cultural. Pluralism. If I were translating these terms to a person from another culture, let's say to a person of the Wakamba tribe who lives in Machakos, Kenya; if that person were to ask me what cultural pluralism in the American craft movement was, what would I say? How would I explain it? I would use simple language and metaphor.

America is my country. This is how I would begin to explain to the person from Machakos about cultural pluralism in the American craft movement. America is my country. It is a large country composed of fifty states and appendages united as one political entity whose assemblage is dedicated to liberty and justice for all. It is a land where men and women of all races, religions, creeds, colors, ethnic backgrounds, and sexual orientations are free to pursue life, liberty, and happiness. This is what I would tell the Mkamba person from Machakos, that these are the values on which the American dream is built. Many of these values, I would have to explain, do not really exist in my country. They exist in the dream part of the American dream, the ideal part. I would have to explain that when the ideals hit the street and you are a poor, uneducated Black woman with children, in the winter in Harlem on 125th Street and Second Avenue, or a nineteen-year-old Shoshone male hanging from a noose tied by your own despairing hands in the Wind River County Jail, in Wyoming, terms like *freedom* and *equality* and *equal opportunity* are replaced by other terms, like *racism, sexism, and fascism.* At this point, my Mkamba friend might ask, "What do racism, sexism, and fascism have to do with cultural pluralism?"

As I considered my friend's question, I would slowly realize that what I have to say about cultural pluralism and the American craft movement is contained within the meaning of the word *America.* The solution to the problem is within the problem. We don't live on how things are. We live on how things appear to us.

The American craft movement purports that a work of art, an eloquent object, is not to be defined by the materials of which it is made. In other words, there is no royal standard, no ruling definition that dictates what is and what is not a viable piece of art, just as there is no racial or ethnic standard for who is and who is not an American. If a piece is expressive, if its message is unique and well-told — whether with mud and sticks or with oil on canvas — then it is eloquent and it is a work of art. The preamble to the Constitution of the United States proposes that an individual need only *be,* to be sacred. The objects that the individual creates need only convey their creator's story, his or her unique message, in a strong, honest voice, to be art. As a Jewish saying puts it, he who speaks with a burnt tongue speaks to God. And it does not matter how the voice speaks: in poetry, in clay, in rock, beaded, woven, nailed, pinned, or glued. The criteria for the existence of art lie in the clarity, honesty, and uniqueness of the voice.

Cultural pluralism, as I would define it to my Mkamba friend, is a group of people like the Wakamba, assembled in a society, who live together, separate and individual, with as many stories, colors, smells, and voices as there are individuals. Cultural pluralism means that all people have the right to be who they are: male, female, heterosexual, homosexual, Black, Puerto Rican, Bannock, Shoshone, Chicano, Ukrainian, Jew, Catholic, Mormon, Baptist, atheist. It means positive coexistence rather than grim assimilation. *Pluria in omnia,* not *e pluribus unum.*

Now, ain't that American?

At this point, my Mkamba friend might ask, "If America is all these things that you have described, free, diverse, individualistic, subjective, allowing the pursuit of happiness, then why are you spending all this time saying that it is what it already is? Why does the craft movement have to prove itself to an elitist tradition if America opposes elitist traditions? Why do you define cultural pluralism the same way that you define America?"

I would not reply. I fear I protest too much.

Michael Lucero
Untitled, 1978 (facing page)
Earthenware; hand-formed clay petals over wire armature underglazed and painted,
72 x 24 x 20
Seattle Art Museum, Seattle, Washington, Long Term Loan/Promised Gift, The Sidney and Anne Gerber Collection

Reminiscent of Carlos Casteneda's "allies," a large, anthropomorphous nature spirit inspires shock and wonder. A small, monkeylike, childlike animal accompanies the larger being. The browns and greens of the being's body and its texture create a natural effect as if, upon closer scrutiny, what you had just seen was not a *man* at all, but something made of the forest floor. The floating effect of the heavy object is a wonderful touch representing the relationship of matter to spirit, and is responsible for much of the shock value.

Jaime Suarez
Vestment of Earth and Time,
ca. 1980
Clay, 12 x 30 x 4
El Museo del Barrio, New York, New York

The power, beauty, and mystery of nature are dealt with in this piece. The earthen colors and their illumination is so like the sun on rock that one can almost feel the generated heat. Clay is the perfect medium to portray earth. Earth and time are vestments, clothing for this world of ours. They give form to our consciousness.

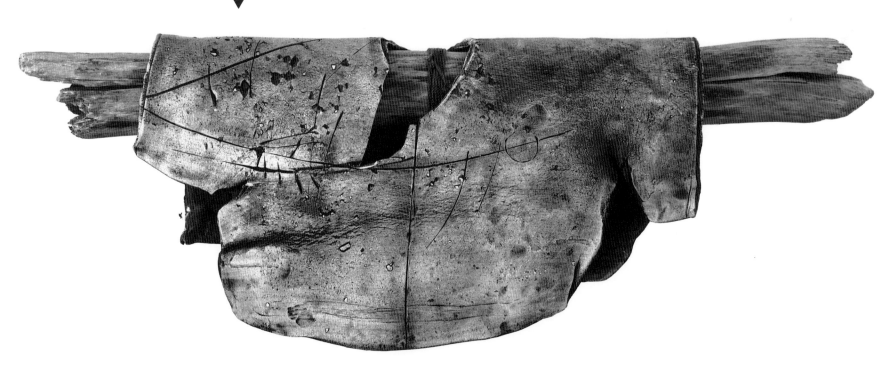

Michael Lucero
Rainier, 1984 (two views)
Earthenware, painted, 20 x 24 x 22
Collection of Michael H. Schwartz,
New York, New York

Lucero's work centers on the human
body; his "dreamers," like *Rainier,*
on the head. It is natural that the
head should fascinate ceramic
sculptors: the cranium is the
ultimate humanistic vessel — literally
the container of thought.
Constantin Brancusi explored the
formal and expressive potential of
the sleeping, disembodied head in
his series of *Sleeping Muses.* His
smooth, egglike heads were secret
containers of dream-content forever
kept from the viewer. Picasso, too,
was absorbed by the magical
inaccessibility of sleeper's dreams.
Lucero's heads are superimposed
with landscape and tactile surfaces.
The landscapes reveal the sleeper's
dream (inside becomes outside), but
meaning remains poignantly out of
reach.

It does not begin with the question, Is this object an example of fine
art, or is this object an example of an applied art?

It does not begin with the question, Is this object an example of the
production of an idea, or is this object an example of the performance of
a function?

It does not begin with the question, What are the traditional
European rules to which this object must conform in order to be
considered a work of art?

It does not begin with any of these. It begins here, with the pen on
this page, with the clay in my hands. It begins round like the moon and
the sun, like a lump of clay, and it revolves in my hands like the earth. It
begins with the story I am telling.

The color! It begins with the color, the red swath on the stone, the
red splash on the canvas, the pool of red on the earth. This is my body.
This is my blood. This is my story. Let me tell you my story! Let me carve it
in stone. My story is in this fabric. Feel it! It is in the warp and the weft.
This is my body. This is my blood. This is the eloquent object. I am
eloquent in the sacredness of my being. There is no other like me. I create
myself as I create the object. Look! I am painting myself into this picture. I
am shaping my world with this clay. I am blowing the glass and my
reflection in it is fragile, delicate, transparent. I have a story to tell. This is
where it begins.

Elie Wiesel tells a story about the great Rabbi Israel Baal Shem-Tov
who protected his people by going to a certain place in the forest, lighting
a fire there, and saying a special prayer. God would hear him. Later, when
the rabbi's disciple, the Magid of Mezritch, had need of heaven's help he
would go to the same place in the forest. Though he did not know how
to light the fire, he could say the prayer, and heaven heard him. Still later,
Rabbi Moshe-Leib of Sasov would go into the forest. He did not know
how to light the fire, nor did he know the prayer, but he was in the place
and God answered. Last it fell to Rabbi Israel of Rizhyn to intercede with
God for his people. "Sitting in his armchair, his head in his hands, he
spoke to God: 'I am unable to light the fire and I do not know the prayer;
I cannot even find the place in the forest. All I can do is tell the story, and
this must be sufficient.'" And it was sufficient.

"God made man because he loves stories."[2]

Sam Hernandez
Wood Krell, 1981
Redwood, elm, pigment,
31 x 21 x 16
Rena Bransten Gallery,
San Francisco, California

Hernandez uses primitive tools and techniques to carve the wood for his sculptures which evoke personal experiences and encounters with people, events, and language. He began using the zigzag serpent pattern in his work in 1977. The surfaces of his forms are organized around geometric shapes and elements which are covered with an elaborate network of adz marks (the scars left by the blow of the tool). He paints the honed wood, rubbing the pigment's surface so that it becomes rich as beeswax.

When a young Sioux warrior went out into the world, he carried with him his shield. On his shield was depicted his story, his color, his animal spirit, his place in the four directions, his name — his individuated name that denoted his personal qualities, heroic exploits, unusual abilities, unique physical attributes, visionary experiences, and other aspects that pointed to his singularity. When this warrior met another on his journey, he would raise his shield, his face, his heart, his name, his work of fine art, his story, his eloquent object, his crafted shield to the stranger and, in turn, the stranger brandished his shield. By exhibiting these pictures of their souls, each displayed on a brain-tanned hide, these men spoke to one another clearly and honestly.

Fine or crafted art? Decorative and social? Sacred or secular? Idea or function?

Jamake Highwater describes a sixteenth-century engraving by an anonymous artist that depicts a vessel at anchor and a landing party of European gentlemen in fine clothes. As they disembark they are observed by a group of dignified, Europeanized Indians. A second drawing described by Highwater shows something very different: "Indians gasping in amazement as a floating island, covered with tall defoliated trees and odd creatures with hairy faces, approaches."[3] This drawing was made by an Indian.

Highwater tells about the reactions he got when showing the pictures to different viewers.

> When I showed the two pictures to white people they said in effect: "Well, of course, you realize that what those Indians thought they saw wasn't really there. They were unfamiliar with what was happening to them and so they misunderstood their experience." In other words, there were no defoliated trees, no floating island, but a ship with a party of explorers. Indians, looking at the same pictures, pause with perplexity and then say, "Well, after all, a ship is a floating island, and what really are the masts of a ship but the trunks of tall trees?" In other words, what the Indians saw was real in terms of their own experience.[4]

Was it a floating island or a ship? Or even, as Highwater goes on to suggest, neither an island nor a ship, but a shimmering complex of molecules as seen by some imagined alien visitor to our earth, someone not subject to our form of thinking, our continual conversion of "the fluid, sensuous animation and immediacy of the world into illusory constructs such as stones, trees, ships, and stars."[5]

Here's another example of how we see and how it affects what it is we are seeing:

A friend of mine in the Peace Corps in Kenya was stationed with the Masai near the Amboseli Game Preserve. He became good friends with a Masai man named Ole Kaidongo. Peter was his English name. He was an exception among the Masai because he had been chosen by his father to leave the tribe to attend the white man's school in Nairobi. Consequently, Peter Ole Kaidongo was an alienated man. He had participated in the circumcision rites of his age clan and so was regarded as a man in the eyes of his tribe, but there was an underlying suspicion of him because of his long absence and the strange ways he had learned in school. Peter was a man between cultures. He was in his native land, with his native people, but he lived in a white man's house outside the *manyatta,* and his boss was a *Kikuyu.*

My Peace Corps friend, Tom, and Peter Ole Kaidongo spent a lot of time working together. They vaccinated cattle, operated the chemical dip for goats and cattle, watched the movements of the local herds and, as is the case in Africa, *tembea tu* — just walked around.

Peter was distressed by the growing rate of alcoholism among the members of his tribe, and by the slow withering of his ancestral lands as the political climate changed within Kenya.

There was another problem, too; the tour buses that traveled through Peter's land each day brought hundreds of tourists with hundreds of cameras and hundreds of shillings which they gave out to the Masai who stood at the side of the road to pose for photographs.

It is, of course, the belief among the Masai that *kupiga picha* — if one's picture is taken, that person's spirit is stolen by the camera.

It seemed that the crowds of Masai standing at the side of the road were growing in numbers every week. Men and women dressed in their traditional regalia, stood *walevi,* drunk, waiting for the next group of tour buses to stop, so they could receive more shillings, have more pictures taken of them, and buy more *pombe* or *changaa* — booze.

On one of these hot afternoons, as Tom and Peter drove past a group of Masai on the road, they came up with a plan.

Peter dressed as a traditional Masai. He took off his Western-style clothes, wrapped a red cloth about him, and tied it at the shoulder. He took up his spear and club, and slipped on the sandals made of rubber tires. Tom helped him spread the red ocher through his hair. Tom gave Peter his camera and Peter concealed it under his cloth. They drove to a spot along the Pipeline Road, a popular tourist bus route. Peter got out and Tom concealed the car some distance away, hiding himself in a cluster of rocks within earshot of Peter. It was not long before a tour bus stopped.

The tourists were American — most of them part of a religious group from North Carolina. Peter played the game well. He posed with various members of the group, an old lady with blue hair, a teenage boy. He posed between identical twins, two blonde girls about eighteen years old. The comments he heard were typical of American and European tourists:

Tourists in Kenya, photographed by George L. Aguirre

Maisai women with traditional neckware, photographed by George L. Aguirre

"He's not wearing any pants! Harry, ask him where he left his pants!"

"Oooh! His ears are gross, aren't they? Why do they do that to themselves?"

"The tour book says all they eat is blood and milk and cow urine. The poor thing just doesn't know any better."

"Mom, what's cow urine?"

"Why do all these primitive people like to get dressed up in beads and shells?"

"What's that stuff in his hair?"

And more. One guy tried to buy Peter's spear for five shillings (eighty cents) and a bag of cowry shells.

When their picture taking was finished and the Americans were returning to their air-conditioned bus, Peter brought out the camera, and asked in the King's English (he had not yet spoken a word to them in English, Kiswahili, or Masai) whether he could snap some photos of their group.

They were surprisingly willing, dumbfounded of course, but polite. Peter took pictures of them in several poses and combinations. As he clicked the camera, he spoke to them. One man, pink and sweaty, had about six inches of his jockey shorts exposed in the back. Peter asked him why on earth he wore such a thing — wasn't it awfully hot and constricting? He asked the women why they wore brassieres. "Why do you have buttons on your collars? Is that some sort of religious custom? Why do men wear pants and the women skirts? What is the pattern of your blouse? Does it have some social or political significance? Why do you smell that way? Is it because you are white, or do you rub some sort of strange grass on you?"

Tom showed me the pictures that Peter Ole Kaidongo had taken that day. They are eloquent objects. A group of people stand, squinting into the sun, smiling.

We don't live on how things are. We live on how things appear to us.

Rafael Ferrer has created an eloquent object. It is entitled *Yo, Yo, Yo, Yo,* or *Me, Me, Me, Me.* It is composed of mixed media, and in art terms that means it is one of those new pieces that are challenging old European traditions.

Ferrer is a Puerto Rican living in the United States. His piece is a sailboat with a bright sail, beaded in the style of pre-Columbian Indians. The word *Yo* (Me) appears on colorful swatches attached to the sail, and the word *Tierra* is written vertically along the mast. What is the story? Puerto Rico is an island. A ship is a floating island. *La tierra* means *land*. A ship looking for land? A floating island in the sea, looking for *terra firma?*

Rafael Ferrer
Yo, Yo, Yo, Yo, 1975
Mixed media, 105 x 106 x 9½
Nancy Hoffman Gallery,
New York, New York

The title of this work, *Yo, Yo, Yo, Yo* (Me, Me, Me, Me) is emblazoned on the broad triangular canvas sail of the vessel. Ferrer's boat is an emblem of the artist afloat in the sea of his culture, the artist as voyager — explorer of self, geography, and time. Other works by Ferrer incorporate specific geographical references, not always Latin American. Ferrer has also made kayaks, oars, maps, and drums — parts of a fantastic "meta-history" of his native Caribbean.

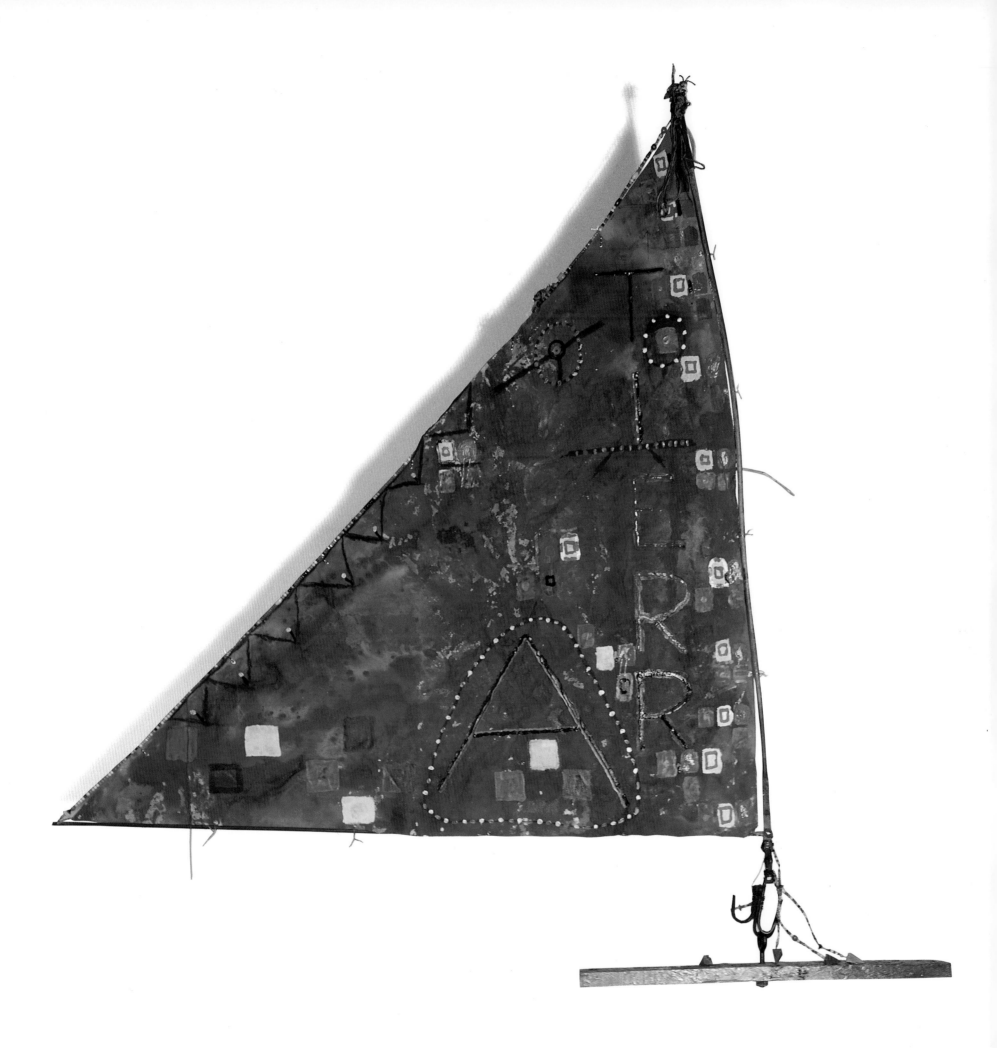

James Tanner
Seeing Eye, 1984
Clay, glazed, 22 x 17 x 5
Collection of Judith Onofrio,
Rochester, Minnesota

From a patterned, multi-colored
throng of images, thrust forth the
dramatic features, red nose and red
mouth, of an African man. The eyes
are apparent, yet camouflaged
within the background. The mixture
of textures symbolizes the
marketplace, the overwhelming
grids of African life.

A Puerto Rican man living in a foreign culture, feeling like an island, a
stranger, filled with nostalgia, looking for some earth - a home. Yet there
is great adventure. He is awash on the endless sea affirming his existence:
I, I am. I am an artist. I am the object. I create myself as I create this
object, eloquently. I am alone in this country. Alone because I am the child
of another culture. Alone because I am an artist. Here on this ship, on this
endless sea, with my brightly colored sail, I look into my soul, I look into
the soul of the world, and I discover myself, my vessel. It is not unlike
other ships, other floating islands.

Jaime Suarez has created a piece he calls *A Vestment of Earth and
Time.* The material he has used is clay. In fact, Suarez is reintroducing clay
to America. (European influences in the past have wiped out the use of
clay as a viable material of artistic expression.) Clay has been labeled as
primitive and *functional.* Suarez, the head of a group of artists in Puerto
Rico called *Grupo Manos,* is showing us, eloquently, the stories one can
create from the bowels of the earth. What is the story? A vestment is a
garment worn in a religious ceremony. This vestment is made of clay.
There is a human form somewhere within its shape. The robe suggests the
one who wears it. The overwhelming sense of the work is its elemental
mystery. It is as if the artist has left the human junk pile for the wonder of
the natural world. Gold shines from the earthen tones with a primal light,
much like the sun upon a rock at sunrise or sunset, an ephemeral moment
when elements meet and create magic.

Or perhaps the form I see is an entity, but not necessarily a human
entity. There is a life force hovering about, possessing the vestment, or
maybe it is death; whatever, the piece itself points to that which is not
there.

The vestment is of earth and of time; that is, earth and time are the
clothing we put on. They give form to our consciousness. As Highwater
reminded us, "common sense thinking is a kind of short-hand." We use it
to convert the world "into illusory constructs such as stones, trees, and
stars."6 What is the story?

Jaime Suarez is home in his native Puerto Rico. He tells us of visceral,
personal connection with the land, the trees, and how the light hits the
land and the trees. His medium is the land itself. His eloquent object is
made of earth; thus earth is used to describe earth. There is silence. There
is a temple. There is the sound of nature. Jaime Suarez is reintroducing
more than just clay to us in the United States. He is reminding us of our
substance. And in doing so, he plays the artist's, the magician's, ultimate
trick: what we are perceiving is yet another interpretation of what we
perceive as real.

James Tanner also uses the traditional necklace to define the head.
The head in his piece called *Seeing Eye* explodes from the backgrounds of
the marketplace and its countless number of changing images and colors.
An African nose and lips, red, push out of the clay, out of the earth, to
assert the individual, to assert the head, the center of emotion. The viewer
gets the feeling of being watched, like a prey is watched, the figure in the
piece stalking you like a hunter. What is the story?

Seeing Eye deals with the African individual and his or her relationship with contemporary American culture. The figure bursts forth violently, red, angry, born from the cultural background. The head emerging with the ornate necklace symbolizes traditions and how they define the individual; how the feelings, the head, the center of emotion, describes itself in the decoration of the necklace. But it is the *seeing eye* with which we are dealing here, even though the nose the lips and the adorned neck are most prominent. The eyes lie just beneath, undercover. Beware. The warrior watches you. He is silent. And he sees all.

These artists, like all true artists, have gone to the roots of their beings, despite the fear, the dread, the folly. The artist then tells the world, honestly, in a strong voice, what was found there. What treasure? What nightmare?

As the artist goes to the heart, so the culture must go to the artist, who is the heart of the culture. Through the artist, the culture is defined, changed, reinforced, destroyed. Without the artist there will be no huge singing. We will have no thread to connect us together, as a culture, without our modern-day shamans, soothsayers, magicians, or pied pipers. The only rule the artist must follow is the one his own heart dictates. Thus, a healthy culture is one whose myriad people, artists, are free to explore their beings. Only in this way can there be truth, can there be a light in our eyes that says *I am.* The whole is only as great, is only as genuine, only as eloquent as the sum of its parts. Of all human activities, it is artistic creation that best expresses a civilization.

By the way, who is this ogre of European elitism that causes us to shriek and tear our hair? None but ourselves.

"The life I am trying to grasp is the me who is trying to grasp it."[7]

NOTES

[1] Jamake Highwater, *The Primal Mind* (New York: New American Library, 1981), title page.

[2] Sam Keen, *To A Dancing God* (New York: Harper and Row, 1970), p. 83.

[3] Keen, p. 7.

[4] Keen, p. 7.

[5] Keen, p. 8.

[6] Keen, p. 8.

[7] R. D. Laing, *The Politics of Experience* (New York: Ballantine Books, 1967), p. 190.

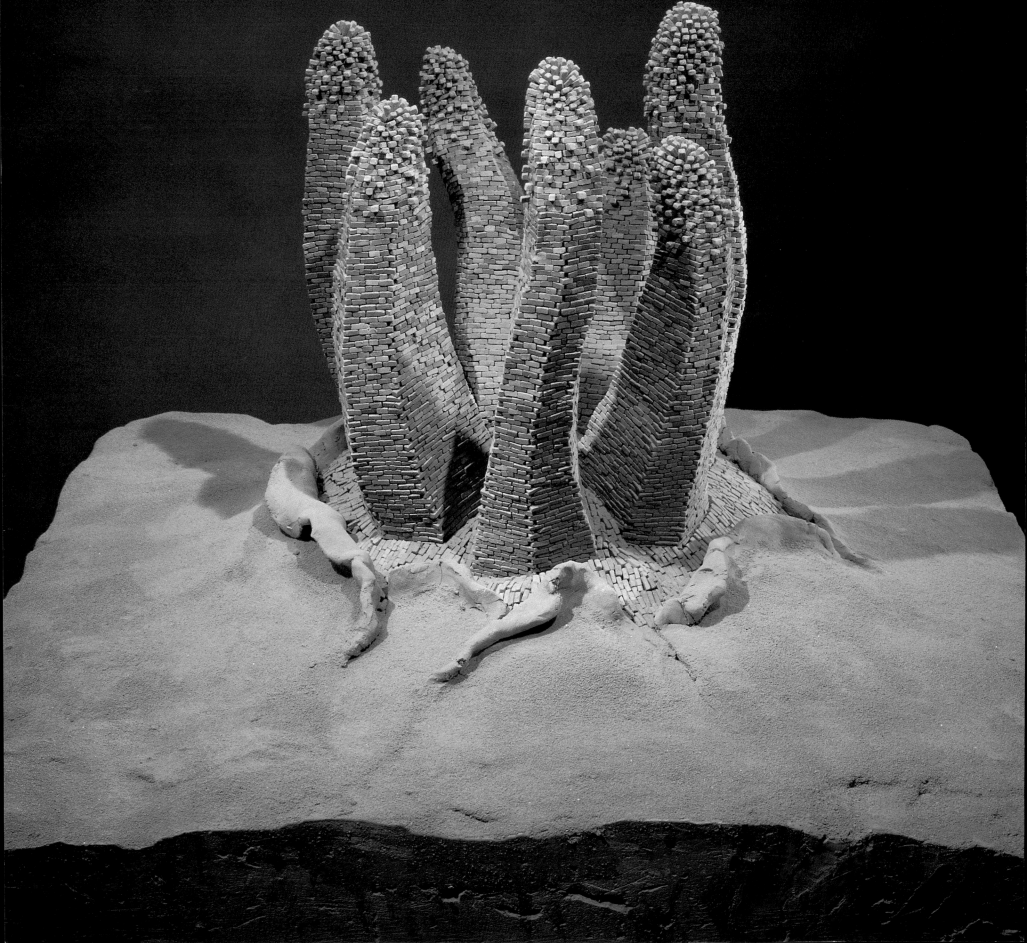

ARTIFACT AND FICTION

RONDA KASL

Charles Simonds
Growing Towers, 1983
Unfired clay, 18 x 24 x 24
Leo Castelli Gallery,
New York, New York

Growing Towers is part of an ongoing sequence of "fantasies about the formal and functional analogies between the body, plant, and the built," says Simonds. "They are mixed metaphors for evolution." Unlike much of his earlier work, the towers do not directly resemble ancient and/or vernacular architecture, but they are similarly informed by a pervasive interest in myth and ritual, the earth as a sacred site, society as a collective dream. The bristling, phallic, fingerlike towers fuse the picturesque image of ruins invaded by vegetation, and the precarious image of the building instinct gone berserk. As initially rigid forms sprout and grow tall, they are "swayed" by time, history, or politics. Willingly or unwillingly, human architecture "returns to nature." (Conversation with the artist, summer 1986)

Tinseled roadside shrines, imaginary dwellings and ritual places, talismans, instruments of navigation and unlikely vehicles of travel — we scarcely hesitate to accept the veracity of these artifacts. We recognize them even though they are sheer invention, deliberate fiction. It is a fiction articulated by explicit allusion to tradition, to craft, to function, and, by extension, to purpose — that is, to the material or spiritual necessity answered by an object. Not only do we imagine this to be a necessary art, the implication is strong that the maker of such objects plays a necessary, well-defined role in society and that the thing he has made is the product of a coherent culture. Neither the meaning nor the value of what the artist has made is in question. Yet, this is a pliable fiction. It would be ridiculous to assert that these inventors of shrines and amulets and shelters share exactly the same program, the same aesthetic concerns and expressive means. Even though I mean to insist upon the allusion to traditional craft materials, processes, and purposes as a property of these objects, they remain part of a loose category. Their imagery is often loaded with additional layers of specific, often highly idiosyncratic meaning — superimposing, in effect, a variety of intensely personal iconographies and mythologies on top of the original one. Consider, for example, Ken Price's extensive Mexican curio-shop tableau, Rafael Ferrer's fantastic "meta-history" of Puerto Rico, or Charles Simonds's invisible "Little People."

Ken Price's work has been marked by a sustained interest in the conceptual limitations (and possibilities) of ceramic objects. The exquisitely made dome- and egg-shaped works of the early 1960s, lacquered with brilliant, Dayglo colors, are latter-day Fabergé: precious curiosities. Price made them when he and his Southern California compatriots, Peter Voulkos and John Mason among others, were energetically challenging traditional attitudes toward the ceramic medium. The efforts of Voulkos and Mason paralleled and were in many ways indebted to the

Ken Price
Unit 3 (Happy's Curios),
1972-1977
Ceramic, wood cabinet
70 x 21 x 21¼
Los Angeles County
Museum of Art,
Los Angeles, California,
Gift of Betty M. Asher

achievements of painters of the New York School such as Franz Kline and Philip Guston. Unlike Voulkos and Mason, who were creating works that emphasized unprecedented scale and raw, expressionistic surfaces and colors, Price persisted in making objects that were small, precious, and extremely refined in terms of sheer technical skill; "L.A. finish" or "fetish finish" it was called. Price formulated his challenge to the conventions of clay usage in the native tongue of the craftsman, not that of the Abstract Expressionist painter. Craftsmanship had become a thematic issue.

Price's long-standing interest in the thematic possibilities inherent in traditional ceramic forms — notably the cup — is perhaps not unrelated to this attitude toward technical achievement. Beginning in the early 1970s, he pursued the formal and conceptual possibilities of the cup theme in a witty, highly sophisticated manner. Although the cup is his point of departure, the works cease to be cups at all and are, instead, about cups. I doubt that it is coincidental that Price was simultaneously working on *Happy's Curios* 1972-1977, a work that has been characterized as "about pottery."[1]

Happy's Curios is an ambitious homage to Southwestern American Indian and Mexican folk pottery traditions. Although Price originally conceived it as a single continuous tableau, a curio shop, it was unfortunately never exhibited in that manner. In the end he broke it down into different *Units,* each one recognizable as a distinct type, a separate culture: *Town Unit I, Death Shrine 3, Indian Unit.* Psychologically, the *Units* are part natural history museum diorama, and part craft museum homage to the anonymous craftsman. They constitute a quasi-anthropological act of classification through stylization. Serious business, anthropology — or were we talking about art? Ken Price is indeed serious: *Happy's Curios* is a skillful and self-conscious emulation of the form, the style, the humor, the very essence of Mexican and Southwestern folk pottery. Price said about *Curios* that in the beginning he was "just making them — without any particular plan — and then I thought it would be really nice to have a hundred of them instead of one."[2] By simply making them, Price became interested in mastering a repeatable style or type. It was this quest for a repeatable style, and the "easy, off-hand, but utterly assured"[3] command of it that is central to the meaning of *Curios.* And yet Price seems in pursuit of something other than the convincing imitation of the outward forms, colors, and design motifs of an indigenous pottery tradition. *Happy's Curios* is about self-identification rather than imitation. Maurice Tuchman wrote in the catalogue for the exhibition of this work:

Happy's Curios began with an intense and disciplined effort of psychological projection: Price identified himself with the folk artists who make roadside monuments and the artisans who produce pottery in over 200 villages throughout Mexico. This effort of will is central to understanding Price's intentions in the enormous labor that was to ensue. Price imagined becoming, as it were, many types of individuals.[4]

Happy's Curios is both funny and wise; provocative too, particularly in comparison with the tiresome arguments that crop up around it about pots versus sculpture, art versus craft. Perhaps it is true that *Happy's Curios* challenges categorization, or, depending upon one's point of view, moots the entire argument — but precisely how Ken Price accomplishes all this is the most provocative question of all. We must recognize, I think, that *Happy's Curios* is not simply about pottery, but that it is about indigenous pottery. The implication is that indigenous pottery is authentic pottery, and authentic pottery is, or can be, art. In an interview with Susan Wechsler, Price described the attraction of Mexican folk pottery:

I always liked the hand factory aspect of the Mexican culture; these makers don't think of themselves as artists. If you ask them what they're doing, they'll say they're running a ceramic factory. Mexicans really like their stuff decorative on all levels, it's not like the mainstream of Western art. Their work is a combination of Indian and Spanish — there's a strange combo. It creates a wonderful folk art that's so powerful, crazy, great, strong, it's hard not to be impressed by it — it's so authentic.[5]

Ken Price
Red, 1961
Ceramic, polychromed, wood base,
15¼ x 16
Museum of Art, Rhode Island School of Design, Providence, Rhode Island, National Endowment Fund

Red is among Price's earliest works, a series of intensely colored dome-shaped sculptures pierced by small finger-like protrusions. Price's *Domes,* as well as the slightly later egg-shaped forms are disconcerting; the forms are somehow elemental and primordial, yet their surfaces are saturated with hard, bright, "industrial" color — often automobile lacquers. These works, with their hard outer shells, mysterious orifices, and vulnerable inner tendrils, owe something to Surrealist biomorphism, but there is also an allusion to natural oddities that is even more strongly present in the slightly later *Specimen* series.

Ken Price
Death Shrine 3, 1972-1978
Mixed media, 101 x 108 x 72
The Art Institute of Chicago, Chicago, Illinois

Ken Price likes the imagery that surrounds death: it is black and white. The large-scale, architectural *Death Shrines* are a part of the *Happy's Curios* series. These complex works incorporate cups that are skulls or icons in shrines or altars inspired by Shinto shrines and Mexican folk art. Price's work is reminiscent of roadside and cemetery altars and memorial shrines, especially those associated with the Day of the Dead in Mexico. After spending five years on the *Happy's Curios* series, Price said he "did what we did in Vietnam at the end . . . called it a victory and got the hell out." (Joan Simon, "An Interview with Ken Price," *Art in America,* 68 [January 1980]: 104.)

Ken Price
Red Zig, 1979
Glazed porcelain, 6½ x 5¾ x 2⅝
Collection of Rene and Veronica
di Rosa, Napa, California

Price made *Red Zig* after 1977,
when he finally concluded the
Curios project. In *Red Zig* he
returned to a consideration of the
abstract sculptural possibilities of
brightly glazed ceramic forms. The
works which followed, small clusters
of sharp-angled geometric volumes,
have been described as "exploded
cups." They maintain the intimate
scale of the earlier cups, even
though the formal configurations
allude to a kind of architectural
monumentality. More recently, Price
has exhibited works which are
reminiscent of his earlier interest in
natural forms.

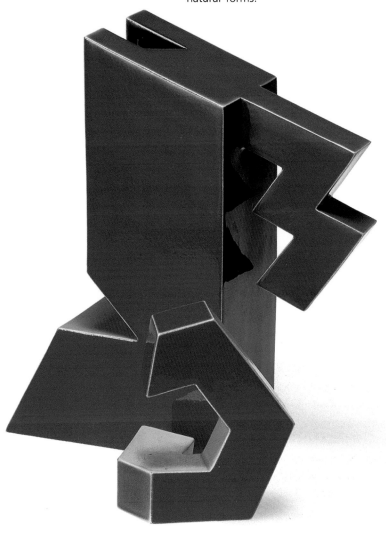

Why did an artist of Price's stature spend five years working on such a project? One must wonder at the effort, determination and skill required to affect convincingly an indigenous style — a style, moreover, that is valued precisely because it is considered unaffected, innocent, authentic. The irony was not lost on Price, who remarked, "After all, it's funny for a guy like me . . . to try to make them look the same."[6] What does it mean to seek through skill and discipline — through craftsmanship — that which cannot have been gained through upbringing? These are complicated questions, and there is surely more than one answer. On the one hand, Price's project reflects his sincere admiration for Mexican folk pottery. Yet it also suggests an anxious veneration of that which is in danger of being lost, or, perhaps more accurately, a self-conscious, willed effort to recover or recreate what is already lost to a generation of craftsmen trained in university classrooms.

The critic Jean Cassou has described the modern artist's "nostalgia for a *métier*,"[7] his lack of training in the traditions of his own art and his confused awareness of the "necessity for a work of art to manifest and maintain itself as a rich and organic product of workmanship."[8] It is an awareness, peculiarly modern, of the necessity to maintain art as the product of a coherent culture, one in which the artist is assigned a social role and art possesses an authentic function. *Métier,* Cassou observed, marks precisely the meeting place of art and society; *métier* is the mastery of craft that makes a work of art "recognizable and acceptable in the monumental unity of a culture;" and it is under the guise of craft that "artistic creation enters the realm where society encounters it."[9] Ken Price seems aware of the necessity described by Cassou, and he grasps its nature: craft is more than acquired skill and style is more than convention.

The invented sociological context implicit in Price's *Curios* is paralleled, more blatantly, in the work of Charles Simonds. Simonds seems even more keenly aware of the necessity for works of art to manifest themselves as the products of a coherent culture. He has pursued this awareness to great extremes, both physically and conceptually, in an extensive series of performances, films, environmental works and objects. In films and performances such as *Birth* (1970) and *Body<−>Earth<−>Dwelling* (first performed in 1971), he has enacted an intense psychological and biological relationship with the earth. Simonds's attitude is shaped, at least partially, both by his upbringing as the child of two Vienna-trained psychoanalysts and by his strong interest in Southwestern American Indian cultures.[10] In the film *Birth,* Simonds buries himself in the earth and is symbolically reborn from it. In subsequent performances, most notably *Body<−>Earth<−>Dwelling,* he invents an anthropological aspect as well. Covering himself with clay, he transforms his own body into a landscape and builds tiny dwellings there.

These are the creation myths of the Little People, an imaginary and invisible people whose settlements and ritual places cling like Anasazi pueblos to the ledges, crevices, and crumbling walls of New York's Lower East Side. First appearing in SoHo in 1970, the Little People soon "migrated" to the Lower East Side where they established themselves in apparently considerable numbers. Simonds built hundreds of dwellings there — tiny structures made of half-inch bricks and red New Jersey clay. Simonds has literally invented an entire civilization; he has formulated their beliefs, their values, their history, created their landscapes and constructed their dwelling places. The dwellings of the Little People, Simonds says, "articulate the earth, how people live on it and what they believe about it."[11] He has encouraged the viewer to relate these dwellings to American Indian precedents, "because, like the Indians, the Little People's lives center around belief, attitudes toward nature, toward the land."[12] His conception of these places is a narrative one: the Little People move in, build their dwellings and temples, inhabit them for a time, and then move on, abandoning them to decay. The dwellings articulate both place and time; they "exist as something from the past, remnants of another people's existence frozen out of some memory or internal image and then laid out in real time."[13]

In *Three Peoples* (1975), Simonds chronicles three races of Little People, three distinct civilizations: Linear, Circular and Spiral.[14] Each of these peoples possesses a distinctive architecture that is the outward manifestation of their beliefs — an emblem of their relationship to the earth "and what they believe about it." The architecture Simonds described in *Three Peoples* finds its most detailed and tangible expression not in the street works but in certain of the objects, or "landscapes with life architectures,"[15] that Simonds has also created. The emblematic nature of this architecture is made explicit by many of Simonds's titles: *People Who Live in a Circle. They Excavate Their Past and Rebuild It into Their Present. Their Dwelling Functions as a Personal and Cosmological Clock, Seasonal, Harmonic, Obsessive.* In this case, the dwelling is formed of two concentric masonry rings whose construction advances in cyclical, clocklike

Charles Simonds
People Who Live in a Circle. They Excavate Their Past and Rebuild It into Their Present. Their Dwelling Functions as a Personal and Cosmological Clock, Seasonal, Harmonic, Obsessive., 1972 (below)
Clay with sticks and stone,
8⅜ x 26¼ x 26⅛
The Museum of Modern Art, New York, New York, Kay Sage Tanguy Fund.

Spiral People, 1974 (above)
Red and gray clay, with twigs and soil, 11¼ x 28¹/₁₆ x 25¾
Allen Memorial Art Museum, Oberlin College, Oberlin, Ohio, Special and Miscellaneous Funds in Honor of Robert Fuller

Simonds's work with earth, raw clay, and growing things is seen primarily in public places — from the streets of inner-city neighborhoods to parks and museums. Since the mid-seventies, the themes of civilization and growth (and decay and rebirth) have dominated his sculptures.

fashion around a central dome. The Circular People who inhabit this architecture abandon one section of it to decay as each new one is built, all the while excavating and sorting the remains of the previous dwelling and incorporating it into the new one. At the center of the circular construction is a dome-shaped, unambiguously sexual form that is the spiritual focus of the civilization — the site of an annual reenactment of original creation. Completion of each new section of the dwelling is timed to coincide with the winter solstice and with the annual ritual of rebirth inside the "womb-dome." This is a cyclical "life architecture" that reflects an analogous "recapitulation and reworking of personal memories into myth and history."[16]

Simonds's use of clay in these constructions and in the environmental works is significant. He has described clay as "a sexual material — symbolically as the earth and physically the way it behaves."[17] This property of the medium, as the "*prima materia* of life,"[18] is, he has said, the focal point of his personal/universal mythology. Witness the examples already cited: the artist being reborn from the earth, sculpting a landscape and propagating a race of Little People on his own body. This attitude toward materials, and toward artistic creation in general, as sexual or biological metaphor is not an unfamiliar one. It appears frequently in the works of a number of contemporary artists, particularly among those with

Michele Oka Doner
Quonom, 1984
Bronze, 15 x 21
From the collection of Becton-
Dickenson, Paramus, New Jersey
Courtesy of the artist,
New York, New York

Michele Oka Doner's studio with
Seed Pods, New York, New York
Photograph courtesy of the artist

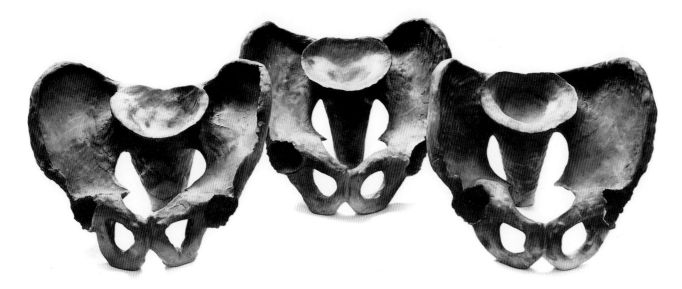

a primary interest in process. Michele Oka Doner's *Pelvis* sculptures and *Seed* pieces come to mind. In Charles Simonds's work, however, the sexual or biological aspect is allied with another that I have called anthropological, in which the artist is concerned with the material, clay specifically, as "the most traditional art medium."[19]

Simonds is by no means the only artist to exploit the contextual resonances of his medium toward metaphoric or symbolic ends. No other artist, however, has articulated these concerns so fully, so explicitly, and on so many levels. Nor has any other artist been so keenly aware of the time-and-place-bound implications of an idiom so self-consciously time-less and intensely personal in its vocabulary. Indeed, Simonds has declared his intention of using it as "an investigative tool to fracture the present."[20] The Little People coexist with parts of our environment and our past. Their Lower East Side dwellings interact with and enrich the indigenous culture, manifesting a strong social, communal, and markedly political aspect. On one level, Simonds acknowledges that the dwellings can be viewed as a reference to an oppressed people, the American Indian; on another, he uses the dwellings of the Little People as a political tool to activate and energize the inner-city neighborhoods where he has worked. And just as the Little People infiltrate and become part of the life of an actual community, so too Charles Simonds, as an artist, assumes a traditional identity and role within that community — a role, moreover, in conscious opposition to one defined by the economic structure of the "art world."[21]

Another artist whose works express a deep concern with the enactment of a traditional role within the life of a community is Houston Conwill. Around 1974, Conwill began to treat ceremonial or ritualistic themes that related to his own cultural heritage. With the salient example of Romare Bearden before him, he set out, according to the critic Judith Wilson, "to tap the spiritual lifeline of Black history."[22] He soon abandoned the medium of paint on canvas in favor of large sheets of latex embossed with patterns, textures, and potent emblems: cockroaches, rats, bones, fish, alligators, cowry shells, *x*s. He manipulated the skin-like sheets of latex in a manner that recalls and paraphrases traditional African decorative techniques: body-scarification patterns, cloth and leather appliqué, assemblage. In 1975, Conwill exhibited a series of *JuJu Bags*,

Michele Oka Doner
Pelvis, 1977
Smoked clay, 14 x 23 x 21
Detroit Institute of Arts, Detroit, Michigan, Founders Society Purchase, Mr. and Mrs. Walter Buhl Ford, II Fund

Doner chose to make the pelvis pieces because the pelvis is a vessel, a basin, a container of life. She arranged them in a group of three as they reminded her of the three graces on the Acropolis. For these and other bones pieces, Doner studied bone structure in anatomy books and simplified the design to suit her vision.

Michele Oka Doner
Tattooed Child, ca. 1968
Porcelain, 19 x 13
Collection of Arthur and Gloria
Rosenstein, Del Mar, California

When Doner made her *Tattooed Forms* in 1968, she was not thinking specifically of napalmed babies in the Vietnam war, news of which was just filtering into the consciousness of the American people. But this moving series of "maimed" figures was immediately adopted by the antiwar movement in Ann Arbor, Michigan. The armless (harmless) child doll is clearly a victim, but the spirals on its brow (one standing for death; the other reversed, standing for rebirth) suggest that within this fragile figure lies a life force not easily subdued.

also made of embossed latex sheets. These very large pouches — some are as large as three by five feet — contain magical substances and objects. Much like the protective charms of Africa, which often contain pieces of paper inscribed with quotations from the Koran, many of Conwill's *JuJu Bags* contain inscriptions borrowed from traditional blues lyrics.

In *JuJu Funk* of 1975, the spiritual or ritual context implicit in the *JuJu Bags* was fully articulated — as was the imagined social identity of the artist. Conwill is not only the maker of "magical" objects, he is the priest or shaman who presides over the ritual itself. *JuJu Funk* was performed in a sacred space defined by a length of red carpet. At one end of the carpet stood the ceremonial throne of the artist/priest, at the other end was a latex-wrapped gutbucket, a ceremonial vessel hung with tiny JuJu bags. Conwill's gutbucket was allusive in a culturally specific way — referring, we are informed, to courage (guts), to survival and sustenance (a reference to the gutbuckets in which Southern Blacks collected chitlings), and to the cultural legacy of Black music (the gutbucket, or washtub bass). 23 *JuJu Funk* was the first of several similar rituals performed between 1975 and 1978 by the artist, often assisted by his wife, Kinshasha. In the course of these performances, Conwill invoked the spirits of his ancestors, recounted histories of his people, and called upon the spirits of the unborn. The goal, he said later, was to "throw energy back into the community."24

After 1978, Conwill became increasingly interested in creating a symbolic or sacred architecture, and began a series of works that culminated in 1980 in *Passages: Earth/Space H-3* (page 261). Outside an Atlanta art gallery, Conwill excavated a nine-cubic-foot chamber with forty-nine rectangular niches carved into its walls. Into some of these niches he placed cylindrical time capsules filled with what he calls "petrigraphs" — scrolls of cast latex; into others he placed small JuJu bags. The petrigraphs and JuJu bags employ the vocabulary of embossed symbols he developed in earlier works. Conwill's earthen architecture is unmistakably funerary, tomb-like; yet while it clearly alludes to death and to the passage of time, it also evokes strongly the generative forces of the earth. Conwill's subterranean chamber is at once womb and tomb, marking birth and death even as it commemorates the passage of historical time. One is reminded of the dome-wombs of Charles Simonds's *Circular People,* though *Passages* lacks Simonds's fantastic narrative elaboration. Conwill's work is at the same time both more abstract and more culturally specific in its iconography.

The fiction Conwill articulates is of a special sort; these installations and ritual artifacts differ in a crucial respect from many of the other works discussed here. Conwill's JuJu bags and time capsules, after all, perform an actual ritual function: although this may not be precisely traditional, it is authentic in the sense that it springs from the spiritual necessities of a real community, not an imaginary one. This is in contrast to, say, a *Death Shrine* by Ken Price. True, Conwill's work remains on a fundamental level the refined and highly conceptualized product of his own vision; yet the cosmology, as it were, is not entirely invented, either. It is largely an

Michele Oka Doner
Figure with Staff, 1985
Clay, 17 x 5 x 2 (Figure)
and 20 x 2 x 1½ (Staff)
Collection of Fred and Michele
Doner, New York, New York

In *Figure with Staff*, Doner returns
to the bound forms of her earlier
work. They are swathed protectively,
either in shrouds, or in swaddling,
or in armor. The armless figure is
sexless, suggesting the androgynous
Greek *kouroi*, unearthed with
missing head and arms but still
accompanied by the staff of life,
thus still a "hero." The repetitive
striations parallel those on
ancient female idols and their deep
connections with nature and time —
elements in all of Doner's evocative
sculpture.

Houston Conwill
JuJu Installation (detail), 1977
Mixed media, 60 inches in diameter
Courtesy of the artist,
New York, New York

Rafael Ferrer
Yo, Yo, Yo, Yo, 1975
Mixed media, 105 x 106 x 9½
Courtesy of Nancy Hoffman Gallery,
New York, New York

inherited one, an authentic spirituality dependent in many ways upon the particular traditions and experiences of Southern Blacks. The primary function of works such as *JuJu Ritual,* or *Easter Shout,* of 1981, and *Cakewalk,* of 1983, is to maintain and strengthen that tradition, that communal sensibility and originality.

In a manner quite different from Conwill, Rafael Ferrer has often looked to his own cultural origins, which are Caribbean, as a source of content and imagery in his art. Ferrer's extensive "meta-history" of Puerto Rico is more extravagantly referential. His works of the 1970s — kayaks, maps, drums, oars, leaf-stuffed anacondas — incorporated a wide range of geographical, historical, and autobiographical references. The fictions Ferrer creates are as culturally specific as Conwill's *JuJu Ritual.* Consider *Yo, Yo, Yo, Yo,* of 1975 ; the words of the title are emblazoned on the broad triangular sail of the vessel. Ferrer's boat is a fantastic emblem of the artist as voyager — explorer of self, geography and time. Other works by Ferrer incorporate specific geographical references — Madagascar, Patagonia, Tierra del Fuego — references that are, as frequently as not, something other than Latin American. It is the quality of his imagination that we recognize, the richly inventive, allusive, García Márquez-like sense of fantasy that Ferrer seeks above all to express. It is a quality that the critic Carter Ratcliff called "tropical":

He may evoke the jungle (see the anaconda, the faces on the paper bags, ponchos, and drums), the beaches of the Caribbean (the maps, the marooned rowboats, the decorated oar), the debris of equatorial cities (the tableau of ironing board, hat and wall panel) or he may, as I've said, refer to other regions of the globe; but his ultimate concern is with the dramatic, relentless impulse to live, propagate and survive which pervades the climate of his childhood, hence the climate of his imagination as well.[25]

Houston Conwill
Louisville, 1983
Earth, wood, mirror, pigment,
96 x 96 x 8
Collection of Kinshasha Conwill,
New York, New York

Louisville is part of a complex and ongoing work about "funk cosmology" that incorporates ritual, game, dance, and ceremony. First shown in a 1983 performance/ installation called *Cakewalk*, it was one of four earth-covered triangles standing for four cities: Memphis, New Orleans, Atlanta, and Louisville — energy points "from which sprang much of the cultural-political strategizing of Black America." They also represent the mound, the mountain, the female "home," or the grave. (The earth was gathered from the gravesites of "wise people" in Louisville.) The mirror nestling at the center exudes a cloudy, ghostly image that takes the viewer into other lives. Conwill says "the mirror is surrounded by the monumental past. By checking yourself out in the mirror, you check or measure yourself ideally against wisdom of the ancestors." (Rosalind Jeffries, "Cakewalk: Secular Mana in Delicious Strides," in "*Cakewalk* by Houston Conwill," exhibition brochure, [New York : Just Above Midtown/Downtown, Inc., 1983], p. 13).

The climate of Ferrer's imagination is as unsentimental as Conwill's is romantic. Ferrer is shrewdly aware of the cultural and political dilemma inherent in his seemingly reckless borrowings from non-Western or "low" cultures. In works such as *Tierra del Fuego,* 1973, and *Andean Kayak for Pablo Neruda,* 1973, Ferrer combines Eskimo, Andean, and Tierra del Fuegian references with Western ones. He incorporates an elegiac reference to Neruda in one work and a portrait of Charles Darwin in the other. Alien and unspoiled? Hardly. Indeed, Ferrer parodies the tactics of "primitivizing" modernism. His artifacts are the tawdry wreckage of colonization and subjugation, altogether unidealized in their depiction of the violent collision between "high" and "low" arts. Ratcliff has argued perceptively that Ferrer's works "reverse the premises of primitivism" by forcing an awareness of the distance that separates "us" from "them." [26]

Salvatore Scarpitta would abolish the boundaries. Long since removed from ordinary use, Scarpitta's sleds allude to past comings and goings, migrations, mythic voyages. "A sled is in the recall of every man. It isn't necessarily in the North. It isn't necessarily in the South," he said in 1977. Sleds, Scarpitta points out, have been pulled over the cobblestones of Madeira. They might be pulled over the sands of the Sahara, too. And why not? Why not have sleds that are made from hockey sticks, broken chairs, crutches, obstetrical gowns, shoelaces? Invented sleds. Useless sleds. Scarpitta's sleds declare themselves to be archetypes, and not just because we recall the form; we recall the technology as well — wrapping, knotting, binding. These activities have biological resonances in Scarpitta's work: "Put the skin on!" [27] The skin of webbings, wax, rubber, and resins holds the sled together, brings it to life, gives it authenticity. Scarpitta has compared the process to skin grafting, saying of the sleds that his task is to "somehow heal them and make them homogenous." [28]

These works, too, make anthropological and archeological references. Scarpitta has said that he aimed "to take over that certain archeological furniture affair that utilitarian things sometimes have." [29] The sleds are obviously not intended to be representationally accurate: even so, one can hardly avoid thinking of them in terms of real sleds. This sense of authenticity does not, however, depend on a rational program of borrowing from Native American Indian sources; it arises instead from his intuitive handling of the materials, his collaboration with them. The difference is sharp between this approach and Ken Price's rationality. Craft, Scarpitta observed in 1975 in an interview with Rose Slivka, "is not the result of the predetermined object, but of the stalking, the tracking. I had to tail these things. Craft comes out of stalking the result." [30]

Consider the process by which the sleds were made. Think of Scarpitta, as he has thought of himself, as Robinson Crusoe. In 1977 he described a process of living and working with the materials at hand, "in a certain ambience of possiblity that could come about just through the medium — handling what was most domestic to me." [31] He began with no preconceived program, and gradually came to recognize the thing he was making — first as an automobile frame and finally as a sled. "So there's this wood frame there, like the answer to this is 'Why the wheel?

Why wheels? Why wheels?' You've been dragging your emotions around the world for fifty-six years. 'Why drive it? Drag it, that's what you're doing.' So I dragged it and it was right. It's a sled. There's no question about it — it's a sled."[32]

Thus it cannot really matter that these sleds do not move, have never moved, that the runners are really hockey sticks or split skis and the webbings are shoelaces dipped in resin. The sleds are the more evocative for having been made from what Scarpitta calls his own "flotsam and jetsam."[33] The materials have their own specific histories, and contribute additional layers of intimacy, memory, and metaphor: sled, stretcher, cradle. This is familiar wreckage — healed by splinting and binding, recalled by stalking.

One comes upon a similar sense of intimacy, and an awareness of the stalking, in many of the process-obsessive works of Jackie Winsor. In works such as *Bound Square*, 1972, and *Bound Logs*, 1972-1973, Winsor has unraveled heavy rope and then used it to bind together rough-cut log constructions. The kinship between the bound forms of Scarpitta and Winsor is obvious. Their works share not only a similar process of wrapping and binding, but a strong element of body reference as well. To be sure, the psychological tensions produced by Scarpitta's *Sled Log* and Winsor's *Bound Logs* are of a different order. Winsor's forms do not, like many of Scarpitta's, allude to the binding of wounds and the splinting of bones, but to the physical nature of her process and what she has called the "muscularity" of the rope.[34] Significantly, however, the two artists share an emphasis on physical labor — bound logs, gouged plywood, splinted poles. These are objects whose fabrication not only required strenuous labor, but whose outward forms are evocative of that labor — art as the product of workmanship, quite literally *works* of art. Clearly, this is not simply an issue of process. Winsor and Scarpitta are also, like Simonds, involved in the articulation of a social identity.

That Scarpitta's sleds should be found so strongly evocative of the artist's labor and the object's purpose, and of the implicit presence of both within an invented social and historical context, is a characteristic they share with the other works examined in this essay. It is a fiction one encounters, albeit with inevitable shifts of emphasis, in Ken Price's *Curios*, Charles Simonds's imaginary dwellings, Houston Conwill's ritual objects, and Rafael Ferrer's boats. The list might have been much, much longer.

What conclusions are we to draw from this proliferation of fictional artifacts? One thing is certain: by means of such objects, artists insist that the creative act is, or ought to be, integral to society, and of value to society. We are anxious to believe that these objects possess some cultural meaning, though, it goes almost without saying, the culture in question here is not the prevailing one. It is an imagined one, and it is often a non-Western one. This is, finally, an art of loss and displacement, one arising from pervasive dissatisfaction with Western culture. It is tempting to view this as an escapist fiction. Such an intepretation, while applicable in general, is not precisely correct in many cases, and herein lies the encouraging aspect of this phenomenon. This need not be a nostalgic art,

Jackie Winsor

Bound Logs, 1972- 73 (facing page)
Wood and hemp, 114 x 29 x 18
Whitney Museum of American Art,
New York, New York
Purchase, with funds from the
Howard and Jean Lipman
Foundation, Inc.

Double Circle, 1970-71 (below)
Rope, 21 x 54
From the Colorado Collection,
University of Colorado Art Galleries,
Boulder, Colorado

Winsor uses only materials that are
natural and unaltered — wood,
rope, bricks — but the physical
work and time that are required to
build her objects become important
aspects of the finished works.
Double Circle is made entirely of
rope, a material which the artist
likes because of its repetitive
familiarity and muscularity. Little
threads are the basic unit that make
up the form and the resulting
interrelationship of part-to-whole is
emphasized by its large scale. The
taut layering of the rope produces a
sense of tension in comparison with
the stillness of the central core, and
the relationship between rope form
and "empty" core reflect a
characteristic concern of the artist
with the dichotomy between interior
and exterior spaces.

or a passive one — consider Rafael Ferrer's audaciously critical imagery, or
Charles Simonds's concrete political agenda, or Houston Conwill's effort to
"throw energy back into the community." By means of such objects, the
community might somehow be changed or reconstituted; it might be
made whole.

NOTES

[1] Maurice Tuchman, *Ken Price: Happy's Curios* (Los Angeles: Los Angeles County
Museum of Art, 1978), p. 7.

[2] Joan Simon, "An Interview with Ken Price," *Art In America,* 68 (January 1980): 101.

[3] Tuchman, p. 8.

[4] Tuchman, p. 8.

[5] Susan Wechsler, *Low-Fire Ceramics* (New York: Watson-Guptill Publications, 1981), p.
116.

[6] Simon, p. 101; cf. Wechsler, p. 116.

7 Jean Cassou, "The Nostalgia for a *Métier*," *Art History, an Anthology of Modern Criticism,* ed. Wylie Sypher (New York: Vintage Books, 1963), pp. 399-409.

8 Cassou, p. 407.

9 Cassou, p. 406.

10 Daniel Abadie, "Charles Simonds" (interview), in *Charles Simonds,* exhibition catalogue (Buffalo, New York: Buffalo Fine Arts Academy and the Albright Knox Art Gallery: 1977), p. 7.

11 Charles Simonds, "Microcosm to Macrocosm/Fantasy World to Real World," *Artforum* 12, no. 6 (February 1974): 36.

12 Simonds, 1974, p. 38.

13 Simonds, 1974, p. 38.

14 Charles Simonds, *Three Peoples* (Genova: Samanedizioni, 1975).

15 Simonds, 1974, p. 37.

16 Simonds, 1975, p. 15.

17 Abadie, p. 13.

18 Abadie, p. 23.

19 Abadie, p. 7.

20 Abadie, pp. 13-14.

21 Simonds, 1974, p. 39.

22 Judith Wilson, "Creating a Necessary Space: The Art of Houston Conwill, 1975-1983," *The International Review of African Art,* 6, no. 1 (1983): 50. See also Yvonne Cole Meo, "Ritual as Art: The Work of Houston Conwill," *Black Art: An International Quarterly* 3, no. 3 (1979), pp. 4-13.

23 Wilson, p. 52.

24 Wilson, p. 53.

25 Carter Ratcliff, *Deseo,* exhibition catalogue (Cincinnati: The Contemporary Arts Center, 1973), p. 17.

26 Carter Ratcliff, "On Contemporary Primitivism," *Artforum* 14, no. 3 (November 1975): pp. 63-65.

27 *Salvatore Scarpitta,* exhibition catalogue (Houston: Contemporary Arts Museum, 1978), unpaginated.

28 Scarpitta, 1977.

29 Scarpitta, 1977.

30 Rose Slivka, "The Sleds of Scarpitta," *Craft Horizons* (August 1975), p. 26.

31 Scarpitta, 1977.

32 Scarpitta, 1977.

33 Scarpitta, 1977.

34 See Lucy R. Lippard, "Jackie Winsor," *Artforum* 12, no. 6 (February 1974): pp. 56-58.

NEO-PRIMITIVISM AND THE SACRED

EDWIN L. WADE

Dominic Di Mare
Letter Bundle, 1976
Handformed paper, hawthorn wood, raffia, linen thread, natural and black wood beads, 9 x 13½ x 4¼
Courtesy Helen Drutt Gallery, Philadelphia, Pennsylvania

The structural form of this piece reminds us of ancient Middle-Eastern libraries with scrolls placed upon racks. However, these scrolls contain no words; they exist as metaphor. Di Mare says "these letter bundles . . . were really meant to be held, not read. Although they're letters, they have no words because what I'm dealing with has no words. How in the world could you describe a bird's song in words?" (Mary Fuller, "Paper, Wood, and String of Dominic Di Mare," *Craft Horizons* [June 1977], p. 54).

Ours is a difficult time in which to speak of spirituality and the sacred. In a society where values are conditionally enforced and contingency determines behavior, where there are no validating rituals of consensus, any overture toward the divine (the most elusive of human pursuits) must of course be suspect. And yet, as proven by society's continual manufacture of commercial surrogates for the sacred — from TV evangelists and faith healers to self-enlightenment seminars — even in our disenchantment we feel a vast, unsuppressable hunger for the "something more." Because of the nature of contemporary society, the concepts of spirituality and the sacred have been abused, they are suspect, and much of their original meaning has been drained from them. And yet the quest for union with the sacred is neither futile nor ended. The spiritual pilgrimage remains the most inspirationally compelling of aesthetic journeys, and there is emerging evidence, in the form of neo-primitive artistic expression, that a new quest has begun.

The silent goal of this exploration is to invoke spiritual contemplation through the material acknowledgement of our immutable, shared humanity. The quest is non-denominational, non-ideological, anything but dogmatic. It involves a convoluted biological and mental journey back to archetypal beginnings — back to primal hearths in which can be forged a new pan-humanistic symbology suited to our increasingly global society.

Yet seeing what is before us has never been harder. We are submerged beneath a flood of information, objects, ideas, and assumptions, all easily recast to serve contradictory ends. This is the legacy

Margaret Bourke-White
At The Time of the Louisville Flood,
1937
Margaret Bourke-White, *Life
Magazine* © Time, Inc.

The postmodernist concept of hard
versus soft fiction is poignantly
suggested in this 1937 photograph
of Louisville flood victims waiting in
a relief line beneath the naive
fantasy of the American Dream. The
hard fiction is that the "American
Way" is open to all; the soft fiction
is that there are exceptions,
sometimes made by race.

of our conditional, postmodern society, in which context alone determines
value, morality, and meaning. How did we get here? Spiritual concerns
have been fundamental in the evolution of human society and the
material expressions of these concerns are as diverse as the beliefs of man.
Yet within Western civilization, especially with the advent of Enlightenment
philosophies (Marxism, rationalism-modernism) that extolled the
perfectability of man, utopian dreams led to an increasing secularization of
society. The production of viable sacred arts has become less and less a
part of our aesthetic thinking during the twentieth century.[1]

The profound emotional and intellectual disruption caused by the
barbarism of World War II accelerated a postwar distrust of Enlightenment
ideals. The West was fallible: technological progress might not be the key
to human advancement; it might even threaten human survival. Family
values were disintegrating, religious beliefs factionalizing, poverty, racism,
terrorism accelerating. Modernism and its pervasive secularity proclaimed a
"better life" while condoning the wholesale, yet "regrettable,"
displacement of Third World and small-scale societies. In America there
was the specter of nuclear annihilation, the political and moral debacle of
Vietnam, presidential resignation, and the marketing of trendy "I'm okay"
entrepreneurial philosophies. In Europe and other parts of the Western
world, a creeping nihilism seemed to bleed away initiative.[2]

One response to the erosion of Enlightenment beliefs was the
emergence of the present postmodernist dialogue. Filled with the bitter
energy of the betrayed, postmodernist thinkers stripped Western ideals to
the hypocritical core, revealing their inherent contradictions. Ours was
revealed as a contingency society, in precarious balance between "hard
fictions" (ideas, institutions, and values thought to be immutable and
underpinning the quality and meaning of our way of life) and "soft
fictions" (the exceptions to the rules, rationalized and adapted constantly
to suit the present need). There was constant tension between the two —
the hard fiction of the Old Testament commandment "Thou shalt not kill,"
for example, versus the soft fictions which have allowed the bloody history
of Christian sectarian wars. The very word *fiction* connotes the
postmodernist assumption that all our ideas are manmade, all are a result
of the human groping toward order, none is divinely ordained. Honor,
integrity, charity, the attributes of a "good man" — though still part of our
social mythology — were expendable under the right conditions. What
was left was the nihilistic domain of self-parody.[3]

Nevertheless, the scourging of antiquated notions about progress,
social evolution, and cultural and temporal boundaries has had some
beneficial effects. From the jumbled, atemporal parts of a deconstructed
world, postmodernists have reassembled significant messages. Shattered
were the old definitions: right and wrong, beauty and meaning, art and
craft. Instead we are seeing "a critical deconstruction of tradition, not an
instrumental pastiche of pop- or pseudo-historical forms, with a critique of
origins, not a return to them. In short, [postmodernism] seeks to question
rather than exploit cultural codes."[4]

An attitude of universal questioning and suspicion of tradition, although liberating in the individual quest for experience, is not conducive to the creation of sacred objects. It is too singular, isolated, and arbitrary in its construction of reality. If an object is sacred, there is consensus among its perceivers as to its significance, even if the responses to it may range from dread and awe to suspicion. Not surprisingly, the void in values within postmodernist society has begun to be filled with meaning drawn from a new optimism, a form of deconstructionist pan-humanism. This movement toward revitalization is heterogenous, mixing Western and non-Western intellectual conventions and value beliefs. Its potent presence is more and more evident throughout the fields of literature, architecture, music, the plastic and graphic arts, and philosophic, social and aesthetic criticism.[5]

From the fusionary synthesis of electronic "space music" (for example, Stephen Meakus's "East of Night," which fuses melodic patterns from Spanish, Near Eastern, and Japanese traditions, requiring the invention of a special multiple-stringed guitar) to the ahistorical reformulation of architectonic forms (as seen in Michael Graves's new wing for the Whitney Museum, which blends classical, Gothic, and modern elements), pan-humanistic works all share certain basic traits. First, pan-humanistic artists intentionally deconstruct conventional classifications of aesthetic style. They select freely from among all the aesthetic inventions of mankind, from the most ancient to the contemporary, then break them down to their evocative, universal qualities. They are not interested in social, scientific, or art-historical definitions of cultural types; that is, they don't care whether a work has been classed as orginating within a group thought to be primitive, civilized, agrarian, pastoral, non-Western, Western, Oriental, Occidental, feudal, egalitarian, etc. They have abandoned the prejudicial viewpoint that restricts the ability to appreciate aesthetic sophistication wherever it may be found. Likewise, time designations (Early, High Baroque, Iron Age, Reformation, etc.) are rejected as inspirationally stifling. Pan-humanist artists and thinkers do not accept the traditional academic view that an understanding of historic context underpins the communicative power of art. The strength of their approach lies in their grasp of the pan-cultural structure of artistic communication. In their way, they are aesthetic anthropologists. They have discerned the formal structural relationships between symbolic intent, compositional rules, and personal artistic freedom that combine to create distinctive styles. They operate on the basis that pattern and cultural values are fundamentally interdependent and mutually supportive. The most evocative of the resulting aesthetic structural units are then recombined into a new form — a form that, although it is nontraditional, can move us in a traditional way. This new form is a hybrid, the product of cultural and temporal cross-fertilization, and it is filled with hybrid vigor and vitality. Using tone, pattern, scale, materials, motifs, composition, metaphor, allegory, or symbol, these recombinations fuse the archetypal past with the present, and in doing so symbolically reaffirm the universal creative act.

The universe of interpretation possible with a pan-humanistic approach provides a logical foundation for neo-primitivist inventions of

Whitney Museum of American Art, New York, proposed expansion model, Madison Avenue facade, Michael Graves, Architect. Courtesy of Michael Graves.

Karl Bodmer
Mandan Shrine R 19
Watercolor on paper, 10¼ x 7⅞
Joslyn Art Museum, Omaha, Nebraska

In the 1830s European explorer artist Karl Bodmer recorded the appearance of totemic shrines among the Mandan Indians who lived along the Missouri River in North Dakota. Bodmer's depictions give a sense of the stark and monumental presence these shrines must have had when erupting out of the broad, open plains. Graves's totem staffs are intensely powerful objects, but, like other contemporary art objects, they are seen in the sterile white-walled galleries of our culture.

Nancy Graves
Totem, 1970 (right)
Animal skin, steel, gauze, wax, oil paint, latex and acrylic,
102 x 36 x 36
Collection of the artist,
New York, New York

Graves's formative works in the 1970s have a hard neo-primitivist purity that suggests actual anthropological totemic effigies of the past; more chillingly, they also suggest the future, as if they were part of a coming apocalyptic era that would complete the circle of civilization.

sacred object-symbols for a future society. Neo-primitivism has thus emerged as a first step in the speculation on such matters. Neo-primitivism works on two levels: the biological and the social. The primalists approach the human condition from a preintellectualized, or biological, perspective. What is this sentient species that kills and eats, that reproduces? they ask. They evoke the viewer's contemplation through stimulation of our animal perceptions and reactions. On the social level, neo-primitivism addresses these biological issues through assimilation, ritualization, giving them a cosmological framework. Both levels of neo-primitivism are atemporal, but can evoke the suggestion of a primordial, anthropologically/ archaeologically defined origin. The artist uses visual statements tensely strung between dialectical oppositions which are left purposely ambiguous in order to inspire the viewer's initial confusion and ultimate

Houston Conwill
Passages: Earth/Space H-3, 1980
Site work in Atlanta, Georgia,
108 x 108 x 108
Courtesy of the artist, New York,
New York

Conwill excavated this chamber
outside an Atlanta art gallery. Into
its walls are carved forty-nine
niches: Conwill placed in the niches
cylindrical time capsules containing
cast-latex scrolls and JuJu bags
made of embossed latex sheets.

Graham Marks
Untitled, 1979
Earthenware, 31 x 29½ x 29
Collection of Daniel Jacobs,
New York, New York

The monumental scale which Marks
has chosen endows his works with
an aura of mystery; they seem to be
organic yet their size hugely exceeds
that of similar forms found in
nature. They are like the giant fruit
of a tree long fossilized, or the
prehistoric nests of monster insects.
Marks's works exert their hold on
the mind's eye as much by their
ambiguity as their imposing physical
presence.

contemplation. The power of the works lies in their deep sensory
messages (death, decay, regeneration, killing, birthing, fear, wonder, etc.).
Neo-primitivism is also an analytic tool focusing on the efficacy of an
object's emotive communication (a topic to be explored later), especially
when non-Western aesthetics are incorporated, and allowing us to
separate the "hype" from the real thing. Kirk Varnedoe notes correctly that
such neo-primitivist work "has looked to anthropological models of tribal
and prehistoric integration of art and society as curative for separation or
alienation of art from its viewers and for the consequent undermining of
art's relevance and power."[6] However, Varnedoe has misconstrued the
significance and nature of this influence. It is not simply that neo-
primitivism is more authentically primordial, tribal, or, in other words,
primitive, than those "merely formal incorporations of tribal art by early
Modernists such as Picasso"[7] (or Paul Gauguin, Paul Klee, Man Ray, Ernst
Kirchner, Max Ernst, and Alberto Giacommeti). The true neo-primitive
object is both new and old, it is a synthetic creation emotively inspired by
archetypal forces. Such objects are not conceptually linked to historical
primitivism, nor are they aligned stylistically to it through imitative
"masking"[8] in the costume of tribal design. Neo-primitivist "artifacts" are
not symbolic or visionary in the Modernist sense but are allegorically
emotive generalizations without specific iconic reference. The works of
Nancy Graves — especially her totem staffs — Deborah Butterfield's fetish
objects, Richard DeVore's killed vessels, Graham Marks's vegetative clay
containers, and Houston Conwill's earth chambers all resonate with
cultural and temporal suggestions, yet purposefully avoid any definable
symbolic association. Picasso's literal incorporation of the sculptural planes
of African Fang and Pende masks into his *Les Demoiselles d'Avignon* in
1907 or Gauguin's use of Marquesan design motifs in his paintings
especially from 1896 onwards, demonstrates an intellectual process
fundamentally different from the emotive transformation of universal
"collective representations" practiced by the neo-primitivists. Their effect is
to reopen the humanist dialogue concerning the role of spirituality in
culture and in individual creative life. The underlying assertion is that,
while the aesthetic formulations of man's inspiration are always in stylistic
flux, they are ultimately reducible to a common core. Each particular
formulation, whether Western or non-Western, literate or nonliterate,
prehistoric, ancient, Medieval, enlightened or benighted, is a potential
solution to the problem of discerning meaning by instilling meaning. Each
one is the dialectical validation of pre-rational, unprovable, suprahuman
phenomena — magic, shamanism, or divine cosmogony, through the
secular creation of *mana*-imbued works which become testaments of
sacred presence.

As we have seen, the raw communicative power of sacred objects
exudes an ahistorical, pan-cultural, atemporal presence, propelled by
evocative archetypes: blood, deities, totems, tombs, bones, fire, earth,
stone, wood, fetishes, temples, life, death, birth, and age. They are man's
racial memories of his first "collective representations" of reality.

What the sacred consists of, elementarily, is objects, things. These objects do not possess their sacredness intrinsically; it is projected on to them. This happens because the objects are used as symbols; they are among man's earliest symbolizations. And the first and immediate designata which are symbolized by these pristine object-symbols are feelings, affects. These feelings, which exist long before they are ever coherently conceptualized into mana words, are collective affects or excitements aroused during group activities. More than that, they are feelings that are partly perceptions and also tremble at the edge of cognition — of society. Society makes itself felt for the first time in this excitement, which is mana. . . . sacred objects are . . . ultimately symbols of society.[9]

James Turrell
The Roden Crater Project
On site location, Arizona
Courtesy of the Skystone
Foundation, Flagstaff, Arizona

How are we to separate those fictitious neo-primitivist works touted as "ceremonial," "primordial," or "shamanistic" in conception, yet once again only dressed up in borrowed motifs, from contemporary creations that actually function on the precipice of sacrality? Consider James Turrell's *Roden Crater,* an actual, 500-foot-high volcanic cone whose interior bowl is 1000 feet in diameter, occupying an area that is three-quarters of a mile wide in the barren Arizona desert landscape: the artist has subtly altered this natural phenomenon by the addition of a spiral walkway and planetary viewing points and tunnels carved into the stone. *Crater's* immensity and its minimal and nondestructive modification suggest both immeasurable age and the possible unity between man and nature. Such works suggest that in other times, and perhaps even still, they could be sacred objects or sites concerned with earth and sky, the stars and man. Turrell's cosmological concerns, and those of other neo-primitivists, are, I suspect, compatible with those of the builders of Mayan temples and Egyptian pyramids; the process is the same for all cultures and all periods. In our time, however — when art is thought of as something that can fit into a gallery — these necessarily vast constructions, which inhabit isolated and remote regions, are unavailable to us. What traditional sacred objects and neo-primitive artworks share most importantly (and the key to the issue of perceived sacrality) is a spontaneous fusion between material object and subjective associative mental image. As with beauty, sacredness is in the eye of the beholder, and by perceiving an object to be sacred, we make it so. And the more ambiguous and archetypal the object is, the greater will be the viewer's propensity to perceive it as sacred, the greater will be the consensus among many viewers of its sacred nature, and the more power, or "otherness," will accrue to it. Wonder, dread, rapture, or ecstasy: all can be the feelings of the viewer, acknowledging an object's affecting presence.

An interpretive material image of God does not create divinity (the particular belief is preexistent in the form of tradition), nor does a belief in God create an affecting icon, a material image which is communally communicative on the deepest symbolic level. Nevertheless, belief and image are mutually inseparable, as with the Hindu Trimurti, an inseparable unity which is yet able to be considered separately as Brahma, Vishnu, and Siva. In art — particularly in the sacred traditions, inclusive of certain neo-primitive works — sacrality is synonymous with intuitive-interpretive recognition. The process is a personal, communicative, transference ritual of perceived power through the identification of nonlogical sacra.[10]

The details of the message vary depending on the perceiver's background and inclination, yet if the object-symbol is effective, it demands an associative response in its viewer. The most effective objects have ambiguous symbolic and physical trappings that allow many interpretations of perceived residing power, thus affecting the broadest audience. Here then is the common denominator for the most ancient personal objects of power, the Australian *churingas,* North American Plains Indian medicine bundles and shields, and Polynesian *tikis.* As they are acknowledged to be sacred objects by more and more members of the

William Wyman
Temple 27, 1979
Lowfire white clay, 15 x 37 x 4
Collection of Sheila and David
Franklin, Lexington, Massachusetts

During his last two years Wyman produced intense spiritual icons, such as slab-constructed pyramids and temples with surfaces which were often devoid of color, muted, or bone dry. *Temple 27,* made in 1979, is a moving work of this period. As with others of this series, it seems to ask more questions than it answers.

José Rafael Aragón
Bultos, between 1838 and 1851
Wood, 66 inches in height
The Taylor Museum, Colorado
Springs Fine Arts Center,
Colorado Springs, Colorado

The Catholic tradition of the
depiction of saints has continued in
areas colonized by the Spanish from
early colonial times to today. New
Mexican sacred figures (*bultos*) are
throwbacks to the late Middle Ages;
since New Mexican colonialists were
isolated from European traditions
from the early seventeenth century
onward, their sacred images did not
evolve into the "pretty" and did not
undergo association with worldly
wealth. Instead they have retained
their original forcefulness and
passion. These crude but powerful
images are painful and genuine;
wounds gape; bloody tears are
shed.

James Surls
Needle Man, 1980 (facing page)
Pine and oak, 118 inches in height
Collection of Martin Sklar,
New York, New York

Surls creates characters —
anthropormorphizing his sculptures
with fantastic figures. These
personages have the roughness of
technique characteristic of the hand
carving local to his native east Texas,
yet they have balance and grace of
form. In *Needle Man,* Surls shapes a
corkscrew body that takes on a
needlelike tapered form. The
projecting, spiky elements around
the head and outstretched fingers
burst forth with uncontrollable
energy. Here the eye of a needle
becomes the swirling eye of a
tornado, the entire sculpture
seeming to spin with energy and
fury. Ungrounded (it hangs only
from a wire above), it is suspended
in air like a storm.

society, the objects evolve — through the force of group consensus — to
become collective sacred representations and eventually icons.

Gaston Bachelard, drawing on the earlier work of phenomenologist
Eugene Minkowski, explored a similar issue in his phenomenological
approach to describing the "poetic image."[11] Bachelard's arguments are
illuminating for the issue at hand — the relationship between the symbolic
object and the symbolic mental image it sparks in the mind of the viewer.
Ultimately, his logic is directed toward a phenomenology of imagination,
central to poetic inspiration, but it is equally applicable to three-
dimensional creations.

> I shall have to make it understood that this relation [the
> relation of a new poetic image to an archetype lying dormant
> in the depths of the unconscious] is not, properly speaking, a
> causal one. The poetic image is not subject to an inner thrust.
> It is not an echo of the past. On the contrary: through the

brilliance of an image, the distant past resounds with echoes, and it is hard to know at what depth these echoes will reverberate and die away. Because of its novelty and its action, the poetic image has an entity and a dynamism of its own; it is referable to a direct ontology.[12]

Both Bachelard and Minkowski believed in a universally operational "élan vital,"[13] which is applicable to our search for manifest, yet intangible, power. Minkowski describes the "élan vital" in the metaphorical language of Thoreauean naturalism:

If, having fixed the original form in our mind's eye, we ask ourselves how that form comes alive and fills with life, we discover a new dynamic and vital category, a new property of the universe: reverberation (retentir). It is as though a well-spring existed in a sealed vase and its waves, repeatedly echoing against the sides of this vase, filled it with their sonority. . . . with penetrating deep waves which, although not sonorous in the sensory meaning of the word, are not, for this reason, less harmoniously resonant, melodic and capable of determining the whole tonality of life. And this life itself will reverberate to the most profound depths of its being, through contact with these waves, which are at once sonorous and silent. . . . It is not a material object which fills another by espousing the form that the other imposes. No, it is the dynamism of the sonorous life itself which by engulfing and appropriating everything it finds in its path, fills the slice of space, or better, the slice of the world that it assigns itself by its movement, making it reverberate, breathing into it its own life.[14]

This quality of retentir is also true, to a degree, of all great art, as it alludes to the intangible inspirational aesthetic presence which moves the viewer into a contemplative plane of abstraction. Yet qualitatively, as Claude Levi-Strauss observed, there exists a fundamental difference between the image resonating from the core of sacred and so-called primitive art and that of the academic traditions.

Professional or academic art internalized execution (which it has, or believes itself to have, mastered) and purpose ("art for art's sake" being an end in itself). As a result, it is impelled to externalize the occasion (which it requires the model to provide) and the latter thus becomes a part of the signified. Primitive art, on the other hand, internalizes the occasion (since the supernatural beings which it delights in representing have a reality which is timeless and independent of circumstances) and it externalized execution and purpose which thus become a part of the signifying.[15]

Neo-primitivist works intellectually internalize the event or occasion being manifest. The physical object and the materials it is made from are the veneer which clothe a known (but immaterial) text. In true sacred traditions, such works are but temporal vessels of immemorial power, to be discarded when they are ritually deactivated. An example is the creation and refurbishing of a Katcina mask among the agricultural Puebloans of the American Southwest, in which the artist neither creates a sacred object nor evokes sacrality. In making a Katcina mask, he creates an alluring physical form which, if successful, can attract supernatural power. It is hoped that the Katcina mask will attract an immortal Katcina spirit, giving it a desirable temporary location; if so, the mask wearer, now spirit-possessed, can effect positive blessings for the fertility of earth and ultimately for sustenance of the people. If the crops fail, it is not the gods who are called into question, but the purity of the people's devotion and the suitability of an intended sacred vessel to create a bridge between the sacred and the worldly.

In his religious zeal and potent imagery, Fra Angelico created a corresponding physical and cognitive aesthetic instrument that allowed an audience which shared his conviction — but not his gift for visualization — to use his artistic bridge between the two domains.

An important aspect of such event-oriented sacred objects, whether new or old, is the audience's awareness that the perceived visual statement is but a component of a larger construct; an ideational and ritual material culture complex. Whether a New Mexican *bultos,* a Mayan incense burner, a Christian cross, or James Surls's *Needle Man,* it is not the single work that embodies the most potent physical distillate of spiritual power, but its fusion with a broader encompassing ceremonialism. Out of this communal understanding comes a total experience far more significant and affecting than any of its isolated associative parts. Clearly, the opulence of a Byzantine reliquary or the heroic dignity of a Benin bronze are aesthetically compelling. Yet in and of themselves, extracted from their functional, symbolic context, they have been emotively diminished. This realization is not new. Yet, an interesting reversal of this proposition also exists, in which some neo-primitivist works, such as Robert Morris's *Observatory* and James Turrell's *Roden Crater,* though they exist entirely outside any larger complex, elicit in the viewer the sense of a preexisting ritual context, which then amplifies the associative emotive power of the single artwork.

Turrell's construct immediately demands dialectical contemplation of earth/air, old/new, natural/manmade, cosmic/planetary, oppositions that fit comfortably within the mental templates of most world religions. The particulars of specific ritualism are provided by the viewer, since actual referential details are irrelevant to the operational presence of the work. The viewer's imagining of such ceremonialism creates the reverberations (rententir) with which the object is amplified and made known.

Minkowski's poetic "auditive metaphor, retentir" is equivalent to the neo-primitivist's allegorical use of references to sacred images or their reducible components, which triggers cognitive associations with sacrality.

Robert Morris
Observatory, 1971, first version
Earth, timber, granite, steel, water,
230 feet across
Collection: Destroyed
Courtesy Leo Castelli Gallery,
New York, New York

They are the nonmaterial "élan vital resonating from visual archetypes that embody various combinations of inferred monumentality, symbolic reduction, and component symbols. Their effect is to stimulate mental abstraction and empathy, among other responses.

Such an artwork is concerned with transformation, not transfiguration. Western mainstream and academic painting remains bound to the aesthetics of transfiguration, purely and ideally, translating that which is intellectually, albeit emotionally, perceived into symbolic visualizations. Neo-primitivists, along with some of their precursors in the craft-arts movement, have re-embraced passionately the alchemic transformational qualities of materials, as well as the metaphoric implication of the creative act of transforming. For them these are allegorical of universal power and prelogical sacred or magical icons. Such concerns are not exclusive to the neo-primitivist, as witnessed by the nonrepresentational paintings of James Havard, who attempts to create the illusion of space and depth as components of sacred Puebloan images (Katcina beings) using a two-dimensional media. The transformational concerns of artists such as M. C. Escher and Max Ernst are self-apparent,

Morris is concerned with the delineation of man's relationship to the cosmos. The *Observatory* is like a fulcrum for the alignment of stars, celestial phenomena, and earthly events. Stylistically, it reminds us of neolithic structures from Greece and Crete and of the stone menhirs scattered throughout Celtic lands.

Howard Ben Tré
Column 38, 1986
Cast glass, lead, gold leaf, copper,
brass, 95 x 28 x 12
Courtesy of Charles Cowles Gallery,
Inc., New York, New York

An eerie timelessness pervades Ben
Tré's works. His early works of the
1970s were weighted more toward
the archaic: small vessels of cast
glass with the preciousness of
excavated ritual objects. Architecture
has been the subject of Ben Tré's
recent work, but his great cast
columns could not be further from
traditional architectural ornament.
They speak of the architecture of
ruins where space retains the order
imposed on it by the architect's
mind long after the substance of his
building is destroyed. Ben Tré's
columns can reach over seven feet
in height. With the solidity of stone
rendered in glass, they are like
haunting, majestic remnants of the
cathedrals of the future.

as are the Jungian and psychoanalytic issues which propelled the Surrealists and Dadaists. Nevertheless, the transformational power of their imagery was diluted by the limitations of their medium. Physical references to magic, religion, or cultic primordial forces best occupy a tangible dimensional space or nesting of spaces. Celtic Stonehenge, a Norman cathedral, a Sioux medicine wheel, a Cheyenne visionary butte, a Shinto shrine, or the secular-sacred Greco-Roman temple monuments of Washington, D.C. — all are associated with sanctified space and permanence. The monumentality and inferred permanence of contemporary works by earth sculptors Richard Long, James Turrell, Robert Morris, and Michelle Stuart (page 217), among others, draws directly on this

Howard Ben Tré
Blenko Project #5, 1981
Glass sculpture, 20 x 15 x 13
Collection of Jean and Hilbert Sosin,
Bloomfield Hills, Michigan

Ben Tré's ambitions forced him out of the studio context to seek the facilities of glass factories, first Blenko in West Virginia, then Super Glass in New York. He brings to the factory floor meticulously constructed molds developed from initial free sketches through detailed mechanical drawings. He lines sections of his molds with sheets of copper and the heat of the molten glass which is ladled in causes the copper to fuse with the cooling substance. The inclusion of metal heightened the mechanistic character of his first solid glass forms of the early 1980s.

Mimbres Burials, ca. 1920s
Photo courtesy of the Department
of Anthropology,
University of Minnesota

In this ancient Mimbres burial
uncovered by the University of
Minnesota in the 1920s on the
Galaz site in Southern New Mexico,
a "killed bowl" is found in its
inverted position over the body.

force of space, scale, and dimension. Other neo-primitivists have understood this principle, and it has also shaped the forms of their works, especially William Wyman's sepulchral temple tombs, Howard Ben Tré's monolithic glass artifacts, and James Surls's spirit constructs.

All these works, ancient or modern, share a connection to basic primordial psychology. Drawing from pan-global, prescientific archetypes — whether Cro-Magnon cave paintings and clay animal fetishes, New Guinean totem figures, or Egyptian and Minoan architectural units — the new empathetic forms still allude to actual cultural contexts, as though Butterfield's totem horses and Graves's totem staffs were true anthropological components of an ancient hunting society's religion. The objects' mystique suggests that they were worshiped and revered as magical simulacre fashioned from earth, wood, stone, yet animistically capable of generative power. Wyman's tombs, Long's stone circles, Ben Tré's architectonic relics — all are archaeological fragments of a phenomenally vibrant domain, past or future. They share a monumentality of perceived scale, elevating them emotively to the heroic and the sacred. All are objects of awe, not elegant as much as forceful, not eloquent but subliminally echoing racial memories. They are phantasms of déjà vu.

An essential component of this shared gestalt or psychology is an understanding of the emotive power of referential ambiguity or dissociation seen in some of the most powerful of ancient sacred arts. Certain neo-primitivists also use this jarring device. Bowls with intentionally pierced bottoms, sacred scripts in invisible or totally private glyphs, death imagery associated with birth, earth elements fused into animate forms, fragile glass cast into weight-supporting architectural units — these purposely combine contradictory or ambiguous materials and messages. Such visual devices are commonly used in small-scale societies during initiation or rites of passage, when the novice is confronted with alternative realities and encouraged to deconstruct the rational principles previously organizing his life and to reconstruct from chaos a new knowledge and order.[16] Hermaphroditic New Guinean fertility figures, African Nembi earth monster masks, or Conwill's *Passages: Earth/Space H-3* (1980), an earth chamber with time capsule scrolls — all operate within the symbolic parameters of William James's "law of dissociation," which holds that "what is associated now with one thing and now with another, tends to become dissociated from either, and to grow into an object of abstract contemplation."[17]

DeVore's killed bowls, with their multiple levels of meaning, provide an example with which to close this discussion. *Bowl* is an apparently functional ceramic container with a broken bottom. From this functional/ nonfunctional contradiction comes a set of associations: a discarded object, accident, or loss of purpose. Yet the bowl is in pristine condition, devoid of any signs of wear or use. Likewise, the overlapping concentric holes piercing the bottom appear intentional. Why? What use is this vessel that can't hold substance? Perhaps that is the immaterial message to contemplate. This artwork is a bowl in form only. On another level it is an aesthetic construct which purposely rejects function. Yet drawing upon

Richard DeVore
Bowl, 1978
Stoneware, low fired overlays,
4¾ x 11¼
Collection of Karen Johnson Boyd,
Racine, Wisconsin

archaeological knowledge, we recall ancient and historic Puebloans of the American Southwest ceremonially interred ceramic vessels as part of their mortuary rituals. The prehistoric Mimbres of southern New Mexico are known to have ritually "killed," or pierced, the bottoms of bowls to be stacked over the face of the deceased. This contemplative association reverberates from DeVore's vessel. As a piece of contemporary art perhaps this object rejects material function but in a spiritual context, substance, "élan vital," is immaterial, and sacred vessels are osmotic membranes stretched over dimensional portals to other worlds. In that sense, this object, like the sacred sandpaintings used in a Navajo ceremony, is supremely functional. The object now communicates functional/ nonfunctional, secular/sacred, modern/ancient, tangible/intangible, as well as numerous recombinations such as utilitarian/secular/non-functional versus nonutilitarian (aesthetic)/sacred/functional. The information inherent in the object is infinitely expandable; it allows the audience to instill it with their own perceptions. True to the nature of ancient or so-called primitive art, the object exists beyond the parameters of its creator's intention or the immediate concerns of the culture which nourished him. It has transcended into a universal communicative presence which demands contemplation and denies the whim of style.

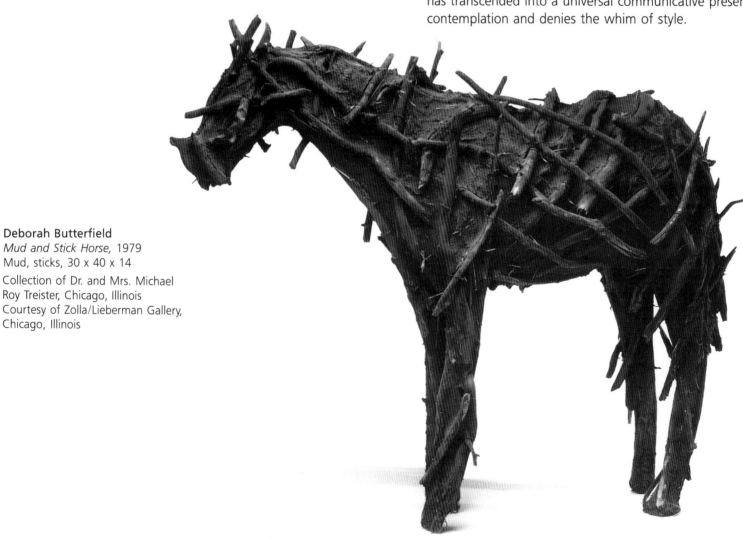

Deborah Butterfield
Mud and Stick Horse, 1979
Mud, sticks, 30 x 40 x 14

Collection of Dr. and Mrs. Michael Roy Treister, Chicago, Illinois
Courtesy of Zolla/Lieberman Gallery, Chicago, Illinois

NOTES

[1] The role of spirituality in contemporary society and its manifestation through the arts have obsessed many modern writers and artists. Artists such as Vasily Kandinsky, for example, created elaborate metaphysical models in an attempt to track the elusive course of the spiritual. However, at the core of many of their constructions lies a common omission, a failure to draw the distinction between the spiritual and the sacred, and between the individual versus the societal response to the two. Couple this with a general loss of historical perspective and an attitude of confrontational individualism supplanting social tradition, and it is understandable why modern Western societies have so much trouble perceiving and using the sacred. In part, the problem evolved from, and has accelerated, the deconstruction of meaning in our language. The terms and corresponding concepts "sacred" and "spiritual" have been so manipulated that they have been rendered almost useless.

Foreshadowing the self-defined world of the twentieth century, Dutch and French Symbolists and German Expressionists embarked on personal quests to manifest the spiritual. Continuing the search were Abstractionists, Dadaists, Surrealists, through today's avowed postmodernists. In the course of this exploration, increasingly marred by the claims of commercially motivated art journalism, the subjective process of spiritual investigation came to be confused with the creation of viable sacred arts. The sacred and the spiritual are autonomous phenomena; though related, they are not mutually dependent. Spiritual rapture does not require the presence of a sacred object. Thus, Kandinsky could explore his "stimmung" of "total realism" and "total abstraction," even to an ultimate purity of aesthetic "silence," obliterating the very corporeal mantle of art, yet the result would not necessarily qualify as sacred. In seeking to escape the material, the artist had overlooked one inviolable tenet of the sacred — that it is tangible, and must be perceived to be acknowledged. The premise of ascendancy, the movement towards a higher order of ethereal being, is pivotal to the spiritual but superfluous to the sacred. The sacred object occupies space unconditionally; it operates through contrast and comparison. Its power lies in the tension between what is known and what is not known, between that which is intellectualized and that which is felt.

Sacred arts, whether neo-primitivist or of other origin, share a common declarational quality. They cause within the perceiver a recognition that something compelling and evocative is operative within an object, place, or thing. This perception of resident presence, or power, does not require referential group agreement as to its message or content, but only unsolicited basic acknowledgment of its existence.

[2] Can civilization, or at least the one our Enlightenment ancestors believed they were building, survive on secular values alone? An increasing number of contemporary thinkers doubt that it can. Sociologist Daniel Bell believes that the sanctifying power of traditions (avowed and practiced by the group as a whole) must be either reintroduced or reinvented for the survival of Western civilization. Bell predicts that the necessary revival will be based on neo-Protestant ideals, but it would seem that other alternatives are equally viable.

[3] Gerhard Hoffman, *Social Criticism and the Deformation of Man: Satire, the Grotesque and Comic Nihilism in the Modern and Postmodern American Novel,* in *American Studies* 28, No. 2 (Munich, West Germany: Wilhelm Fink Verlag, 1983).

[4] Hal Foster, *The Anti-Aesthetic: Essays on Postmodern Culture* (Port Townsend, Washington: Bay Press, 1983), p. xii.

Bakongo, Congo
Male Nail Fetish Figure
Wood, metal inserts and blades, gum, magic substances, ivory, 14½ inches in height
Philbrook Museum of Art, Tulsa, Oklahoma, Gift of Lawrence Gussman, 1982

This male nail fetish is used among the Yombe in the Congo as a ritual object. Nails and other metal objects are driven into it during divination and protective rites: so pierced, the object becomes a conduit for power.

[5] Postmodernism and the pan-humanism it has engendered are simply organizational approaches. Except in the view of a few proponents, they are not social movements, and it is likely that some of their practitioners would not acknowledge their involvement with either method. Historically, these approaches punctuate the attitudinal changes that have increasingly influenced twentieth-century thought. Neither approach is consistently applied, as will be shown in our analysis of neo-primitivism, an outgrowth of pan-humanism. For example, Nancy Graves moved through a neo-primitivist phase early in her career, but now she is exploring other aesthetic avenues, whereas Deborah Butterfield persistently digs into the animistic properties of her *Horse* constructions. Designation of individual works (not artists) as postmodern or neo-primitivist is based on certain shared characteristics. Although I have touched on some of those qualities in reference to postmodern and pan-humanistic expression, it is not my intent here to document those approaches, but rather to explore neo-primitivism, which has arisen from them. Consequently, their analysis is brief, concentrating on important shared traits.

Manifestations of postmodernism can be seen in the plays of Peter Weiss (*Marat Sade),* Carl Off (*Antigone*); the architecture of Aldo Rossi, Mario Botta, Philip Johnson, Michael Graves, Louis Kahn, and Peter Eisenman; the social and aesthetic criticism of Jurgen Habermas, Daniel Bell, Peter Buger (*Theory of the Avant-Garde*), Jean Baudrillard (*L'Échange Symbolique et al Mort*); Paolo Portoghesi and Charles Jencks (especially *The Language of Post-Modern Architecture*); the wide-ranging muscial compositions of the Residents and the German industrial-sound composers Einsturzende Neu Bauten; and some of the choreography of Twyla Tharp (especially *The Catherine Wheel*) and others.

In the realm of pan-humanism, which weds cultural patterns from throughout history into new, structurally coherent forms, are the compositions of Swiss harpist Andreas Vollenweider; German composers Stephen Meakus and Deuter (especially Stephen Meakus's East of Night and Deuter's reformulation of Japanese and Indic styles in Multiple Flutes from the album *Nirvana Road* and Flute and Synthesizer from the album *Ecstasy*); and Americans Herbie Hancock (Cantata) and Lucia Wong (House of Sleeping Beauties); collage artist Magdalena Abakanowicz, Susan Zurcher, the Hopi sculptor Charles Loloma, and others.

[6] Kirk Varnedoe, "Contemporary Explorations," in *Primitivism in 20th Century Art* (New York: The Museum of Modern Art, 1984), p. 681.

[7] *Varnedoe,* p. 662.

[8] Frederick Jameson, "Postmodernism and Consumer Society," in *The Anti-Aesthetic: Essays on Postmodern Culture* (Port Townsend, Washington: Bay Press, 1983), p. 114.

[9] Daniel O'Keefe, *Stolen Lightning: The Social Theory of Magic,* (New York: Vintage, 1982), p. 188.

[10] W. Lloyd Warner, *The Living and the Dead: A Study of the Symbolic Life of Americans* (New Haven: Yale University Press, 1959).

[11] Gaston Bachelard, *The Poetics of Space* (Boston: Beacon Press, 1969).

[12] Bachelard, p. xii.

[13] Bachelard, p. xiii.

[14] Bachelard, p. xiii.

[15] Claude Levi-Strauss, *The Savage Mind* (Chicago: University of Chicago Press, 1968), p. 29.

[16] Victor W. Turner, "Betwixt and Between: The Liminal Period in Rites of Passage" in *The Proceedings of the American Ethnological Society* (Seattle: University of Washington Press, 1964).

[17] William James, *Principles of Psychology,* vol. 1 (New York: Henry Holt, 1918), p. 506.

Deborah Butterfield
Horse #6, 1978
Sticks, mud, steel armature,
108 x 144 x 24
The Oakland Museum,
Oakland, California,
Timken Fund

Beginning in the early 1970s Butterfield first made horses of wire and steel armatures covered with paper-mâché, following the natural model closely. As she came to experiment with mud, common sticks, weeds, and other materials, she also departed from realism to create more dramatic and expressive effects. *Horse #6,* hiding or trapped in a thicket, seems at once to be a caged animal; a burdened, encumbered being; or a ghost image appearing from behind a veil that protects and obscures it. Butterfield continues to create horses, more recently using scrap metals with which she directly builds the forms.

Buffalo effigy, Sioux or Cheyenne, ca. 1860-1880
Carved wood, tufted fiber tail
8¾ x 7 x 2⅞
The Philbrook Museum of Art,
Tulsa, Oklahoma

Male and female buffalo effigies of wood were placed at the base of the sacred Sun Dance pole in the ceremonial brush arbor. They petitioned for fertility of the buffalo, upon whose survival the equestrian hunters of the Plains depended.

Sherry Markovitz
Autumn Buck, 1982
Paper maché, oil paint, beads,
36 x 15 x 21
Collection of Bill and Jan Bascom,
Seattle, Washington

ARTIST INDEX

Hank Murta Adams
Detroit, Michigan

Born in Philadelphia, Pennsylvania, 1956

B.F.A., Painting, Rhode Island School of Design, Providence, Rhode Island, 1978

Neda Al Hilali
Santa Monica, California

Born in Cheb, Czechoslovakia, 1938

Studied with Bernard Kester

B.A., Art, University of California at Los Angeles, Los Angeles, California, 1965; **M.A.,** Art, University of California at Los Angeles, Los Angeles, California, 1968

Anni Albers
Orange, Connecticut

Born in Berlin, Germany, 1899

Studied with Martin Brandenburg

Diploma, Bauhaus, Weimar — Dessau, Germany, 1930; **Honorary Ph.D.,** Maryland Institute, College of Art, Baltimore, Maryland, 1972; **Honorary Doctor of Letters,** York University, Ontario, Canada, 1973; **Honorary Ph.D.,** Philadelphia College of Art, Philadelphia, Pennsylvania, 1976; **Honorary Ph.D.,** University of Hartford, Hartford, Connecticut, 1979

Laura Andreson
Los Angeles, California

Born in San Bernadino, California, 1902

Studied with Olive Newcomb, Gertrud Natzler, Anita Delano, Barbara Morgan

B.A., Education, University of California at Los Angeles, Los Angeles, California, 1932; **M.F.A.,** Painting, Columbia University, New York City, New York, 1937

Robert Arneson
Benicia, California

Born in Benicia, California, 1930

Studied with Antonio Prieto

B.A., Education, California College of Arts and Crafts, Oakland, California, 1954; **M.F.A.,** Ceramics, Mills College, Oakland, California, 1958

Ruth Asawa
San Francisco, California

Born in Norwalk, California, 1926

Studied with Robert Von Neumann, Josef and Anni Albers, Buckminster Fuller

Honorary Doctorate, California College of Arts and Crafts, Oakland, California, 1974; **Honorary Masters,** Academy of Art College, San Francisco, California, 1983

Michael Aschenbrenner
New York, New York

Born in Pomona, California, 1949

Studied with William Warehall, Curtis C. Hoard, Joe Moran

B.A., Ceramics and Printmaking, California State University, San Bernardino, California, 1974; **M.F.A.,** Studio Art, University of Minnesota, Minneapolis, Minnesota, 1978

Rudolf Arne Autio
Missoula, Montana

Born in Butte, Montana, 1926

Studied with Frances Senska

B.S., Art, Montana State University, Bozeman, Montana, 1950; **M.F.A.,** Sculpture, Washington State University, Pullman, Washington, 1952; **Honorary D.F.A.,** Fine Art, Maryland Institute, College of Art, Baltimore, Maryland, 1986

Larry J. Beck
Seattle, Washington

Born in Seattle, Washington, 1938

B.A., Painting, University of Washington, Seattle, Washington, 1964; **M.F.A.,** Sculpture, University of Washington, Seattle, Washington, 1965

Howard Ben Tré
Providence, Rhode Island

Born in Brooklyn, New York, 1949

Studied with Dale Chihuly

S.A., Ceramics, Portland State University, Portland, Oregon, 1978; **M.F.A.,** Sculpture and Glass, Rhode Island School of Design, Providence, Rhode Island, 1980

Christina Bertoni
Pascoag, Rhode Island

Born in Ann Arbor, Michigan, 1945

Studied with Richard DeVore

B.F.A., Painting, University of Michigan, Ann Arbor, Michigan, 1967; **M.F.A.,** Ceramics, Cranbrook Academy of Art, Bloomfield Hills, Michigan, 1976

Dempsey Bob
Prince Rupert, British Columbia

Born in Telegraph Creek, British Columbia, 1948

Studied with Freda Diesing, Walter Harris, Vernon Stephens, Earl Muldoe, Ken Mowatt

Studied Design at Kitanmax School of North West Coast Indian Art, Hazelton, British Columbia, 1972; Studied Advanced Carving at Kitanmax School of North West Coast Indian Art, Hazelton, British Columbia, 1974

Robert Brady
Berkeley, California

Born in Reno, Nevada, 1946

Studied with Viola Frey, Hal Riegger, Robert Arneson, Vernon Coykendall

B.F.A., Ceramics, California College of Arts and Crafts, Oakland, California, 1968; **M.F.A.,** Ceramics, University of California, Davis, California, 1975

Karen Breschi
San Francisco, California

Born in Oakland, California, 1941

Studied with Seymore Locks, Sam Richardson, Richard Shaw, Tony De Lapp

B.F.A., Ceramics, California College of Arts and Crafts, Oakland, California, 1963; **M.A.,** Sculpture, San Francisco State University, San Francisco, California, 1965; **Ph.D.,** Psychology, California Institute of Integral Studies, San Francisco, California, 1987

Deborah Butterfield
Bozeman, Montana

Born in San Diego, California, 1949

Studied with Roy DeForest, William Wiley, Robert Arneson

B.A., University of California, Davis, California, 1971; **M.F.A.,** University of California, Davis, California, 1973

Alexander Calder

Born in Lawnton, Pennsylvania, 1898; died 1976

Studied with George Luks, John Sloan, Boardman Robinson, DuBois

M.E., Mechanical Engineering, Stevens Institute of Technology, Hoboken, New Jersey, 1918

Wendell Castle
Scottsville, New York

Born in Emporia, Kansas, 1932

B.F.A., Industrial Design, University of Kansas, Lawrence, Kansas, 1958; **M.F.A.,** Sculpture, University of Kansas, Lawrence, Kansas, 1961; **Honorary D.F.A.,** Maryland Institute, College of Art, Baltimore, Maryland, 1979

John Cederquist
Capistrano Beach, California

Born in Altadena, California, 1946

B.A., Crafts, California State University, Long Beach, California, 1969; **M.A.,** Crafts, California State University, Long Beach, California, 1971

Judy Chicago
Benicia, California

Born in Chicago, Illinois, 1939

Studied with Oliver Andrews

B.A., University of California at Los Angeles, Los Angeles, California, 1962; **M.A.,** University of California at Los Angeles, Los Angeles, California, 1964

Dale Chihuly
Seattle, Washington

Born in Tacoma, Washington, 1941

Studied with Hope Foot, Warren Hill, Harvey Littleton, Doris Breckway

B.A., Interior Design, University of Washington, Seattle, Washington, 1965; M.S., Fine Arts, University of Wisconsin, Madison, Wisconsin, 1967; M.F.A., Glass, Rhode Island School of Design, Providence, Rhode Island, 1968

Lolita Concho
San Fidel, New Mexico

Born in Acoma, New Mexico, 1918

Studied with Dorothy Dunn

Houston Conwill
New York, New York

Born in Louisville, Kentucky, 1947

Influenced by Sam Gilliam, Romare Bearden

B.F.A., Painting, Howard University, Washington, D.C., 1973; M.F.A., Painting, University of Southern California, Los Angeles, California, 1976

Lia Cook
Berkeley, California

Born in Ventura, California, 1942

Studied with Ed Rossbach

B.A., Political Science, University of California, Berkeley, California, 1965; M.A., Textile Design, University of California, Berkeley, California, 1973

Ken Cory
Ellensburg, Washington

Born in Kirkland, Washington, 1943

B.F.A., Metals, California College of Arts and Crafts, Oakland, California, 1966; M.F.A., Sculpture, Washington State University, Pullman, Washington, 1969

Margret Craver
Boston, Massachusetts

Born in Pratt, Kansas, 1910

Studied with Baron Erik Fleming, 1938

B.D., Design, University of Kansas, Lawrence, Kansas, 1929

Margaret De Patta

Born in Tacoma, Washington, 1903; died 1964

Studied with Lazlo Moholy-Nagy and Armin Hairenian

Stephen DeStaebler
Berkeley, California

Born in Saint Louis, Missouri, 1933

Studied with Joe Brown, Ben Shahn, Jacques Schnier, Peter Voulkos

A.B., Religion, Princeton University, Princeton, New Jersey, 1954; M.A., Art, University of California, Berkeley, California, 1961

Richard DeVore
Fort Collins, Colorado

Born in Toledo, Ohio, 1933

Studied with Maija Grotell, Naomi Powell, Wallace Mitchell

B.Ed., Education, University of Toledo, Toledo, Ohio, 1955; M.F.A., Ceramics, Cranbrook Academy of Art, Bloomfield Hills, Michigan, 1957

Dominic Di Mare
Tiburon, California

Born in San Francisco, California, 1932

Self-Taught

Michele Oka Doner
New York, New York

Born in Miami Beach, Florida, 1945

Studied with John Stephenson, Oleg Grabar

B.S.D., University of Michigan, Ann Arbor, Michigan, 1966; M.F.A., University of Michigan, Ann Arbor, Michigan, 1968

Velma Davis Dozier
Dallas, Texas

Born in Waco, Texas, 1901

Studied with Vivian Aunspaugh, Boardman Robinson, Eric Helman, Floyd Keith

B.S., Painting, Texas Women's University, Denton, Texas, 1932; M.A., Art, Columbia University, New York City, New York, 1933

Ruth Duckworth
Chicago, Illinois

Born in Hamburg, Germany, 1919

Studied with Hans Coper

Honorary Ph.D., DePaul University, Chicago, Illinois, 1981

Jack Eugene Earl
Lakeview, Ohio

Born in Uniopolis, Ohio, 1934

Studied with John Klassen

B.A., Art Education, Bluffton College, Bluffton, Ohio, 1956; M.A., Ceramics, Ohio State University, Columbus, Ohio, 1964

Robert Ebendorf
Highland, New York

Born in Topeka, Kansas, 1938

Studied with Carlyle Smith, Robert Montgomery

B.F.A., Jewelry, University of Kansas, Lawrence, Kansas, 1958; M.F.A., Design, University of Kansas, Lawrence, Kansas, 1963; Diploma, Creative Metals, State School for the Applied Arts and Crafts, Oslo, Norway, 1965

Alma Eikerman
Bloomington, Indiana

Born in Pratt, Kansas, 1908

Studied with Karl Gustav Hansen, Ossik Zadkine, C.F. Wilm, Baron Eric Fleming

B.S., Kansas State College, Emporia, Kansas, 1934; M.A., Columbia University, New York City, New York, 1942

Wharton Esherick

Born in Philadelphia, Pennsylvania, 1887; died 1970

Studied with William Merritt Chase, Cecilia Beaux

Rafael Ferrer
Philadelphia, Pennsylvania

Born in Santurce, Puerto Rico, 1933

Studied with E. Granell

Mary Frank
New York, New York

Born in London, England, 1933

Studied with Martha Graham, Max Beckman, Hans Hoffman

Viola Frey
Oakland, California

Born in Lodi, California, 1933

Studied with Mark Rothko

B.F.A., California College of Arts and Crafts, Oakland, California, 1956; M.F.A., Painting, Tulane University, New Orleans, Louisiana, 1958

Michael Frimkess
Venice, California

Born in Los Angeles, California, 1937

Studied with Peter Voulkos, William Green

Larry Fuente
Mendocino, California

Born in Chicago, Ilinois, 1947

Influenced by Salvador Dali

Studied at Kansas City Art Institute, Kansas City, Missouri

Effie Garcia
Santa Clara, New Mexico

Born in Santa Clara, New Mexico, 1954

John G. Garrett
Los Angeles, California

Born in El Paso, Texas, 1950

Studied with Neda Al Hilali, Bernard Kester, Vasa

B.A., Drama, Claremont Men's College, Claremont, California, 1972; M.A., Design, University of California at Los Angeles, Los Angeles, California, 1976

Sidney (Sid) Lee Garrison
Houston, Texas

Born in Wichita, Kansas, 1954

Self-Taught

Arthur González
New York, New York

Born in Sacramento, California, 1954

Studied with Robert Arneson, Manuel Neri

B.A., Painting, California State University, Sacramento, California, 1977; M.A., Painting, California State University, Sacramento, California, 1979; M.F.A., Clay Sculpture, University of California, Davis, California, 1981

Peter Gourfain
Brooklyn, New York

Born in Chicago, Illinois, 1934

B.F.A., Painting, Art Institute of Chicago, Chicago, Illinois, 1956

Francoise Grossen
New York, New York

Born in Neuchatel, Switzerland, 1943

Studied with Bernard Kester

B.A., Textile Design, School of Arts and Crafts, Basel, Switzerland, 1967; M.A., Textiles, University of California at Los Angeles, Los Angeles, California, 1969

Nancy Grossman
New York, New York

Born in New York, New York, 1940

Studied with Richard Lindnez

B.F.A., Pratt Institute, New York City, New York, 1962

Trude Guermonprez

Born in Danzig, Germany, 1910; died 1976

Studied with Anni Albers, Marguerite Wildenhain

Studied at School of Art, Cologne, Germany, 1930-1931; School of Fine and Applied Arts, Halle/Saale, Germany, 1931-1933; Textile Engineering School, Berlin, Germany, 1933; Studied Scandinavian Weaving Techniques, Helsinki & Hämeenlinna, Finland, 1937; Studied Swedish Weaving Institutions, Stockholm & Insjön, Sweden, 1946

William Harper
Tallahassee, Florida

Born in Bucyrus, Ohio, 1944

Studied with Kenneth Bates, John Paul Miller

B.S., Art Education, Western Reserve University, Cleveland, Ohio, 1966; **M.S.,** Art Education, Western Reserve University, Cleveland, Ohio, 1967; **Certificate,** Cleveland Art Institute, Cleveland, Ohio, 1967

Duayne Hatchett
Buffalo, New York

Born in Shawnee, Oklahoma, 1925

B.F.A., University of Oklahoma, Norman, Oklahoma, 1950; **M.F.A.,** University of Oklahoma; Norman, Oklahoma, 1952

Anthony (Tony) Hepburn
Alfred Station, New York

Born in Stockport, England, 1942

Studied with Ian Auld, Hans Coper, Lucie Rie

N.D.D., Terra Cotta, Camberwell College of Art, London, England, 1963; **A.T.D.,** Philosophy, London University, London, England, 1965

Samuel (Sam) Rudolph Hernandez
San Jose, California

Born in Hayward, California, 1948

B.A., California State University, Hayward, California, 1970; **Honorary Degree,** University of Sonora, Hermosilla, Mexico, 1972; **M.F.A.,** University of Wisconsin, Madison, Wisconsin, 1974

Sheila Hicks
Paris, France

Born in Hastings, Nebraska, 1934

Studied with Rico LeBrun, Josef Albers, Dr. George Kubler, Anni Albers, Junius Bird

B.F.A., Yale University, New Haven, Connecticut, 1957; **M.F.A.,** Textiles, Yale University, New Haven, Connecticut, 1959; **Honorary Degree,** Rhode Island School of Design, Providence, Rhode Island, 1985

Donald Wayne Higby
Alfred Station, New York

Born in Colorado Springs, Colorado, 1943

Studied with Fred Bauer, John Stephenson

B.F.A., Art Education, University of Colorado, Boulder, Colorado, 1966; **M.F.A.,** Ceramics, University of Michigan, Ann Arbor, Michigan, 1968

Rick Hirsch
Boston, Massachusetts

Born in New York, New York, 1944

Studied with Frans Wildenhain

B.S., Art Education, State University of New York, New Paltz, New York; **M.F.A.,** Ceramics, School for American Craftsmen/Rochester Institute, Rochester, New York

Mary Lee Hu
Seattle, Washington

Born in Lakewood, Ohio, 1943

Studied with Richard Thomas, Hans Christensen, Brent Kington

B.F.A., Cranbrook Academy of Art, Bloomfield Hills, Michigan, 1965; **M.F.A.,** Southern Illinois University, Carbondale, Illinois, 1967

David R. Huchthausen
Smithville, Tennessee

Born in Wisconsin Rapids, Wisconsin, 1951

Studied with Harvey Littleton, Joel Phillip Myers, Richard Dahle

A.A., University of Wisconsin, Wausau, Wisconsin, 1973; **B.S.,** University of Wisconsin, Madison, Wisconsin, 1974; **M.F.A.,** Illinois State University, Normal, Illinois, 1976

Ferne Jacobs
Los Angeles, California

Born in Chicago, Illinois, 1942

Studied with Arlene Fisch, Mary Jane Leland, Olga de Amaral, Dominic Di Mare

M.F.A., Claremont Graduate School, Claremont, California, 1976

Kreg Kallenberger
Tulsa, Oklahoma

Born in Austin, Texas, 1950

B.F.A., Ceramics, University of Tulsa, Tulsa, Oklahoma, 1973; **M.A.,** Ceramics, University of Tulsa, Tulsa, Oklahoma, 1975

Jun Kaneko
Omaha, Nebraska

Born in Nagoya, Japan, 1942

Studied with Jerry Rothman, Peter Voulkos, Paul Soldner

M.F.A., Ceramics, Claremont Graduate School, Claremont, California, 1970

Louis Brent Kington
Makanda, Illinois

Born in Topeka, Kansas, 1934

Studied with Carlyle Smith, Richard Thomas

B.F.A., University of Kansas, Lawrence, Kansas, 1957; **M.F.A.,** Cranbrook Academy of Art, Bloomfield Hills, Michigan, 1961

Jody Klein
Waltham, Massachusetts

Born in Akron, Ohio

B.S., Painting, Kent State University, Ohio; **M.A.,** Printmaking, Kent State University, Ohio, 1965

Howard Kottler
Seattle, Washington

Born in Cleveland, Ohio, 1930

B.A., Ohio State University, Columbus, Ohio, 1952; **M.A.,** Ohio State University, Columbus, Ohio, 1956; **M.F.A.,** Cranbrook Academy of Art, Bloomfield Hills, Michigan, 1957; **Ph.D.,** Ohio State University, Columbus, Ohio, 1964

Sam Kramer

Born in Pittsburgh, Pennsylvania, 1913; died 1964

Studied with Glen Lukens

Studied at University of Southern California, Los Angeles, California, 1936

John Mason
Untitled, 1984
Ceramic with glaze,
33 x 38 x 5¾
Collection of the artist,
Los Angeles, California,
Courtesy of Wanda Hansen,
Sausalito, California

Dominick Labino
Born in Fairmount City, Pennsylvania, 1910; died 1987

Honorary D.F.A., Bowling Green State University, Bowling Green, Ohio, 1970; **D.F.A.,** University of Toledo, Toledo, Ohio, 1979

Stanley Lechtzin
Melrose Park, Pennsylvania

Born in Detroit, Michigan, 1936

Studied with Richard Thomas, Philip Fike

B.F.A., Crafts, Wayne State University, Detroit, Michigan, 1960; **M.F.A.,** Cranbrook Academy of Art, Bloomfield Hills, Michigan, 1962

Marilyn Anne Levine
Oakland, California

Born in Alberta, Canada, 1935

Studied with Jack Sures, Peter Voulkos

B.Sc., Chemistry, University of Alberta, Edmonton, Canada, 1957; **M.Sc.,** Chemistry, University of Alberta, Edmonton, Canada, 1959; **M.A.,** Sculpture, University of California, Berkeley, California, 1970; **M.F.A.,** Sculpture, University of California, Berkeley, California, 1971

Lucy M. Lewis
Acoma Pueblo, San Fidel, New Mexico

Born 1895

Roy Lichtenstein
Southampton, New York

Born in New York, New York, 1923

Studied with Hoyt L. Sherman, Reginald Marsh

B.F.A., Ohio State University, Columbus, Ohio, 1946; **M.F.A.,** Ohio State University, Columbus, Ohio, 1949

Marvin Lipofsky
Berkeley, California

Born in Barrington, Illinois, 1938

Studied with Harvey Littleton

B.F.A., Industrial Design, University of Illinois, Urbana, Illinois, 1961; **M.S.,** Sculpture, University of Wisconsin, Madison, Wisconsin, 1964; **M.F.A.,** Sculpture, University of Wisconsin, Madison, Wisconsin, 1964

Ken Dawson Little
Norman, Oklahoma

Born in Canyon, Texas, 1947

B.F.A., Texas Tech University, Lubbock, Texas, 1970; **M.F.A.,** University of Utah, Salt Lake City, Utah, 1972

Harvey K. Littleton
Spruce Pine, North Carolina

Born in Corning, New York, 1922

Studied with Nora Braden, Maija Grotell, Dominick Labino

B.D., Industrial Design, University of Michigan, Ann Arbor, Michigan, 1947; **M.F.A.,** Ceramics, Cranbrook Academy of Art, Bloomfield Hills, Michigan, 1951; **Honorary D.F.A.,** Philadelphia College of Art, Philadelphia, Pennsylvania, 1982

Charles Loloma
Hotevilla, Arizona

Born in Hotevilla Hopi Reservation, Arizona, 1921

Journeyman Certificate, School of American Craftsmen, Alfred, New York

Michael Lewis Lucero
New York, New York

Born in Tracy, California, 1953

B.A., Humbolt State University, Arcata, California, 1975; **M.F.A.,** University of Washington, Seattle, Washington, 1978

Susan Lyman
Provincetown, Massachusetts

Born in Boston, Massachusetts, 1949

Studied with John Stephenson, Jackie Rice, George Zirbes, Sherri Smith

B.F.A., Ceramics, University of Michigan, Ann Arbor, Michigan, 1971; **M.F.A.,** Ceramics, University of Michigan, Ann Arbor, Michigan, 1976

Samuel (Sam) Soloman Maloof
Alta Loma, California

Born in Chino, California, 1916

Studied with Millard Sheets, Self-Taught

Sherry Markovitz
Seattle, Washington

Born in Chicago, Illinois, 1947

B.A., Art, University of Wisconsin, Madison, Wisconsin, 1969; **M.F.A.,** Printmaking, University of Washington, Seattle, Washington, 1975

Graham Marks
Bloomfield Hills, Michigan

Born in New York, New York, 1951

Studied with William Daley, Robert Turner, Wayne Higby, Val Cushing, Ted Randall

B.F.A., Philadelphia College of Art, Philadelphia, Pennsylvania, 1974; **M.F.A.,** New York State College of Ceramics, Alfred, New York, 1976

Maria Martinez
Born in San Ildefonso, New Mexico, 1886; died 1980

Influenced by Nicolasa Pena

John Mason
Los Angeles, California

Born in Madrid, Nebraska, 1927

Studied with Peter Voulkos and Susan Peterson

Alphonse Mattia
Westport, Massachusetts

Born in Philadelphia, Pennsylvania, 1947

Studied with Daniel Jackson, Tage Frid, Bob Worth

B.F.A., Dimensional Design/Furniture, Philadelphia College of Art, Philadelphia, Pennsylvania, 1969; **M.F.A.,** Industrial Design/Furniture, Rhode Island School of Design, Providence, Rhode Island, 1973

Richard Mawdsley
Carterville, Illinois

Born in Winfield, Kansas, 1945

Studied with Carlyle Smith

B.S. Ed., Kansas State Teachers College, Emporia, Kansas, 1967; **M.F.A.,** University of Kansas, Lawrence, Kansas, 1969

Harrison McIntosh
Claremont, California

Born in Vallejo, California, 1914

Studied with Glen Lukens, Richard Petterson, Marguerite Wildenhain, Bernard Leach

Studied Ceramics at Claremont Graduate School (special student), Claremont, California, 1949-52

John McQueen
Alfred Station, New York

Born in Oakland, Illinois, 1943

Studied with Adela Akers

B.A., Sculpture, University of South Florida, Tampa, Florida, 1971; **M.F.A.,** Weaving, Tyler School of Art, Temple University, Philadelphia, Pennsylvania, 1975

James Melchert
Oakland, California

Born in New Bremen, Ohio, 1930

Studied with Peter Voulkos

A.B., Art History, Princeton University, Princeton, New Jersy, 1952; **M.F.A.,** Painting, University of Chicago, Chicago, Illinois, 1957; **M.A.,** Decorative Arts, University of California, Berkeley, California, 1961

John Paul Miller
Brecksville, Ohio

Born in Huntingdon, Pennsylvania, 1918

Studied with Baron Eric Fleming, Kenneth Bates, Viktor Schreckengost

Certificate, Industrial Design, Cleveland Institute of Art, Cleveland, Ohio, 1940

Richard Minsky
Kew Gardens, New York

Born in New York, New York, 1947

Studied with Daniel Gibson Knowlton

B.A., Brooklyn College, Brooklyn, New York, 1968; **M.A.,** Brown University, Providence, Rhode Island, 1970

Judy Moonelis
New York, New York

Born in Jackson Heights, New York, 1953

Studied with Rudolf Staffel

B.F.A., Tyler School of Art, Temple University, Philadelphia, Pennsylvania, 1975; **M.F.A.,** State College of Ceramics, Alfred, New York, 1978

Ron Nagle
San Francisco, California

Born in San Francisco, California, 1939

Studied with Peter Voulkos, Henry Takemoto

B.A., San Francisco State University, San Francisco, California, 1962

Gertrud Natzler
Born in Vienna, Austria, 1908; died 1971

Studied with Franz Iskra's Workshop, Vienna, 1933

Studied at Handelsakademie (Commercial School), Vienna, Austria, 1926

Otto Natzler
Los Angeles, California

Born in Vienna, Austria, 1908

Studied with Franz Iskra's Workshop, Vienna, 1933

Studied at Lehrestalt fur Textilindustrie, Vienna, Austria, 1927

Manuel Neri
Benicia, California

Born in Sanger, California, 1930

Studied with James Weeks, Elmer Bischoff, Nathan Oliveira, Richard Diebenkorn

Alfonso Ossorio
East Hampton, New York

Born in Manila, Philippines, 1916

Studied with Carleton Coon, Edward Forbes, George Stout, Wilhelm Kohler

A.B., Harvard College, Cambridge, Massachusetts, 1938; Studied at Rhode Island School of Design, Providence, Rhode Island

Albert Paley
Rochester, New York

Born in Philadelphia, Pennsylvania, 1944

Studied with Stanley Lechtzin

B.A., Sculpture, Tyler School of Art, Temple University, Philadelphia, Pennsylvania, 1966; M.F.A., Goldsmithing, Tyler School of Art, Temple University, Philadelphia, Pennsylvania, 1969

Thomas (Tom) J. Patti
Plainfield, Massachusetts

Born in Pittsfield, Massachusetts, 1943

Studied with Roudolph Arheim, Sybil Moholy-Nagy, Rowena Reed Kostelow, William Katavolous

B.D., Industrial Design, Pratt Institute, School of Art and Design, New York City, New York, 1967; M.I.D., Industrial Design, Pratt Institute, Graduate School of Art and Design, New York City, New York, 1969

Richard Perry Posner
Seattle, Washington

Born in Los Angeles, California, 1948

Studied with Paul Marioni, Marvin Lipofsky, Jim Melchert, Dennis Leon, Paul Harris

B.A., Sculpture and Art History, California State University, Chico, California, 1973; M.F.A., California College of Arts and Crafts, Oakland, California, 1976

Ken Price
South Dartmouth, Massachusetts

Born in Los Angeles, California, 1935

Studied with Peter Voulkos

B.F.A., Fine Arts, University of Southern California, Los Angeles, California, 1956; M.F.A., Ceramics, New York State College of Ceramics, Alfred, New York, 1959

Martin Puryear
Chicago, Illinois

Born in Washington D.C., 1941

B.A., Painting, Catholic University of America, Washington, D.C., 1963; M.F.A., Sculpture, Yale University, New Haven, Connecticut, 1971

Dextra Quotsquyva

Born in Polacca, Arizona, 1928

Terry Rosenberg
New York, New York

Born in Hartford, Connecticut, 1954

A.A., Miami Dade Community College, Miami, Florida, 1974; B.F.A., University of Miami, Coral Gables, Florida, 1976; M.F.A., Alfred University, Alfred, New York, 1978

Alison Saar
New York, New York

Born in Los Angeles, California, 1956

B.A., Scripps College, Claremont, California, 1978; M.F.A., Otis Art Institute, Los Angeles, California, 1981

Betye Saar
Los Angeles, California

Born in Los Angeles, California, 1926

Studied with Don La Viere Turner

B.A., Design, University of California at Los Angeles, Los Angeles, California, 1949

Lucas Samaras
New York, New York

Born in Kastoria, Greece, 1936

Studied with Alan Kaprow, Meyer Shapiro

B.A., Rutgers University, New Brunswick, New Jersey, 1959

Italo Scanga
La Jolla, California

Born in Lago, Calabria, Italy, 1932

Studied with Charles Pollack

B.A., Michigan State University, East Lansing, Michigan, 1960; M.A., Michigan State University, East Lansing, Michigan, 1961

Salvatore Scarpitta
Baltimore, Maryland

Born in New York, New York, 1919

Miriam Schapiro
New York, New York

Born in Toronto, Canada, 1923

Studied with Victor de'Amico, Mauricio Lasansky, Paul Brach

B.A., State University of Iowa, Iowa City, Iowa, 1945; M.A., State University of Iowa, Iowa City, Iowa, 1946; M.F.A., State University of Iowa, Iowa City, Iowa, 1949; Honorary D.F.A., Wooster College, Wooster, Ohio, 1983

Marjorie Schick
Pittsburgh, Kansas

Born in Illinois, 1941

B.S., Art Education, University of Wisconsin, Madison, Wisconsin, 1963; M.F.A., Jewelry Design and Metals, Indiana University, Bloomington, Indiana, 1966

Cynthia Schira
Lawrence, Kansas

Born in Pittsfield, Massachusetts, 1934

B.F.A., Textiles, Rhode Island School of Design, Providence, Rhode Island, 1956; M.F.A., Textiles, University of Kansas, Lawrence, Kansas, 1967

Bruce Schnabel
Los Angeles, California

Born in Philadelphia, Pennsylvania, 1951

Studied at Temple University, Philadelphia, Pennsylvania, 1969-1970; University of California, Berkeley, California, 1970-1971; California College of Arts and Crafts, Oakland, California, 1970-1973

June Theresa Schwarcz
Sausalito, California

Born in Denver, Colorado, 1918

Joyce J. Scott
Baltimore, Maryland

Born in Baltimore, Maryland, 1948

Studied with Carol Westfall, Twin and Nike Seven Seven, Art Smith

B.F.A., Education, Maryland Institute, College of Art, Baltimore, Maryland, 1970; M.F.A., Crafts, Instiuto Allende, San Miguel Allende, Mexico, 1971

Kay Sekimachi
Berkeley, California

Born in San Francisco, California, 1926

Studied with Trude Guermonprez, Jack Lenor Larson

Stanley Lechtzin
Electrofibula #90 E, 1984
Electroformed silver gilt, black nickel, pearl, 6½ x 3½ x 1½
Collection of the artist, Melrose Park, Pennsylvania

Mary Shaffer
Washington, D.C. & Providence, Rhode Island

Born in Walterboro, South Carolina, 1947

Studied with Jack Massey, Hilda Goldstern, Jack Burnham, Anne Truit

B.F.A., Illustration and Painting, Rhode Island School of Design, Providence, Rhode Island, 1965; M.F.A., Sculpture, University of Maryland, College Park, Maryland, 1986

Richard Shaw
San Francisco, California

Born in Hollywood, California, 1941

Studied with James Melchert, Ron Nagle, Robert Arneson, David Gilhooly

B.F.A., Ceramics, San Francisco Art Institute, San Francisco, California, 1965; **M.A.,** Ceramics, University of California, Davis, California, 1968

Charles Simonds
New York, New York

Born in New York, New York, 1945

Studied with James Melchert, Harold Faris

B.A., University of California, Berkeley, California, 1967; **M.F.A.,** Rutgers Univeristy, New Brunswick, New Jersey, 1969

Thomas (Tommy) Simpson
Washington, Connecticut

Born in Elgin, Illinois, 1939

B.S., Northern Illinois University, Dekalb, Illinois, 1962; **M.F.A.,** Painting, Cranbrook Academy of Art, Bloomfield Hills, Michigan, 1964

Arthur Smith

Born in Brooklyn, New York, 1923; died 1982

Studied at Cooper Union, New York City, New York

Richard Zane Smith
Ganado, Arizona

Born in Augusta, Georgia, 1955

A.A., Art, Meramee Junior College, Kirkwood, Missouri, 1975

Paul Soldner
Aspen, Colorado

Born in Summerfield, Illinois, 1921

Studied with Peter Voulkos

B.A., Bluffton College, Bluffton, Ohio, 1946; **M.A.,** University of Colorado, Boulder, Colorado, 1954; **M.F.A.,** Ceramics, Los Angeles County Art Institute, Los Angeles, California, 1956

Rudolf Staffel
Philadelphia, Pennsylvania

Born in San Antonio, Texas, 1911

Studied with Jose Arpa, Xavier Gonzalez, Hans Hoffman

Therman Statom
Los Angeles, California

Born in Winterhaven, Florida, 1953

B.F.A., Rhode Island School of Design, Providence, Rhode Island, 1975; **M.F.A.,** Pratt Institute of Art and Design, New York City, New York, 1978

Robert (Bob) Stocksdale
Berkeley, California

Born in Warren, Indiana, 1913

Self-Taught

Michelle Stuart
New York, New York

Born in Los Angeles, California, 1940

Studied with Diego Rivera

Studied at Chouinard Art Institute, Los Angeles, California and New School of Social Research, New York City, New York

Jaime Suarez
San Juan, Puerto Rico

Born in Hato Rey, Puerto Rico, 1946

Studied with Alexander Giampietro

B.A., Architecture, Catholic University of America, Washington, D.C., 1969; **M.A.,** Urban Design, Columbia University, New York City, New York, 1971

James Surls
Splendora, Texas

Born in Terrell, Texas, 1943

Studied with Julius Schmidt

B.S., Painting, Sam Houston State College, Huntsville, Texas, 1966; **M.F.A.,** Cranbrook Academy of Art, Bloomfield Hills, Michigan, 1969

Toshiko Takaezu
Quakertown, New Jersey

Born in Pukapo, Hawaii, 1922

Studied with Maija Grotell, Claude Horan, Marianne Strengell, William McVey

B.S., University of Hawaii, Honolulu, Hawaii; **M.F.A.,** Cranbrook Academy of Art, Bloomfield Hills, Michigan, 1951

Henry Takemoto
Los Angeles, California

Born in Honolulu, Hawaii, 1930

B.F.A., University of Hawaii, Honolulu, Hawaii, 1957; **M.F.A.,** Los Angeles County Art Institute, Los Angeles, California, 1959

James L. Tanner
Janesville, Minnesota

Born in Jacksonville, Florida, 1941

Studied with Harvey Littleton, Amos White, Don Reitz, Hal Lotterman

B.A., Florida Agricultural and Mechanical University, Tallahassee, Florida, 1964; **M.S.,** University of Wisconsin, Madison, Wisconsin, 1966; **M.F.A.,** University of Wisconsin, Madison, Wisconsin, 1967

Lenore Tawney
New York, New York

Born in Lorain, Ohio, 1925

Studied with Marli Ehrman, Alexander Archipenko, Marta Taipale, Emerson Woelffer

Peter Voulkos
Berkeley, California

Born in Bozeman, Montana, 1924

Studied with Frances Senska, Jessie Wilber

B.S., Montana State University, Bozeman, Montana, 1950; **M.F.A.,** California College of Arts and Crafts, Oakland, California, 1952; **L.H.D.,** Montana State University, Bozeman, Montana, 1968; **Honorary D.F.A.,** California College of Arts and Crafts, Oakland, California, 1972; **Honorary D.F.A.,** Otis Institute of Parsons School of Design, Los Angeles, California, 1980; **Honorary D.F.A.,** San Francisco Art Institute, San Francisco, California, 1982

Patti Warashina
Seattle, Washington

Born in Spokane, Washington, 1940

Studied with Robert Sperry, Harold Myers, Rudy Autio, Shoji Hamada, Shinsaku Hamada, Ruth Penington

B.F.A., Ceramics, University of Washington, Seattle, Washington, 1962; **M.F.A.,** Ceramics, University of Washington, Seattle, Washington, 1964

Horace (H.C.) Clifford Westermann

Born in Los Angeles, California, 1922; died 1981

Studied with Paul Weighardt

B.F.A., Art Institute of Chicago, Chicago, Illinois, 1954; **D.F.A.,** 1979

Margaret Agnes Wharton
Glenview, Illinois

Born in Portsmouth, Virginia, 1943

Studied with Richard Keene, Ray Yoshida, Jim Zanzi, Jack Burnham, Ree Morton, Jenny Snider

B.S., Advertising, University of Maryland, College Park, Maryland, 1965; **M.F.A.,** School of the Art Institute of Chicago, Chicago, Illinois, 1975

Jackie Winsor
New York, New York

Born in Newfoundland, Canada, 1941

B.F.A., Massachusetts College of Art, Boston, Massachusetts, 1965; **M.F.A.,** Rutgers University, New Brunswick, New Jersey, 1967

J. (James) Fred Woell
Deer Isle, Maine

Born in Evergreen Park, Illinois, 1934

Studied with Robert Von Neumann, Arthur Vierthaler

B.A., Economics, University of Illinois, Urbana, Illinois, 1956; **B.F.A.,** Education, University of Illinois, Urbana, Illinois, 1960; **M.S.,** University of Wisconsin, Madison, Wisconsin, 1961; **M.F.A.,** Art Metal and Graphics, University of Wisconsin, Madison, Wisconsin, 1962; **M.F.A.,** Sculpture, Cranbrook Academy of Art, Bloomfield Hills, Michigan, 1969

Beatrice (Beato) Wood
Ojai, California

Born in San Francisco, California, 1893

Studied with Glen Lukens, Gertrud and Otto Natzler, Viveka and Otto Heino

William Wyman

Born in Boston, Massachusetts, 1922; died 1980

B.S., Massachusetts College of Art, , Massachusetts, 1950; **M.A.,** Columbia Universtiy, New York City, New York, 1951

Fumio Yoshimura
New York, New York

Born in Kamakura, Japan, 1926

Studied with Ryuzaburo Umehara

M.F.A., Painting, Tokyo National University of Arts, Tokyo, Japan, 1949

Claire Zeisler
Chicago, Illinois

Born in Cincinnati, Ohio, 1903

Studied with Alexander Archipenko, Lazlo Moholy-Nagy, Bea Swartchild

Honorary Ph.D., Moore College of Art, Philadelphia, Pennsylvania, 1981

GENERAL INDEX

PHOTO CREDITS

Vito Acconci: *Maze Table*, 179. Roy Adams: *Leitungs Scherben*, 101. George L. Aguirre: *Tourists in Kenya; Masai Women with traditional neckware*, 235. Argentum Photographic Services: *Plaque*, 198. Ryusei Arita: *Peter Voulkos working*, 82. Dirk Bakker: *Eel Hive*, 134; *Pelvis*, 247. William H. Bengtson: *Leopatra*, 102. Norinne Betjemann: *Yellow Rock Falls*, 123. Jon Bolton, Jr.: *Temple Series*, 70, 71; *Double Finger Ring*, 41. Joe Boone: *Bottle*, 19. Margaret Bourke-White: *At the Time of the Louisville Flood*, 258. Thomas Brummett: *Letter Bundle*, 256. ©Dick Busher: *Cylinder*, 162; *Pink Sea Form Group with Gold Braun Wraps*, 168. Eduardo Calderon: *Autumn Buck*, 278. Michael Cavanagh: *Double-Bulged Bowl with Lid*, 72. Richard Cheek: *Parlor of Oak Hill*, 165. Geoffrey Clements: *Reconstruction #12*, 170; *Frontal*, 166; *Bound Logs*, 255. Lia Cook: *Translucence*, 49. ©Tom Crane: *Rock Chair*, 180. Grey Crawford: *Richard's Piece*, 51; *By the Lake Where Time Stands Still*, 221. Anthony Cunha Photography: *Untitled*, 6. Susie Cusher: *Square on Square*, 172. Bevan Davies: *Yo, Yo, Yo, Yo*, 237, 250. D. James Dee: *Figure with Staff*, 249; *Artemis*, 33; *Rose Gate*, 175. M. Lee Fatherree: *Holy War Head*, 59; *Red Zig*, 244; *Untitled*, 86; *Horse #6*, 276; *Pendant*, 76; *Pin*, 127; *Grandmother Figure*, 200; *Mandy's Motto*, 74; *Cup with Box*, 57; *Verdeyama*, 84; *Another Look at my Beef with the Government*, 143; *A Letter from Robbie*, 199; *Couch*, 108; *Plate*, 25. Ignacio Gaerlan: *Study for Virginia Woolf Plate*, 42. Claude Gaspari: *La Fourche*, 115. Margaret Harman: *La Luz I*, 75. Lewis Harrington Photography: *Red Bird*, 193. Mark Haynes: *Olla*, 120. Paul Hester: *Orchestral Toy*, 47. Eva Heyd: *Roc Pendant*, 127; *Amiyose*, 87; *Neckpiece*, 40. eeva-inkeri: *Vestibule*, 174. Peter Iverson: *Equilibrium I and II*, 29; *Rain Rattle*, 150; *Shield IV*, 27. Jerry Jacka Photography: *Bracelet*, 206. Bruce C. Jones: *Portrait II*, 178. K&L Custom Photographic Services: *Louisville*, 251. Marcia Keegan: *India Truck*, 38. Jerry Koblecky: *Porcelain Drawing on Paper*, 20; *Library Steps with Elephant and Donkey Finials*, 30. Dick Krueger: *Mud and Stick Horse*, 274. Lassiter and Shoemaker Photography: *Luster Glazed Porcelain Hollow Form*, 113; *Old Woman Face Mask*, 214; *Neckpiece for the Back*, 91; *Drawings from the Colored Smoke Machine Series*, 149. Abel Lewis: *William Morris*, 160. Vincent Lisanti: *Hustler's Delight*, 60; *Untitled Basket*, 222. ©Neil MacDonald: *Claire Zeisler in her apartment*, 222. Pete McArthur: *Cha Cha*, 210, 211. Scott McCue Photography: *Seated Figure with Yellow Flame*, 55; *Seated Figure with Striped Right Arm*, 55. John Chang McCurdy: *Untitled*, 262. Colin McRae: *The Liberation of Aunt Jemima*, 209; *Typewriter*, 96. Michael McTwigan: *Io*, 121. Paul Macapia: *Airstream Turkey*, 14. Matrix Gallery, Austin, Texas: *Dem*, 200. Maxwell & Bellis Photographers, Inc.: *Book*, 177. Steve Meltzer: *The Egyptian*, 87. Bruce Miller: *Serpent Table*, 117. John Paul Miller: *Pendant/Brooch*, 72. Rudy Miller: *Aunt Jemima Pancake Mix*, (Designer, Frank de Raffele & Associates; Design Director, Max M. Lomont, The Quaker Oats Company), 208. Kevin Montague: *Double-Bulged Bowl with Lid*, 72. B. Moore: *California Loop*, 53. Peter Moore: *Totem*, 260. Peter Muscato: *Galesteo Book II*, 217. Don Myer: *Sevillanas*, 24. ©Steve Myers, 1987: *Pictorial*

Lake, 100. ©1983 National Geographic Society: *National Geographic Magazine*, Cover, April 1983 Issue, 37. Richard Nicol: *Bracelet #37*, 46; *Neckpiece #8*, 63; *Untitled*, 99. Joseph Painter: *Vase*, 190; *Vessel*, 191. ©Douglas M. Parker: *Scribe*, 182. Marlen Perez: *Winter Wheat*, 106. Andrew Dean Powell Photography: *Hors d'Oeuvre Table*, 181. Duane Powell: *Headdress #5*, 93. Adam Reich: *Juggler*, 37. Wm. G. (Gerry) Riggs: *Gold Ruby Loop with White Lines*, 80. Marlin Roos: *Air Machine #19*, 194. Charles Rumph: *Two Figures on a Stand*, 109. Douglas W. Schaible: *Blenko Project #5*, 271; *Untitled (manganese prunted vase)*, 32. E.G. Schempf: *Midland Winter*, 218. Schenck & Schenck Photography, Claremont, California: *Covered Jar*, 61; *Platter*, 125; *Sanbon Ashi*, 83; *Vase*, 97; *First Kumu*, 26; *Walking Man*, 82. Schopplein Studios, San Francisco, California: *Huddle*, 166; *Cup with Silkscreened photo of Peter Voulkos*, 85; *Loop #1*, 45. Fred Scruton: *Tiki Chair*, 184. William Bennett Seitz Photography: *Rabbit Chairs*, 182. Eric Shambroom Photography: *The Man*, 192. Darrel Spector: *Ceramic Sculpture #11*, 56. Larry Stein: *Table with Gloves and Keys*, 117. Andreas Sterzing: *Give Me Liberty or Give Me Romance*, 183. Rick Stiller: *Male Nail Fetish Figure*, 275. Stone and Steccati Photographers: *Bowl*, 31. Bill Svendsen: *Fiesta Basket*, 5; *Santa Monica/Atlantis*, 220. Ivan Dalla Tana: *Van Chrome T.V.*, 184. William Taylor: *Proposed Expansion of Whitney Museum of Modern Art, New York, New York by Architect Michael Graves*, 259. Michael Tropea, Chicago, Illinois: *Simple Gift*, 39. James Turrell: *Roden Crater*, 263. Malcolm Varon, New York, New York: *Untitled*, 204; *Ecology Krater II*, 138; *Untitled*, 50; *Untitled*, 133; *Page I*, 223. Denis Velez: *Vestment of Earth and Time*, 231. David Wharton: *Needle Man*, (Photo Courtesy Dallas Museum of Art), 267. ©Don Wheeler, Inc.: *Punk Walrus Inua (Poonk Aiverk Inua)*, 207; *Jar*, 34; *Pin*, 98; *Portable Souls*, 148; *The Colored Smoke Machine*, 149; *The Colored Smoke Machine*, 152; *Bowl*, 119; *Metamorphosis II⁴*, 77; *Interlock System³ #287*, 196; *Titanic Series #268*, 196; *Red/Blue Twisted Arc*, 66; *Jar*, 120; *Pin*, 128; *Bird Trapped in Shadows*, 228; *The Double Cross*, 131; *The White Boy's Gone Crazy*, 131; *For The Souls*, 130; *Kool-Aide Kocktail*, 130; *Seeing Eye*, 238; *Class of '78*, 44; *Come Alive, You're in the Pepsi Generation*, 44. White Line Photography, San Francisco, California: *Mask*, 136; *Domus #5—Harbor Lights*, 135. Ellen Page Wilson: *La Rosa Negra*, 202. Dick Wiser: *Roden Crater*, 263. Bruce Wrighton: *Apparition Canyon*, 104.